Getting By In A Silent World

The Life and Times of Jack The Barber

By Jack L. Cooke

© 2005, 2009 Jack L. Cooke

All rights reserved. Permission to reproduce in any form must first be secured from Jack L. Cooke, 735 Deveron Crescent, Unit 215, London, ON N5Z 4X8.
jlcooke@sympatico.ca

Cooke, Jack L., 1928-

Getting by in a silent world: the life and times of Jack the barber / by Jack L. Cooke.

ISBN: 978-0-9808983-2-3

1. Cooke, Jack L., 1928- 2. Deaf--Ontario--Biography. 3. Barbers--Ontario--Biography. 4. Ontario--Biography. 5. Canada--Biography.

I. Title.

| HV2577.C67A3 2005 | 362.4'2'092 | C2005-903854-3 |

The History Press
94 Lillian Crescent,
Barrie, ON L4N 5H7
Tel: (705) 728-5802 Fax: (705) 728-0048
www.thehistorypress.ca
publishing@thehistorypress.ca

1		Contents	3
2		Preface	7
		Chapter 1	
3		Happiness Is The Journey	11
4		A Bad Experience	15
5		Surviving The Heat	15
6		The Tornado In The 30's	19
7		A New Furry Friend	21
8		Rabbits	22
9		The Orchard	23
10		Tramps Of The 30's or Someone's Son	24
11		A Wondrous Gift	26
12		Cold Winters and Cutting Wood	26
13		Winter and Car Care, Roads and Travel	27
14		Going To School	30
15		My School Days	31
16		"A Lesson Learned"	36
17		Motherwell Village by The Thames	38
18		Sunday	41
19		Horse and Buggies, Cars and Radios	43
20		My Dad and The Butcher Knife	48
21		Farm Cats	50
22		Life as "The Only Boy"	51
23		Len My City Cousin	53
24		The War Years	56
25		Saturday Nights	51
26		My Grandfather Cooke	58
27		My Grandpa and Grandma Butson	59
28		Fur and Feather Barn Pest	61
29		I Lose My Hearing	62
30		Making Maple Syrup	63
31		The Day We Player Hooky From School	64
32		High School and The Aftermath	64
33		Shirlyan My Kid Sister	66
34		The Long Trip Home	67
		Chapter 2	
35		Those Early Years The Booming 40's	67
36		I Meet my Uncle Fred Butson in Winnipeg	72
37		I Meet Uncle Frank and Aunt Rosena McNee	78
38		Wib and The Duncans Of High River	88
39		My Aunt Becky (Norris) Kiel	92
		Chapter 3	
40		Growing Up and Times To Remember	97
41		My First Car Accident	101

42	"Fall Fever and Westward Ho"	107
43	Home Again	112
44	Friends to Remember – People I Worked For	113
45	The First TV Set	117
	Chapter 4	
46	The Real West	119
47	The Henry J Kaiser Fraser	135
48	Jerry Baltesson Came East To Visit	138
49	Ron Smith, Jerry Baltesson and I Drive West	139
50	Amos Graver and Maple Island	146
51	A Western Trip 1955	148
52	Dad and Mom by Boat To England	155
53	A Western Trip 1957	158
54	The Old Farm Was Sold 1961	182
55	Barry White and Diane	185
56	Dad and Mom Buy The Taylor Farm	188
	Chapter 5	
57	Off To Barber College	190
58	George, Dot, Mark, Aunt Em and Penny	194
59	My First Barber Shop 1963	199
60	Jack and Bob Go West	203
61	"The Crazy, Crazy Colourful 60's"	208
62	"The Executive House" 362 Dufferin Ave.	210
63	Regina Mundi College	211
64	Mrs Murdock and Her Christmas Cake	212
65	Some Strange Encounters	213
66	Of Friends and Friendships	216
67	Jack and Allan Have A Bad Day	219
68	Unpleasant Encounters	219
69	Mr Mrs Bull's 50th Wedding Anniversary	220
70	Barry and Diane White Are Doing Well	221
71	Two Hockey Greats, Daryl and Dino	221
72	A Fateful Tragedy	221
73	Time For Dad and Mom To Retire	222
74	Bob Takes Leave	223
	Chapter 6	
75	Life At The V O N House	225
76	Dad and Mom and Nancy - Go West	233
77	The Sad Tale of My Friend "A New Canadian"	236
78	Jack Loses His Shop and Starts Out New	239
79	For All Of Us Life Moves On	242
80	The Dream Car: My 1983 Camaro Z 28	243
81	The London YM CA Burned Down	244
82	Barbershop Tales	245
83	Dad and Mom Move To Ritz Villa	249

84		Wm. Bull Passed Away	250
85		Lenora and Grace Travel East	252
86		My Mom Passes Away	253
87		Mike and Gigs Chubak Pull Up Stakes	253
88		I Trade My Z 28 For A Grand AM Pontiac	254
89		The V O N Decide To Move	256
		Chapter 7	
90		The Berkeley Apartment Building	258
91		A TV Caption Machine	261
92		At 92 Dad's Health Was Failing	261
93		Carl Quits As Custodian	263
94		Stranger Than Fiction	264
95		Jack Takes On A Garden	266
96		Getting Taken	266
97		Mandy My Manx Cat	269
98		Mr Buchanan Comes Around	269
99		Mr Buchanan Has A Stroke	271
100		Mrs Buchanan Passes Away	271
101		My Aunt Maude	273
102		The California Holiday Trip	275
		Chapter 8	
103		" Coasting Thru My 60's"	290
104		On Reaching 65	292
105		My First Old Age Pension Check	298
106		Mr Buchanan Passes Away	298
107		I Think About Buying A Condo	299
108		Yvonne Has A Deal	301
109		"A Friend" Olive Sutherland Passes Away	302
110		Deke and Cathy	302
111		I return To Oyen	309
112		Don Sutherland Sr. Passes Away	315
113		Bill and Jean and Jack Fly West August 1998	316
114		Buying a Condo	317
115		I Bought A Computer	322
116		Yvonne Moves To London	324
117		My Manx Cat Mandy Dies	327
		Chapter 9	
118		A Great Canadian Holiday Trip 2001	329
119		I Drive North To Fort McMurray	342
120		Time For Another Kitty	353
121		Don The Computer Guy	355
122		Life Moves On	355
		Chapter 10	
123		"A Time To Reflect"	358
124		A Special "Thank You"	360

About the Author

Jack the author, was born in Stratford, Ontario, Oct. 17th, 1928. He spent his growing up years on the old farm on the Mitchell Road near the village of Motherwell, Fullarton Township, Perth County, Ontario.

In 1942 at the age of 14 he contracted scarlet fever, which destroyed his hearing and any chance of a normal life or to further his education.

At the tender age of 15 he more or less fled to western Canada in search of a way of life, and perhaps a chance to find himself.

He fell in love with the west and its people and for a time a whole community adopted him. In it he found uncles and aunts, friends and neighbours all who became his very own. He has kept those ties a lifetime.

Returning to the east and unable to find steady work because of his hearing loss he was encouraged to become a barber by Dickie Thorne, the local shoe store man in his home town of Mitchell. For over forty years Jack cut hair in south London. This is the story of the life and times of Jack the Barber, *Getting By In a Silent World*.

Preface: In A Silent World

I was born a child of the thirties thus I view a much larger dimension of life than those who were born after me. I know the difference between the necessities of life and the luxuries. I am better able to appreciate the good things life offers us today, yet able to mourn the loss of what we left behind.

There was a time when no one locked their doors, a time when milk was delivered to your house every morning, a time when the mailman picked up letters and delivered mail to your door or mailbox six days a week. A time when the simple words, "Going to town" made your heart race. I remember when the whole family followed friends or uncles and aunts all the way to the car to see them off, to say "Good byes" because we knew we loved them.

I was born at a time when your work always came first before yourself, when one dollar a day was good pay if you were lucky enough to find a job, and the word 'holiday' was only for the rich and not yet in our vocabulary.

While I am aware now there were hardships at that time, we did not feel oppressed by it. It was simply the way we were. This was life, as we knew it in our home and in our community. Our family, friends and neighbours all shared the same problems, the same joys, sorrows and accomplishments.

A motto on our Perth County billboard as you enter our county said, "Together We Rise" … and we did.

Now when I look back I know that in spite of all we have today we had something then which is missing in our lives today. Perhaps it is simply the joys and appreciation of little things we did for each other or perhaps just the satisfaction of doing things "well" the hard way, of hearing or saying the words "Thank you" and knowing the true meaning of it.

No one thing changed my life so much as my hearing loss due to scarlet fever when I was twelve years old. All plans for a future were suddenly dashed. The world at that time, more so than today would not accept a deaf person. It won't adapt to you. Somehow you have to learn to deal with it.

This is the story of a boy entering a Silent World. Then of a young man struggling to find a place in that world against the odds. It is also the story of the people who touched his life along the way and made that world more manageable in one way or another for better or worse. I have few regrets.

I know now, "Life is but a journey that takes you from here to there."

What you find at the end of the journey depends a lot on the road you <u>had</u> to travel, and whom you met to influence your life along your way. At the *tender age of fifteen my travels took me afar from home to Western Canada at a time the country was still very young. I travelled its dirt roads and crossed its muddy streets; I rode horse back in the hills looking for cattle. I have spent days under the hot prairie sun picking rock from newly broken land. I have dug goose pits and climbed mountains. I know the intense pride the west feels of its past history and I am very much aware of its vibrant pulse and its impatient heartbeat for its future. I loved the west then and I still love it today, but my journey led me back to beautiful old London on the Thames River in the heart of South Western Ontario. It is here I found a place I feel I can call home, but my first home, the place where my heart will forever be is on the old farm on The Mitchell Road, the place where I was born and raised.*

Those years of growing up in the thirties and forties are well documented in the first few chapters of my book, followed by those in between years of my teens and twenties. For a time it seemed my life was an endless tortuous journey from east to west and back home again searching for my place in life. My love for Alberta and the west and my ties to my home, the old farm on The Mitchell Road were always in conflict. I realize now I was led on a long journey, a journey that moulded and enriched my life.

It was my old friend Albert Norman, the painter in Mitchell who hired me in the late fall of 1962 when I arrived home from the west with no job and no place to stay. It was also that fall that Dickie Thorne the local Mitchell shoe store man planted the seed for me to become a barber. My only regret might be I wish I had started to barber ten years earlier as I had finally found my calling – a place in life where I could earn a living and at the same time enjoy my work. It was a place warm in the winter and cool in the summer.

For about forty years through good times and bad I managed to keep my shop operating while time took its toll on the many businesses all about me.

Now in my later years I could not imagine my life without that journey which brought me in contact with all those I learned to love and respect. I have tried not to lose track of the many people I have met on my life's journey, but many have passed away and the rest of us are getting older.

It is to you my dear friends and to my sisters and families I dedicate this book, for the many ways you touched and enriched my life. God Bless.

There was a beginning and there will be an end.

Our yesterdays are our history,

and our tomorrows

remain a mystery.

Today is a gift.

Author Unknown

Chapter 1

HAPPINESS IS THE JOURNEY

"Milestones" are seldom recognized along the way as we live our daily lives. It is only when we get older and look back, that we will recognize them. Looking back now, I see a whole generation that for a time was stripped of hope and plans for a future, afraid to enjoy the present for fear of jinxing their future. By assuming nothing good will ever come your way again you will never be disappointed, never have your hopes dashed again. The thirties did this to many people and perhaps it took a war to make them rise above it.

Although I left the farm a long time ago I have never regretted that I was raised on a farm, living and sharing in a farm community. It left me with a different vision than most city people have in many ways and that vision has enriched my life. When I drive down the highway or out into the country I don't just see trees, I see the maples the ash the oak and walnut, and I see that the elms are making a comeback. I see the hawthorn and the willow, and the locust. I look at the field crops and I see the winter wheat and the barley, oats and the corn and soybeans, and canola. I don't just see grass, I see timothy and alfalfa, clover and grass and more. I recognize dozens of kinds of weeds, flowers and shrubs, all because I grew up with them on the farm and they were our everyday language.

Farming was actually more than just a job or occupation, it was a home and a way of life. Each morning you wake up not only to your family but to your livestock and to your whole community, with commitments to all. No clear line separates your work from your community commitments. It is an old model of living, which has been handed down for centuries. You don't just own the farm, you own an active place in your community. When you are born on a farm you will learn to love the land under your feet, and it will always be the place you will call home, the place where you were born.

I was born in a rural area of Southern Ontario, October 17th in 1928. I didn't realize the years were drifting by so fast until now as I grow older. Sometimes I stop to wonder, just how I got from there to here, for when I look back to those early years I remember a world so much different from the world we live in today. My thoughts drift back to a long, long, time ago to the old farm on the Mitchell Road where I grew up in Fullarton Township in Perth County, Ontario. My grandfather George Cooke came from Peterborough England in the late 1880's. He first farmed in the Woodstock area and then rented this farm on the Mitchell

Road in 1899 from Wm. Bothwell. He later bought it and the sixty acres to the south, which had a lot of bush and swamp on it.

The Old Cooke Farm Home on the Mitchell Road

The earliest memories in my life were of long hot sunny summer days with the smell of wood smoke constantly in the air. My grandfather who owned the farm was clearing land and burning brush and stumps down on what we called "The Sixty." Many great trees of ash, maple, elm and oak that were thought not straight enough logs for lumber were piled and burnt. In the evening I would walk with my grandfather going from stump to stump checking them to see if they were burnt out enough to pull with our team of horses using a logging chain. Many a tug or whipple tree got broken while clearing stumps and rocks from the land. Perhaps it was then that I learned to love the smell of wood smoke and earn my lifetime love and admiration of horses

Dad, John Wilfred Cooke was born in Woodstock, Oct. 21, 1898.

Mom, Mary Reta Butson was born at Cromarty or Staffa area July 10 1900.

Sept. 30th 1926 my dad John Cooke married my mom Reta Butson, and they worked the farm along with my grandparents. Laurine was born Oct.10, 1927 and I was born Oct. 17/1928. Like all young folk my dad and mom longed for a place of their very own. So in 1929 they bought the Barr farm that was actually the other half of grandpa's sixty. They delayed moving into the house because they were able to rent it to a friend Jack Young. They simply needed the income so it seemed the best thing to do. In the year 1930 my dad caught polio, and came very close to losing his life. It was many years before he actually made a full recovery and regained his health. The great depression of the thirties descended on everyone and by 1932 they had to give up the new farm. They sold it back to Mr. Barr. I would only be four years old but I remember my mom crying, as she felt her hopes and dreams were dashed for a home of their very own. They didn't enjoy sharing the house with older folks; they wanted and needed something of their very own.

March 15, 1931 my sister Pearl was born.

April 21, 1932 my sister Jean was born.

The Barr Farm

Springtime an then summer were seemingly a long and endless time of great joys for me. Each spring my Uncle Georges bush across the Mitchell road from our house and barn would announce that spring had indeed arrived once more. We watched as suddenly the bush sprang forth in a shade of green which deepened into foliage each day. Wild crab-apple trees burst forth in bloom attracting busy bees. Soon the he whole bush resounds with the croaking and thrilling of hundreds and hundreds of frogs, throbbing a chorus of happiness Every now and then the bull frog added a rich loud crock perfecting a country in harmony as we knew it. First the spring calves would be born and I would greet each one with great affection and they would respond to my touch. Then there were little pigs. I use to scratch behind the mother sow's ears and made good friends with them. Thus I was not afraid to enter the pen to pet the little ones. But not all mother sows want to share their family with you, so take care. Don't make them squeal or you might have to make a hasty retreat!

Cats and kittens were another thing, and it seemed that our mother cats came from a long line of great lovers and the neighbourhood toms had a very happy and carefree nightlife. Our farm cats often had two or three litters a year. It was kind of sad to see these beautiful kittens born knowing you cannot keep them. The sooner they were made to disappear the easier it was for mother cats and little boys too.

The Old Farm Buildings on the Mitchell Road – art by Jack

A trip to The Village Store was always a wonderful treat and a break from the farm. I still remember the great roll of brown paper sitting on the counter and the white string hanging down from the ceiling. There was a bobbin of white string sitting near by from which the string went up to the ceiling and through an eye, then across the ceiling above the roll of brown paper and through another eye, dropped and was left floating in the air. It was great to see the store owner pull on the brown paper from the roll and wrap your purchase and while holding onto it reach for the string and somehow the package sort of make a circle on the counter before your eyes and a tie was made and your purchase handed to you all in one smooth movement.

We bought most of our gas at this village store. The gas pump was out in front of the store veranda. It was a two-glass chamber atop a towering bottom. There was a white globe on top of the glass chambers telling you the brand name at Motherwell was White Rose, other brands I remember best were Texaco, Supertest, B.A. A long handle was attached on either side of the tower, and you swung the handle back and forth to pump the glass chamber full of gas. Each chamber held ten gallons of gas and had numbers and lines on the side of the chamber. One chamber held number one gas and the other number two gas. You just took the hose off the side of the tower and put it into the car gas tank and squeezed the handle and watched the gas lower itself in the chamber until it touched the line or number you wanted. Everyone always thought they got a full measure of gas for their money.

A Bad Experience

One beautiful sunny summer morning when I was perhaps six or seven years old a group of neighbour men arrived at our farm in a jolly mood. I knew several of them as they had helped my dad from time to time as farm people did at that time. I had no idea what was going to take place, but I always enjoyed it when company came so I was out there to welcome them.

I was not ready to see what I saw that day, but I realize now it was just a part of farm life, as little boys had to grow up and accept such things as life and death. They came out of the barn in a group and the one man had a rope in his hand. The other end of the rope was looped around the hind leg of one of my dad's fat pigs. By pulling the rope to the left or right they could guide the pig and make it go in the direction they wished to guide it. You can lead a horse or cow, but you cannot lead a pig. You drive or follow it.

By now I had noticed this strange rope and pulleys hanging in the maple tree. But I didn't have a clue what it was for. The men were in a jolly mood, laughing and prodding the poor pig that was squealing like mad. I remember the morning was still so fresh and full of promise for all living things. The warm sun shone down upon the farmyard below and I stood in the shade of the great maple witnessing the intrusion upon a small boy's life. What was about to happen would live in my mind's memory forever. About mid-way across the yard one man took out a huge butcher knife and put it under the pig's throat and drew it across. Blood gushed out so bright, so red. The clear shrill squeals it had been making ended with horrid gurgling sounds! To add insult to this terrible scene one man jumped on the pig's back and rode him to his death.

As a little kid I stood there in shock. I felt much, much too young to witness death in this manner. I could not understand the joy these men seemed to find, " in the killing." They pulled the dying pig over to the block and tackle and pulled it up by its hind legs until it was off the ground. I was still standing frozen to my spot. The man took the knife and slit the pig down the belly and all the insides rolled out onto the ground. I had seen enough. Too much for a small boy, but such was life, on farms in those early years. It was all a part of growing up. I think back now and I wonder if my dad should have sent me to the house until it was over, as I would much rather have lived my life, free of this memory.

Surviving In The Heat

Most farms did not have a refrigerator. A few had what was called an icebox, which looked like a fridge and was kept cool by a block of ice. This worked very well, but there was a lot of work involved in getting and keeping ice. In the winter men would go to the Thames River and cut huge blocks of ice. I have seen the ice ten to twelve inches thick on the Thames River. They sawed the ice with special handsaws into twelve-inch squares and called them " Blocks. " They lifted the blocks out of the water with great ice prongs and piled then onto bob sleighs. Then with a team of horses drew it home. It would be a very heavy load and the team of horses were allowed to stop every so far to catch their breath.

The gravel roads were usually snow packed most or all of the winter, so bob sleighs could travel down the road most of the winter without a problem.

Once home the ice was put in what was called an icehouse, often when possible built into the side of a hill. Wood sawdust was then shovelled over the ice as it was piled in the icehouse layer by layer. The sawdust was also put down between the blocks so they would not freeze together. Sawdust is a wonderful insulator and the ice would keep in the icehouse all summer.

Freezers had not been invented yet so the farmers out of necessity invented what they called beef rings and pork rings so they could have fresh meat each week. It worked like this. A number of farmers agreed to each raise a pig or a steer to a certain weight to be ready to slaughter on or about a set date. Now there are just so many correct cuts in either a beef or pork animal and you would receive one of each of these cuts until you had used them all up, and then you were out of the ring unless you put another animal in. These rings were used mostly in the hot summer, when it was impossible to keep meat very long in the heat. I remember my mom always kept the best cuts of meat for the grain threshing gangs, as men needed good food when they worked hard. In the winter one could manage to get by with perhaps pork in a wood barrel of salt brine in the cellar or maybe culling out a few fat hens, which had gone into retirement and stopped laying eggs.

The summer of 1936 was very hot. In fact, it was one of the hottest heat waves ever recorded by Environment Canada. For twelve days the temperature exceeded 40C or near 110F. No one had air conditioning at that time, and many people died of heat exhaustion. Records tell us 1,180 lives were lost in Ontario and Manitoba that summer. In 1936 that was a lot of people from our small population. The heat meant that our cattle and farm stock needed more water, and our barn well could not keep up with the demand.

Two Clevis and a Neck Yoke

Grandpa and I got the job of hauling water from the house well to the barn. We put two wood barrels on a flat stone boat. Every farm had a

stone boat in those days. Its main job was just that, hauling stones off the fields, but it came in handy for many other jobs. It was usually made of rock elm lumber, as it had to be tough and made strong. They used two elm wood skids or runners about eight feet long placed about three feet to forty inches apart with heavy boards spiked down across them. Then the front and rear boards would be of heavier elm plank bolted to the skids to hold it perfectly square in spite of heavy loads and rough use. A hole was bored in the centre of the front plank into which a clevis with a heavy steel ring was placed. A second clevis was attached through the ring to a wippletree, which was then pulled by one horse. If you used two horses then you used a double tree, to which two wippletrees were attached.

I remember that grandpa had a long down drainpipe like the ones, which came down from the eave troughs on the corner of the house or barn. He attached the elbow over the pump spout and the other end into the barrel. It worked well. When grandpa got tired pumping I took over for a while, and sometimes we both pumped together. When we had both barrels full we draped a burlap sack over the top of the barrel and then dropped a barrel hoop over each to hold the water from slopping out over the top. This worked well. We usually kept a third horse around for small jobs as the team might be in need in other places. Older, more or less retired horses earned their keep doing these kinds of odd jobs. In our case first it was old Frank then old Doll that got the job. Two barrels of water were a heavy pull for an old horse.

The summer of 1936 I remember the house was so hot at night that I slept out on a cot on the front veranda, and in the morning I would count the mosquito bites. However one night I got attacked from within. It seems a bumblebee had made a nest in the old mattress on the cot and I was crowding him a bit so he stung me on the bum. It was then I learned just how come they were called.... bum-ble bees.

During the hot, hazy mid-summer days when the heat was extreme the cattle would find relief from the sun in the shade of the great elm trees which dotted the country side. The farmers usually left at least one of these large trees in every field, just for the purpose of shade for the cattle and horses. If you searched for the tallest of all these great elms within your eye sight you would most likely see a Red Tail Hawk perched on the tallest branch in the centre of the tree. They surveyed their territory and only he and his mate were allowed in that area. We often watched as these hawks drifted high in the sky, drifting around and round in great circles hardly ever having to move a wing.

The great trees are long gone because of the Dutch elm disease that crossed the cities, towns and countryside a number of years ago. We lost the hawk to pesticides about the same time. Both are sadly missed. The elms you see today are seedlings from the trees we lost, and it will be many, many years before they reach the height of those majestic trees of yesteryears, probably never in our lifetime.

In the late afternoon you would find the cows under the great elms trees contentedly chewing their cud, and not wanting to be disturbed. Sometimes cows will come when you call them, but it is usually only when they feel there is something special in it for them. To call the cows you shout. "Co boss. Co boss," (don't ask me why) about a thousand times. Every now and then you would send the dog to round them up. The dog is usually only too eager to do the job, and at times he feels a lazy cow needs a little nip here and there to hurry her along. A cow with a full bag of milk cannot run very fast. A good dog usually just nips on their heels. The next time you go for the cows and call "Co boss Co boss" the cows would be more likely to come, but cows like little boys have short memories and without fear of punishment they don't always do as they are told.

Dad's 10 / 20 McCormick Dearing

My dad had a tractor for as long as I can remember. The first one I remember was a10/20 McCormick Dearing with steel wheels and lugs. It seemed there were many of these tractors all around the country, and I never heard of an unhappy owner so I think it was a good tractor. Farmers though had a love affair with their horses and they could not believe the day would come when there would be no need for a workhorse down on the farm. The team worked great in the bush, getting around trees and certainly as long as they had a threshing machine the team of horses worked better picking up sheaves from the stooks than a tractor. The first change came when they cut the wood spokes on their wagon wheels down and put on steel rims and rubber tires. This made the wagons much lower and better to load hay or pitch grain sheaves onto. The rubber tires also made the loads much easier for the horses to draw, but it took great courage to finally cut the wagon tongue short and hitch the tractor to it.

The Tornado - In The 30's

It was in the mid 1930's that I witnessed the awesome and destructive power of my first ever tornado. We had no early warning of it as at that time the battery powered radio was used reverently for little else then the evening news.

The day dawned much like any other summer's day in the thirties, hot and dry. My grandparents who lived in one part of the house had asked dad to drive them to Woodstock so to visit with my grandma's sister, my Aunt Miami. My mom was going to stay home with we four kids. It was a wise decision I would think as dad and mom along with four kids and my two grandparents would make a crowd.

In the early afternoon the sky to the northwest started to darken up. Soon we heard long rolling thunder amid flashes of lightning. I remember standing on the sidewalk with mom and my sisters watching black rolling clouds approaching from the north west. As the weather had been hot day and night nearly all the windows in the old brick house were open. When a storm approached the first thing you had to do was rush around to every room in the house and close all the windows.

My mom ushered us into the safety of the house and then ran up the staircase to shut all the windows throughout the house. This gave me a good chance to get back outside to watch the action. I was fascinated at that time by a good thunder storm as I still am today. I stood on the veranda hugging the post next to the steps. I had little fear. God was putting on this great show just for me. The rain poured down and the wind roared as it picked up debris and tree branches and hurled them through the air. What a show. I was simply thrilled from head to toe until my mother grabbed me by the shirt collar and literally tossed me into the kitchen.

I am sure by now my mom expected it was more then just the usual summer thunderstorm so she probably expected the coming of a tornado. Mom knew the old back kitchen built onto the house was not the safest place for us to stay, so she herded us into the front hall where we all sat on the lower steps.

Soon we heard a terrible banging coming from the dining room. After a second and third and fourth bang we all left our sheltered spot and ventured close behind my mom into the dining room to find out what was making the noise. When we looked out the dining room window onto the front veranda there was Billy our huge old billy goat who had been on a chain pasturing in the laneway. We kids were afraid of him as he always was mean tempered and ready to charge us if we came close. He was now terrified by the storm and wanted inside. He banged his head on the front door as only a billy goat can do. Mom knew he would break the door down and come in, if she could not get him to go away.

There was a large pot of very hot water on the back end of the kitchen stove. Mom carried the hot water to the dining room door and opened it and threw it on poor old Billy's head. He dashed off the veranda shaking his head and we didn't see him again until after the storm.

A loud crash came from the back kitchen area and we could feel a cool draft flowing into the house. It seemed to be coming from the woodshed door off the kitchen. Mom opened the woodshed door and found that the old apple tree which had stood near the rear of the back kitchen had blown down and the top of it came through the woodshed door. Of course I was excited and not a wee bit unhappy, I would not have missed all this for the world.

Now with the tree in the woodshed mom took us back to the front hall steps. It grew dark and the wind howled while the house shook. Then suddenly it was over.

Going out the kitchen door onto the veranda, I was shocked to see the roof of our driving shed lying on the sidewalk which extended from the veranda steps. The north east end of the barn roof had just disappeared. Everywhere I looked trees were uprooted and damaged. Once a row of tall spruce trees lined the south side of the laneway and maples on the other. All of the spruce were now downed and only a tall lonely pine tree survived. It still stands on the old farm to this day. The maples were very badly damaged. Our once great orchard which my grandpa had been so proud of had been hit hard. Over half the apple trees were uprooted.

Meanwhile dad and my grandparents were driving home from Woodstock. Apparently along the path of the tornado. They were wondering just what they would find when they arrived home. They saw much destruction along the way, barns flattened and houses destroyed, trees uprooted or with broken limbs. When they finally arrived home I think they were actually relieved to find the barn and house still standing. I remember all the neighbours turned up the next day to cut up the downed trees. My dad and grandpa went to the bush and cut a number of straight long poles and flattened the one side to be used on the roof of the driving shed. I think they salvaged most of the sheeting from the old roof on the lawn. I can still hear the pounding of the many hammers on nails as the neighbours worked diligently side by side on the roof. Soon it was done and time for the shingles to go on. The wonderful aroma of the new cedar shingles filled the air. I know all the neighbours came and worked together for free. That's the way it was, the way we were. Such tragedies always brought out the best in everyone in the community. It takes years to recover from the damage done to trees from a tornado so it is best to go right out and plant a number of trees. Someone down the road will enjoy them

The billy goat survived and was soon enjoying the pasture along the lane once more. The many huge flat top stumps left from the trees that were cut down along the lane were his domain. He stood on top of the stump and reared and shook his angry head and challenged anyone who dared to come near.

A New Furry Friend

Farm boys soon earned the job of "Getting the Cows" I was very small when I was first told to Go... Get the Cows and the cows were very big. The odd one would challenge a small boy alone, so a good dog was a real help. I had Toby a wonderful cattle dog and a good friend. He was like most farm dogs at that time, tan and black with a splash of white on his face and throat. These dogs were referred to as farm dogs and they were everywhere. When they first arrived here in Canada from England and Scotland they were not recognized as a breed. They were not at all like today's border collies, but were a much heavier and a more muscular dog. They were very protective of children and live stock and also very territorial. As yet there was no dog food, as we know it today so along with skim milk at milking time they were fed table scraps, stale and left over food. They caught the odd rabbit and hunted for mice, to complete their diet.

These dogs proved to be an ideal farm dog, staying happy and healthy. For some reason they were a popular dog up until the 1940's to 60's when they started to disappear.

One evening when Toby and I went to the field for the cows we met the most beautiful black cat in the lane. She wasn't actually that big, but square set with short legs and large paws and green eyes. I think what I remember most was her luxurious coat of short coal black hair. She was plump and healthy and very friendly. We made friends right away. Perhaps she had wandered too far and got lost and now needed a home. We went on to get the cows and the cat followed me closely, then back to the barn together where she seemed to fit in right away. She got along well with the dog and all the other cats. I named her Tiny I think mostly because of her short legs. She spent much of her time hunting mice around the buildings and afar in the fields, the kind of cat a farmer really needs to keep his buildings free of mice. We called them "mousers." Thus she earned her keep and always remained in very good condition, and sadly this in the end was what got her killed.

In early spring my mother got her usual flock of little day old chicks. There is nothing so beautiful as baby chicks - just a ball of warmth and fluff, totally innocent and unafraid, they seem to be born without fear. We all know chickens spook, but that is something they learn later. At first they were put in a Colony house, with a brooder stove in the centre. A brooder is a kind of pot-bellied stove with a steel hover fitted over top of it to keep the heat down on the floor. The first ones I remember were coal fired, and had to be watched very closely as it was easy to get the colony house too hot or let it get too cold. A huge thermometer hung on twine from a nail in the rafter to just a few inches off the floor next to the hover. The temperature down there was supposed to be kept over 80 degrees. The little chicks would settle into a ring around the hover area to sleep. If it got a bit too warm they crowded out from the circle and if it got cool they crowded in. Ha! Life seemed so simple to a baby chick. You dashed out from the heated area to get a drink of cool water from the water fountain, then grabbed a free meal from the hopper, took a quickie poop and dashed back under the hover area again to keep warm.

When they grew too big for the colony house we put them in what they called shelters in the field. These were actually just roosts on wire with a v roof on top. The droppings fell through the wire and collected below. Every so many weeks you had to tip the shelter over and fork the droppings into the manure spreader and spread it out on the pasture field. At first you enclosed the area where the shelters were with chicken wire held up by wooden or iron stakes, which were driven in the ground. After a few days when the chickens got use to calling the shelter home, you could raise the chicken wire giving the chickens freedom to run a bit farther afield from home. For a while you had to watch to see that they all returned to the shelter at night. I can see my mom out there now with one hand on either side of her apron shooing chickens in under the wire fence, so they would go into the shelters for the night. Once they were all in you shut the doors on either end of the shelter. This was a nightly job; one mom usually did by herself.

She did however let me carry water several times a day out to the fields for her chickens. To this day I always say I got my long arms from the thousands of pails of water I carried to those darn chickens!

We began to find dead chickens at the shelters almost every morning. Something was killing our chickens. After some thought my grandfather said, " It must be that fat cat Tiny as all the other cats are lean."

Tiny must have felt that something was not just right as she kept her distance when my Grandfather and my dad tried to catch her. Grandpa asked help from my sisters and me but we declined, as we loved that cat. But in the end they caught her and she was killed against the barn wall, amid the wails of us children. Tiny was such a loving and beautiful animal, a pitiful ending for such a good and loving cat. Needless to say, the killing continued, and in the end they found out it was skunks visiting the shelters during the night, and pulling the chicken out through the wood slats in the doors. I have never forgotten this ill ending, for such a loving and beautiful, hard working cat.

Rabbits

A distant cousin gave me two white rabbits. They made great pets but it was some time before I would trust Toby alone with my rabbits. I had often seen him chase down and catch many jackrabbits and cottontails and shake them senseless by the scruff of the neck and then devour them with great gusto. To him I felt all rabbits white or not, were food.

For meat farm dogs were expected to catch their own. Most dogs lived on table scraps plus bread and milk. Needless to say many dogs were always hungry and suffered from maltreatment and malnutrition. Toby though was breed apart from many dogs and was a plump and loving dog, with a luxurious coat of hair. He did have his pride, so he would have nothing to do with my pet white rabbits and they grew very bold and often nipped him on the heels. After he got use to the rabbits, and the rabbits got use to running free. I no longer locked them in at night. So as rabbits, they were free to do, whatever it is that rabbits do, when free to do as rabbits do. But like all rabbits, come morning, you should find them home asleep ... exhausted from doing whatever it is that rabbits do.

Toby had this special spot where he liked to spend his time sleeping at night, which was in front of the door of the little shed where my dad stored his barrels of gas and fuel oil. In the early morning the sun would shine down on the door and reflect the heat and add to his comfort. I would look out of my bedroom window first thing in the morning and see my two white rabbits snuggled up against Toby, taking in his warmth over night and then the warmth from the early morning sun. The rabbits looked for all the world, at peace and safe, comfortable and happy. But the minute Toby heard some one up in the house he was out of there, as he well knew, no self respecting farm dog got caught in bed.... sleeping with rabbits. The rabbits eventually disappeared but I am sure Toby had nothing to do with it. Secretly I think he grew to enjoy them.

The Orchard

Our orchard as I remember it had many large old and over-grown apple trees. These were trees that really looked like apple trees. By that I mean trees with large trunks and low spreading limbs, which invited children to climb and play. These strong limbs were also just right for swings of all sizes. As a small child I spent many hours lazily dreaming while sitting on a swing under the shady old apple tree. My grandfather had at one time shipped many wooden barrels of apples to England from these trees. Unfortunately he did not understand how to manage an apple orchard very well and most of the trees were non-productive. Grandpa was a true farmer and he liked livestock and field crops. While he did enjoy his garden with a patch of rhubarb he was not interested in growing apples or other fruit.

Every spring I would anxiously a-wait for the blossoms to appear. As a child I looked upon this with wonder and delight. There in our orchard for a number of days each spring were ever-blooming clouds of blossoms from one end of the orchard to the other. Robins sang cheerfully as they made their nest or fed their young amid the great bundles of blossoms. Fragrant scents drifted down to us under the trees. We walked under the white blossoms and their many shades of pink, which in the distance drifted off into a soft purple hue. The drone of busy bees and happy song of birds filled the air and made all this seem, ... a promise for a fruitful year.

For some reason most or the trees never bore fruit. However there were always all the apples we needed for ourselves. Spies for pies, harvest apples for applesauce and moms great apple pudding, Snows for early eating and Thomas

Sweets and Russets, which kept well all winter. In the mid summer there was a wonderful eating apple we called Yellow Transparent and in the late summer a red apple called St Laurence. Almost every farm in our area started out with an orchard, which over the years grew old and" slowly died off.

"Tramps of the 30's or Someone's Son

During the thirties there were a lot of people without jobs- many boys in their teens and young men in their twenties and even husbands left home so there was one less mouth to feed. The only way a woman could get what one might call welfare today, was if there were no adult males living in the house... so many sons and husbands in great despair left home so the family or wife and kids could get a government check to keep them from starving. This government regulation broke up many families, and put so many men out on the road to nowhere. It only added to the country's despair, as there were no jobs to be had anywhere.

These young men and others not so young were put out on the road, and this perhaps brought out the worst in some of them. True there were some that were not to be trusted, some even dangerous, but for the most they were just some one's son or husband that had no other choice. There were no jobs and no such thing as Unemployment Insurance at that time for them. When one of these poor chaps came down the road and the men were in the field or away, the women, alone in the house with children were afraid to open the doors to them. We called them tramps. Many were desperately, hungry and had no food, no money and no place to sleep at night. Most people were afraid so locked their doors and pretended not to be home when a stranger came a-knocking… In cold weather some would steal into your barn late at night to sleep near the livestock for warmth. Unfortunately nearly all men at that time smoked, and they liked to smoke just before they slept so it was thought that many barn fires were caused by these so called tramps.

One evening in mid summer as we were doing our evening chores, a man (a tramp) walked in the lane from the road and asked if we would give him supper or some food. He didn't look like the average tramp. He looked like some one's son, and we felt sorry for him. That didn't mean a free meal as most people had trouble just feeding their own family. My dad said if he cleaned out the horse stable while we were milking the cows he could have supper and even stay the night with us if he wished. Our horse stable was about six single horse stalls long, but only four were in use.

In the summer the stable's work often got left while men worked in the fields so there was a nice pile of manure in each stall. My grandfather got a kick out of the way this guy went about cleaning out the stable. It was easy to see he was not a farm hand to start with as he started at the door and worked back to the far end of the stable. To clean out horse manure (buns) most farmers used a special home made tool. One was called a push board and the other a huge rake with wood peg-like teeth. Both were about 16 inches wide and 6 inches high, to which was fastened a long wood pole handle. I don't ever remember seeing these tools sold in a store, but many of the neighbour farmers also had them so I expect they were home made. You sort of raked the horse buns from the straw then pushed them into a pile and lifted them with a fork into a wheelbarrow. But a farm hand would never push the manure away from the front door and then load it into a wheelbarrow and carry it back towards the door out onto the manure pile. You always cleaned stables from the far end and worked towards the door. It just made sense.

Mom saw that the young man had enough to eat and after supper he noticed mom's piano in the dining room. He asked if it would be OK if he played it. This was the first time I ever saw a man play a piano. Men played mouth organs, guitars and the violin, but few played the piano. I still remember the way he played that piano. He made it rock! Later we all sat around listening to the radio for a while and then the evening news. It was getting late and we were soon going to be ready for bed. The man got up and walked out the kitchen door. It seemed a natural thing for him to do as we thought he went outside to relieve himself before retiring. At that time we didn't have inside plumbing so we didn't think anything of it.

But we got anxious as time passed and he never came back in. Our real concern was that we hoped he had not gone to the barn to spend the night as he smoked and we didn't want him smoking in the barn. We had no hydro or electric power at that time, so my dad lit a lantern and he and I went off to the barn to search. Now my Grandparents lived in one half of the big farm home, well not exactly half, actually a bedroom, kitchen and the front parlour. They used the front hall and door to come and go.

I remember, walking close to my dad who was carrying the lantern and I was scared to death that we might have to confront this young man and I was aware my dad had never fully recovered from polio, and I was not very big to be of great help if things didn't go well. At the foot of the stairway to the upstairs of the barn we looked up and suddenly saw a dark movement. Dad raised the lantern, and to my relief it was grandpa. Grandpa was a small English man about 5 foot 8 or 9 in. going on six foot six. He never backed down from anything and no matter what was done, cleaning stables, cutting wood or stooking grain; he always had to be the best man, after all he WAS English.

He often demonstrated how he could take a dry Canadian thistle and crush it in his bare hands, as his hands were so callused from hard work from using hand tools the thistles would not penetrate them. I have seen him do this many times. So there he was in the dark at the head of the staircase going into the up stairs of the barn to look for the tramp, all alone. I have often thought ... how brave he was for a small man and so very plucky, but then again maybe it was not really such a smart idea to go there in the dark alone. We never saw the young man again. I often wondered what happened to him. Somehow I felt he was OK. I wished him well as I am sure he was just someone's son.

A Wondrous Gift

Do you believe that there are times in life, when you may witness something, you can't explain to others something so pure, so wondrous that it will stay with you all the years of your life? In your heart you have this strange feeling that just for the moment or for a few minutes God granted you a gift, of a wondrous vision of beauty that would be yours to keep for as long as you live. When I was perhaps 10 or 12 years old, I was awakened in the night because of the brilliant light shining in the bedroom window. Looking out the second story window of the old farm house into the little field between the house and the road I saw the most beautiful shafts of moonbeams coming down from all sides between the rows of spruce trees, which edged in the little field. The moonbeams seemed to be setting a stage for the perfect central scene... Then, to the orchard side beneath the spruce I saw two fawns emerge very slowly and cautiously into the shafts of moonbeams. It was as if the beauty of that wondrous light that surrounded them enchanted them too. Soon they felt safe and they began to dance, to jump and run amid the moonbeams. How can I describe it to you? It was heavenly. I know I witnessed something special that night. I tried to tell my dad and mom about it in the morning, but I know they felt it was just a kid's dream, but I knew it was for real.

Cold Winters and Cutting Wood In The 30's

Winters in the thirties and forties were quite another thing, it always seemed that Christmas came almost half way into winter as the snow came down so early and stayed so late, until spring finally arrived. There were huge banks of snow piled up everywhere around the buildings. Only the tops of the cedar fence posts projected out of the snowy fence lines, while most of the fence itself was hidden below in the snow. We used Fahrenheit to tell the temperature in those days and for weeks on end the temperature would drop to minus 35 or 37 below. This today would read well over minus 50 C below.

I remember how happy my dad was one day when he came home to tell us the good news. He had won the contract to supply the local school with a large number of cords of wood for the school furnace the following winter. This meant a great deal to help us out with our farm income. A cord of wood could be cut in lengths of, one foot, two feet or four feet long, but when it is piled to measure it should measure four feet high and four feet wide and eight feet long, this is one cord or 128 cubic ft. Most school had wood furnaces that burnt wood cut two ft. long. The wood would be split open with an axe and steel wedges, and then piled with great care to dry all summer. Late the next fall it would be taken to the school and piled in cords measurement, some in the school basement and the rest behind the school. I always loved the smell of dried firewood in the basement.

That winter my dad hired a young man to help him do barn chores in the early morning and then cut wood for the rest of the day. But when the temperature went down to minus 36 F he thought it was too cold to go to the bush to cut wood. The young man said,

"Well that's all right but I have to get paid just the same or I will need to find another job,"

My dad told him,

"Well if you have to be paid, then we have to cut wood," I was very young not more then six or seven but I clearly remember seeing them off to the bush. They donned their bush clothes in the horse stable. There, great heavy winter overcoats hung on wood pegs. They didn't have the kind of winter clothing we have today. These very heavy felt winter overcoats made of pressed wool were donned over jackets and sweaters. Under it all was their heavy wool winter underwear; two pair of wool socks in rubber boots, which were standard winter wear for farmers.

The last thing they did was to cut holes in burlap sacks to put over their heads to keep their faces from freezing while walking from the barn to the bush. They found that once they got deep into the bush and out of the wind they didn't seem to feel the cold as long as they worked. So as the hired man had to work hard to stay warm, my dad got a lot of wood cut that winter. One evening I remember they brought up a couple of beautiful pheasants that were frozen solid. It was a cruel winter for nature and during those cold winters in the thirties most of the pheasants and deer died from the cold and too much snow to reach feed.

Winter and Car Care, Roads and Travel

When the first frost arrived car radiators were drained of their summer water and filled with a combination of alcohol and water. Then it was tested so it would withstand cold winter temperature as low as -35 to -40 degrees below F. For some reason it had to be checked constantly as it boiled over, evaporated or just plain disappeared. Soon after the last spring frost was passed everyone drained the car radiator and the car motor block with great care and re filled the car with water. They would try to save this radiator fluid for the next winter. Often it was poorly stored in dirty or open cans and by fall it was terrible looking stuff to put back in the radiator. It was nothing to see car radiators boiling over just because of poor radiator maintenance.

Most cars in the early thirties did not have a heater and a trip into town in the winter meant stamping your feet on the floor boards to try to keep them from freezing. Buffalo robes kept the upper part of our body warm in the back seat but your feet always froze. Eventually the old buffalo robes went out of style and car blankets became a big hit and everyone carried one on the back seat of your car winter and summer. All cars then were rear wheel driven and the tires were made of a very hard rubber, which were not good for winter driving. The hard rubber gave them poor traction, so a set of car chains for your rear wheel was an absolute necessity in the winter, as most roads; especially side roads had lots of snow on them.

When you got stuck and spun your wheels you would easily break a chain link, thus you must always carry some black wire and pliers in the car trunk to fix your chains. There is nothing more provoking than being all dressed up in your Sunday best and having to get out of the car and fix those darn car chains. It was a wet, cold, dirty job in the best of times. There were times when it would almost drive you crazy driving into town hearing those chains bang bang banging on the underside of the fenders, all the way to town and home again. Some times I thought my dad was much deafer than I was, as he didn't seem to mind.

We were lucky we lived on a county road as perhaps once or twice a week a truck with a snowplough on it would eventually come and "Open the road." News of the arrival of the snowplough travelled fast on our party line telephone.

"The plough is coming, the plough is coming," and everyone would start to look for it. In some places the huge banks had to be hit several times before the plough could get through, and there were times of defeat and some roads just had to wait till spring before they got ploughed out.

The roads we enjoy travelling on today have been built up high over the years, allowing most of the winter snow to blow across them. The first roads more or less followed the lay of the land and the snow drifted in from the fence line. The small snow ploughs at that time just shoved the snow aside making a pathway down the centre of the road. Every time it was ploughed out it would blow back in higher from the bank it threw up. Today we have high roads and also the huge ploughs hit the snow and throw it far back into the ditch.

One winter we had been snowed in for nearly two weeks. Dad had made several cross-country trips to the village store for basic groceries, and tobacco. The mail was being delivered from farm to farm, so all we had to do was walk through the fields to the neighbours when they called us on the phone to tell us we had mail. Actually we were not badly off.

After a week or more at home on the farm and the plough was still "Broke Down" we were all getting cabin fever and were sadly in need of an outing. As an only brother stuck at home with three sisters it was driving me nuts!

Our great neighbours Ed and Joy Smith had asked us to come for supper if the roads were open. All that day we looked up and down the road for a plough, but it never came. By night we kids were greatly disappointed to say the least. When dad came in from the barn after chores he said,

"Get dressed, and dress warm because I'm going to hook up the bob sleighs and we will go to visit the Smiths." I am happy we had that bob sleigh trip, as I have never forgotten it. There were many great banks of snow across the road, from bank to bank. They called these up and down banks pitch banks or pitch holes. The horses foundered in the bank of snow and then pitched forth into the hole beyond. All the time the two bobs on the bob sleighs kind of cushion or ride out, over the rough ride. It was sort of like riding a slow but violent roller coaster, so a real fun and exciting thing to do. It was fun, and all we had to do was hang on. It was music to my ears to hear my sisters laughing yelling and hanging on for dear life.

Ed and Joy and son Ralph, lived about two or three miles away down a side road, I don't think Ron was born yet. They knew we were coming, and it was comforting for us to see the lamplight glowing in the kitchen as we arrived. I remember Ed was on the way out the door as we arrived to help dad unhitch the team and take them to the barn to be stabled. Stabling your neighbour's team of horses with great care was a part of common courtesy when visitors came for the evening.

Most people parked their cars at the end of their lane at the road, neatly piling the snow high on either side with scoop shovels. It seemed the drivers on the snowploughs took great pride in seeing how much snow they could push into your entranceway each time they passed by your lane. It was hard work shovelling. Snow blowers had not been invented yet. Those that lived on the side roads as we called them, would often park their cars some where near a county road or highway so they could get out, and in to town to shop when the main road was open. Many winters we were snow bound for days waiting on a snowplough, as it would be "broke down." Some winters it seemed the plough was always "broke down"

The local village stores were kept well stocked with all the main things people needed. These stores were our lifelines when things got bad. Most country general stores were also a post office. The store served as a community centre, a cross road for news in the community. It was a gathering place for winter weary farmers where smiles were fast and time was slow. No one was expected to come home from the local store with just groceries; they also brought home the latest news.

Mail men, were a breed apart from those who serve us today. In the winter they delivered by horse and cutter when there was too much snow for cars, and in their honour we invented the old saying, "Neither rain hail sleet nor snow held up the mail." When the horse and cutter could not get through, the mail still did as he came on foot and delivered it to a farm close to you where you could pick it up. Our Mailman was Bill Pelling from Fullarton. They don't make mail men like him anymore.

Going To School

In spite of the cold and snow most children walked to school. We didn't have super light and warm clothing like the kids have today. Often mothers made wool mitts out of the tops of worn out men's socks. My mom would skilfully use the top of the sock for the wrist and then with her sewing machine round out the hand and sew in a thumb and presto a wool mitt. Two mitts, one over the other would keep your hands warm. Our winter coats would be made of a very heavy felt material, which was made of pressed wool. It was heavy and actually weighed us down. All sweaters of course were made of wool and were a must to wear during the winter.. Often one wore a jacket over a sweater, over a sweater. It was often said,

" It is cold out, so bundle up." and bundle up we did, because we had to.

Everyone wore a long, long scarf and it was often the most colourful thing we owned. There was a certain way our mothers taught us to put them on. You off centre it on your forehead to start then throw the one end over your shoulder and around your neck. Then do the same with the other end. Then bring the one end up across your chin almost covering your mouth. Now do the same with the other end. Take each end now around your neck again ending up to one side. There was a special huge safety pin used to hold the scarf snug. You could then pull the top down low on your forehead and the bottom up over your mouth. All kids learned to do this with ease while jabbering away. In very cold weather it saved you from frostbite. But even bundled up in all those heavy clothes we would soon get cold if we just stood around too long, so it was important to always keep on the move.

For school nearly every boy wore tall or short laced up rubber boots with felt insoles on the bottom as otherwise they were very cold. Two pairs of wool socks were needed to keep your feet warm if you were going to be outside for long. If we got cold we often said, "Let's run, I'm getting cold." The run would increase our blood flow and increase our body heat, and for a wee while we could forget the cold...Such was life, we accepted it, and that was the way we were.

We would arrive at school with rosy cheeks and frost-bitten ears and nose and hands tingling from the cold. We gathered on the open furnace grate taking in the heat to warm our frozen body parts and dry our mitts and clothes. Soon we forgot about the cold outside until it was time to go home. School in those days began at 9:A.M. with a fifteen min. recess at 10.30 A.M. and 3.00 P.M. and a noon hour lunch break of one hour from twelve to one. The children were encouraged to play outside, except for the coldest days. I guess with fifty some kids playing under one roof it was almost necessary to occasionally put the kids outside for the teacher's sanity. The small children were out of school at 3:P.M. but the older ones stayed until 4:P.M..... everyday. Nowadays we see busloads of High school students in the middle of the afternoon going home or to a sport event and the teachers complain they are over worked and underpaid.

"My School Days"

In 1934 I started public school. I can still remember that morning. It was a bright and sunny day and Bill and Stanley Morrison came in the lane way to meet me. Bill was one of the older boys in school and he looked out for me during noon hour and recesses and saw that nothing bad ever happened to me. He remains a life long friend. Things were very rough and tumble in schools in those days and kids were not only teased but hurt. Teachers just could not get their work done and know all that was going on. The huge red brick school that I went to at Motherwell was built in 1916 and was the envy of every other school section in the township. It was the third and last school built in the Motherwell area.

The first school was built in 1847 and made of logs 20 ft by 22 ft. and was built near the Thames River at the foot of the west bank. In 1864 a new white brick school was built well down the road west of the river and Motherwell village. It was a beautiful school but after over fifty years of service it was replaced in 1916 with the huge red brick school that I went to.

The first thing I would notice as I arrived at school would be the two cement staircases going up on either side to the two huge front doors. High above the left door was the word BOYS and high over the right door was the word GIRLS, and God forbid any guy or girl that ever took a short cut and entered the wrong door. Make no mistake, it was sin, a great sin and there was no tolerance at that time for any kind of unisex ideas. Boys were boys and girls were girls and as far as public school went there was no encouragement for close encounters. That would have to wait. (I'm the fourth guy in the second row from the R behind the little blond.)

Pupils At The Motherwell Public School 1938

Motherwell Public School In 2005

Once in a while when for some reason we were going to be late for school or if it was raining, my mom would drive us in the old 1929 model A Ford. If there were any kids on the way walking, mom would pick them up to so they too would not be late or get wet. I remember how the kids would run away from the rear end of the car when they got out yelling.

"Run she is going to take off." It was a bit embarrassing at the time, but I use to love telling mom's grandchildren about this many years later. Mom would deny it, but it was true, she would gas up the motor fearing it might stall, and then she let out the clutch and spin the tires. Dirt and gravel would shoot out from behind the car. If you didn't get out of the way in time you got showered with dirt or gravel.

The school had a huge basement with two big wood furnaces, one on either side. Two-foot long blocks of firewood were pilled across the north end of the basement from wall to wall and from the floor to the ceiling. There were two lunchrooms at the front between the two stairwells, one for boys and one for girls. Each had two rows of small wood lockers with wire fly screen fronts attached onto the wall. Two long benches were against the other wall with two rows of coat hooks above. There was a glazed over window in each room facing the front of the school which didn't let much sun light shine in. At that time it seems school was not supposed to be a cheerful bright or sunny place. Upstairs the desks were placed in rows one behind the other attached to the hardwood floor from front to back. The Primer class sat on the east side one behind the other, with the smallest child at the front. Then first class, second class, then Jr. Third and Sr. third, followed by Jr. forth and Sr. forth with fifth class sitting on the west side of the school. When I started school almost every seat was occupied as there were over fifty pupils attending.

My first teacher was, shall I say, "Of The Old School." She was old-fashioned prim and very stern and she thought she had to rule by fear. A large leather strap was kept draped over the front of her desk as much as to say,

"Don't you dare?" She never left her desk without her pointer in hand. She would walk, no **strut** up and down the aisles between the rows of desks, pointer in hand looking for an idle child. She expected you to work and pay no attention to her or to those around you while she was sneaking up on you from behind. You were not allowed to turn your head, to see where she might be and if you did you got crack over the knuckles or on the head or ear with the pointer. I don't think there was a single pupil, who escaped her. Sooner or later we all had an appointment with her pointer.

My second year of school was so much different. We had a new teacher, a Miss Smith and I was rather amazed to find out we no longer had to fear the teacher. Miss Smith was an excellent teacher and we could actually relax, learn and enjoy school. Our Miss Smith is still living today as I write this and she is kindly thought of by all of the pupils she taught. I would also like to kindly mention my last teacher Miss McMillan with whom I still keep in contact. After I lost my hearing to scarlet fever she gave me special attention. Perhaps at the time I didn't know how to appreciate it, but I do today.

The upstairs was one great big room with a platform going across the front from wall to wall and behind it was a black board all the way across. On both sides was a row of large tall windows. At the back there was a teacher's room and a library room and two staircases, one for the boys and one for the girls.

The teacher's desk sat dead front centre on the platform, with an eagle eye view of the whole room.

I always liked the smell of our schoolhouse. I am not sure just what it was? Paper and books and school supplies? We used a slate board and a slate pencil for most of our general schoolwork. But I remember how much I loved a brand new scribbler or workbook as we called them. There were two kinds. The scribbler had soft grey paper, which was used for arithmetic, and another kind had smooth white paper, which was used for subjects like geography and literature. The wood desk we sat in was not intended to be too comfortable, but even then a few guys managed to steal a few winks of sleep. Our desktops each had a groove across the front for a pen or pencil. On the right side was what was called an ink well, a small glass chamber sunk into the wood and a flip up steel lid to let you into the ink well. The small kids started out with just pencils, and later on learned how to use a pen with a single nib. These pens made the kind of writing you see on all those scrolls in old books. It can be absolutely beautiful. Most kids had ink spills sooner or later on their clothes or desk and almost everyone had ink stained fingers Sooner or later you would have to grab a blotter and soak up that blot of ink you made. With kids it was inevitable. Later on after you mastered the pen and nib you started to use the fountain pen, but nothing writes like those old fashioned pens with nibs if you master the art and know how to do it. It was still years later that the first ball pens came out. It was then that truly good penmanship went out the window.

There was little time taken from school hours for sport activities, and teachers never took school time to upgrade themselves, and at that time I never heard of a parent teacher's night. The teacher worked through the trustees and vice versa. School for both pupil and teacher was serious business, and neither was ever allowed to forget it. Few pupils learned to like it and most longed for the day when they could escape. It was largely about an education driven by fear of the teacher and the school board or powers that be, with little thought given to make it entertaining or enjoyable. Still most teachers did their very best, as they too, were caught in a strict system and bore a heavy workload

I found that even with such a demanding workload they showed individual attention to those in need. When I started school, we had one teacher teaching eight grades or classes. I never heard of a teacher striking in all the years I was in school. Not only did teachers teach you while in school, but also they were expected to be still in charge of you on the way home from school until you reached home. In the summer many of the boys got caught swimming or fishing in the Thames River on the way home from school. Without a written note from your parents this was a no no, and if the teacher caught you she would send you home. The next morning you might even get called to the front of her desk and asked to explain yourself. She left no doubts in the minds of all you had sinned.

Once about a half dozen of we boys decided to go swimming in the Thames River south of the Motherwell Bridge and beyond the rapids. We were <u>almost</u> out of sight; except for a spot at the very west, end of the bridge and we were all frolicking in the water having a great time when some one shouts,

"*There's the* teacher." Six nude boys streak ashore, and dressed in great haste and made fast tracks for home. I bet the teacher still chuckled over that one for years,

The Thames River, Looking South from the Motherwell Bridge

but as they say, "Boys will be boys."

Sometimes in the winter the teacher allowed us to take our sleighs or toboggan down to the riverbank on our noon hour to play. It was on such an occasion that I got a broken arm. I had a rather cumbersome handmade sleigh, one that my dad had made to haul bags of feed to the barn from the road with when our lane was blocked with snow. I had just started down the hill when a faster toboggan rammed my sled and made it change course. There had been an old lime kiln dug into the hillside at one time many years ago and my sleigh dove over it and from there it was a more or less a shear drop onto the river ice.

Thames River, Looking North from the Motherwell Bridge

Somehow I landed with my arm twisted behind me and I was in a lot of pain. The kids gathered round and sort of rolled me onto my sleigh and pulled me back up hill all the way back to the school. The teacher came down to the boy's coatroom and tried to take a look at my arm. But it seems my arm had somehow jackknifed inside my leather jacket sleeve. And try as they might they could not get my arm out of the sleeve. My Aunt Maude in Detroit had given this jacket to me. It had been her son's until he outgrew it and it was now my prized possession, and I could see it was in great danger.

The teacher took a large pair of shears and began cutting up the sleeves and I bellowed and she thought I was in great pain. My pain was not so much from my broken arm as it was from having my leather jacket sleeve cut up. But the teacher didn't realize that until many years later. The arm was broken and Dr. Pridham and nurse Mrs. Churchill set it in his office in Mitchell. I still bear a scar on my left wrist from this accident.

It was a wonder there were not more serious accidents on that hill for as I said, Boys Will Be Boys, and all boys must have fun. Tony Gettler a neighbour boy had one of the best bobsleds in the community. It was a privilege to be invited for a ride on it. We would use the hill on the west side of the bridge when it was packed with snow. We would travel all the way from the top of the hill down past the store and far beyond. You steer a bobsled from the front bob, usually with your feet but Tony would lie face down on the bobsled with his hand on the front bobs to steer. Then perhaps four or five boys would sit on top of him from front to back. All with their feet locked up inside of the arms of the guy in front. Someone would be stationed at the foot of the hill to signal that all was clear, that is no cars or sleighs were in sight. Then with a good push off from behind down the hill we would fly sweeping across the bridge at a mighty speed and at times gliding far beyond the village store. What a ride?. What a rush? We knew now what a great thrill was and that we were brave and fearless. Again we would have a long walk back up the hill for yet another ride.

The Old Motherwell Bridge Looking West

Teachers were also expected to take an active place in the community, that is, they might teach a Sunday school class in the local church or sing in choir or even help with the Church Christmas Concert. To be sure we got much better mileage out of our teachers in those days, and fewer complaints. A teacher's life was very much committed not only to the school children but to the community, but one might say a good teacher got a just reward in one respect. They won a lifetime of respect from the students they taught.

At school we learned many things besides our A B C's, so one might call it a lesson in culture. I'm not sure if that is what you would call it or not. Our community had been divided in 1925 when the United Church came into being. Fifty percent of the community did not wish to join the United Church so they left and built a new but smaller church right next door to the school. So our community found itself split half United and half Presbyterian. This caused a bitter feud among the older generation. But the children in the school got along well together and they wondered what the fuss was all about. I expect the teachers we had at that time had a lot to do with this.

It showed us that with proper guidance ... and when teachers or parents did not instil unkind thoughts, kids are able to sort things out and get along just fine. I myself never seemed to suffer because my family was English living in a very Scotch community, and while my parents went to the United Church many of my best friends were Presbyterians.

This third school survived until September 1967 when the students attended the new South Perth Centennial School on the Mitchell Road. The old school was sold to a Mr Jack Lancaster of St Marys for $4,700.00 plus $200.00 extra for the bell.

"A Lesson Learned"

One day I came home from school with a very burning question for my dad. It was nearing Federal Election time and I was hearing pro's and con's on Liberals and Conservatives from kids in school and I wanted to know if we were Liberal or Conservative. It had to be one or the other, so I reasoned as everyone took a solid stand on these important issues. The way I looked at it was, our neighbours the Morrisons were Liberal and drove Ford cars and went to the Presbyterian Church. On the other hand the Browns were Conservatives, they drove Chev cars and went to the United Church.

It seemed everyone followed the family line generation after generation and his or her kids swore to do likewise. So it was only logical that we had to be something, but then my dad was different in many ways. For instance he loved cars and he had gone through several different kinds of cars all of them pretty old as he just could not afford a new one, but he loved his wheels. Right then he owned a Durant. He had proudly driven it home from Mitchell one day and my mom would not speak to him for weeks, as to mom a car was just something that got you from A to B and cost you money. But in answer to my question re-Liberals or Conservatives: Dad gave me the best piece of political advice I have ever received. Dad said,

" We are not anything, so don't marry yourself off to a political party, as money and power always corrupts people. So you must vote them in knowing, in time you will have to vote them out when they go corrupt." I have found this to be 100 percent true. Yet most people still don't seem to see the big picture as they refuse to see the writing on the wall. The government has gone corrupt, and its time for change. Just vote them in and expect to have to vote them out. Don't marry them Show no mercy. Thanks Dad for the truth. It makes my political life much easier.

"Motherwell Village," by the Thames

The Village Store at Motherwell

In the summer time I used to love the view of the Motherwell village as you came down the hill from the west. Great maple trees lined the road on both side forming a canopy over top. The west end of the steel bridge a commanding sight, above the Thames River below. There is something that seems just right, about an old steel bridge over a river that fits into a perfect pastoral picture with a village. The rumble of your car tires as you cross over the wooden planks disturbs the stillness and silence below. In mid- summer a blaze of multi-colour greeted you once you crossed the river. A cloud of coloured hollyhocks blazed the way of the south side ditch, from the bridge to the blacksmith shop. Bert Brown the village Blacksmith planted them there to hide a lesser view. Bert also had great lawns and many flower beds around his house and yard on the north side of the road. No one did more to make the village a pleasant place to live or visit than Bert Brown.

For many years during my childhood "The Village Store" was run by Ernie and Bessie Watson who were old school friends of my dad. It was there that all family and community and political problems got thrashed out in front of the counter. I like to think everyone benefited from the good old fashion pro and con and went home just a wee bit wiser, whether it was in the interest of the village, the township, the county, the province or country. Nothing was ever too complicated or difficult in those days that it could not be solved right there in the village store.

Bert Brown's Blacksmith Shop - Motherwell Village

Bert Brown's House In The Motherwell Village

To the west of the house towards the river Bert Brown had a large Old English garden which continued to bloom from early spring through to late fall. Great beds of tulips and daffodils and narcissus greeted the village each spring. Many kinds of perennials and bi-annuals which were strange to the rest of us bloomed all summer long into fall. Most farmers or farmer's wives settled for the traditional oldies such fiddlehead ferns and peonies in the spring and phlox for the summer and perhaps a day lily. Most spectacular was the blaze of Bert's hollyhocks and delphiniums

The Motherwell Store – in 2005

Once the active centre of the Motherwell community, "The Village Store" now stands vacant in 2005, abandoned to its fate. Warm memories flood to my mind of the place this store had in the lives of all who lived in the Motherwell community.

Perhaps we remember best the friendly jingle of the bell over the door as you entered. Or was it the welcomed heat as you came in out of the cold in the winter? Perhaps it was the smell of dry goods on shelves and counter such as only found in a country store. Here, there were always friendly smiles and pleasant conversation awaiting you The store was no doubt the heart of the community, the school the mind and the church the very soul. Put together, you have a community.

How does one put a value of our historic past which for a time served us so well? It was from this village store we received our daily needs and in many winters it proved to be our very life line as we would be snowed in for weeks.

It was in this blacksmith shop we had our horses shod and our plough points sharpened. It was here we had our broken machinery welded and wagon boxes made. It seems in the end we just walked away and let it fall in ruin, but has it not always been so. Every now and then I wander north along the river "Thames" and through the village "Motherwell" and sit a spell and think of those yester-years when all was well in Motherwell. Ah, old memories run deep.

The Motherwell United Church (Mitchell Road)
Sundays

    Sundays were, like life in slow motion. It was truly a day of rest. We got up a bit later and spent a little bit more time at the breakfast table. We planned the day yet there was no distraction from what Sunday was meant to be, a day when one shows thankfulness and respect to God for the blessings he bestowed upon us all week. There was no Sunday movies or shopping malls or even television as neither had been invented yet. If you didn't make too much noise you might be allowed to play "Andy Andy Over" over the summer kitchen after church.

    The church played a very important part in the lives of everyone in the community. You were expected to send your kids to Sunday School every Sunday and the parents were expected to turn up for the Church service, which followed. If you missed two or three Sundays in a row your standing in the community was at very low ebb. I didn't mind Sunday School so much as our Superintendent George Urquart had a great voice and loved to sing. He gave us lots of hymns to sing, long ones with half a dozen verses. He never tired of the oldies like,

"Jesus loves me this I know" "The old rugged cross" "Jesus keep me near the cross" and of course "Onward Christian Soldiers" My first and best Sunday School teacher was Mrs. Leslie Brown a dear sweet little old lady who let me talk my head off to her in class. She learned first hand all about the rabbits that came to our orchard every night to eat the frozen apples left on the ground. Or how many deer were seen on our wheat field, and how many pheasants came to eat the frozen corn silage beside the silo. She learned a lot from me every Sunday.

After Sunday School came church and dad and mom would turn up in their Sunday best, dad wearing his old navy wedding suit and my mom like all the ladies covering her hair with a large brim hat. They would stand talking to neighbours before the service began. Eventually we all climbed the staircase to the upstairs part of the church and walked down the aisle one after the other in single file. Dad would be in the lead followed by mom, then my three sisters Laurine, Pearl and Jean and I would bravely bring up the rear. When dad came to our pew, which was mid way along the north side wall, he would turn around facing his family with his hand outstretched to the top of the seat. One by one we all slid in taking our places leaving mom next to dad and then Jean the youngest next to mom. Dad of course sat on the outside next to the aisle protecting his family from all within. Church seats in those old churches were never intended to be too comfortable. Maybe they were supposed to be a part of our redemption. The seats in our old church were pure torture cutting into the centre of the back. I am sure someone must have had a great sense of humour when he built them, then came out to watch us suffer every Sunday, year after year. .

Mr. Anthony was our minister for many of those early years in the thirties; he was a short, round, bald man with a paunch up front, and a voice that droned on and on. Sometimes it faded away entirely and just when you thought he was done, finished, left, he came back with vigour and added more hell fire and sin. At my tender age I didn't understand much of what he said, but I had it figured we were all in very deep trouble. He loved to pray great long long prayers and the congregation loved it even more as a respite to rest their weary heads on the rear of the seat in front of them. Oh they didn't just plop their heads down there right away. It was a gradual thing; their heads would slowly but surely sink until their heads rested on the back of the seat in front of them. I found all of this, of great interest and I wondering whose head would touch wood first; my money was on Harold McKay.

In front of us sat two brothers and two sisters, about my dad's and mom's age. They were great farmers and very good neighbours. Every Sunday the one brother had lots of razor cuts on his face and neck. He would tear off small pieces of newspaper and stick them on the cuts to stop the blood from flowing. Our first safety razors were anything but safe and our first blades were called Blue Gillette. If you had a bad complexion or were in great haste to shave you would take lots of flesh off your face with great ease and suffer great pain. As I was not getting much out of this hell fire and sin stuff, I would concentrate on the pieces of newspaper on my neighbour's face and neck. I would lean forward and try to read his face. My dad chastened me when I got home; he said I should not try to read the funnies during the church service. I found it very much more entertaining then the hell fire and sin stuff. Long before the prayer was over some of the greatest guys I ever knew would be resting their heads on their arms on the back of the pew in front of them…sound asleep. While going to church was considered a must to maintain your social standing in the community, it also seemed our daily lives were lived in full view of the whole community. Thus a man was judges not by his wealth but by the straightness of his furrow and a women by her garden or her needle work.

Horse and Buggy's Cars and Radios

When I think of my dad and cars I remember how he loved to tell the story of his very first car. It seems he was able to talk his dad into buying a new model A Ford in 1925. My grandmother had two sisters living in Woodstock they liked to visit. My Grandparents would set out in the early morning with the horse and buggy to make this round trip from the farm at Motherwell to Woodstock and back. It was a very long and tiring trip of maybe over fifty miles one-way. They would arrive home very late in the evening exhausted from the day's trip yet they still had chores to do. With this car they were able to drive down to Woodstock and back with more time to visit, yet home in good time to do the milking, and other night chores.

Getting Home After Dark

They marvelled at this new convenience, and how it was going to change their lifestyle forever. My grandfather himself never drove a car or a tractor in his lifetime. He left that to dad, besides he loved his horses. At this time my dad was courting my mother at Munroe some seven miles north of the farm. He asked my grandpa if he could take the car to see my mom. My Grandfather promptly said,

" No, it has had enough for one day. Take the horse and buggy," and with that he threw the buffalo robe over the hood of the car and said, " Let it rest "

Our first radio was a box twice as long as it was high; I would say it was ten inches high and twenty inches long. The front had several dials that lit up with wondrous lights of colour when it was turned on. It was a thing of great beauty and total mystery. We as children were not allowed to touch it. It sat on a small table in the northwest corner of the huge dining room. I have to admit I paid it a few sneak visits when everyone was out of the house. A few times I even turned it on to watch its magic lights light up. There was a large horn like speaker with a long cord attached to it. Dad would carry the speaker out to the kitchen every night when he came in from work after the evening chores. He would have to go into the dining room and turn on the radio. Then we all gathered around the horn in the kitchen and listened in fascination, as it was "Pure Magic."

My grandparents lived in one part of our old farm home and each night after the news was over I would go in and tell my grandpa the latest world news hot from the radio. I soon found out that the more exciting the news was the happier my grandfather seemed to get. I loved my grandfather and I liked to see him happy so I poured it on. I would try to make it a bit more interesting for him. Grandpa came from England and he longed for news of home so I tried to help him out if there was a bad fire in London and 6 people died I would make it an even dozen. If there was a wind storm in Liverpool, and took out a block of houses I would have it take out 3 blocks of houses. I was getting along fine, or so I thought until my Grandfather started to ask my dad for more detail of these strange happenings. Oh boy! I was caught and they called it a lie, which made me very sad and I was asked to explain what was going on. Well I said I found out that I could make my grandpa real happy by telling him larger stories. Dad and Mom were really provoked with me and they explained that this was just like lying. I promised never to do this again not even to make my grandpa happy. I wondered if they would ever trust what I said again?

One cold winter day we had gone to St.Marys to shop. I decided to just sit in the car and wait on them to return. I remember that it was very cold and I soon wished I had gone with them somewhere inside where it was warm. But I sat in the back seat of the car stamping my feet to keep them warm and watched the few people walking on the street. We were parked mid way on the first block on the north side facing west. A door opened a short distance down the street and a man looked out and then looked up and down the street as if to see if all was clear. He re-entered and then directly backed out carrying one end of a table. The table had a heavy green throw draped over it, the kind a lot of people threw over their pianos in those days to keep the dust out. When the first man took a step backward, and down onto the sidewalk ....just for a moment the throw shifted and I could see two dangling arms and feet hanging down, from under the table. There was a man tied up under the table and that was why they had a throw on while they moved it. The two men loaded it onto a truck which was sitting there and drove off to the west over the bridge and out of sight. I have thought of this many times since and wondered just what was going on. When my folks came back from shopping I was all excited and tried to tell them what I had seen. They thought I was still telling wild stories like I had been telling my grandpa and so they would not believe me. This was a lesson for me and I could see that when people know you tell lies they wont believe you when you tell the truth ... a lesson learned.

My folks were English and the community of Motherwell was totally Scottish. When my grandfather arrived from England he was not actually welcomed into the community. Young people today tend to forget that this country was settled in block or areas, of nationalities. The Germans settled mostly to the north and east of the town of Mitchell. The English settled at Munro and Carlingford and the Scottish in the Fullarton and Motherwell and Staffa area and the Irish in the Dublin area west of Mitchell. This kind of block settlement went on all over the country. It was a good idea at the time as then they could help each other out best in their own language, while they gradually learned to speak English. In the early days a young man did not venture alone out of his own territory to parties or dances in another community, as he was not always welcome. If he did so he had to mind his manners and keep his mouth shut. Many a bloody fight got started over nothing other then you were out of your own territory and not wanted there.

It is truly wonderful that we survived all that, to arrive at where we are today with intermarriage of all people in all areas of the country. At that time it just didn't seem possible it might ever happen Catholics and Protestant just never married without getting kicked out of the family-sad but oh so true.

For a few years in the late thirties my sisters and I were lucky as the neighbour's daughter often got a ride to school in her Uncle Bill's old truck. You will find this story hard to believe but I swear it is true. Our neighbours had a long laneway, which filled with snow so the uncle parked his truck at the road between two great stone gateposts. In those days when it was so cold, most cars or trucks were very hard to start first thing in the morning. The car or truck motors would just not turn over, as they were frozen stiff. This Uncle Bill would carry a sack of straw out to the road every morning and push it under the truck motor and light it on fire. There was a bit of bush between the neighbour and us. My sisters and I would be standing at the road, freezing, while waiting on our ride. All the time we were watching for the smoke, as then we knew Bill was heating up the truck motor and hopefully it would start and soon be on their way. Uncle Bill started his truck this way on many cold winter mornings for years. Now I don't recommend this procedure for today's cars or trucks, but it worked for him so please don't knock it.

The thirties and early forties were desperately cold, which made life on the farm all the harder. What made matters worse was there was very little money to be made at farming. Fat hogs at over 200 pounds would dress out at maybe 170 pounds and at 28 cents a pound would earn you about $47.00 each. From this they would deduct the cost of shipping and handling, so you ended up with maybe $42.00. Little pigs eight weeks old would sell for about $5.00 or $6.00 each, and there were times you actually could not sell them at all. Eggs sold for about 28 to 30 cents a dozen for grade A large. They were packed into thirty dozen crates. You could not expect more than eight to nine dollars a crate after they were graded by hand. If you could sell a fat hen for a dollar it made your day, but that might mean you had to eat salted pork out of the barrel for supper. If you have never tasted salted pork out of the barrel then you have never lived, and if you have... you're lucky to have lived to talk about it. Absolutely nothing taste so vile as salted pork from a barrel. We ate it not because we liked it, but because our parents didn't give us a choice.

While these prices will seem almost impossible for you to believe today, you also need to know that bread sold for ten cents a loaf, and a gallon of gas sold for twenty-eight cents. You could hire a man for one dollar a day or twenty-five dollars a month if you gave him room and board.

It was not an easy life being a hired man on a farm. He would be up at six AM to do barn chores and then after working all day in the fields he was expected to help milk cows by hand each night. That was room and board. It was in a sense as if he were one of the family and thus expected to work the same hours as everyone else. The difference was of course he got paid $1.00 a day. As for the family on the farm it seemed they got free board and were able to hang onto the farm. Sometimes we envied the hired man as he had few expenses and no bills to pay and we would see him in town on Saturday night blowing his money at the local bar. He would be back to work on Monday morning looking a bit the worse for wear. He would be broke and waiting for next weekend's pay check to do up the town. Ah, such was life.

I remember my dad hiring a very young man. He was asking a dollar a day, but not room and board. My dad told him that no one was paying a kid a dollar a day. He explained that his mother and several kids were living in the old Dow house on the side road alone and the money was to go to her to pay the rent and to help feed the kids and he wanted to be at home with them every night. Dad hired him and never regretted it. That is the way we were.

In many ways we were lucky as we had lots of good firewood in our bush to keep our furnace going. Then my mom and my grandfather were good gardeners so we always had a good garden, and an orchard full of apples. In the fall we dug our Irish Cobbler potatoes, which in those days were huge and free of scabs and stored them in the cellar. There were carrots in a barrel of earth, turnips in the barn root house, and lots of apples both for eating and to make applesauce and pies. We never tired of mom's apple or raspberry pudding at our noon time dinner.

There was an open area in our bush where trees had been cut out and it was now overgrown with new kind of crops. First in the springtime the fiddlehead ferns would show their wonderful heads then grow and spread out. Wild flowers such as the bloodroot, hepatica and dogtooth violets and mayflowers grew in the opening. The red and white trillium and the Jack in the pulpit and tiger lilies all lobbied for space. But once the wild raspberry plant got started it soon overgrew everything else and within a few years there would be lots of berries to pick.

In mid summer, usually in July, mom would don a pair of dad's overalls and shirt and a straw hat, and gather my three sisters and me to go to the bush to pick wild raspberries. Every once in a while my dad might need some help from me but my mom would say,

"You can have the three girls but I want Jack as he can pick more then the three girls put together." Now picking raspberries in the bush in mid summer was no picnic for us, but it was for the mosquitoes. Some times we literally got eaten alive, but you could not go home until all the pot and pails were full. As time went by, with the heat and the mosquitoes we all got tired and cranky and mom would give us a little pep talk and say,

"Just one more pail full each and we will go" Then it would be, "Now if we top this basket or pot up we are done." It always seemed to work. Pearl was a very good berry picker, but Laurine and Jean knew when enough was enough and would go and sit in the car and wait on us. Mom would make lots of home made raspberry jam and the rest as fruit in quart jars; some times we picked thirty to forty quarts in a picking. Some winters we had as many as 150 quarts of raspberries on the shelf in the basement. That's enough for lots of puddings and raspberry pies. My three sisters and I still love our raspberry pudding turned upside down with whip cream for special occasions.

My Dad and The Butcher Knife

My dad often had to fill in for my mom while she was at the Women's Institute meeting at the Motherwell United Church. It seems occasionally while trying to save all the little kids in China they had to stay late at the church for supper. Actually, the ladies came well prepared to stay for a long, long time in their good old fashioned way with a potluck supper. Soon steaming bowls of heavenly food were on the table and perhaps for dessert one of Mrs. Nairn's masterpieces, which was a dark chocolate cake.

Meanwhile back home on the farm, dad would come in from doing the early evening chores to find four hungry kids on his hands. Each kid was just as hungry as any little kid in China, or so it seemed to dad. My dad was self-taught in his very own ways of survival and he never changed in a lifetime. He would head straight to the knife drawer in the old kitchen cabinet and out came that old magic Butcher Knife. None of us were allowed to touch it! We all knew there was something very special about a butcher knife. It was not a thing for kids to handle. To tell the truth we didn't give a lot of thought to why, for in those days kids did as they were told and asked few questions. One thing we did know was my dad could work wonders with a Butcher Knife and nothing else to get a whole meal.

My mom made those wonderful large round loaves of home-made bread, yeasty in flavour and spongy to the touch, with an aroma my sisters and I would gladly die for today. With his Butcher Knife dad would slice the whole loaf and then place it on the table without a plate. My mom would never do this so we thought it was, as kids would say today, "real cool."

Then there was a large bowl of home-made butter, which we kids helped to make by taking turns shaking cream in a large jar. The cream of course came from our very own cows, with old Boots and Bessie being kindly thought of.

Next we all followed dad with the Butcher Knife into the cool unheated front hall where on the floor sat a huge round wooden cheese box made of elm thinly sliced from great elm logs right there at the local box factory in Fullarton village. The box was made to hold three large round cheeses, each about four inches high and eighteen or twenty inches across. The cheese was made in the Stacy cheese factory right next door to the box factory. Beside the cheese box sat a full-size cream can, which in the fall was filled with local honey. We all loved to sneak into the hall with Knife, as when he sliced off generous pieces of cheese or a large curl of honey there were always a few small pieces for us.

Of course when mom was home we were not to tell her as it was called piecing before mealtime, and that was a no, no, but I'm sure my mom knew all about it.

The butcher knife worked well in the cream can too, and soon large golden curls of honey filled a bowl. Then we would follow dad and the butcher knife back to the kitchen where dad lit the coal oil lamp and soon a warm glow settled over the kitchen table. Dad would have his tea and my sisters and I would fill our glasses with our own milk.

Then we gathered around the table in the glow of the lamplight, knowing enough not to touch anything until the blessing was said. We thanked the Lord for this his blessing, and for dad and the butcher knife, and please God don't forget those starving little kids in China.

While there was always a shortage of cash I never remember being hungry. There were always homemade scones and tea biscuits on hand in our kitchen and a fresh chocolate cake every weekend. My mom was a good cook and I know she worked hard to see that we didn't know hunger. But just the same I was aware many people did know hunger - especially all those little kids in China, so I always had to clean up my plate, no matter how full I was. "Eat it up; the little kids in China are starving." Oh yes, I worked hard to save a lot of little kids in China.

Mom bought sugar and flour in one hundred pound bags and would bleach these sacks to get the printing out and to also make them whiter. From these sacks my mother and all the neighbourhood ladies made tablecloths and bed sheets and pillow covers. As children on the farm at that time we were not at all worldly. What you have never had or known about, you never miss. So all that we had we were thankful for, and we didn't feel we missed much. It also seemed all our neighbours were in the same shoe. There were a few people in our community that we knew had money, and I respect these people to this day, as at that time they never flouted their wealth nor measured their friendships in dollars.

My mom spent many evenings doing needlework and crocheting by lamplight. It is something I fondly remember. When the neighbour ladies came to visit she would show off her needlework and crocheting to them with great pride. She was really good at it. Every winter mom set up her quilting frame in the dining room and she would spend hours in there alone quilting, but once in a while mom would ask her friend Joy Smith, or my Aunt Pearl Butson for help.

We did our chores, ate our supper and did our home work all by lamp or lantern light. I always found it fascinating to watch my grandfather or my dad light a lamp or lantern from a hand rolled newspaper taper. They would tear off a small piece of newspaper and roll it from one corner tightly into a taper. Then lick the end with their tongue to make the end stick so it would not unroll. The taper was lit by sliding it under the lid on the stovetop, or if the kitchen lamp was already lit, they stuck the taper into the lamp chamber.

There is nothing more comforting than looking into your kitchen window from the outside of your home at lamp light within. It has a certain glow that is mellow and warm and caressing. We took coal oil lanterns to the barn and hung them on wires or nails from the ceiling beams. We moved the lantern from nail to nail as the chores proceeded. We needed a lot of lantern light when the days got short and dark in fall and winter. We milked the cows then separated the milk in the cream separator and fed the pigs and did all the nightly chores by lantern light. This meant going up into the hayloft and forking hay down the chute for the cattle to eat below. Kids handled lanterns everyday so I often wonder why there were not more barn fires than there were through out those years

Farm Cats

The farm cats all appeared in the cow stable at milking time like clockwork. They all sat around patiently waiting while you milked the cows. Some times when your favourite old cat was close by, you would aim a squirt of fresh cow's milk at her. She soon learned how to catch it in the mouth, but it would splash all over the cat's face. After she enjoyed the treat she would have to wash up. Sometimes several other cat friends would volunteer to help out. I never passed up the chance of squirting milk at one of my sisters just to watch them run! My dad would scold me for wasting good milk. But when you are a brother with sisters there are things that you just naturally have to do.

After the milking is done, you start up the cream separator, which was turned by hand to separate the cream from the milk. This became my steady job very early in life. I had to keep a sharp eye on the flow of the cream, as I could not hear the bell that rings when your speed is down. The bell rings because you are turning the handle too slow and your cream will not test 32 percent butterfat, as it was supposed to make butter. While working with the separator it was hard to keep the cats out of the skim milk pail and they were always under you're feet trying to outwit each other to get the first lap of fresh milk.

Have you ever seen a half dozen or more farm cats drinking fresh warm skim milk from a milk pail? It is a sight to see. The milk foam on the pail can be four or five inches above the top of the pail. In order to drink milk the cats have to submerge their heads through this foam down into the skim milk several inches below. The cats up to their shoulders in foam will surround the pail and you would think they were a bunch of headless cats. One wonders how they manage to drink and breathe submerged in so much foam. Farm cats depended largely on this skim milk morning and night as the mainstay of their diet, as they get no other food unless they hunted for it. Thus they sit and drink and drink until they are very wide and can hold not one lap more. Then they all sit around and wash each other up before finding a comfortable manger to sleep off their milk-full tummies. Good farm cats were well worth their board as they kept the mice and rats and sparrows out of the barns and other buildings. These are all treasured memories I have of those early years of out farm, our community our school and our church.

While one would not want to return to those days, I am glad that I was there to experience it. Because of those tough times when we had so little we can better appreciate all the good things that we have today. Our neighbours and us shared many of the same problems caused mostly by hard times and the lack of knowledge to better ourselves and perhaps even our unwillingness to make change. But we worked hard with what we had and helped one another, and we survived those thirties. There is a saying,

"Tough times never last, but tough people do" and I know from experience, that this is true. Almost a hundred percent of those people in Motherwell that I grew up with made good at what ever they chose to do with their lives, and now we have this special bond that keeps us forever together. We feel that we lived in times that put us to test; we passed that test, so now know each other's and our true worth.

Life as "The Only Boy"

Being the only boy on a family farm, means that all the odd jobs fall on you alone. It means that seven days a week you have to be available all of the time and as long as you're needed you don't really have a life of your own. The chores you are given to do will gradually increase, as you get older and stronger. You are a free hired man, and if you are not getting an education you will feel trapped with no future. As the only boy there will be no time for ball games or hockey games as 7 PM is milking time and the cows are waiting. When there are several boys in a family you might take turns getting off, but as an only boy you are trapped.

My dad did not play any sports, nor had his father, and neither my grandfather or my dad could see why anyone would waste their time playing games as there was no money to be made there at that time. It only meant one less pair of hands to hoe corn or to milk cows. In all those early years on the farm I never had a bike and my dad never bought me a bat or ball.

At school I liked football. We called it rugby, but I have never owned a football of my own. Other than to play ball on the school play ground, I played neither on a ball team nor on a hockey team. It was out of the question because as the only boy I was needed at home

When I first arrived home from school during the winter months my first job was to load blocks of wood from the woodpile onto my sled and draw it around the house to the furnace room window. I was to throw in enough wood to last the night and all of the next day. Being a kid I usually tried to take as big a load as I could and often much of it would fall off before I got there. As I had just walked home from School I might still be cold so I didn't appreciate the nightly job. But it had to be done and I was the only boy to do the job. It would be many years before my sisters got liberated and asked to help me.

As I grew older there were times that I felt a great need to do something for myself. This something might take me away from the farm and the farm duties I was expected to do. I was made to feel very guilty for leaving my dad and mom with all the work for even an evening. I know I felt trapped, more I felt because I was just needed, and not appreciated. For years I tried hard to please my dad and mom, but it seemed as if they thought if they said any good things to or about you then you might get a big head and get hard to handle. It was important to keep your kids humble and not too worldly. Kids should never have an opinion of their own on anything, especially one that is different from your parents.

My dad got up on the wrong side of the bed every morning. All the years that I was home on the farm he would call me each morning, never in a gentle voice of a father, but in a loud demanding voice of the boss. The voice said,

"Get up!" I well knew he meant NOW. I stumbled forth sleepily and he would say, the only 3 words that he would utter until after the early milking was done and he sat down at the breakfast table. The words were,

"GET THE COWS." All morning we would by-pass each other doing chores together but he would not talk. He never said an unnecessary word let alone a kind word before breakfast. It was as if he was angry at the whole world and me. I never got use to this. Somehow I always felt it was because of me and I should do better. Somehow I should please him. It was not that I didn't love my dad; it was more that I didn't understand him, and at times I know I even feared him. My dad was just not a morning person. It was not a healthy way to start off every day.

I think this is why I became so unsettled in my early youth and at the times I did not understand myself. It was as if I was needed but not wanted here. My dad had a very quick and uncontrollable temper, which made me afraid of him. One morning, just after we finished milking the cows he attacked me with a claw hammer leaving me with some very bad bruises, two of which were on my head. At the breakfast table my mom asked me what happened. I was too ashamed and perhaps even afraid to tell her the truth so I told her I fell down the steps at the barn. She never did find out what happened.

Every morning after breakfast, my dad had to go to the village store for tobacco. He never bought more then a day's supply at once. I never could understand why it would not make sense to buy enough tobacco to last 2 or 3 days or a week but of course I was just a dumb little kid who didn't understand adult ways. He would always ask mom if she needed anything before he went. My mom always tried to keep her grocery bill down, so as not to run up a bill. But men had to have tobacco and no one thought to question it, even if you had to do without food to keep the grocery bill down. Don't ask me why. Remember I was just a dumb kid.

Before he left for the store he would tell me the things he wanted me to do while he was away. There were other farmers doing the same thing. They gathered at the store, while their sons were doing their work at home. It's called "Being the Boss" or was it "Shooting the Bull?" How long they stayed depended on who all came in. When he arrived home he would tell mom all the local community news, which was of course always welcome. Then he would complain to me that I had not got enough work done while he was away. Well perhaps I could have done better but one got very tired of working so often alone. The trips to the store every morning and then afternoon trips into town while I was left to work always bugged me. Sons were not allowed to complain; it was looked upon as being ungrateful.

The good thing was dad lived to be 93 years old and those last few years we grew very close. I would see his face light up when I arrived at their door. There were times I knew he wanted to right things between us as he mellowed with age. He told me that I had been a good son a number of times, and that he was proud of me. Then one day he told me,

"Jack I wish I had a chance to do it all over again and things would be a lot different between you and me." That was the nicest thing he ever said to me. I remember answering,

"Well dad lets just be thankful we have had these last few years to get to know and appreciate each other," but I am getting ahead of my self here.

Len, My City Cousin

One summer in about 1937 or 1938 my mother's brother who lived in Stratford sent his oldest son out to the farm for the summer. His name was Len and he would be 16 or 17 at the time. Of course I was quite happy to have him there, as I had always wanted a brother. But I didn't enjoy that summer very much because Len knew all kinds of crazy things to do that got us into trouble. Of course Len got off as he was a city kid out on the farm and didn't know any better but I was a farm kid and should know better. So almost everyday I got a whipping from my dad, and I do mean I got a proper pounding. I remember dad saying that I must enjoy it or I would not get into so much trouble so I could not accuse my dad of not having a sense of humour.

One morning just as dad was leaving to go to the village store for tobacco, he told Len and me that we had to dig a hole in the orchard and bury a dead calf. I don't remember how the calf had died but I do remember it was dead and stiff as a doornail. Dad showed us the spot were he wanted it buried under an apple tree, straight out from my grandparents kitchen window. I could see my grandpa looking out at us.

It had been quite dry that summer and the old orchard sod made hard digging. The sun grew hot and the ground seem to get harder the deeper we dug. Finally Len says it is deep enough, but I said I didn't think so. I was only about ten so not exactly an expert on digging graves. Len suggest we drag the calf over and see how it fit. Mmmm this sounded like a good idea. We did that and there was no way it would fit, as the hole was not long enough or wide enough and definitely not deep enough. So we went back to more serious digging. We decided to water the hole and see if it made the soil any easier to dig. Well, maybe it helped some, but it got us pretty wet and muddy.

Finally very tired and all sweaty wet and muddy, we decided enough was enough, and as long as it was buried who cared how deep. We dragged the calf to the hole again and sort of rolled it in. It didn't look very comfortable with its feet-sticking straight up in the air. So we pushed them down as best we could close to its body. Dad still was not home and we wanted to have it all covered over before he did or we knew we would have to dig the hole deeper. All was going along very well though and finally we had it buried. We decided to pack the earth down a bit with our feet. So we stomped on it.

Suddenly the calf's two front legs popped up out of the grave under us. Mmm this was not good. We tried to push them back down again but without any luck. Finally Len had a great idea. He asked me to run to the woodpile and bring back the axe. We took turns chopping the calf's legs off. Then dug another hole and buried them. We didn't think anyone would ever know about this. It seems my grandfather was watching all this from his kitchen window and he was rolling in laughter. Even dad saw humour in it and I didn't get my usual pounding. For years my dad told all our friends about the day Len and Jack buried a calf.

The War Years

I remember the day the Second World War started. Germany had already taken over Czechoslovakia and on Sept. 1st, 1939 attacked Poland and two days later were at war with France and Britain. Canada officially declared war Sept. 10th. We had just started back to school in September of 1939 when someone came to the school door to tell the teacher, and the teacher relayed the message to us. We were now at war with Germany! As children we could not possibly grasp the meaning of this or how it was going to affect history or our very own lives. Let us say that in 1939 the world we lived in was rather small, and close to home. Germany seemed a long ways away and we were safe here in Canada. I remember hearing several of my Uncles who were veterans of the First World War talk endlessly about war every time we visited them. As a child I got rather upset with the fact that the conversation always got around to the war, which to me was fought many years ago, long before I was born. Now I know it was something they had experienced and had to talk about in order to deal with it.

Soon we heard news of our neighbour sons enlisting, first a trickle and then a flow. I began for the first time in my life to see uniformed men and boys at the village store or on the street in town. Patriotism was born to the look of crisp new uniforms and to the sound of marching feet. But none of these young men were aware of the kind of war that lay ahead of them. Canada actually had no military at all in 1939. We had to start from scratch. Germany was years ahead of us with military equipment we never dreamed of.

In 1939 Canada was largely a rural nation of eleven and a half million people. Now in the year 2004 it has a population of about thirty three and a half million. The city of London had a population of seventy six thousand in 1939 but now in the year 2003 it has a population of about three hundred and fifty thousand.

This war was a tragedy to all sides with a terrible loss of property and life, but it changed Canada forever. Within five year's time we were a different nation and it was unbelievable. From a sleepy nation plagued with seemingly hopeless unemployment and poverty we made a complete about turn to prosperity. Everywhere people were working spending money and creating more jobs. We had one of the largest air forces in the world, and a navy to be proud of. The nation had finally awakened from its slumber. There is a verse in the Old Testament, which has universal truth. It says, "Where there is no vision the people perish." It is sad it took a war to awaken us, to make us pull together and find our vision.

In the nineteen forties things got a lot better out on the farm. The second world war effort, caused farm production to increase along with good prices for their products, to feed England and the armed forces built up from all the "at that time" British Empire.

For the first time ever farmers felt they could step out and enlarge their farm enterprise. Canada had secured a contract trade agreement with England for all the, bacon and eggs we could produce. My mom was in seventh heaven and she increased her flock of hens from about a hundred and fifty, to three hundred, and then to five hundred. Our evenings were now largely taken up with a wet cloth in hand cleaning hen eggs, a job none of us seemed to enjoy.

Up until now I don't think any farmer who farmed ever gave thought of doing it to make money. It was more often not a chosen way, but rather an inherited way of life, which might allow you to earn a decent living but nothing more. Farming was not thought of as a real job. It was said some people left the farm and got a job. Others never had a job, as they farmed all their life. This was probably the reason why my mother never had any Canada pension when they retired. She was a farm wife and while she kept a house and raised 4 kids and helped with all the farm work from driving the tractor to the milking the cows she didn't have a job, or so the government said and so could not pay into Canada pension. "Go figure."

Saturday Nights

We lived for Saturday night when we would all pile into the family car and head off to town, but first we each had to have our weekly bath in the old round galvanized steel tub. In the summer we bathed out in the wood shed. And in the winter mom used the clotheshorse with a sheet on it to hide us in the tub in a corner of the kitchen. Water was heated in a large copper boiler on the wood-burning stove in the kitchen. There would also be a copper water reservoir built into the rear of the stove. Shoes were shined and hair was combed and we donned our next to Sunday best to do up the town in style. As kids we were very happy and very excited as we lived for these Saturday night outings. Once a week we were able to break free from our long work-a-day week on the farm.

On getting out of the car I was given 25 cents and my sisters 10 cents. Every one knows girls don't need as much money as boys. We would search the town for the best buys. There were B B Bats for one cent each and gum balls two for a penny, liquorice cigars and pipes for a penny each. A hot dog cost a whole five cents and an ice cream cone the same.

Mother's brother and wife, my Uncle Loril and Aunt Pearl always went to town early on Saturday nights and took my Grandmother Butson to town with them. They would find a parking place along main street so my grandma could sit in the car and watch for her friends to go walking by. Your neighbours would be there and all your relatives and friends from near and afar, and to add some mystery many, many, strangers you had never met. The streets were packed as many of these people came to town only on Saturday nights. You could not walk straight down the street you had to dodge back and forward through the crowd much like you would today in a really crowded mall before Christmas. Oh the kids all loved it and they walked down one side of the street crossed over and back on the other side, around and around. You see at that time Mitchell was very much just a one block long town. Often the Salvation Army would be playing in the band shell in central of town and there would be a good crowd surrounding it singing hymns.

While I enjoyed the music I was much more a Roy Rogers and Gene Autry fan at the Plaza Theatre, so off to the show I would go every Saturday night. Children were not allowed to enter the theatre at night without an adult accompanying them. Thus we would have to stand out in front of the show looking for a friend or friendly face and ask if they would take our money and buy our tickets for us. Most of the time they would if you promised not to sit with them. Ha ha.

There is one thing I should tell you about the movies at that time and that is all the bank robbers and crooks were much more polite in those days. You see they would never think of interrupting Gene Autry or Roy Roger in the middle of a song. It was always as the last few notes of the song drifted off into the sunset that the shots would ring out... and some one would exclaim,

"It's the bank, it's being robbed." So Gene on Champion or Roy on Trigger would gallop off, with their guitar slung on their backs, and their big white hats on their heads. They always drew their guns and shot the sky full of holes as they went after the bad men. Like the Mounties they always got their man. Then too, it was always easy to tell a bad man from a good man, as the bad men always wore black hats and the good men white. The good man never lost his cowboy hat while galloping after the robbers, and a good fistfight never even ruffled the good guy's hair, nor dirtied his clothes.

I would meet my dad and mom and sisters after the show was over, usually about eleven o clock. On the way home we would stop at Mrs. Elliott's store on the edge of town and buy a <u>Brick</u> (Quart) of ice cream. As we didn't have a refrigerator we had to eat it as soon as we walked in the door. Mom would hold onto the ice cream out the car window. She thought she was keeping it cold, because her hand got so cold. But as we know now it was the worst thing she could possibly do to keep it frozen. But that is the way it was, and that was the way we were. Mom would divide the ice cream into six pieces and we all sat around the table and ate it very slowly as it was a real treat and not something we got very often. Needless to say ice cream tasted much better in those days.

On the street corners there were often crowds of people talking in a foreign language, and many people complained about it. Now I know that it was because many of the older folks found it hard to learn English without any kind of help and while the young learned English at school, they spoke German or whatever, when they were with their older family members or neighbours of their community. It took many years for this country to come to terms with our different nationalities, as it was inbred in all nations everywhere for generations not to trust other kinds of people. I believe it was the high schools that led us out of this dead lock. Ron was Scottish and he met Nancy at high school who was German and they fell in love. Today they have children and grandchildren. They are great Canadians and we are all very proud of them.

As things got better farmers started to put in, inside plumbing, built in cupboards and running water. Those that didn't have hydro put in hydro and bought refrigerator and electric stoves. I worked hard on the farm all week and on Saturday night I got 25 cents. I was able go to more Gene Autry or Roy Rogers movies. Children paid eighteen cents and adults forty-three. The three cents on each was the government amusement tax. Most often I went to the show with my neighbour Stanley Morrison who was a great fan of Gene and Roy. Sometimes when my dad and mom would want to go home early Stanley's brother Bill would meet us coming out of the show. He always wanted to go across the street to Bill Hoflick's for a hot dog and a coke before heading home The problem was that after the movie I only had 7 cents left from my quarter, and a hot dog was 5 cents and a coke was another 5 cents. So I would just order a hot dog. When Bill found out why I never had a coke, he would just say give me your money and let me buy for us all and he would pay that three cents. I know today that does not sound like much but it was at that time, and I have not forgotten Bill for doing it. On top of that he had to drive me a half mile farther down the road to take me home. Without a doubt I knew I had a good friend and neighbour in the Morrisons.

"My Grandfather Cooke"

In 1941 while the Germans were dropping what they called blockbusters on London and other English cities, my grandfather lay in bed dying of cancer. His greatest concern seemed to be, what will happen to his dear old England as by now we realized this war was a long ways from being won. When the war started he was sure it would be over in a short time as he thought no one had the might to stand up to old England This turned out to be a different kind of war; one the world was not prepared for. I was 12 years old and I loved my grandfather dearly. He was perhaps the only person in the world in whom I had no doubts, I just knew he loved me. I remember sitting beside his bed and how he said Jack (A) (he always called me Jack- A)

"Jack A I'm not afraid to die. I am ready to go. But I would give anything to know what is going to happen to dear old England." He also asked me not to forget him and I promised him that I would not. I still remember being at our old public school when the teacher answered to a knock on the school room door. The teacher came back in and told my three sisters and me our dad was waiting for us. In my heart I knew even then what had happened but to a child death is a distant thing. You have to see it close up to truly believe it. I remember walking into my grandpa's bedroom and seeing and knowing that life had flown from this lifeless body. It struck me then, my grandpa was dead. I fell on my knees and cried.

I find myself driving up to the old cemetery in St Marys every year with a pail of suds and water and a brush keeping my grandparent's stone clean. After my grandfather passed away my grandmother spent the winters in Detroit with her daughter my aunt Maude and the summers with us on the farm. I dearly loved my grandma so summers were a special time.

My Grandpa and Grandma Butson of Munro

The Butson Farm Home at Munro

Their Wooden
Well Pump
by Jack

I don't remember very much about my Grandpa Butson, as he died while I was still very young. When I visited them it seemed he was always out at the barn doing chores or in the field. I feel he never gave me a chance to get to know him. On the other hand my Grandma Butson doted on me. I was well aware that cousin Reggie my Uncle Bob's oldest son and I competed for first place among all the grandchildren and believe me there were many. I do believe I should have given the spot up willingly to Reggie as he lived closer to them and I know he helped his grandma a lot more then I ever did. In fact I think about all I ever did for her was eat her chocolate cake and smell her flowers, but wait,.. I <u>was </u>a cute little varmint.

Would you believe it, my Grandma Butson always had a chocolate cake sitting on the kitchen table along with the sugar bowl, the salt and pepper shakers and a special kind of container with a thumb flip up lid, filled with maple syrup. The maple syrup was always on the table just in case there was an apple pie around.

Grandma's Chocolate cake was heavenly and always a thing of great beauty and if you didn't have at least one piece my grandmother would think you were sick. The cake was constantly replaced as a house hold necessity just before the last piece disappeared.

Two things I always think of when I think of my Grandma Butson. The first being of course her chocolate cake and the second would be her flower beds. It was Grandma Butson that got me interested in flowers. She had beds all around the old white clapboard house, big wide beds four to six feet out into the lawn. Then there was a huge mound of earth across the front of the house perhaps 15 feet wide and 30 ft long. The centre of it was easily 3 ft. higher than the lawn that surrounded it. I think it had to be the soil that came from the basement of the house when it was dug. Rather than haul it all away with horse and wagon they covered it with top soil……gave it to grandma, and …..called it a flower bed.

A vast lawn in front of the house ran all the way to the road (which was the 23 highway). Down each side were flower beds, and a huge chestnut tree spread across the lawn at the road. All this grass had to be cut with a hand pushed lawn mower. The older grand kids who lived close by often had the job, then after they grew up cousin Reggie took over the chore. I have seen his blisters.

Cars on the 23 highway often drove by slowly just so they could look, but many people came in to visit her just to see her flowers. Every time we visited in the summer she would take us out to see he flowers and do a walk around. I always loved that. However, grandma and mom would stand in one spot talking for ten or fifteen minutes about a certain flower, plant or bush. All the while I would be ten plants ahead begging and waiting, waiting, waiting. I would beg them to catch up. Saying, "Hurry up mom, hurry, come and see this one it's a butte."

I was fascinated by what my grandma could do with flower and flower beds, but grandma would not be hurried. She took her time telling my mom all about this or that plant, - where it came from, how long she had it and how well it flowered last year. I am sure my mom had heard it all many times before but that didn't really matter. This was one thing they both had in common – a great love for, flowers.

While they both loved their flowers I'm sure they each secretly knew this walk around was a very special time for them together. Mother and daughter. Perhaps what they didn't realize at the time was that I would remember all this as well. It was special to me too.. Ah! pleasant memories of my Grandma Butson.

"Fur and Feather Farm Pests"

It seemed that every farmer in those days had problems with farm pest. Squirrels would invaded the barns in search of easy food. They chewed holes in the barn siding, tore open sacks of feed, tantalized the cats and dog and in general made a mess. Young boys would find sport on week ends with a rifle shooting squirrels. Next to squirrels, groundhogs in your grain field or meadows were a constant nuisance. It was dangerous to gallop a horse across a pasture with high grass as the horse could step in a groundhog hole and break a leg. The most agitating problem I believe though was when you were cutting a field of grain. If you didn't know or see where the hole was your binder cutting bar would run aground on the mounded earth around the area breaking the guards, teeth and blade, shutting you down while you made repairs.

It was not uncommon to see a farm truck with a couple of farm boys driving slowly down a country road in the evening or a Sunday afternoon in search of groundhogs to shoot. While I am squeamish on the kill today, at that time it was considered a sport.

Foxes had all but disappeared in the thirties but made a comeback in the forties, and were killing chickens in the spring and summer months. They were wily, crafty creatures and hard to shoot. Often there would be a den of young ones and the best way, or perhaps at that time the only way to be rid of them was to dig them out. The end was not a pretty sight, but that was how it was and everyone accepted it.

Few farmers had much love for crows or black birds as they would walk down a row of corn taking out the corn seed one after the other until they had their fill. You could not get close enough to shoot them and a scare crow soon became a bird perch. In the end poison corn seed became the only choice. Starlings in the mail box were an endless messy problem as were sparrows in the sheds and barn.

A barn is usually home to a few pigeons and I don't think any farmers minded a few, but for some reason some barns seem to appeal to pigeons more then others. Our neighbour's barn was one of those. I remember well my cousin Arlo Cooke and a neighbour Vernon Roger coming by early one Saturday morning asking me to come along with them to our neighbour's barn to catch pigeons. They both had a sling shot but I was not allowed to have one. I would be about twelve or so. As I was always a climber they wanted me to climb the ladder on the end of the barn to the hole in the gable end and catch any pigeons which tried to escape. I wrapped my legs onto the ladder and I caught handfuls and handfuls of pigeons but I didn't enjoy what I was asked to do. That was to ring their necks and throw them down. I still remember that day with shame as I have always loved pigeons.

"I Lose My Hearing"

In the early forties most farm women were raising large families. Four, six and even eight children were not uncommon. I had three sisters who have always been very close to me and we are even closer today. They have given me all I have in the line of <u>family.</u> Every winter it seemed the school got hit with some kind of diseases. We had whooping cough, measles, flu and chicken pox. When you have 4 or 6 kids in the house down with the flu it was much like running a hospital. Scarlet fever came to us in Dec. 1942.

My three sisters and I had Scarlet Fever in the early winter of 1942. Where it came from we will never know. We were the only family in the community to get it. The school Christmas concert was called off and the school closed for several weeks. We were immediately put under Quarantine, with a big official looking sign placed on the farmhouse door. My one sister Pearl and I lost our hearing because of this. No one thing ever changed the lives of my sister Pearl and me as much as our hearing loss. While it did affect our hearing right away, making school work very difficult, the nerve endings in our ears were damaged so severely that they just kept dying off steadily over the next several years, until we both were almost 100 percent deaf. For Pearl and me this was an all-new world we had to learn how to deal with. Pearl used to play the piano and she had to give that up.

Music also meant a great deal to me. I used to sing first at school and church concerts and then at music festivals and I never got anything but a first prize for my singing. On the farm I sang from dawn till dust. I sang to the cows. I sang to the horses and to the pigs. Perhaps it was because I spent so much time working alone, I don't know. Life for me seemed much happier with a song. I do know all this singing all day long expanded my vocal cords allowing me to sing like the birds.

Mom swore the cows would not give down their milk if I were not there to sing to them. I was asked to sing at weddings and funerals and at talent shows, but as time went by it got so I could not hear the piano when I went on stage. I remember one of the last times I ever sang in public. It was in the Crystal Palace ballroom in Mitchell and half way through the song I forgot a line in " My Bonnie Lassie " and then I could not seem to get back with the piano as I didn't hear the music. It was very embarrassing. But the worst was that most of the people in the audience didn't know that I was deaf so they really didn't understand what had happened.

I also played the piano by ear and for a while I would play the song in an octave lower so I could hear while I practiced. But as time went on I had to put my ear right down on the piano itself to hear anything. Well, I finally had to give up my music. It was much like losing my left arm. I am a lefty you see. There was a time I knew every song that was sung in public, both old and new. Today I have no idea what the songs sound like, but I find the words of most songs offending and the English terrible. If they honestly can sing why do they have to sing profanity to get attention and dress weird and shake their butts while making asses out of themselves and then insult us by calling it entertainment?

As I had been doing quite a bit of singing I had bought every new popular song that came out. Today I have no idea what happened to all my music, it disappeared. I especially miss a little black book in which I had neatly written down every song I ever knew, I carried it with me all the time.

Making Maple Syrup

In the springtime on the way home from school we would visit Roger's sugar shanty, in the bush next to the road. They always made us feel welcome and would give us a big dipper full of hot maple syrup to sample. We would pass the dipper one to the other until it was empty, then they would offer us more. We always got all the syrup we could drink.

We also found out to that if you drink too much hot maple syrup you would end up making a hasty run for the outer house. Of course the Roger brothers knew all about that and I guess thought it a joke. Sometimes we ventured into the shanty during a cold spell when no one was there, just to see if there was some syrup left in the pans we could drink. We often found the sappy syrup in the evaporator frozen over, and mice tracks frozen in the ice along with a few of those little brown droppings. Still it did nothing to stop us from breaking through the ice so we could enjoy a cold treat. We lived dangerously in those days and I have fond memories of my visits to the Roger's sugar shanty.

We had a lot of maple trees in our lane way and down the road on the front of the farm. So I talked dad into letting me tap these trees and boiling the sap in the orchard. My Uncles lent me a syrup pan to boil it in. I managed to scratch up enough money to buy spiles. As for pails I used anything I could lay my hands on, mostly five and ten pound honey pails or beehive corn syrup pails right down to bacon powder tins. It was an odd assortment. I would rush home after school to find everything running over. I got no help from dad but my sisters occasionally helped me out to gather sap. We gathered the sap in the milk pails and stored it in dad's cream cans out in the orchard where some nights I boiled till near midnight until it was well down towards syrup. Dad would come out and get me and tell me to shut down and get off to bed. My agreement with dad was that I didn't take any of his firewood in the wood yard beside the house. There were always lots of branches that came down from the trees during the winter. So in a way dad got an early spring clean up but I have to admit I burned every thing wood that was not nailed down.

Mom not so willingly finished the syrup off on the kitchen stove in the back summer kitchen. The problem was the steam makes the wallpaper come off, and she thought that was bad. The syrup however was extremely good, and I made a number of gallons.

The Day We Played Hooky From School

I always fell in love with spring- the freshness of the morning air- the forest all about us green once again, and the morning sun warming us as much on the inside as it did on the out. It was such a morning on my last year of public school that I talked my two sisters into playing hooky from school for the day. I had never played hooky before and I might add never since.

We were walking past Roger's bush when it donned on me that on a day like this no kid should have to sit in school. Laurine was in her first year of high school, so I just had to talk Pearl and Jean into it. They readily agreed with me that it was a great idea for a day like this. For the first few hours we enjoyed our new found freedom and the freshness of the forest all about us. We played about looking for wild flowers, frogs or anything that crawled. But as the day got warmer the mosquitoes came out looking for their morning breakfast and it was so good they stuck around for lunch. They looked at my sisters and me as a newfound smorgasbord. We swatted and swatted but more and more hordes of wild and hungry mosquitoes descended onto us. My sisters were crying, buckets of tears and I knew I was to blame, but what could I do. If we went to school now we would have to explain to the teacher and going home now to face dad and mom was out of question. So we had to stay in the bush until the kids got out of school. After they passed the bush on their way home we left and hurried home. While we didn't enjoy the day one bit we thought at least we had got away with it. I knew my sisters would not tell on me. Late that night a girl in my class at school phoned my mom to find out why we were not in school that day. Caught! There was hell to pay and my sisters and I never played hooky again.

High School And The Aftermath

I started Mitchell high School with great hope that somehow I could get my education. I realized with my hearing loss it was not going to be easy. During my last year in public school Miss McMillan had worked very closely with me. I remember her telling me that she was not going to let me fail my grade eight. I could not expect that kind of help in high school. What made high school so difficult for me was that most things were taught verbally and I just could not take reliable notes and keep up. I remember asking a number of my friends for their books after school so I could take them home and copy, but after all too many times they had to say no to me, as they had to have their books at home at night to study. So I was getting farther and farther behind as the weeks went by.

About Easter on my first year in high school while sitting in class, there was a loud pop in my ears and then, a great silence. I remember looking around me. It felt as if everyone had left the room and I was just sitting there alone. There was no scuffing of feet, nor rustle of paper, just silence. It was scary. So I went up to the teacher, Peter Pidgeon and tried to explain to him that my hearing, which he already knew was bad, had finally left me all together. He sent me to see Doctor

Pridham. The doctor told me to take my books home, that I had to stay away from school and loud sound for a while. One eardrum was totally shattered full of holes and the other one in bad condition. At that time not too much was known about such things. The public in general all had the theory that when you were deaf you bought a hearing aid and if you had poor eyesight you bought glasses. I had hoped a hearing aid would help me, but I found out that when you lose the nerve endings in your ears a hearing aid was of no use to you.

Loud noises hurt my ear drums. Long hours of noise on a tractor or around machinery left me with what I would call a dead head for a long time after. My head just felt separated or aloft from my body. It was as if I was floating or walking on air. Tractors in those days did not have mufflers; they barked out real raw power, which heightened our senses. The louder they sounded the more power the farmer felt he had. The roar and vibration of the grain threshing machine going full blast and ready to receive a load of grain sheaves was high on the list of assault on my ears. The one that bothered me the most though was the grain grinder. It had two steel plates within which were gradually tightened together as the grain funnelled down onto them. They screamed out a loud torment and a terrifying noise. How I dreaded the day that dad would tell me that we were going to chop, which meant to grind grain into chop to feed our pigs and chickens. The noise of the two grinding plates coming together sent a deadly message screaming into my already dying eardrums. Yet the job had to be done and there was no thought at all given to what more damage such loud noise might do to my already damaged eardrums.

I think I have always been allergic to dust in any form and the fine dust from the chopped grain sent me wild with itch. I itched from head to toe. It didn't seem to bother my dad one bit, and of course when it didn't bother him he could not understand why I made such a fuss about it. The more I itched the longer he chopped grain. My dad would carry the grain from the granary to the hopper on the grinder in a bushel basket while I kept the chop (ground grain) away from the grinder by shovelling it back into a pile. When the hopper was full I held the bags as dad shoved them full of chop with a scoop shovel. You had to lift the bag a number of times, as it was being filled and let it slam back down onto the floor to pack the chop down in the bag. This of course sent large volumes of flour into your face and added to the misery. As soon as we finished I would head off to the house for a much needed shower.

I kept hope that by the next year, my hearing would be better so I could go back to school, but this was just the first part of the slow deterioration of my hearing caused by Scarlet Fever. Things were only going to get worse, never better. If I had the right contacts at that time I would have found out that I could have had my high school education paid for by the government, at The School For The Deaf in Brampton. It seems neither the school system nor the government reach out to those in need, but it was there for those who were more informed and the privileged in society, but I was just a farmer's son.

Shirlyan, My Kid Sister

On August 13th 1942 Aunt Maude gave birth to a daughter Shirlyan. My Aunt Maude's first husband Jack Noble came from London Ontario. He had died of pneumonia and my Aunt Maude then married Guy Starks. Each had a son about the same age from their first marriage. Aunt Maude had Jack Jr. and Uncle Guy had Bill. At this time Jack was in the US Navy and Bill was in the US Marines. This little girl was an adored sister to both Jack and Bill and it seemed she was God's blessing to seal this marriage and make it a ……united family.

Uncle Guy worked for General Motors and Aunt Maude had just opened up her very own Hairdressing Shop, "Alice's Beauty Shop." Together they had just bought a new house at 20243 Alcoy St. and a new baby had not been planned for. At the age of 41 my aunt had not expected she would have another child. They considered Shirlyan a miracle and somehow they would make it work.

In order to make the mortgage payments on the house my aunt had to keep her shop open. So in the end what happened was this little girl Shirlyan came up to the farm in Canada and spent a lot of time growing up along with my sisters and me. We loved her as a kid sister, and to this day we feel she is one of the family.

She would follow me everywhere, often in old rubber boots, which came up to her hips. She asked question upon questions, about things most city girls never ever though of, questions like,.

"But Jack, why do all the little pigs have curls in their tails?"
"But Jack, who puts the curls in?"
"But Jack, how do the little pigs know which titty is their own?"

She had a pet hen called Pecky that was blind in one eye. She loved that old hen and carried it about. Old Peck came to the house door several times a day just to be with her. Then there was Suzy the pet cow who stood still to be petted. At this time we had a huge rough looking half Collie half German shepherd dog. Most people were afraid of him, but to Shirlyan the dog was just a part of the family

When my dad went to the field with the tractor to work the land she would go along for the ride and fall asleep at his feet lulled by the warmth of the sun pouring down from above and the tractor roaring from within. All the while dust fell upon her making her look anything but that little city girl her mom thought she was.

On Saturday nights she got her weekly bath just like the rest of us and went to Mitchell to see the city lights and to do up the town. Even though she was very young I don't remember her ever getting homesick. It seemed she was surrounded by people who loved her. Her dad and mom came every other week end to see her.

Shirlyan, married Dan Hurt her twelfth grade sweetheart, and moved to California. They had two children Scott and Michele, both married with children.

A Long Trip Home

One summer day my dad told me he had bought a model L Case tractor from a farmer away down south of London near a place called Delaware and he wanted me to drive the tractor home. Well as I was just fifteen this would be quite an adventure. I had been driving dad's 10 / 20 McCormick Dearing on the farm so I was sure I was up to it. But I was not very worldly about the roads very far afield. I had been to London a number of times with my dad but I didn't know much about the roads to anywhere other than to St Marys, Mitchell and Stratford. To this day I don't know how he came to trust me to do this.

On the way down my dad explained the route I would have to take to drive home. He would see me onto what was the old highway going from London south to Windsor, then leave me to make my way home driving north. I remember feeling very grown up, that my dad would trust me. I would come back to London on what is now Wharncliffe Road and follow it all the way to Western Road behind Western University, coming out to Richmond Street, just north of the old bridge over the Thames River. Then I was to proceed north, on # 4 through Arva and Birr to Elginfield and turn right there onto #7 going towards Stratford. A quarter of a mile down that highway is the # 23 highway going north which I would take home going through Whalen Corners to Woodham, Kirkton, and on until I reached the old red brick Mt Pleasant United Church on the 11th line where I would turn right and follow through until I reached the Mitchell Road. Once there I would be almost home as we were the second farm north of the corner.

Dad's Second Tractor

But once we arrived at the farm there were unforeseen problems. The model L Case was a huge brute of a tractor on steel with a large stick hand clutch. Even as a boy I was always very strong, but I had trouble handling that hand clutch. The only way I could move it was to stand up high and try to jerk the stick using two hands. On a busy highway this was not good. So they solved the problem by putting a 3 ft. gas pipe atop the clutch stick. To stop I would have to stand as high as possible and grab the top of the gas pipe and jerk it with all my might.

Now picture this: The tractor was on steel wheels with huge steel lugs. Is it any wonder my dad would not drive it home nor could not find anyone else to drive this tractor well over 50 miles from Delaware home to Motherwell? It was a bone-shattering trip and I stood up for most of the way. They didn't have mufflers on tractors then either and the noise was deafening.

I was to stay on the shoulder as much as possible but driving through London I had to drive over people's driveways and across side streets. Not everyone was happy to see this kid and his monster tractor cross their driveway tearing up their oil and gravel driveways. However all went as well as could be expected until I got to Elginfield.

By now it was late in the afternoon and there was a nice fresh stretch of fresh black top laid from Elginfield east to the 23 highway. It had been rolled to perfection and looked simply beautiful in the late afternoon sun. The problem was Jack had to cross over it to turn down the 23 highway to go home, amid dozens of angry waving arms and shouting voices trying to get me to stop or to go away. I proceeded to cross at high speed, the lugs tearing great wads of black tops out of the freshly laid highway and throwing it hither and yonder. I looked behind as I roared off down the 23 as I was expecting the whole herd of trucks to follow me. It must have been their worst nightmare to have this happen at anytime but especially at the end of their day. To this day I am both very sorry and more than a bit amused by what happened. I am sure they all had something to talk about that night at their supper table.

The war was still on in Europe in 1944 and great grain crops were growing once more in Western Canada. But there was a great shortage of men to harvest it. The government offered a plan to send all able bodied men out for free by train. They called it " The Harvest Excursion Train." Whole trainloads of men left Toronto on these harvest specials bound for Winnipeg dumping a human cargo in to the Winnipeg Union Train Station to be placed where needed. It was on one of those trains I found myself the end of August 1944 when I was fifteen coming sixteen in October. I know my dad and mom were worried and in despair and I was deaf, strong willed and thought I was grown up but so alone in my Silent World.

Chapter 2
THOSE EARLY YEARS - THE BOOMING 40'S

The great drought had ended and good crops were once again growing all across Canada in the forties. The price for almost everything from a bushel of wheat to a dozen eggs or a pound of pork was the best we ever had. Things were very good again down on the farm. When all is said and done and things are going well I don't think there is a greater feeling of reward than that which comes to the farmer each fall when he has his harvest off.

In the spring he prepares his seed bed and sows his crop with care. All year he watches it grow; he prays for rain when it is dry; he gives thanks to the Lord when it rains. When it is ripe he works long hours cutting and stooking, then hauling it to the barn with his horses and wagon to be threshed. A great stack of straw would be built in the barnyard with great pride. The granary would be full and over flowing. Then came a feeling of thankfulness to God and pride in yourself, along with this a great feeling of contentment as finally you had time to relax from the usual long days of labour.

By 1944 the population of Canada had grown to 12 million. Almost fifty percent of Canadians lived in the country. Only a mere 20% of the rural homes had electric lights and appliances. Almost all homes were heated by wood or coal. Due to hand pumped presser systems over fifty percent had inside running water.

The harvest was off on our farm and I had answered a large advertisement in the Stratford paper where the federal government was asking for harvesters to travel to western Canada, to help harvest the huge 1944-grain crop. As I was not sixteen for almost two months yet I had not expected that I would be accepted. But word arrived that I could go. So I packed my two huge and battered old black cardboard suitcases with all my worldly belongings, as actually I had no intentions of coming home. This was I thought, my escape from my everyday life of drudgery on the farm into adventure. Every young man seems to have a great need for adventure in his life. For the next number of years many young men and some not too young found adventure going west on the harvest excursion train, working and seeing the country and making new friends.

The train left Stratford in the afternoon with a number of younger chaps and a few older men, none of which were of military age as they were all off to war fighting Hitler's army all over Europe. The train picked up more harvesters as it stopped at each and every station along the track to Toronto. This was going on all across the province. When we arrived at the huge train station in Toronto we were herded like cattle into a wing where everyone settled down for a long wait for the train to Winnipeg. All the time more men were arriving from all over Ontario, and some even from Quebec and on down east. I remember thinking they were a very rowdy looking crowd and as I had led a rather sheltered life in a rural community I was not exactly comfortable among them.

Soon after the train left Toronto it got dark, I remembered that mom had packed a few sandwiches for me to eat on the train, and I was glad she had the foresight to do this. All around me it seemed other mothers had done the same. A man would come through the train hawking sandwiches and pop and bars, from a small tray, which hung from a strap around his neck. But of course every thing he sold was at two or three times the price it normally sold for in stores. The train stopped at every little station along the way, picking up eggs and cream and dear knows what, and dropped off newspapers and mail, groceries and machine parts and repairs.

Not every car on the train had a bathroom. The cars with bathrooms were placed every so far apart so that you had to walk through maybe six or eight cars one-way or the other to find a bathroom. There was constant traffic up and down the aisle all night. Every time the door on either end of the car was opened a rush of cool night air shot down through from one end of the car to the other. This alone was bad enough, but the train's coal fired engines spewed black soot from its smoke stack. So every time the door was open soot came in and clung to your hands face and clothing. By morning we looked a bit like a trainload of chimney sweeps. The seats were not at all comfortable, even to just sit in for a long trip. Sleep of course evaded us as the train had violent start-ups and stops all night loading and unloading cars. There were loud shouts and voices of anger, laughter and rushes of cold air with showers of soot. We were certainly not travelling first class, that's for sure, but then at that time no one expected much of anything for free from the government.

Morning found us in the far north, deep in wilderness amid trees and lakes, such as I had never seen before. I was enchanted with the great expansion of space and the sheer emptiness, and the mystery of the unknown. We travelled all day, stopping at all the small villages and towns taking on and delivering. Those start-ups and stops were apparently meant to leave no one standing on their feet. Our bodies ached from being abused. All day we slowly wound our way through Northern Ontario and then night descended upon us. By now I had bought some food from the vendor as he travelled down through the cars calling out the name of his wares,

"Sandwiches! Bar's! Pop!" A chap told me when the train stopped at some of the larger stations they sold sandwiches and things inside at a much better price. But I was a bit nervous about leaving the train as I might not hear the "All Aboard! All Aboard!" call. However I was able to watch the other boys and men and made sure I headed back to the train on time.

Late that second night as we neared the lake head a great fog rolled in, and engulfed our train. We could see nothing from our windows until we pulled into strange stations, - its lights dimly showing its structure. I would see the forms of Indians standing on the station platform amid a swirl of fog. In some way it seemed unreal as I stared out my window at them wondering. Where do you come from? What are you doing here? Why are you standing there on the train platform staring at us? Then something seemed to click inside me and I felt I was in their shoes and was looking into the train seeing all those boys and men, wondering, who are you, what are you doing here, where are you going? And then the train would start with an 'All Aboard' and lurch ahead and they were left behind. Somehow I felt, there were just so many feet and a windowpane between us It's sad we had to remain strangers, and maybe we could have been friends. I always remembered those Indians on the platform in the fog and their silent questioning stance.

The train rolled into Winnipeg on a Sunday, the afternoon of the third day. A human cargo of travel- weary passengers was dumped into the city's Union Station. We were tired and dirty with clothes we had slept in. Again we were herded into a wing. As it was Sunday we were told we would not be going out until Monday morning. It was then and there I decided to leave the crowd and find the rest room and clean up.

Before I had left home my mom told me that her father, (my grandfather Butson) had a brother Fred in Winnipeg. They knew he had once worked as a barber in the Union Station in Winnipeg. But it seems she had lost track of him over the years.

I washed myself up as best I could in the restroom and then went to see if I could find the barbershop. I found it but it was closed, as it was Sunday. There was a black man cleaning the shop and he came to the door to chat with me. I asked if by chance he happened to know a Fred Butson. He was sure he recognized the name but it was from many years ago. He said if I could wait for a few minutes he would check on the name and get back to me. Before long he came back and told me Fred Butson had worked there for several years many years ago. And he understood he now had a shop in the basement of the Confederation Life Building in the heart of down town. This was great news for me!

I have no idea now, how much money I had on me at that time, but I know it would not be much. Also as a farm boy I knew absolutely nothing about travelling in the big city on streetcars, buses or taxis. I did know though it would cost me money, -money that I didn't want to spare just now so I had better walk. A stranger pointed me in the right direction towards the heart of the city near Portage and Main where I would find the Confederation Life Building. As it was Sunday almost every single place was closed. I am not sure just what I hoped to do when I got there. But with two large heavy suitcases I started to walk. Every once in a while I had to put them down and rest, for as I said I had all my worldly possessions with me and they weighed a ton. I never did learn how to travel light. I remember chatting with a policeman who was curious about my heavy suitcases. Maybe he thought I had robbed a bank as was carrying the loot. I told him I was searching for my uncle and his barbershop, which was in the basement of the Confederation Life Building.

Sometimes now I wonder why he didn't load me in his police car and deliver me to the building just to be nice. But no such luck. I finally arrived and every door was locked up tight. I sat on my suitcases trying to think of what I should do now. I remembered my mom had told me that he had been married but his wife died of pneumonia a long time ago. So I reasoned, - well if he had no wife then he likely ate lunch at some restaurant or lunch counter in this area so maybe I should look around.

I started visiting all the eating-places and for a while it seemed as if it was not a very good idea. Then I noticed a small lunch counter place in the Leland Hotel. I went in and sat at the counter and waited for the waitress to come. I told her I was from Ontario and I was searching for my great uncle, a barber who worked in the barbershop in the basement of the Confederation Life Building. She asked me to describe him. Well the truth was I had never met him so I described my Grandfather Butson, saying he would not be too tall perhaps even a bit on the short side with white hair and a neat white moustache.

"Yes, I am sure he comes in here for lunch." We searched for his name in the phone book, but his residence was not listed, he was only listed at the Barbershop address. In those days not everyone had phones in their apartments, but there would be one down the hall for everyone to use to call out. She told me there was a taxi driver who works out of the hotel and I should wait until he comes in as, "your Uncle always ask for him when ever he needed a ride home from work."

I waited patiently for quite some time and finally he did arrive, and yes it was a Fred Butson and a barber whom he often drove home. He said,

" I will take you to the location where I let him off, but I don't really have his address." He drove me to a corner of a beautiful tree lined street with a long row of apartments on either side with great wrought iron balconies, and let me out. As I paid him he pointed in a northerly direction and said,

"He always walks that way." I looked up and a short way down the street on the second floor balcony was a man looking down at me. Something within me tingled as I looked up at him and I said to myself, "That's my uncle."

I Meet My Uncle Fred Butson In Winnipeg

I walked into the entranceway, of a walk up apartments, and looked at the names listed as residents. Sure enough there was a Fred Butson. I could not believe my luck. But was it "just luck?" I have asked myself that question many times over the years. Was it possible for a fifteen-year-old farm boy to find his uncle in a city of several hundred thousand? Or do you believe in a Guardian Angel?

Moments later I knocked on the door and there was my Uncle exactly as I had described him. He looked at me and said,

"You are the young man that just got out of the taxi"

"Yes, I said and, do you know Leonard Butson?"

"Yes he is my brother", he replied.

I asked him if he remembered Reta Butson and he said he did, so I told him I was Reta's son Jack Cooke from near Mitchell Ontario. He said in all the years he had been in the west no one from home had ever come west to see him. He was so happy to have someone from his family come to visit him.

I stayed for about three or four days, during which he took me to a different place to eat every day and proudly told every one I was his grand nephew visiting him from down east. We walked the wide streets of downtown Winnipeg together and I found out it is a great city full of grandeur and beauty and proud of its place in Canadian history, "the gateway to the west." I loved the huge hand carved stone and the great round pillars in the historic old buildings, many of which still stand today. Winnipeg is truly the Chicago of Canada with its wide streets, historic buildings and oh yes.... the wind.

He took me down to where the Assiniboine River enters the Red River, then we walked up the riverbank path to the parliament buildings high up on the bank. There I saw all the magnificent statues, which surrounds the parliament building and grounds. He pointed out the golden boy a-top the parliament buildings dome facing north, to where Manitoba was told their future would lay. Not in the south nor the east or west, but to the north.

Assiniboine Park Winnipeg

The next day we took the bus out to the Assiniboine Park, where we crossed the Assiniboine River on the footbridge into the park. Never in all my young years had I seen so many flowerbeds or such a variety of flowers and colours, as I saw that day in the " English Gardens." My thought went back to Ontario to my mom and my Grandmother Butson both of whom loved their flowers. If only they could have been with Uncle Fred and me right then! Uncle Fred had packed a lunch and we sat on a park bench, and chatted while we ate our lunch. He was easy to chat with and much like my Uncle Roy, my mom's brother. I would remember this day that I spent with my Uncle Fred in the Assiniboine Park forever.

I spent a day with him in the huge barbershop, and he proudly introduced me to all his customers. It was his own business and there were about six or so barbers working for him. I watching him cut hair and chat with his customers. I could see that he enjoyed his trade and he had the respect of his customers. He made a great impression on me. I will always remember him as a kind, wonderful person, and I am sure he had a lot to do with me becoming a barber.

I guess you might say Uncle Fred too, had his own story to tell, and it was a bit like my own or many others. He was born on a farm near Staffa here in Ontario to a large family. He didn't feel there was any future for him on the farm but felt very uncomfortable about leaving. He said he always had the feeling he was the black sheep in the family as he packed his bag one night and left without saying goodbye. He just didn't know how else to leave it all behind.

Sometime later he ended up in Manitoba working for the railway laying tracks. On weekends he started cutting hair for the men with whom he worked. It was not long until he earned the name of, "The Barber," and some time later he left the railway and opened a Barber Shop in Indian Head Saskatchewan. But after a time he realized he would earn more money cutting hair in a big city like Winnipeg than in a town like Indian Head. So he headed back to the big city, the great city he learned to love.

Barbers in those days didn't have to take a course and be licensed as they do today. Usually the trade was handed down from father to son and they called it the grandfather plan. When the time came for all barbers to be licensed, those who were already cutting hair were granted a license by all provinces under what they called the grandfather plan.

Having worked for the railway cutting hair he found a job quite easily in the Union Station Barber Shop in Winnipeg. But after gaining experience he wanted his own shop. Records show me he took over at the Confederation Life Building Barber Shop in 1920 and was there until after 1950.

Uncle Fred saw me back to the Union Station and managed to get me back on the train with a group of harvesters heading farther west. I said a sad farewell to my Uncle Fred and promised I would come and see him again someday. For a short time he took me in as family. This meant very much to me.

Once more I found myself back on a train, but this time I had no idea where I was heading. My ticket said Angusville but whoever heard of Angusville? However in late afternoon the train pulled into a small town called Angusville towards the Saskatchewan border and south of the Riding Mountain National Park. The park rising in the north is a part of the Manitoba escarpment, a spectacular rise of forest parkland teeming with nature. It is also surprising to find out that it is the exact geographical centre or crossroads of the North American continent

A group of farmers were waiting at the station for us. They looked just a bit different from people I was use to seeing, as they were small in stature tanned or brown with very smooth skin. I soon found out they were Ukrainians. A farmer by the name of Puska hired me. When I arrived at his place I was surprised to find that a couple of guys working for him had been on the train from Ontario. They were from Barrie. These people were apparently doing very well as they had a new house, a good barn and other good buildings. They also had good cattle and horses and the land was black and fertile with a big crop to be threshed.

The next day I found myself working with a beautiful team of matched sorrel Percheron horses and a fine wagon. I was loading my own sheaves. Now this was a first for me. In the east one man pitches sheaves up onto the wagon and the other man stands on the wagon and builds the load. True they build beautiful wagonloads of grain in Ontario. But in the west every man has to learn to build his own load. It is fast and efficient and you soon learn to make good looking loads all by yourself. After all, the trick is to get the sheaves to the threshing machine; it's not a beauty contest.

The country was a beautiful mixture of cleared land and clusters of poplar and the ever presence of the Riding Mountains in the north. I promised myself I would go there some day, but as yet I never have.

We were working with a good crop and good equipment and the food was exceptional. There was just one problem; these people did not have much respect for the men. Two older sons stayed with the machine and pitched all the loads off. They kept the machine full to the tilt all the time. You just drove your team up beside the machine and left it. The one brother would climb up on it and start to feed the machine. They fed the machine from both sides. You took the empty wagon back to the field. They demanded everyone work hard and faster and faster. They were constantly shouted at us to get the hell in to the machine and load our wagons faster. We were tired of body and sore of muscle by the end of the day, and no one was very happy. We were very glad for a few hours of respite before going off to bed.

I remember taking a walk outside one night, with one of the chaps from Barrie just before retiring. We were amazed that no matter which direction you looked there was not a single light to be seen. There was not a neighbour for miles in any direction. We really did feel far off the beaten path and of course at that time we were.

The old house had been made ready for the harvesters and served as a bunkhouse. I found it of great interest. It rested amid a grove of tall poplar, which provided a great setting for it. It was made of fine straight logs, and perfect in its structure, and was still in excellent shape. It was of course the first home of the homesteaders. The mortar between the logs was still very white and tight and in the best of condition. Imagine my surprise when they told me their parents had made this mortar by hand from cow manure mixed with lime. Everything about these people seemed to spell hard work and efficiency.

After a few days my nose started to bleed. I had always had a problem with nosebleeds when I worked too hard and got over- heated. I was losing a lot of blood, as it would not stop bleeding as long as I had to work like this. So I felt I was in an impossible situation.

I was just fifteen coming sixteen in about two months. I was use to hard work, but not being driven like this. I felt very weak and faint from loss of blood so much so I just could not work any longer. I took stock of my options, and I thought the best thing to do was to go on to a place called Lumsden in Saskatchewan. My mom had a cousin there. His name was Earl Butson and he was a nephew of my Uncle Fred, and of all things, he owned a Barber Shop. I had met Earl and Beulah his wife once when they visited my dad and mom on the farm back in Ontario. I thought perhaps if I had a week's rest I could maybe find a place to work where the "master" was not so demanding.

They didn't like the idea that I was leaving and I was a bit shocked when the lady in the house struck out at me, saying,

"It is because we are Ukrainian, isn't it?" "You don't want to work for us."

This of course had nothing to do with it. So I told them the truth- that the men were all farm boys in Ontario and were use to hard work but they were being driven too hard and were not being respected. I told them they would likely lose more men before the harvest got off if they didn't treat them better. This sobered them. I did however leave there as friends. Looking back now I feel they treated others as they had been treated themselves all their lives.

I took the bus from Angusville to Lumsden, which took me first to Regina and then north. I was the only person on the Greyhound bus when I first saw the Qu'Appelle Valley. I remember how the bus driver pulled over onto the shoulder of the road and let me get out so I could take some pictures with my camera. I understand it was once a great river, perhaps an ice river, travelling from Alaska south toward the American border. You will find many kinds of rock in this valley not found anywhere else on the prairies. These rocks came down the ancient waterway from Alaska.

After travelling on flat prairie the valley is a sight to behold. Lumsden itself was a very pretty little town nestled comfortably in the historic Qu'Appelle Valley.

There is a story they told me about the name Qu'Appelle. They say long ago some people Indian and perhaps French were camped for the night in the valley. During the night they heard a voice calling out, which sounded like a child crying. A searching party went up and down the valley searching and shouting,

"Qu'Appelle," "Qu'Appelle," which means, to call, or who calls.

My cousins made me welcome and I remember spending days walking about the town and the valley. Fall was in the air and the leaves were turning colour and the hills that surrounded the town turned to a soft grey as only natural prairie grass does. I always remember high on the hillside to the north east of town there were large stones, which had been placed, and then white washed. It could be seen for miles. It spelled out McGravins Bread, a local brand. I also remember that there was a small restaurant right across the street from my cousin's house and barbershop. Although I didn't have money to spare I could not resist going over there for the odd banana split, which cost me 35 cents, a luxury I could not afford.

About a week later I travelled north on the train to Davidson Saskatchewan to a brother of my grandmother Butson, my Uncle Bob Norris. No! He was not a barber. He owned a Machinery Dealership on Main Street. I only stayed a few days as my Uncle had a bad bout of flu and I didn't want to catch it.

I had heard there was still some harvesting in Alberta to be done, so I rushed off on the train.

Uncle Fred Butson had a sister Rosena, living at Excel Alberta. So I decided to take the train out there and call on them and hopefully find work. By now I was in need of some cash. Maybe I had too many banana splits? The train from Davidson had to go first up to Saskatoon and then back down to Excel. It is actually on a route from Saskatoon to Calgary. I sent a telegram to my Aunt Rosena from Saskatoon telling her I was on the train from Saskatoon and would arrive in Excel late that night. It was starting to get cool at night and the night air coming into the train car from each end every time some one went in or out of the car was giving me a chill. By the time I arrived in Excel I was not feeling well.

It was after midnight, when I arrived in Excel. It was one of those small train station villages you found so often at that time on the prairie. Once it had been a growing hamlet, but the dry thirties had put almost everyone out of business. Just a store and grain elevator and the train station remained. The stationmaster's name was Mr Jim Barker. He met me and asked if I was Mr. Cooke, and I said I was. He told me my Uncle Frank McNee, Aunt Rosena's husband could not drive in to pick me up that night as it had rained all day. They had asked the stationmaster to put me up over night at the station and hopefully the road would be dry enough in the morning for them to pick me up. I was handed a blanket and a pillow and he pointed towards a long bench along the station wall. This was another first for me. I remember he walked out leaving me alone in the dark station with the door wide open to the night. I don't know why he didn't close it, and I left it as it was. I was chilled to the bone, and I knew it was my Uncle Bob's flu. During the night I heard my first coyotes howl out in the darkness and I was sure it was wolves. I was very much alone and scared to death, yet too sick to get up and close the door.

Early the next morning Mr. Barker asked me to come in for breakfast. This was in their living quarters built right into the station. I was thankful for the warmth in there, as I was not at all well. A big bowl of grits was placed before me. I was soon to find out this was a western ritual, eating your grits for breakfast. I believe it was called Red River Cereal. I grew up on oatmeal for breakfast in Ontario. Oatmeal was OK but this stuff had all kinds of ugly looking stuff in it. It reminded me of what came off the back of our old farm-fanning mill back home when we cleaned seed grain in the spring. Everyone told me it would put hair on my chest. Maybe so, but somehow something went badly wrong; I lost what hair I had on my head.

The morning train came in from Saskatoon and Mr. Barker went out to meet the incoming train. Farmers brought their cream and eggs to the station to be shipped to Calgary, so he would have to load that, and there might be machinery parts or store products arriving on the train. I continued to mull over my Red River cereal and was finished when the train left and Mr. Barker came back in.

As you already know, my hearing was getting very bad, but I caught parts of a conversation between Mr. and Mrs. Barker in regards to some money that was missing. The conversation was getting pretty heated and no doubt my face was getting red, as there I was, a perfect stranger sitting at their breakfast table and some money was missing, which had been left on the table. Finally in despair Mrs. Barker (May) said,

"Exactly where did you leave the money?" With his pointer finger he thumped the kitchen table and said,

"Right there on the newspaper."

With that Mrs. Barker rushed to the kitchen stove and we all followed. I can see her now, holding the stove lid plate in one hand and the poker in the other. Looking down into the stove at the burning newspaper she poked at it and the burning money unfolded and we clearly saw the dollar bills in flame. I could read the numbers as they curled and turned to ashes She had burnt the money. It was a very sad day for them but inside me I was relieved. If they had not found this money they would have told everyone I was a thief.

I Meet My Uncle Frank and Aunt Rosena McNee

My Uncle Frank arrived in a model T with mica glass windows on all sides. The car was in very good shape, as he didn't drive it very much. I was soon to feel that it must also have a very charmed life, as my uncle was a terrible driver. He was retired now and getting up in years. But he was still a miniature Paul Bunyon, with a shock of dark hair and a booming voice. I liked him immediately. He was not a bit shy in any way and had a quick and easy smile that was as convincing as his voice. He talked with ease as he loaded my two large suitcases into his car. I was now about to learn why, when it had rained all day, they could not drive their cars.

We started down the road to go to my uncle's farm with my Uncle Frank shouting to me with his booming voice. He was trying to hold the car to the centre of the dirt road but it kept skidding to the slope of the shoulder. I could hear the tires picking up the mud and slinging it against the underside of the fenders. I later learned it is called gumbo, a type of mud that will wrap around your tires and fill the space under your fenders and bring you to a halt. In the distance a small truck loomed, coming towards us. It too was skidding to the right and to the left and back again and caused me great concern as it approached.

We gathered speed as we approached the truck and I found myself hanging onto the seat to keep afloat while my stomach churned. As we came abreast of the truck my uncle swung to the right. We hit the grass on the shoulder bounced over and slipped on down into the ditch. All the time my uncle's booming voice never missed a beat, and I hung on for dear life. My uncle floored the gas pedal and we shot up on the road. But all too fast as we slipped right across the slippery gumbo top and down into the ditch on the far side. It didn't seem to matter to my uncle where he drove as long as he kept up his speed.

If I had not been so sick it would have been hilarious. But I was so very sick and ready to throw up. Regardless of all this my uncle was still talking up a storm. It was as if nothing unusual was happening. We actually drove under a telephone pole guy wire and back up on the road. We did this more or less all the way back out to the farm. There are definitely a lot of advantages to driving in an almost treeless wide-open country when the roads are in this condition. In the end it only served to endear those memories, which I have of my uncle. Needless to say I have never forgotten that first time I met my Uncle Frank and the ride in that grand old model T out to his farm. It was clearly one of my adventures.

We arrived at a very small, unpainted frame house, sitting on a patch of prairie grass. There were no lawns or flowerbeds as I was use to back east, just drabness and packed dirt around the door. Somehow it all blended into the vastness of the land all about me. My Aunt Rosena came out the door to meet us. She was perhaps five foot four and she looked such a little woman, in a very big country. She was a real great aunt to me and I soon learned to love her.

I was embarrassed to arrive in this condition, very sick with flu but my aunt put me to bed and waited on my every need and in a couple days I was feeling my old self again.

Now what does a fifteen year old boy do to find entertainment while visiting an elderly uncle and aunt? - Certainly not watch television, as it had not been invented yet. Truly I don't remember that there was any problem as in the evening we sat in their little kitchen, and they told me all about their lives, while I sat and drank it all in. This is their story, told me as I remember it.

My Aunt Rosena (my grandfather Butson's sister) was born on a farm near Staffa Ontario in the year 1879. She said she always felt like an ugly duckling at home and in the community, as she had a large goitre growing on her neck. It was not at all unusual to see people with goitres on their necks many years ago. These women usually wore beautiful neck chokes to cover the neck area. For some reason I don't ever remember seeing a man with a goitre. We know now it is caused by the lack of iodine in the diet and that is why we use iodine salt today. Aunt Rosena left home to find work as a waitress and somehow she ended up working in a restaurant in Chicago in 1919.

My Uncle Frank was born in Thamesford Ontario in the year 1873, and in 1910 he took a homestead near Excel Alberta. In 1919 he was passing through Chicago on a return trip from Ontario to Alberta and by chance stopped at the restaurant where my Aunt Rosena worked. She waited on his table. When he found out she was from near Mitchell Ontario they found lots to talk about. I guess you might say, one thing led to another and he stayed in Chicago much longer then he had intended to. In the end he talked her into going west with him. He was so big and brawny and she so small and petite.

A few days after I arrived I took a long walk on the half section across the road from the house. From the house, I could see a large body of water far back on the property. It was a slough, which glistened in the sun. A slough is a small or large body of water created by the spring run off from melted snow and spring rains. Cattle drank water from these sloughs in spite of its strong taste. The summer heat would evaporate much of the water and many dry up and leave a white alkaline salt bed behind. I could see the wild ducks flying to and fro from it morning and evening. The land I was walking on was very alkaline and non productive. Later I walked over to the home place with the house and barn on it. It was very rolling with many piles of rock; truly my uncle and aunt had not found a very good piece of land.

Uncle Frank's Stone Fence

All across the front of the home farm there was a pile of rocks, perhaps six feet across at the bottom and five feet high. My uncle and my aunt had drawn all these rocks off the land on the stone boat and wagon. The stone fence was used to hedge in the pasture field and keep the cows from wandering. This fence can still be seen today as a monument to my uncle and aunt's hard labour. I look at it with sadness. I was told later that my Uncle Frank's farm had half the rock of all Alberta on it. I often asked myself why would anyone try to farm on land like this. It is a good question and I don't have an answer to it.

Many of these rocks found in the fields found a new home in a buffalo wallow. Unless you have lived in the west you will most likely have no idea what a buffalo wallow is. Years ago when there were herds of tens of thousands of buffalo on a bald prairie without any trees, the buffalo were in dire straits to rid themselves of their heavy itchy coat of winter hair in the springtime. Fortunately nature helped to solve the problem. It seems the great ice age left a few giant size rocks scattered across the prairies. The buffalo found them to be a good itching post. They would walk around and around the huge rock scratching off the winter hair and perhaps ticks from their hide.

This in turn would kill the grass around the stone and churn the soil into a powder dust. The ever-blowing prairie wind would blow the dust out from around the rock and over hundreds of years gradually lower the rock into the prairie. Great herds of buffalo stood waiting for a turn to scratch the hair off their hide.

When the government opened Alberta for homesteaders they set up a land title office at the town of Brooks, about seventy-five miles west of Calgary. The homesteader would first travel to the land title office in Brooks and pick a section of land. Often it was a piece of land they had never seen. A number would be on a surveyor's section stake in the northeast corner of every section. They would travel overland walking or riding a horse looking for the right section stake, and then claim their homestead. It was very much potluck as some got a much better section of land than others. Alas, Uncle Frank and Aunt Rosena had picked land covered with rock, alkaline soil and sloughs. Little of it was productive.

In 1944 my Uncle Frank was 71 and Aunt Rosena 65. They had retired from working the land and rented the home farm to the next-door neighbour Harry Bull. They did however keep two or three Hereford cows and milked them night and morning from spring to late fall. The milk would be put through the hand turned cream separator, which separates the cream from the milk. Aunt Rosena would churn the cream twice a week and make butter, which she sold, to the neighbour. It was natural for all cows in the west to have their calves in the springtime, thus for a while there was more milk then was needed. During the winter months the cows would be dry and milk from the closest store was miles away. So Aunt Rosena canned whole milk. That is, she boiled it and sealed it in jars for when it was needed. I had a chance to taste some canned milk and I really could not get to like it. It taste exactly like cold boiled milk and not at all to my liking.

Mr. Bull's crop was already combined, and most of his grain was in his bins. Farmers had grain piled everywhere, even in their machinery sheds. The local elevators were full to capacity. Whenever an empty boxcar came in everyone made a fast trip to the elevator with a load of grain.

Mr. Bull needed help with many other fall jobs to ready his farm for winter. He asked my uncle if this eastern lad knew how to stack bundles. Note I said stack bundles. People in the west call sheaves bundles. My uncle explained to me that stacking bundles would be much like what we would do when we built a load of grain on our wagon at home, only this time we would be building a stack on the ground.

This was exactly what I had hoped would happen, as I needed a job. This was also the beginning of a great life long friendship with the Bull family and many others in that community. We stacked oat bundles beside the barn for winter-green feed for the cattle. Farmers and ranchers in the west have long supplemented there winter hay with oat green feed this way. The cattle and horses love it, and as winter-feed it has a rich aroma, which I love when you pull it from the stack to feed the cattle.

Stacking Bundles for Winter Feed

Making a good stack with grain bundles is a work of art. You first lay a row of sheaves all around the outer edge keeping the butt of the sheaf out. Then you lay the centre by overlapping the sheaves from end to end. Always covering the butt of the last sheaf you just laid. Remember to keep the centre well up for if you don't, the rain or melting snow will be able to get into the stack. When moisture gets into the stack it can spoil the green feed as the grain will sprout and create musk and mould. The outer sheaf's butts are always placed out, so the grain kernel won't start to grow. A good stack is like a thatched roof. The rain runs off. When you reach the height you want, you start bringing the outside row of sheaves in each time you start a new round of sheaves. This way you end up with a rainproof stack.

The Bulls had a wonderful garden, and it was Mrs. Bull who was the gardener. At home my grandfather liked working in the garden, and my mom was also a good gardener. It seemed though, that all the eastern gardens I knew were limited to carrots, beans, peas, turnips and potatoes. Mrs. Bull however grew many things in her garden we never grew at home. There were parsnips, cauliflower, and several kinds of squash and among other things a big wonderful red potato she was very proud of, called "Plymouth" There was also a strawberry bed, a row of rhubarb and a raspberry patch. Besides the vegetables and the fruit she grew a lot of flowers in her garden too. No one I knew in the east grew flowers along with their vegetables. Flowers were always grown around the house. In Mrs. Bull's garden there were zinnias, cosmos, marigolds and petunias galore, and an evening primrose that gave off a heavenly scent after the sun went down. There were also rows of gladiolas for cut flowers and a rose bed by the front of the house. Other than that the house was surrounded by well-packed earth. It was there I missed the flowerbeds the most.

Under the ever-watchful eye of Mrs. Bull I learned how to top vegetables well enough to please her so they would keep when stored for winter. While she was a great gardener she was also a fantastic cook and every meal was something to look forward to. As there was no TV yet, they told me I could play the piano. I was still able to hear just enough to play. Once I lost my shyness I would even sing along to the music and they never once complained; in fact I think they enjoyed it. At that time I could play almost anything as long as I knew the tune. However I knew my time at playing the piano was running out and it didn't seem possible, fair or right, that the day would come when I would have to give up my piano.

Mr. and Mrs. Bull always remained to me just that, "Mr. and Mrs. Bull" even though I came to love them both almost as parents. Mr. Bull was English and for some reason he had held onto that thing the English seem to have about correctness. He stood out in a crowd. He was well educated, well spoken, and always well dressed. There was a sense of well being about him and it seemed everyone around him thought he had money, perhaps even at times when he didn't. I respected him and admired him greatly for his knowledge and his sense of humour. That was something my dad never shared with me, a sense of humour.

On Sundays I would go back to my aunt and uncles for dinner or supper. I remember the first time I returned after being away for a whole week. My aunt's table was set fit for a king. She had put on her best tablecloth, her best dishes and best silverware. They had been in Alberta all those years and not one person had visited them from the east. Alberta at that time was far far away. I was the first relative to visit them and she wanted to celebrate. They had been married for twenty-five years and she had managed to save some of her wedding cake, which had been stored away in a special wrap. We had it for supper that night and I couldn't believe I was eating a twenty five year old wedding cake, as it was still moist and good. Years later I inherited the silverware and crystal we used that day.

We got word a cousin of mine from Staffa Ontario was going to arrive at my uncle and aunt's soon and stay for a few days. This was my aunt's nephew and my cousins, Ed and Rita Butson. Little did I know but that my dad and mom had asked them to try to talk me into going home with them. When they asked me to go back home with them I declined, but I also knew that there was not much more work left to do at Mr. Bull's. They told me they thought I might get a job on a farm of a friend of theirs at Pasqua near Moose Jaw Saskatchewan. So in a few days I said good-bye to the Bulls and my aunt and uncle, and I was bound for Pasqua, a small village east of Moose Jaw.

There I met Crosley Chappel and wife. I do believe my cousins thought that if they got me that far on the road home I would give in and go home with them. But it didn't work out that way. It seems my mother had gone to public school in Staffa with Crosley and his sister Eva, both of whom lived now on farms near Pasqua. Eva was now Mrs. Jim Howes. Ed and Rita left for home without me. I did however send home one suitcase full of clothing, mostly summer clothing I would not need. I had found out two very large suitcases were hard to travel with. I stayed on for a short while working for Crosley.

The flat land here stretched out forever to the skyline and one has to see it to believe it. It is called the Regina Plains and you can see over fifty miles in any direction. This rich black land grows some of the best crops in all Canada, and perhaps all North America. The fall work here was pretty well done and there was not much left for me to do, so again I had to consider my options.

Every now and then in your life there comes a moment of truth, a time when you might feel a high or low that you will recall from time to time for the rest of your life. It was a time like that for me. I can see myself now sitting on the back steps at Jim Howe's house with their small dog on my lap. I was feeling very down and I wondered just what I was going to do. I didn't feel quite ready to go home, even though I knew I was homesick. Things were not turning out well for this soon to be sixteen year old boy. But I didn't want to go home with empty pockets. So I thought I better go back to Alberta to find work.

I had once met a rancher named Wib Duncan of High River Alberta when he was visiting some of his cousins here in Ontario. These Duncans in Ontario "Santa and Zoe" had married into my mom's family. One winter when Wib was down visiting, they brought him over to meet us. Meeting Wib was a bit like meeting John Wayne. He wore a broad rimmed well-creased Stetson looking a bit the worse for wear, cowboy boots with pointed toes, jeans that were a might bit tight and a cowboy shirt with snap down buttons. While his dress stood out in Ontario it was standard wear in the High River ranch country. Wib had told me if I ever went west again to visit him at his place. So I decided to take the bus to Calgary and then down to High River. The bus left Moose Jaw late in the evening, which meant I would be on the bus all night. This didn't worry me in the least as I considered it an adventure, remember I was just coming sixteen and I know now there was a lot of empty space between the ears.

Crosley was driving me to meet the bus down the only stretch of asphalt highway in the west in 1944 from Winnipeg to Calgary. It was a fifty-mile stretch of black top from Regina to Moose Jaw. A few miles east of Moose Jaw we came upon a bad accident, and we were among the first to arrive. It seemed that a huge milk truck overturned while trying to avoid a smaller truck that was returning from B.C. with a load of bright red crab apples. The driver of the small truck had been thrown through his windshield and went up the highway on his stomach, taking off most of his clothes and skin. Then his truck caught up with him and came in on top of him. When we arrived he was lying on his back under the truck with his chest under the front axle. He was bleeding badly. Close by there was a milk truck on its side and the milk gurgling out of its tank onto the highway, flowing down onto the man lying under the truck axle. Blood and red crab apples floated and bobbed away in the milk. He was conscious and screamed for us to get the truck off him. More cars stopped and more people gathered, and together we tried to lift the weight of the truck off him. He only screamed more as we struggled with the weight. It seems everyone at that time had bumper jacks and his bumper had been torn off, so it seemed we were helpless to help him.

Finally Crosley said we would have to go or I would miss my bus. By now there were enough people there to do whatever could be done for him. I hated to leave him like that and I often think back and wonder what happened to him. Did he live or die? Whenever I think of this I see his blood mixed with the white milk and the red crab apples floating away, one of those memories I'd rather forget.

When you're sixteen and all alone travelling at night on the bus, everything around you is new and exciting. The main highway west of Moose Jaw was gravel top and not always so smooth. It seemed most of the towns were a short way off the main highway and at that time the bus would leave the highway and drive into town to let passengers off or pick then up and drive back out again. This made travelling very slow. The bus would even stop away out in the middle of nowhere to let a passenger off in dark lonely places or at side roads or waiting car. Talk about service, they had it in 1944. Every now and then we pulled into a strange place with a coffee shop open and waiting on us, and the driver would get out and shout,

"Twenty minutes" and everyone awake and others not so awake, would scramble off the bus for a cup of java, and a chance to use a bathroom. Strangers already seated in the coffee shop would eye us with suspicion and were no doubt curious as to where we were going and why. I am sure each of us had our own story to tell. We travelled all night and sometime the next morning someone on the bus exclaimed,

"Look there's the mountains" and that was my first view of the Canadian Rockies. As we continued to drive west they rose higher and higher on the skyline, looming ever more larger and more beautiful. Sometime in the morning we arrived in Calgary. Even at that time it was a striking city built in a valley along the Bow River and against its magnificent backdrop of the foothills and The Rockies.

When I arrived at the Grey Hound Bus Station, I found that the bus going to High River had already left, but there was an afternoon bus that went part way as far as Okotoks, and then went on to Lethbridge. From Okotoks I would be about twenty or twenty five miles short of my destination. As I was not new to hitch hiking I was sure there would be no problem. I had a few hours to kill before my bus left, so I walked out of the station, and around and about the down town. All about me were men and women, old and young and boys and girls in cowboy hats and cowboy boots and it seemed as if everyone, even the poorest cowboy or Indian had on a new pair or Levis or GWG (Great Western Garment) jeans.

So I decided to arrive in High River in Style. I bought my first and only, cowboy boots in a soft medium tan and a light tan Stetson cowboy hat, with a reverse horseshoe steamed into the top, then a pair of GWG boot top pants and GWG shirt with snap buttons. Looking in the mirror I knew that I was a dude to be reckoned with.

I remember that ride on the bus going south from Calgary on the old highway, which went through all the little towns and villages. It was mostly the mountains that held my fascination as I sat staring out the bus window as the miles went by. I remember we arrived at a corner somewhere just north of Okotoks where the bus pulled over to let me out. After giving me my suitcase the bus drove off east, leaving me standing with my thumb up. I don't remember waiting very long as hitch hiking at that time was a very "in" thing to do, and most people would stop for a young person very quickly and especially for a dude like me.

Along came a real old farm type truck with a stake rack and several barrels of gas on the back held back in place by a chain. It reeked of gasoline. Behind the wheel was an honest to goodness hard working cowboy if I ever saw one. He was well up in years, his skin dark and weathered by the sun and the wind. He was also very cheerful and talkative. I found him to be one of those people that you will never really forget. He of course asked me where I was going and I told him to High River. He told me that was where he was headed. So then he asked me who I was going to see at High River, and when I told him Wib Duncan he was overjoyed, as Wib was a friend of his. I found out later Wib Duncan was a friend of just about everyone he ever met.

This old chap had his very own story to tell, and as we poked along on the highway this is what he told me. He was born in New York City at a time of great poverty for his family. He and his three sisters were put in an orphanage and they found life there unbearable. With not enough food and constant beatings he decided he would run away. Things went well with his escape; whether or not they tried to find him he would never know. He headed south to what he hoped would find him a job and a place in life. Still very young he ended up in Texas working on a ranch. Here he found that there was a wild plan for a cattle drive from Texas to Western Canada. He applied and managed to get a job, with these people. Starting off as a handy man, he later learned to ride a horse and help to drive the cattle. It took months to make the trail ride from Texas to Southern Alberta and during that time he learned all about being a cowboy and he decided that this was the life for him. He made several of those trips before deciding to settle down on a ranch near High River. As he grew old he often thought about his sisters back in New York and wondered just what had happened to them.

So in the early forties he took a trip back to New York City hoping that somehow he could find them. He found that the orphanage where they had been was long gone and no records were available to help him. He didn't want to give up, so perhaps in desperation he decided to try the impossible.

He rented a room in a hotel and had a telephone put in and started calling all the people with the same last name of his sisters had, hoping that perhaps even one out of the three had not got married. I guess there were hundreds and hundreds of names to call and at times he wanted to just give up and go back to High River. Then one day a lady said,

"Yes, that is my name, and yes, I have two sisters by those names and a lost brother by that name." He had found his sisters.

They visited for a few weeks, and he enjoyed the time they spent together, but he did not like the big city. He felt a great need to return to High River. He knew now more than ever before, that in his heart he was a cowboy and High River Alberta was his home. That was his story.

I like to think he lived a full and wonderful life and that perhaps he made another trip back to New York City to visit with his sisters, and then back to Alberta again. Over the years I have thought back many times to that journey in the old truck. It is then I smell the gas fumes and feel the shudder of the stake rack as we travelled south on the old highway. While I was absorbed in the story he had to tell, I could not help but steal a look now and then to the west at those wondrous Rockies.

Foothills of the Rockies

Wib and the Duncans of High River

When we arrived in High River he took me to Wib's sister Mable, Mrs. Neil Ross, where he introduced me as if he had known me all his life. She was a warm motherly woman whom I liked right away. Shortly after a phone call was make and soon Wib arrived to take me out to his Ranch. I was one tired boy, as it seemed a whole lifetime since I had left the Chappels in Saskatchewan. The ride to Wib's Ranch was made after dark so I didn't see much while on the road from the town out to the ranch. I remember getting out of the truck to open a barbed wire gate off the road, to a long winding lane on a downward path to the ranch house and buildings. After a warm welcome from Wib's sister Nell and the hired man Charles over several cups of coffee, they sent me off to bed. I remember I slept like a log, as I felt I was safe and among friends.

The smell of coffee and bacon wafted into my bedroom the next morning and suddenly I knew I was very hungry. They were anxious to hear any news I had of the Duncans in Ontario and of my journey and of my dad and mom. It was a Sunday morning and everyone seemed quite relaxed and in need of rest and conversation. In those days no one would think of working on Sunday. It was the Lord's Day and very much respected by all. I'm sure all farm horses thanked God too.

It seemed the grain crop had gone in late that spring in the High River area, and was then very late to ripen. It was however a very bountiful crop and now ready to be harvested. If I wanted work I had certainly come to the right place. As they needed more help they were glad to see me. Grown up men were hard to come by because of the war, so they were happy to have boys or very young men, anyone who was willing and able. I had been working for five dollars a day for Mr. Bull and had earned eight dollars a day threshing in Manitoba. It came as a surprise to find that Wib was actually offering eight dollars a day, if you worked from sun-up to sun-down about a twelve-hour day. I could just feel a large bundle of money in my pocket. I was very happy about this and glad I had made the trip to High River.

Jack and Wib's Team of Horses

I was awestruck by the view when I walked out of the ranch house in the morning.

The large bungalow type ranch house was built beside the Highwood River. The river's broad cold water flows forever down out of the mountains. Across the river from where I was standing was a wall of rock that was perhaps a hundred feet high. Indians had once used this spot as a Buffalo Jump. They did this by stampeding a herd of buffalo, and then guided the herd toward the cliff where they would fall to their death. A quarter mile west up river, the river swung to the south and the great cliffs on the far side hid the mountains from my view. Behind me was a high natural prairie hill and I could see a roadway cut into its side and I realized it as the one we had come in on last night. The whole setting, the ranch house, the barn the corrals and buildings along with the river and the wall of rock seemed secluded from all else except the Duncans.

On the Monday morning, I was all set to work. I was given the choice of staying at the house or staying in the bunkhouse in the field with the men. I made a wise decision when I chose to stay with the men in the field. I found out later that at times when men from the east came out to work for them, and stayed at the ranch house, the men in the field didn't feel free to associate with them. There were two bunkhouses in the field, both built on low steel wheeled wagons that could be pulled from one location to another. The bunks were built two bunks high on either sides and again across the end. It could actually bunk ten men if needed. A round pot bellied stove sat in the centre aisle at the front near the door. The front bunk was full of wood and coal for the stove, and we found it got very cold late at night so we took turns keeping the fire going all night.

One bunkhouse was about full when I had arrived so I was put in the other one with two lads about my age who were out there together from Quebec. They both spoke English well and we got along together splendidly.

It was now mid October and while the nights were cold the days warmed up so we could work in shirtsleeves comfortably. Each night after the day's work was done you would take the harness off your horses and place it on your wagon tongue with extreme care. In the morning before the sun was up you would have to place that harness on your horse's back and do it up properly in the dark. So be very careful how you lay it down. I was lucky, as I had always enjoyed harnessing horses; anything to do with horses came quite naturally to me. The horses were taken to a water tank close by and let drink, and then tied to the side of your wagon rack where they were fed sheaves of whatever you were threshing at the time. The horses spent the night right there in the field tied to your wagon. I enjoyed that as I would often go out late and see that they were ok and add a few comforting words, as I knew they too had a hard day. When you understand horses you find that some will work better, "with you, then for you." Understanding horses is to love them.

In the morning as we went about watering, feeding and harnessing our horses our eyes would constantly turn to the lights in the cook car. The cook car was like the bunkhouse, a house on wheels. From that direction we detected the aroma of rich coffee and fresh cooked bacon and eggs. Mrs. Ross stayed right there in the field day and night getting the food ready for all these hungry men. There was a cook stove with a stovepipe going out through the roof. Then there were few cupboards and a long table with a bench on either side down through the middle. All of which made the place look a bit crowded even when empty. At the far end was a bunk for Mrs. Ross to rest or sleep. She was a joy to know.

Each morning she greeted us all cheerfully with laughter and chatter. She would soon get to know all the men's names and speak to them personally. Nothing went on in the bunkhouse or in the field that she was unaware of. She saw the joke or humour in the many happenings in and far beyond her cook car. It was not only food she offered but also good old fashion hospitality and perhaps a motherly figure for boys far from home. A good cook is always a vital part of a work crew.

The last load of the night before, would be sitting beside the threshing machine ready to be fed into the feeder well before the sun came up. The men would be in the field loading their wagons before the chill of the cold night had left. On clear mornings they were greeted with the most spectacular sight anywhere on earth. They saw the sun rise on the Rockies. The first rays touching the peaks turning them to various shades of red and pink, orange or yellow depending on the

A letter from my sister Pearl, all for 4 cents

Wib's Old Bunk House

atmosphere. The Duncans treated the men well and everyone worked hard together. It showed me that when you offer men good wages, treat them with respect and feed them well, you got the most for your money.

About this time I was very happy when Wib brought a letter out to the field from my sister

Pearl. I still have that letter today. It has a four-cent stamp on it. Pearl had addressed it to me in care of my Uncle Bob Norris in Davidson Sask. It had been forwarded from there to my Aunt Rosena's in Excel Alberta. Then forwarded again back to Crosley Chapel near Moose Jaw and the finally out to High River. There is no way the post office would give us this kind of service to us today. At that time the post office had the theory that mail at all times had to get to its destination, and all for four cents.

It was Hallowe'en weekend, and some of Wib's work crew wanted a special dinner. It seems several of these boys had worked for Wib other years and on Hallowe'en night they always went to the Hutterite Colony and stole a turkey. Mrs. Ross would not give them her blessings. She warned them she would not prepare it for dinner. In spite of all this, the boys wanted to do it. To make a long story short we had goose for dinner the day after Hallowe'en. It seems the boys could not tell a turkeys from a goose inside a dark building. One boy grabbed something with feathers and they all left on the run. They had come very close to getting cornered and caught by the Hutterites and later found out the Mounties were out looking for the thieves. The boys were very afraid they might get caught, so they burnt the feathers in the bunk house stove and buried the ashes along with the bones well out in the field. We were all afraid, as everyone at that time knew that the "Mounties" always get their man.

By now the mountains and foothills were white with snow as it had snowed up there a number of times. We knew time was getting short to finish the harvest, but we were hopeful as we were nearing the last of the crop.

A few days later a heavy snow came down and the men were more or less confined to the bunkhouse for several days and some were getting restless to go home. The sky was all grey and heavy and threatening more snow. It was cold and wet and we just had a day or two threshing left to do so there was talk of leaving for home. I remember Wib's brother Grant took us all into High River for the day thinking the outing would cheer us up so we would stay. They had not paid us anything yet because they knew if they did some of the men would leave for home. When it came time for dinner that day the two French boys I bunked with didn't have enough money on them to buy their dinner, so I bought it for them. I sometimes wonder if they ever think back to that time now and think kindly of that English lad that paid for their dinner that day............. I like to think so.

After another heavy snowfall, Wib came out to the bunkhouse to tell the men he had decided to let them all go. So he paid us all, but he wanted me to come back to the house for a few days to visit. I don't remember how long I stayed. But soon it was that time again to ponder what I should do next

Jack Enjoying a Day At Wib Duncans

I had an Aunt Becky in Vancouver, a sister to my Grandmother Butson. It was getting cold in Alberta so I thought it might be a good idea to head for the west coast where everyone assured me it was nice and warm.

The Duncans had treated me well and I kept in touch with them for many years until they all passed away. Incidentally Charles the hired man married Nell, and Wib married late in life to a lady who owned a restaurant in High River. While all of them are gone now, I remember them fondly as true westerners and true friends.

I took a bus from High River to Vancouver; by way of the "Crows Nest Pass" It was a trip through a snow-clad mountain wonderland. I was always anxiously waiting to see what was around the next bend in the highway. I don't recall how many hours I was on the bus but I rode it straight through all the way, sleeping when I could on the long bench across the rear of the bus. Vancouver of course was already a great city in 1944 and I was a bit concerned about getting lost. I had my Aunt Becky's address with me so to play it safe I took a taxi to her address. That was my very first taxi ride and I don't mind telling you I felt I had become a real city slicker. Imagine me a farm boy so far from home riding in a taxi in this strange and beautiful city of Vancouver.

My Aunt Becky (Norris) Kiel

My Aunt Becky was married to a Louis Kiel and they lived at 1775 Davie St. which was right down near the beach at Beach Ave. (At that time it was a part of Pacific Ave.) and close to the aquarium and the south entrance to Stanley Park. They had the last house on the north side of the street and were next-door to the Cunningham Drug Store. The house was a huge cream coloured wood clapboard two and a half stories high. It had a great balcony across the front outside its bay windows on the second floor. But it seemed the sea gulls had it spoken for so no one would dare venture out there.

This was actually my Great Aunt, and I had never met her before. But she was a very dear person with great insight and wisdom, which in one way or the other sooner or later found its way to you. She knew I was troubled with what I thought were problems at home and with my hearing slowly diminishing. So she talked to me kindly, saying that although parents didn't always do what was right, they usually did the best they could. She had heard from my mother and assured me that they loved me and missed me.

Uncle Louis and Aunt Becky had retired to Vancouver from Kindersley Saskatchewan, where they had owned a successful hardware business. They seemed extremely comfortable in their retirement. Their house was furnished with old, huge and magnificent furniture. They gave me a room to myself in the basement and with it came the best lot of books I had ever seen outside a real library. Apparently Uncle Louis loved good books. I have always and I still do like books. I was in heaven. My Uncle Louis looked every bit the businessman he had been all his life. He was well dressed with an air of success about him. He was very courteous to me in a stand offish way. On the other hand my Aunt Becky took me under her wing and mothered me as one of her own.

What a wonderful location for their retirement. The air coming in off the water was always clean. English Bay Beach was only a short distance away, and one could walk for miles there, or go for a walk in Stanley Park and in a few minutes leave the busy city behind and be in another world. For a few weeks I made the most of it, even though I knew it would soon come to an end.

We were now well into late fall. I have always loved the freshness of the fall air. I can breath it deep into my lungs and it works magic for me then, even as it does for me today. I spent many hours walking along the beach; winter was in the air and wicked waves crashed the shoreline bringing in drifting logs bleached white as bone and pieces of driftwood and timber of all description. I would look at a waterlogged log or at a hand hued piece of timber and wonder where it came from. If only it could speak it would have a story to tell. While walking in Stanley Park I remember seeing a small pond near the southern entrance where there was a small boat set up on stilts and a sign, which read, "The Lost Lagoon." At the time I thought it referred to the boat, but I guess it was the name of the small inland pond. The story goes that the boat was found on the ocean shore a long, long time ago, and they believe it came from Asia. So they found it a permanent home on stilts beside this little inland pond.

While it didn't get very cold it did rain, and it also has the sloppiest snow in all Canada. It falls like snow but hits you like a glass of ice-cold water. If you get caught out in it your all wet in minutes. By now I knew my life of leisure must soon end. I had to find yet another job, and jobs in the winter in Vancouver were scarce. Many people from far off places leave their farms and the bush and go to Vancouver to enjoy the climate and a few months of city life in the wintertime.

For many, some work would help them to afford staying in the big city. I had been looking in the paper for a job but there were only a few jobs listed. One that caught my aunt's eye was for help wanted on a dairy farm on Lulu Island, which is just off shore in the Fraser River. As I could not hear well on the phone my Aunt made the call and I got the job. They would come to the house to pick me up the next day.

The idea of going back to milking cows was not exactly to my liking, but one can't always be choosey and especially so in the wintertime when you're far from home. There is a bridge, which connects the island to the main land. I don't remember much about the trip out to the island except my driver was very quiet.

When I arrived at the dairy farm house, I was introduced to an older married couple from Manitoba. They had answered an ad in the paper, asking for someone to keep house and cook meals for the men on a dairy farm in B.C. They didn't need to stay on their cash crop farm during the winter months in Manitoba and didn't keep any kind of farm stock. Before long I had the feeling that this was not at all what they had hoped it might be, a warm and cozy winter at the west coast. The weather was always damp and they were not use to the dampness. Thus they always complained about feeling the cold. There were two other boys working there and we all lived together in the house. We got along well together, but our staggering work scheduled bothered the couple from Manitoba with their sleep hours. Three guys in the house getting up at 3:00 am every morning is bound to interrupt anyone's sleep One of the great bonuses of our job was that we all liked our milk, and now we had all the milk we wanted to drink, free.

It was a beautiful dairy as dairies go, two long white wood barns end to end with firewall doors in between. Steel stanchions for the cows and overhead litter carriers to take the manure out. There were also two big wooden silos, in which they kept real smelly pea silage for the cows, and oh how the cows loved it. The cows themselves were Guernsey very kind and gentle critters, with huge udders and were great milkers. We did the milking with the help of several milking machines.

I never did get to see much of the island as I worked seven days a week and none of us had a car to drive. The island had a dyke built all around the outer side of it, to make it possible to farm it. You see everyday when the tide comes in from the Pacific; it backs the water up in the mouth of the mouth of the Fraser River flooding the island. There is a ditch all around the island on the inside of the dyke wall to catch the water, which seeps through. After the tide goes out, the water in the ditch seeps back out into the river. The island is naturally quite wet and only grass and a few things will grow, and one of these few things is a pea, which they grow and used as silage for the cows to eat.

I was never able to learn to live with that job. It was possibly the worst job I had in my lifetime and only because of the hours. All of the equipment we used was the best and the people we worked for were fine and one could hardly complain about the gentle nature of the cows. It was the hours that got us down. The day started at 3 A.M. when we went out to say good morning to the cows, and they all replied:

"Moooo mooove it Buster were hungry," and so on this friendly note our day began. We fed them first and then did the milking. The milking had to be done and in the milk house by 6 A.M. Ready to be taken into Vancouver for the city's morning milk. At seven or thereabout we were expected to be at the breakfast table. We seldom made it on time so our cook was unhappy. If you were born on the farm you know things don't always go as planned, and often go very wrong. So a farmer's timing has to be flexible.

We had an hour off for breakfast and at 8 A.M. we were to be back in the barns to clean the stables and bed the cows down with straw. We were supposed to be finished by 11 A.M. and have from 11 A.M. until 3 P.M. off to eat dinner and to rest or sleep if we could. But we seldom were done with our work by 11 A.M. and even when we ate dinner at 12 noon how could you get much rest before going back to work at 3 P.M? Now as you all should know the cows don't rest on Sundays so you work seven days a week, and I had one day off a month. Yes, one day off a month. There was no union involved on dairy farms in those days.

When my monthly day off came up, I would want to make the most of it. So I would leave for my Aunt Becky's the night before. This way I would have a whole day to spend with them. I had to walk a half-mile in the dark to a train stop; it was just a little platform along the track. I remember every time I went it was dark and a bit scary. The track right there was on a curve and as the train rounded the bend, its headlights were nowhere near you. This stop was seldom used so the train would come roaring around the bend and only at the last minute would he see you standing there dangerously close to the tracks, so as to be seen. I always thought it was going to go on by, but somehow it always managed to screech to a halt at the last minute. On one such trip I confided with my Aunt that I was very unhappy about the hours I had with my job and the pay I received. It was then that my aunt gave me a few words of her wisdom, which has stayed in my mind all these years. I remember the sincerity of her voice and the way she said it, with the emphasis on "Do" She said,

"Jack, I am very sorry about the hours you have to work as I can see it is hard on you. But as far as the money goes I want you to remember this."

"It's not how much money you make, but what you "do" with the money you make." Those words of wisdom have remained with me the rest of my life, and when I chose to be a barber I knew I had to manage the money I made or I would not end up with anything. She encouraged me to go home. I knew if I did I would still have to "Get Up And Milk The Cows" but at least I would have better hours.

After saying a sad farewell to my Uncle and my Aunt, I bought a bus ticket for St.Marys and a long journey home.

The bus I took travelled across the US border into Washington State and on down to Seattle. This was I understood because of heavy snow in the Canadian Rockies. I remember the endless hills as we neared Seattle. We arrived at the Greyhound Bus Station late in the day. I had to sit most of the night in the bus station before my bus left for Chicago early the next morning. When your young it seems a train or bus trip to places you have never been before is very much an adventure. At that time I was very trusting and I could sleep almost anywhere. There was little thought given to the idea that harm might come your way.

I rode that bus day and night across the northern United States. Our first stop was Spokane Washington and then across Idaho to Billings Montana. Then across South Dakota to Illinois and on into Chicago. From there to Detroit and on to London and home to St Mary where I phoned my dad to come and pick me up. It was as if I had been away over night or for the weekend and dad had not missed me. There was no big smile to greet me much less a hug. We travelled home in silence, for as usual my dad had nothing much to say to me. Some things never changed.

I do remember though that something had changed for me, and changed for the better. It was as if while I was away I had grown up, or else my eyes had been open to the beauty of the country all about me. Where before I saw only dirty old brick houses and unpainted barns. I was now able to see the beauty in what had been before me all this time but until now I had not noticed it in this light.

For the first time I saw the beauty in those monstrous old brick houses and the great unpainted board barns. All this was something solid and lasting, built with caring hands. Its beauty to me was so obvious now, yet until this moment I had not seen it. This beauty was everywhere about me. It was in the design of the wood work under the eaves and on the gable ends of the houses. It was there in the elaborated brickwork on which the late afternoon sun shone and added warmth to the colour of the aging brick. It was in the lofty maples which lined the roadsides and shaded the farm buildings. The great unpainted silver grey of the hemlock barns that had always seemed so ugly to me were now wrapped in warmth with colour and charm. Something had awakened within me and I knew it was good.

Chapter 3
Growing Up and Times To Remember

Like all boys, I looked forward to being sixteen and getting my driver's license. At my age now I realize this must be every parent's worst nightmare, having your kid turn 16 and wanting to drive a car. I realize I was rather lucky about this as my dad loved cars and understood my feelings and need to drive. I never thought he would let me drive his 1938 Ford though, as he just had it into Jack Edmond's garage and had its grill fixed and the car repainted.

One day in Mitchell as we were getting into the car he handed me the car keys saying I could drive home. Mom got in the back seat along with my three sisters and dad took the passenger side. I had watched dad shift gears all my young years so I had that down pat in my mind. I did very well and I think my dad was impressed. Soon we were well out of town and on the road home. I was cautiously travelling maybe 30 or 35 miles an hour and my mom kept shouting, slow down, slow down. I think she was just a might bit nervous. Now that is hard to understand as my dad took all corners on two wheels. He always scared me to death as once behind the wheel he was always in a hurry to get to his destination.

The 38 Ford had cable brakes compliments of Henry Ford. When they worked they would lift you right out of your seat when you made a hurried stop, but the problem was they never worked very well, very long. One day I went to cross a very narrow bridge just as a car entered the bridge on the other end. I soon realized the bridge was too narrow for us to pass, so I applied the brakes, but the car kept going merrily on its way. Our cars met grill grinding into grill and my dad's car with its freshly fixed grill was just a bit the worst for wear. I expected much worse from dad when I got home, but for some reason he took it remarkably well.

A few days later he pointed out two of his nicest fat pigs and said,

"I am going to give you these two pigs to keep for sows, you can raise little pigs from them to sell."

Of course this made me very happy, and then a few days later when we went into Mitchell, he drove to Sawyer's Garage and pointed out a 39 Plymouth Coupe car and wanted to know if I liked it. Like it, well gosh darn it, it had wheels on it didn't it?

At that time when you first started to drive you got a beginners permit. Then you could go ahead and drive as long as you had someone with a driver's permit along with you. Later when you had gained some experience at driving you applied for your real drivers permit. Dad made a $100.00 down payment on the 39 Plymouth club coupe, which we bought for $700.00. I was supposed to pay it off from the money I would earn raising little pigs. Talk about counting your chickens before they are hatched, but I guess desperate times create desperate plans. It was many years before I drove one of my dad's cars again.

When I went to get my first real drivers permit I had to take a driver's test.

I had an appointment for the test at Fawms Garage in Mitchell. Dad dropped my sister Pearl and me off at the garage and he left and went on up town. The test was to be done in one of Mr. Fawm's cars. Pearl got in the back seat and Mr. Fawm seated himself in the front passenger side seat. I really didn't know him as my dad always took his car to Jack Edmonds the Ford Garage. I just remember it was all business as Mr. Fawm was not being overly talkative, or very friendly. I suppose because of his job he felt he had to distance himself from the person he was giving the test to. He put me through his usual little jog around town telling me where and when to go and when and where to stop. Of course I had to show him I could park between two cars, and even how to make a u-turn. I was careful to always signal with my hand when I made my turns. We didn't have turning signals on our cars at that time. We signalled by putting our arm out the car window. All the time he held a pencil and pad quietly keeping score. When we arrived back at the garage I was convinced I had done an excellent job. Mr. Fawm admitted I had done well but I forgot to signal with my hand on a certain corner. I was sure I did, but it was his word against mine and right now mine didn't count much. Right then a little voice in the back seat chirped up,

"He did signal, I saw him" my kid sister Pearl rising to the rescue.

Wheels make a great difference in any young guy's life, but wheels also leave your parents with many sleepless nights worrying about your safety and wondering where is my wandering boy tonight?

This was the first of many wonderful cars I have owned, I considered each one of them an experience. I would like to list all of the cars here I have ever owned.

(1) 1939 Plymouth Coupe (2) 1947 Chev Sedan

(3) 1953 Henry J Kaiser (4) 1954 Ford

(5) 1960 Ford Starliner hardtop (6) 1964 Ford Galaxie Convertible

(7) 1968 Plymouth Fury 111 Convertible (8) 1973 Ford Mustang Convertible

(9) 1978 Dodge Magnum (10) 1983 Chev Camaro

(11) 1989 Grand AM Pontiac (12) 1999 Special Edition Ford Mustang

Except for the first two all were brand new cars, I never owned one I didn't love. As you can see I treated my cars like my politics. I never married myself off to any one party. I am hoping there will be at least one more car in my life.

100

My First Car Accident

My first car accident happened while I had this 1939 Plymouth. It was New Year's Eve and I was to pick up the two Stacey boys near Rannock and go to a movie in St Marys. When I arrived at the Stacey farm a neighbour boy Don Nairn was there and wanted to go along. This was ok with me except my car was a club coupe and this model had no back seat and four in the front was a no no. However we couldn't refuse him on New Year's Eve. So once we were in town he was to keep his head down. After the movie we all wanted to drive out to a popular eating-place called the Knotty Pine Inn about a mile out of St Marys on the Stratford side. We were driving behind a Grey Hound bus and as we neared the outskirts of town a car coming towards us was weaving back and forth across the highway. Again and again it pulled over onto our side of the street only to swing back again. They pulled in on the bus in front of us and pulled off, then they pulled over on me and I thought for sure they would pull off as he had been doing.

There was a hard hit and then a crunching sound as this car came down the side of my car. Although I knew my car was damaged my first concerns were for my passengers. Luckily we were all ok. I knew I had to get rid of one of my passengers, as I didn't want to be found with four people in the front seat. However the neighbour boy Don Nairn didn't want to go alone, so I let the second boy go along with him. The second boy would have made the best witness, but he just happened to be on the outside so he left. I couldn't get out my door as the side was crushed in. When we were out of the car we viewed the damage. My car had been raked from the front fender all the way to the rear fender, yet there was no damage done to the front bumper or to the grill. On the highway was a wheel, which had been torn off the car that hit me. Yet there was very little damage done to this car other than to the wheel and fender.

We could see a number of boys getting out of the car that hit us. By now several cars had stopped and we didn't know who was who. Some boys were pitching beer bottles from the car onto the lot, which was along side the street. Someone had called the police and soon a police car arrived. The cop asked us to get into the police car. My friend the Stacy boy and I got in the back seat and the other driver got in the front. We soon found out the policeman was from St Marys and he knew the boy and his family that hit me. The boy was crying and in great distress as he told the cop it was entirely his fault, as he had too much to drink, and was on the wrong side of the road.

Now I had been brought up to have full faith and totally believe in the law. I believed that you just didn't get to be a policeman unless you were honest and honourable. So I trusted this policeman to do what was right. I was now 17. I had done nothing wrong as far as this accident was concerned, so I put all my trust in this town policeman.

The policeman told him to "Shut up or you will get yourself into a lot of trouble".

At that time I didn't realize what I should have done; I just left it to the policeman to handle it right. He told me I could go home. The guy that hit me was still in the front seat of the car with him when I left. After I left I believe he explained to the boy that since I had not asked him to lay any charges against him, then he was free to lay charges against me. All he had to do was say that it was I that was on the wrong side of the road instead of him. He would see that there was not anything in his report about admitting he was on the wrong side of the road, or that he was drunk. I took my car to a neighbourhood friend Jim Evans who liked to do bodywork. He did a very good job of the bodywork and then he added a fresh coat of light green paint.

I came home one day and my mom handed me a letter, it was a court summons I was charged with careless driving and was to appear in court in St Marys. Word got around to a few good neighbours what had really happened and when the court date came up, they were there for me. I really appreciated their support; there was Norman Morrison and Jim Watson and Eddie Smith and my dad. I had no money for a lawyer so I was going to be my own defence. I still had faith in the system and I was sure that if I just told the truth, all would be ok. I was of course scared speechless as I listened to the lies told by this guy, all of which was backed by the policeman. Once when the policeman said something, which was totally an outright lie, I stood up to protest. I found out this was very wrong in a court of law. Every one including the judge pounced on me and told me to sit down and be quiet. I felt totally defeated.

When his lawyer had me on the stand asking questions, he would not let me answer in whole. He placed his questions just so trying to forced me to only answer yes or no so as not to disclose anything. If I tried to say more he cut me off rudely saying,

"Answer the question yes or no." When he was finished I was completely shaken by what we call a justice system and had no fight left in me. The worst was I had lost something very valuable that day, which was my respect and faith in law and justice.

When the time came that I could have said something in my defence I was too terrorized to open my mouth. The judge found me guilty of careless driving and I had to pay a fine.

He did however say that he had the feeling that there was something missing, something that should have been told. I was thankful he made that clear. If only I had the courage to speak up when I should have I might have had that sick cop's badge. This unhappy event has bothered me all my life and I have had to struggle to keep faith in the system. Don't kid yourself; Yes Junior, there is such a thing as a bad cop, but thankfully most of them are good guys.

I was young and energetic and my community life was very full. There was the local United Church Young People's Union and Jr. Farmers and our Motherwell Community club, parties and dances, and of course Sunday School and Church.

I took my place in all this activity even though I struggled with my hearing. Our local Motherwell United Church Young Peoples Union met every Sunday evening in the basement of our Church and our county presbytery met once a month, most often in someone's home from one end of the county to the other. I took my part and had a great interest in all these activities. Eventually I worked up to preside over our local Young People's and moved on to become a member of the board of directors of the Perth County Young People's Presbytery.

Mitchell Jr. Farmers came next, and after serving in almost every office I became the president of the Mitchell Jr. Farmers. I served as president for a number of years. While I was president, Mitchell became the largest Jr. Farmer's organization in Perth County. The membership more then doubled. This was largely because I had a great team of people who were so willing to work hard for me. I demanded a lot from them, I knew it then and I know it today. Yet I believe they enjoyed the results we received by working together. There are times when they share their memories of this with me with pride. On the other hand my dad and mom took no interest in any of the things I did. They did know that it sometimes messed up the milking schedule. Or at times took me away from my farm duties. I did feel guilty about it because sons were supposed to be dutiful to their parents and not think of themselves. This was of course selfish of me. I also knew that as a son I had broken almost every code in the book.

The County Jr. Farmers were asked to present a half hour TV program for the Wingham TV station. As I had been writing local events in the Mitchell paper on Young Peoples and Jr. Farmer activities, they asked if I would write a document on poultry in Perth County, then act as commentator for the show. This was a tall order for me, as at home we didn't own a TV set yet. However I wrote the document and did the show with the help of Ivan Norris and Jack Fisher of the Mitchell Jr. Farmers. I also should credit fifty baby chicks donated to us for the show by Roe's Hatchery of Atwood. I still remember the first few lines of the document. It read -

"It is a far cry today from the first time a cock crowed in the jungle of Burma to the modern poultry houses of Perth County" I still think it as a good line to open with.

In Mitchell a large number of our Jr. Farmers were seated in the gym watching the show. What made me sad though was that while my neighbours the Smiths had a TV set and were going to watch the show, I could not get dad and mom to go to the Smiths to watch it. They purposely would not watch it just to agitate me.

One of the projects our Jr. Farmers took on was a mailbox sign. At the time few farms had a professional printed name on their mailbox and trying to find some one could be difficult to say the least. People might refer to your place as the farm with the big red barn or the one with the large stone gatepost. Believe me I have heard it all. We decided to try to cover the whole township with mailbox signs to fit on the top of your box with a couple screws. I took my clue from the many other members and had my dad's name put on it and then added, "and son." Big mistake, my dad would not let me put it on the mailbox as he said,

"There was no "and son" about it, the farm is mine." Suddenly I didn't feel quite so selfish anymore. Many times in the winter when I felt discontented with myself I would take the shotgun and go for a walk in woods. While I did like to hunt on a rabbit drive, more often it was just an excuse to wander the woods alone and find some inner peace.

I bought my first set of Skis from Ruth (Nairn) Morrison who lived next door. On Saturday afternoons in the winter after the barn chores were done and if there was no rabbit drive, I would go Skiing with Ruth or her sister Norma. We usually skied on the hillside banks of the Thames River at Motherwell. They weren't exactly the Blue Mountains but they served the local purpose. No one drove far to ski in those days, as it was thought of as the sport of the well to do. If it had not been for those old Motherwell hills and Ruth and Norma I would never have learned how to ski. All winters though come to an end, and the first sign that spring is on the way is when the farmers start to tap their maple trees once more for the syrup season.

I took my Uncle Hughes's syrup pan to the bush and dug a hole through the centre of a large beach knoll and lined each side and far end with rocks. Then I shovelled the surrounding earth from the knoll back against the rock thus making an earthen fireplace about two feet high. Then I put some iron bars and steel fence posts across from side to side to rest the pan on. On the rear end I stuck in a stovepipe with a damper and mudded it all in with stones and earth. On the front I put a piece of galvanized tin sitting on a brick on each side so as to make a draft at the bottom. It worked well and I think I boiled syrup there for two or three years. No one ever helped me, but that was OK, it was my project and I was happy to do something on my own.

My agreement with dad was that I could cut down any dead trees or clean up any brush from trees he had cut during the winter, so I usually took the bob sleigh or wagon and horses back with me. That way I could gather the sap in milk cans on the sleigh or bring wood to my fire, and besides the horses were great company. Something can be said about being alone in the bush with your team of horses and especially so after dark. If you watch them you will note that their ears and nose are constantly on the move picking up sound and scent that we are not aware of. They can also get impatient from standing for long periods of time and stomp their feet or snort to let you know it's time to call it quits. At times there can be a lot of communication in silence and especially so when you're out there alone in the woods.

Gathering Sap in the Sugar Bush

The end product of the day was usually a little over a gallon of syrup. When dad and mom got all the syrup they needed for the family I could sell the rest that I made. Syrup in the late forties was selling for $4.50 to $5.00 a gallon depending on its quality. Pan syrup is darker from more boiling than evaporator syrup and has a stronger flavour. I actually like it better, but it does not get the grade mark that evaporator syrup does so it sells for less. How do you know when the syrup is ready to "take off" as they call it? You have a special thermometer and when the temperature reaches 220 degrees F it is syrup and ready to take off. Handle it carefully as syrup is very hot.

After a couple or three years of boiling my own syrup my neighbour Norman Morrison came to visit me. I remember how he propositioned me.

"Jack how many gallons a day do you make here?" I told him that on a good day if I had a good run of sap, I might make two gallons of syrup, but I usually averaged a bit over a gallon. He reminded me that when it gets cold and the sap doesn't run you won't make anything, and on rainy days you will find it hard to work out here in the open, so you would find it hard to average a gallon a day in the end. He wondered if I would leave this and instead work for him. He would give me a gallon of syrup a day or five dollars which ever I wanted. So I talked it over with dad and he thought it would be best if I worked for Norman.

It was the beginning of many years of making maple syrup for the Morrisons. They were happy years as we were the best of neighbours; I also loved the bush and the horses. Norman was a good guy to work for and I could talk to him about anything, from maple syrup to religion and get a straight answer. Norman was a good farmer and at that time I was sure he was making lots of money. For some reason after kidding him about his money, I told him that the Bible tells us that it is harder for a rich man to go to heaven, than it is for a camel to go through the eye of a needle. I heard him chuckling over that, one day when he was talking to my dad. He was not sure how he was to take that. I noted he never did give his money away, but I am sure someday I will meet him there in heaven. I will tell you a little story about him so you will know just what kind of guy he was.

On the way into St Marys one day Norman dropped in to see my dad about something. Before he left dad asked him if he would mind taking fifty dollars to town with him and depositing it in his bank account as he had a payment due on a note. This would save him a trip into town. About two weeks later dad was in town and a man asked him if Norman ever found that fifty dollars he lost. Of course dad knew nothing about it. A few days later when dad saw Norman he asked him about the lost fifty dollars. Norman said that a few days later the money turned up so everything was ok. He said he had been to a machinery dealer looking at some new machinery and he thinks he bent over to look at something and the envelope with the money fell from his shirt pocket. When he arrived at the bank he found the money missing, so he retraced his steps to the machinery agent to look for it, but they could not find it. A few days later the machinery agent was showing someone else the same piece of machinery and he found the envelope and fifty dollars lying on the ground. He called Norman to come and pick it up. This was the way people were then; there was an unsaid trust.

Dad said, "You did put fifty dollars in my account."

Norman said, "Yes, of course, you entrusted fifty dollars to me and I lost it." That was the Norman I knew and the way I will always remember him.

It seemed my dad soon found out very early that he could trust me with money, that just because he gave a few extra dollars I was not going to be in a rush to spend it. So almost every time I was ready to go out, he would say,

"Do you need any money?" Often I might say,

"No I think I'm ok" and dad would hand me a few more dollars and say.

"Well take this just to be on the safe side"

He was always very good with me that way. It seems that over the years my friends have thought that somehow I must have money, as they have never caught me broke. It just might be that I hear that voice of my dear old Aunt Becky saying,

"It's not how much money you make Jack, but what you" DO" with the money you make."

I worked hard all summer and played even harder, thus often I would be rather late in getting home. My dad was always at me saying I should not be burning my candle on both ends. I loved to drive up to Grand Bend on Sunday evenings and go roller-skating. Many of my friends would be there from near and far. It was

Ruth Nairn that introduced me to the Grand March on that roller rink. Ruth was good at guiding me, as I could not hear the instructions. No one had their own roller skates in those days, as the skates just strapped on to your shoes.

" Fall Fever and Westward Ho "

Every time fall came around I would feel the call of the west. In my mind I would see those great fields of waving wheat and the rolling hills of prairie grass, with its cows and calves. After two years at home I needed to go back so I put my name in for the harvest excursion once more.

This time I just took my one large suitcase and a handbag and every thing went much as before. On the train I was seated beside a lad from Gads Hill a village just north of Stratford. His name was Bill Rose. We decided to team up and go to the same place. When we arrived in Winnipeg I really did want to see my Uncle Fred but we were going to be put on a bus and shipped out right away. As the grain crops usually ripens in Manitoba first, before Saskatchewan or Alberta they would not send us out any farther until the crops in Manitoba were harvested.

Again they took us to a large empty area and called out names to places we had never heard of before. We both pictured a far off place with a strange name so when they called out, ten men for Cypress River, I told Bill that sounded good. He agreed so we both put up our hands and we were ushered away together and put on a bus. Neither of us had any idea where we were heading, but then that adds to the excitement. It ended up that is about 95 miles west of Winnipeg on the number 2 highway towards Brandon.

We arrived in the late afternoon in a well treed but sleepy little town well off the number 2 highway. It had a railway track and a row of grain elevators on the south side of the street and a row of shops and stores on the north side. As we pulled up we could see a group of farmers jockeying to be in the front at where they thought the bus might stop. They were desperate for harvest help and they actually rushed up and put there hands on you and tried to pull you away as they asked you to come with them. This man put a hand on my arm and said,

"This one has a bit of muscle. Then he added, "They sure don't send then out like they use to." The war was over but there was still a shortage of mature men to work at the harvest so most of these workers were very young men and boys.

Bill and I went with this man. His name was Marius Aubry, and he spoke just a bit different. He said that he wanted me to work for him and that his neighbour had asked him to bring him a man if possible. When we reached this neighbour's place he stopped at the road and looked at Bill and said,

"Now look this is up to you, if you feel you want to stay or not?" then added, "Things are just as bad as they look, so be careful."

We drove into a yard of mud and rooted dirt. What a sight to see. The place was in shambles. A small sun bleached grey frame house with chickens all about the door and pigs running free rooting all over the yard. There were cans and boxes and boards and machinery parts scattered all over. It looked like the remembrances of a mad twister. The farmer and his wife came out of the house to greet us. We debated the rest of the fall as to which was the dirtiest, the pigs or the farmer and his wife. Bill cowered down in the back seat and said,

"I'm not staying here," to which Marius said,

"OK, I understand I will get you out of this"

This was one of the few Scottish farmers in the area and he said,

"So you brought me some help did you?" Marius told him not many men came in on the bus so he could not get a man for him. At first the Icelandic farmer seemed a bit taken aback and he told Marius,

"You cannot take two men for yourself as I have to have one." So Marius told him the second man was to work for his two brothers. They were going to share him, which for a short time proved true. We left much to Bill's relief.

Down the road a way we pulled into a lane with a barbed wire gate across it…one of those you only saw in the west with a stick and chain on, to tighten it. I jumped out to open the gate and Marius drove through. When I got back in he sat for a few seconds and then turned sideways to talk to us. He said,

"Now I don't know what you guys are use to, or what you are expecting. My place is not fancy but it is clean."

I already liked the man. He seemed honest and open and I respected him for that little speech he gave to us before he took us over the hill. I thought it was a show of a proud and solid character, and of courage and honesty. It turned out that every word of what he said was positively true. We couldn't see anything

Getting the Gate by Jack   from the road, just a winding roadway going up around the side of a hill. As we drove farther on we could see the roof and then the front of a nice looking red-hip roof barn coming into view. Soon we could see the whole of it, sitting at the far end of a large yard, which was surrounded with a growth of shrub trees.

At this end of the yard and nearer to us was a small-unpainted clapboard house, its rear and far side huddled up close to the shrub trees in the hillside. The yard was clear of debris but no lawns or flowerbeds in sight. The packed earth spread all the way from the house to the barn and beyond.

Out of the house came a rather beautiful full figured lady, with a great head of dark hair and a smile that was quick, the kind you would always remember. The instant she welcomed us I knew things were going to be OK here. It was late afternoon by now and they knew we had been on the road for a long time. So they suggested we go into their front room and rest until the men came in from the fields. The men were busy cutting grain with the binders and stooking sheaves.

Once seated in the front room I was aware of the big-framed picture of the Virgin Mary, which dominated the room. I also was sure I had heard a few French words spoken between Marius and his wife Bertha. Suddenly I wondered just what I might have got into. Although I was English, all my life I had lived in a Scottish community. I had heard stories galore about the terrible French, and yet I had never met a true Frenchman. Then I was born in a solid Protestant community and all my life I had heard about the terrible Catholic. What had I got into? Soon we could smell coffee, such as I had never smelled before, and to this day I swear the best cups of coffee I ever had were made by this French woman Bertha. I would give anything for another cup of that coffee.

Shortly after six a group of dark, sweaty but talkative men entered the large farm kitchen. Bill and I were called to sit with them for supper. The food was plentiful and wonderful, but the conversation was in French so Bill and I sat in silence. Suddenly one young man spoke up and everyone turned their heads and looked at us. Then without an explanation everyone was talking English.

This young man who spoke up was Jerry Baltesson. He was a normalite school teacher that year teaching at a local public school. He was boarding at his Uncle Marcel's who was Marius's brother. There was a third brother John there also and they all worked together to make a threshing crew. An older man was at the table too. He was Emile Aubry, the grandfather of the Aubry clan and very much a Frenchman.

Jerry and I remain friends to this day. He is now a retired schoolteacher and lives in a beautiful penthouse in downtown Winnipeg. I asked him what happened that day at the kitchen table. He said that the men always talked in French when their grandfather was present, as he had never learned to understand English very well. When he made them realize we didn't understand a word they were saying, they switched to English for courtesy reasons.

Marius and Bertha had two daughters, Gaby the oldest about thirteen or fourteen and Loraine perhaps twelve. Loraine was one of those children who would never grow up. She was big, heavy set, good natured and playful, but she would never be more then a big baby in her mind. She took a liking to Bill for some reasons and he was a scared to death of her. She would run straight at him only to dive past him at the last minute. Everyone thought it was funny except of course poor Bill. He was sure he was going to get squashed to death sooner or later. She liked me too I know, but never bothered me the way she teased Bill. Everyone was good to Loraine, but it was easy to see she was a heavy load for Bertha her mother. Yet they never complained; they took her along where ever they went never trying to hide her. These people were honest and accepting to the core and I respected them greatly for that.

One Sunday after I had been working for them a few weeks, I walked out to the field as I could see Marius's brother Marcel working on the threshing machine, servicing it and making sure it was ready to go on Monday morning. While working away he asked me a few questions about me and about Ontario. He was born in Cypress River and had never been out of the province. He said,

"Jack I understand down east where you come from there are no French or Catholics. How do you feel about coming out here and staying with us?"

"That would have been a big question, a few weeks ago when I first got here. At that time I would not have known the answer, but now after spending a few weeks with Marius and Bertha I had made up my mind about a number of things. I am never going to judge a person by his nationality or his religion again. I was a stranger to them just a few weeks ago and they have shown me they care about me and when I watch them with Loraine and see how they watch over her and love her, all I know is, whatever God they believe in, it is the same God I believe in."

A number of years later my dad and mom were driving through Cypress River and stopped by to meet the Aubrys. Marcel told my dad and mom about the time he asked me that question and he would always remember the answer he got, and that it made him very happy and that of course made me happy.

I was given two beautiful sorrel Belgium mares to drive; they were actually sisters from one of brother John's mares. Marcel owned the one and Marius owned the other. They both named their mare Lady. They were beauties, exactly alike and they responded to me with loyal affection. I could walk back to the threshing machine without having to climb back up on the load and drive the wagon in. I would walk ahead and they would each put their head to my shoulder, one on either side and would follow me everywhere I went. Everyone thought this was great, and they all took turns asking me how the Ladies were.

Bill eventually went to work for a neighbour, the Diehls, a German family. He left for home before I did and I have never seen him since Cypress River. Some day I think I will drive up to Gads Hill and look him up and find out how life treated him and if he ever got back to Cypress River. Snow came down just before we got the last of the crop off, and I became rather house bound. That wasn't all bad as there was lots of great coffee and homemade bread and buns.

One morning after breakfast Marius asked me if I would mind hitching Gaby's horse up to the buggy for her to drive to school. The school was a good distance away and she used a horse and buggy every day. Of course I said yes, and off I went to the barn. The truth was while as a kid I had ridden in buggies I had never put that kind of harness on a horse nor ever hitched a horse up to a buggy. There is a great difference from hitching a workhorse to a wagon then a driver to a buggy.

I didn't want them to think I didn't know how to do it so I went about trying to do the job, hoping I could muddle through and in the end get it right. I managed to get the harness on the horse all right, and took it out into the yard and backed it in between the shafts on the buggy. Ah! Now what do I do with those strange loops on straps hanging down on the harness, Well the logical thing to do it seemed was to put the tugs through the loop before I fastened the tug to the whipple tree. I did that on both sides and stood back to admire my work. Mmm something seemed very wrong here as the shafts were still lying on the ground. Mmm now what do I do about that. Mmm - Big question?

About then Gaby arrived and she looked at me and she laughed. She had a lisp at times on some words. She was bent over with laugher as she said,

"What is the matter with you? Are you thoopid?" She quickly unhooked the tugs from the whipple tree and pulled the tugs free of the loops, then pulled the horse forward and dropped the loop over the end of the shafts. Then she backed the horse up again and fastened the tugs to the whipple tree.

Boy, I was a great help that morning and they never let me forget it. Years later they still laughed about it. Yes I guess I was "thoopid."

They all thought this was a great joke on me, and everyone told everyone else how Jack harnesses a horse to a buggy. I have told this story to many of my friends and every now and then when they try to explain something to me, and I don't seem to see the point, they say,

"What is the matter with you are you thoopid?" and we all get a good laugh.

The weather in Manitoba stayed wet and cold, so I said a sad farewell to all my new friends at Cypress River and left for home. There were still a few days of threshing left in the fields but with luck they would be able to finish it later. I left by bus for Winnipeg and visited for a couple days with Uncle Fred. He was expecting me and I was happy to see him again. It was a long trip home alone on the train I remember though Southern Ontario looked good to come home to.

Home Again

As my dad always said, I was always burning my candle at both ends. I was always trying to get just a bit more out of life then twenty-four hours or seven days a week offered. I enjoyed the Jr. Farmers organization and the Young People's Union and the church work. Through Jr. Farmers I met Earl and Allan Paulen who farmed just east of Mitchell. My mother and Mrs. Paulen had been school friends and it seemed only natural that Earl and Allan and sisters Betty and Marion and I should become great friends too. The Paulen family was all very musical playing the violins, guitar and piano. I was never good at playing anything really well because of my hearing loss, but I did play the piano by ear. The problem was if I could not hear well I could not play well. However I did sing, and they never seemed to tire of my singing. Betty played for me many times when I was asked to sing somewhere. Later Earl's girl friend Carolyn (Eisler) Paulen played for me.

Through the Paulen boys I got introduced to the Mitchell United Church. They had a wonderful minister at that time, Rev. Robert Watt the youngest of five Watt brothers all of whom were United Church Ministers. He was packing the church full every Sunday, with his wonderful sermons. When I said packing I mean even the balcony and at times people sat in the aisle.

One day after church, Earl and Allan introduced me to Mr. Harley the church organist and music director. They wanted him to hear my voice. Of course it was a little embarrassing to have it happen this way. However he liked what he heard and had me sing a solo in church the very next Sunday. This was the first of many; many times I sang solos in the Mitchell United Church. I joined the choir so I could work closer with Mr. Harley, as he was also a music teacher and there were many things he could suggest to help me sing better. My dad and mother never heard me sing in the Mitchell United Church.

Besides singing in the choir I sang at weddings and funerals. I have sung everything from O Perfect Love, The Holy City, The Lords Prayer and The Birthday Of A King; my favourite for funerals remains "Beyond the Sunset."

All this got me introduced to the many wonderful people within the church and Sunday school, and soon they wanted me to consider teaching a Sunday school class. It appears they had a class of boys all about 15 that needed a teacher. The boys were supposed to be hard to handle. Well I had no problem with any of them. I am happy that every one of those boys made good. I will have to admit that one of those boys gave me a lot of help to get the others to respond. His name was Dean Robinson.

Dean went on to do great things. I believe one of his first real jobs was working for the London Free Press, then with the Stratford Beacon Herald. He also taught journalism at Doon Campus of Conestoga College. Dean has many great books to his credit. I like to think that perhaps somehow at one time I helped him.

After a couple years of teaching Sunday school, the board asked me if I would accept the job of Sunday school superintendent. This was quite an honour as the Main Street United Church had a huge Sunday school. I spent two years at the job.

I tried to balance all this with the farm work at home. If I had a brother it might have helped as my dad and mom relied totally on me. Dad and mom took no delight in what I did off the farm. In a way I can understand, it was just the way we were and what was expected of you at that time. Your work on the farm should always come first. On Sunday mornings in the winter I would be up before six AM and clean the stables, bed the cattle and have the milking done and be at the church in Mitchell by 10.00 AM for Sunday school. Dad was left to feed the cattle at noon. Some parents would have been proud of their son for doing this, as it was church work, but I was made to feel guilty.

Today I see parents who hesitate to ask their kids to even cut the grass, or shovel snow, while they shell out thousands of dollars for their kid's educations. They don't feel their kids owe them anything beyond being a good kid.

Friends To Remember And People I Worked For

Does everyone in his or her lifetime, know someone that years later, when looking back is remembered as a humorous wonderful friend or colourful character? I found such a friend in an older friend of my dad and mom. He was called John G Scott. Everyone referred to him only as John G. John G married Mary F and that is what everyone called them John G and Mary F. They lived in a modest little house in the village of Russeldale, the kind you see in every little village across Ontario with a neat little lawn and flowerbeds and a garden. John G was what in those days was called a drover. This meant he made his living by going from place to place buying and selling. If you had little pigs to sell he knew a buyer. If you needed one more milk cow he could find you one. He loved to barter, but in the end you nearly always could make a deal with him. He was as honest as they came and always stuck to his deal and expected you to do likewise. If you needed help to buzz wood or any kind of trucking job he would be there for you. No job was too small or too big and his price was always fair and right and often free.

One of his more steady jobs was trucking fat hogs to the White Packing Plant in Stratford. He would arrive at our place with his beat up old truck, the rack held together with rope and black wire. Chances are he might need a pail of water for his radiator, or some rope or wire to hold his rack together. He would back up to your loading door. Ours was always the doorway to the horse stable. John G always had this problem backing up as somehow the barn always came up a bit too fast. He would smack into your barn wall hitting it with zest. Backing into a stone barn wall is not the kind of thing most people want to do more than once in a life time, but John G did it every time he came.

We would help him pull out his loading ramp from under the rear of his truck, then get the gates off the side of the trucks where they hung. Then we would place a gate on either side of the ramp and we were then ready to load our pigs. Everything was in ill-repair, but capable of doing the job. This was John G.

He always carried a can of black tar with a shingle stick in it. By drawing the tarred shingle across the fat hog's shoulder or rump he left a mark on your hog so that when he reached the packing plant he knew whose hog was whose.

He brought us all the neighbourhood news and he was never in a hurry to take leave. If you had a problem, he had the time to help you. When he left you knew you had a visit from a friend, not just some trucker making a call. He loved a good joke. One time my dad hired him to truck our wheat to Ferg Levi's mill in Mitchell. Roy Russell, a neighbour had one of the first combines in our area. It was a pull type, which means you pulled it with your tractor and it was driven by the power drive shaft from the rear of the tractor.

One man would have to sit on a platform on the combine and put bags on the bagger of the storage bin. When the bag was full they would be tied and placed on a platform, which was about four foot square. Two bags placed one way and then two went the other way so they would pile firmly and neatly. Every time you made a round and came to the corner where the truck was parked you put your foot on a trip and the platform dumped the bags off. They would roll off onto the ground.

This was one of the first times I had been close up to a working combine and I didn't know anything about dumping the bags, so I climbed up on the platform to be with John G and rode a round of the field. As he neared the corner he said,

"Why don't you sit up there on the bags out of my way?" So I made myself comfortable and watched him tie bags. As we rounded the corner suddenly I went flying off with the bags. He had dumped me. I could see John G laughing with glee as the combine continued on around the field. He laughed about that for a good many years, but somehow it only endeared him to me.

Every fall after the harvest was off I would either find a job locally or go west to help with the harvest. I have always felt that I received a great reward working at various jobs I took as I was always learning something. I was able to use what I learned many times over for the rest of my life.

I worked for Ferg Robinson of Robinson's Lumber Mill in Mitchell for two falls. I had met Ferg by chance when I was quite young, maybe sixteen. A neighbour, Les Brown's barn had burnt down and Robertson's Lumber was building the new barn. All the neighbours turned up to help with the building; I had always been handy with a hammer and Ferg noticed this so he put me in charge of a group of men, most of whom were old enough to be my father. Ferg praised me in front of my dad several times for my ability. For once I thought I saw a glimmer of pride in my father's face. Perhaps there was hope for me yet.

One fall a few years later I asked Ferg for a job, and he hired me right off. My wages were the very best in town, and I was extremely happy, as I liked Ferg and all the Robinsons, my job and my pay check. I got one dollar and twenty-five cents an hour. I worked from eight AM till six PM with an hour off at noon five days a week, and on Saturday morning from eight till twelve noon. This was forty-nine hours a week at a dollar twenty-five. My weekly pay check was $61.25. WOW!. I don't remember anything being deducted from it at that time. Ferg was a good guy to work for and we got along well. He was building a lot of machinery sheds and pole barns at that time. While I was happy in every way, I knew my hearing was a problem for him. Several times I would be working high up on the barn and he would have to climb up to tell me about something, as I could not hear him shouting to me from down below. I knew this was not good but Ferg never complained all the time I worked for him.

There was a small job he took on one fall that I have never forgotten. Just west of Mitchell a barn had burnt down leaving a forty-five foot silo. Since the farmer was now without a place to store his grain he wanted Ferg to build a roof on this silo so he could use it to store his grain. Ferg had a 45 ft ladder that would just reach the top. We pulled all the lumber up by rope from the inside and then built the framework for the roof. It was to be capped or covered with aluminium. All was going smoothly until we came to the very last sheet of aluminium to be nailed down. It was cut to fit at the very peak, but I was now working on the outside of a very steep roof with nothing to hold onto. From the very peak it was well over fifty feet to the hard ground below. Believe me it was scary but I was no chicken. I had to be very careful not to start to slip, as there was nothing to stop me from falling all the way to the ground. No! No! We didn't have any unions at that time, and they didn't interfere with the work of small businesses. In fact we didn't even wear hard hats.

I will never forget the trust I put in Ferg that day. He was on the ladder, which was just under the roofline. His head was jutted up and over the edge of the roof. He spoke very calmly to me and said,

"Now Jack I want you to let yourself slide down very slowly to my hands."

"Don't slide fast as I could not stop you from going over the edge." So I did a slow slide, butterflies all aflutter in my tummy. Then he said,

"Now you will have to come down over the edge on the inside of me to the ladder. Let your feet come over the edge of the roof and I will help you find a ladder rung.. don't lean back. I can balance you but I could not hold you, so go slow and don't lean back." I put my trust in Ferg that day. I don't think either of us ever forgot it.

All car manufacturers had stopped building cars in 1939 in order to build everything from jeeps to tanks for the war. The first cars built after the Second

World War was in 1946. I well remember that one of our neighbours Alex Morrison; a brother to Norman bought a new Chevrolet car for one thousand dollars. A thousand dollars was a vast sum of money in 1946. Now something was about to happen over the next few years with our economy that had never happened before or since on such a scale. Canada came out of the Second World War deeply in debt, but full of hope and high on energy. Once again it seemed Canadians had faith and a future. The boys came home tired of war, eager to marry and settle down and raise a family and get on with life. They took out long term veteran loans and 20 and 25 year amortization mortgages on homes and farms and small businesses at five and six percent. A new house in the city would cost you about $6,000.00 and a 100-acre farm about the same. While the older generation was still a bit timid the young were full of hope, convinced the world was about to change and they were going to be a part of it. Little did they know at the time but for the most their dreams all came true.

In 1946 a kid with a nickel had big purchasing power. It would buy you an ice cream cone or a bottle of pop. It would also buy you an O Henry, Sweet Marie or Nelson chocolate bar. But in 1947 the price for pop and candy rose to eight cents or a sixty percent jump. This was disastrous for a kid with only a nickel. The price of a movie at the local "show" for children jumped from eighteen cents to thirty and for adults from forty-eight to sixty.

Factories, which had been making war equipment, retooled and were soon turning out stoves, fridges, and washing machines and selling them to the new homeowners, "The Veterans." A great miracle was about to happen. We call it inflation, and we are told it is a bad thing…but was it for us at that time?

My neighbour drove his Chevrolet car for several years and then sold it to me about three years later for more money then he had paid for it. I bought it for $1,100.00 with only forty six thousand miles on it. I in turn drove it for three years and sold it for the same money I paid for it. This is called inflation. Over the next fifteen to twenty years the veterans sold their $6,000.00 homes for $12,000.00 to $13,000.00 and bought newer and bigger homes for $16,000.00 to $18,000.00.These are the homes you have to pay $130,000.00 for today, so this is inflation.

Everyone's net value was increased by inflation; our ever-increasing worth in real estate, material things and dollars also increased our credit. Canadians went on a huge buying spree, which kept the factories busy and the pay checks full as better jobs and better pay were always on the upward spiral. Income tax had been invented in 1917 but limped along until after the second war when it was enforced. First it was imposed on office and factory workers wages and then finally extended to the farmers, especially those with milk cheques. The government hired inspectors who roamed the rural countryside forcing reluctant farmers to file income tax forms or go to jail More than one got run off the farm with a shot gun.

But in the end they had to pay. The great miracle was that we paid off a monstrous war debt from taxes on the great increase of our personal worth all because of years of inflation. It is hard to tell that generation that inflation is always bad.

July 9th 1949 my oldest sister Laurine married Oliver McIntosh of Motherwell.

The First TV Set

One morning in the winter of 1951 my sister Laurine's husband Oliver McIntosh came to visit us right after breakfast. He wanted us to go to his place to help him raise an aerial for his television. Now up until right then I had not even heard of a television. I had no idea what it was. So I asked him, "What is a television?" He tried to explain it to me. He said he had this square box with a screen on it, which would sit in the living room, and then there was an aerial sitting atop these water pipes he had welded together. This aerial would pick up the picture and sort of throw it down some wires into the box and then we all could see the picture on the screen. He said all this with a very straight face.

Well now I didn't believe in magic, and it's hard enough at times to believe in God. I found it hard to believe my brother in law would spend his money on such a wild idea as this. Well we had to humour him, so dad and I went down to where he and Laurine first lived in a little house across the road from the old McIntosh homestead. Oliver had welded several old water pipes together and they were lying on the ground on the north side of the house. The foot of the pipe was against the house foundation and the top straight out to the north.

He had the aerial fastened on the top of the pole and off the ground by putting it in his trailer box. One wire went over the back kitchen and was attached to his tractor tow bar. What he wanted dad and me to do was keep a wire tight on either side of the pipe as it went up so it would not jackknife one way or the other. All went well and some how we fastened the pipe to the side of the house and several guy wires fastened to iron stakes in the ground

Now was time for the hour of truth. We all went into the house and sat in front of the box. When they turned it on, it went crazy, with lines going up on the screen, then down on the screen and some times across and every which way, and another. See, I knew the stupid thing would not work. Dad and I left in disgust and started our now late barn chores. About an hour later Laurine phone to tell us they now had a picture. Their Television set was an Admiral. I am not sure of the size but I think fourteen inches and they loved to watch Hockey Night In Canada and I love Lucy shows. This was the very first television I ever saw. It was hard to believe.

Soon after that my neighbours Ed and Joy Smith received their first T V set from their son Ralph who was now teaching school. I often went to visit them in the evening. It was better than the movies as you not only saw a good movie, you had great company to share it with and lots of free coffee and dessert. Joy earned a little pin money on the side by cutting the neighbour men's hair. She charged about fifty cents a haircut. Getting your hair cut was really a nice social evening. It included the haircut and a movie and coffee and lunch. Now that is pretty good all for fifty cents. After a hair cut one evening Ed and I were sitting watching T V with our feet in the oven of the kitchen stove. We were absorbed in a good movie and I think happy in each other's company, when Joy said,

"I smell smoke" The kindling smouldered in the oven and as our feet were resting on it, our socks got a good scorching to. Joy laughed and laughed and said,

"You two would just sit there and catch fire if I didn't come and rescue you"

On May 5,1951 my sister Pearl married Arnold Graver of Rostock. He was a good mechanic and an even better husband and father and Grandfather.

Chapter 4
The Real West

As the summer waned towards the fall in 1952, I got a letter from Mr. Bull telling me there were great crops all over the west and they would need help to harvest it. He wondered if I could come out and help him. He also asked if I could bring someone to work for his neighbour the Sutherlands. When word got out I was going to drive west in my car a neighbour friend Bill Stephens asked to go.

This would be my first trip driving a car to Western Canada as up until now it had been the train or the bus. In a way this was an all-new and exciting trip, but one I would take many times over the next number of years. My dark green 1947 Chevrolet sedan was in top condition for the trip. I had decided to go west via the States, as it was the shorter route. We crossed the border at Sarnia to Port Huron and arrived at Mackinaw Strait late in the after noon. There was no bridge across the strait at that time so we had to wait on a ferry. The cars and trucks are all stowed in the bottom of the ferry and there was a deck above where you could sit and enjoy the trip. We arrive at St. Ignace in Northern Michigan and drove on quite a number of miles before finding a motel for the night.

The next day we drove through Duluth and on to Bemidji, where we stopped to say hello to Paul Bunyan and his famous blue ox. That night we drove late and had trouble finding a vacancy, but a motel manager found us a place out in the country far off the highway with a French family. They were very happy to have a Canadian guest. The next day we crossed the border to Emerson Manitoba and instead of taking the highway up to Winnipeg we turned west to Cypress River.

We had only intended to drop in on the Aubrys for a short visit and then continue on our trip to Oyen Alberta. When a neighbour of the Aubrys heard I was visiting along with a friend he phoned to tell us he needed some help as his son had somehow dislocated his shoulder and could not stook grain. They had a huge crop that year and were in dire straits. They knew we eastern farm lads knew how to stook and as I had worked for Marius one fall he knew we would be good workers. So he offered us $10.00 a day if we would stay and stook for him.

This was great pay at that time so I made a phone call through to Bulls in Oyen to ask if they needed us right away, or if it was OK to stay a few days in Manitoba to stook. Bulls were not at home to take the phone call and when it rang several times Olive Sutherland the neighbour answered it. She assured us that it would be OK to stay, as the crop was not quite ready in Alberta yet. It was not uncommon on those party lines for people to do something like this. In a sense they were just looking out for each other. I always got a kick out of hearing later that Olive called Bulls that night and told them,

"That Englishman you are expecting to work for you called, and is in Manitoba." It was apparently my voice that made her think I was English; I had never realized it was so obvious. Over the years I have often been asked where I came from. This farmer's name was Hutlet and they had a family of five, George, Guy, Annette and two younger twin daughter; all were very much French.

Guy was the son with the bad shoulder. He would bring out coffee, lunch and water to the field while Bill and I stooked grain under the warm sun. I remember the air was exhilarating and fresh and pure. The sheaves we were stooking were free of weeds and neatly bound and we were quite happy to be working out in the field. We also knew we were being very well paid. When Guy came out to the field I remember singing to the tune of the old "Southern Song" that black people use to sing while working in the fields many years ago.

Up in the morning, out in the sun working like the devil

For my day's pay, but lucky old Guy (sun), has nothing to do.

Bur roam about the stubble (heavens) all day.

I was able to see the Aubrys and Jerry Baltesson and family and other friends I had made here on my previous trip. Bill and I enjoyed our stay at Cypress River and left with more money in our pockets than we started out with from Ontario. So we felt we were getting off to a very good start.

In recent years Bill and Anna had visited Cypress River and found George living on the old farm. In March 2005 George and his wife Myrtle came east to visit Bill Stephens and Anna on the farm near Anderson and then came to London to visit me. After 53 yrs it was great to see him once again and to meet Myrtle

When we left Cypress River we drove on to Regina and north to Outlook, Rosetown and Kindersley. Throughout this central area we saw some of the most amazing crops of wheat we would see in our lifetime. Ahead and behind us, great flat fields of wheat stretched to the horizon and then beyond, mile after mile of waving wheat ready to be harvested. We crossed the border at Alsask to Alberta and were now only about thirty miles from Oyen and our destination.

This was the first time I had driven a car out to the Bull farm and for some reason I turned down one road too soon. This road soon disappeared into a dusty trail and seemed to lead us into a farmer's pasture field There we came upon a lonely farmhouse where we pulled in to ask for directions. We found a very friendly and talkative farmer by the name of Howard Davies. He was curious as to where we came from in Ontario. We told him near Stratford thinking he might know where that was. He told us he had once been an English homeboy and when he came to Canada he was put on a farm owned by a Mr Monteith at Sebringville just west of Stratford. He said Mr. Monteith had a daughter, who married a Mac Simpson. Would I happen to know him? It is a strange world, as I not only knew Mac Simpson but also his wife and all of his family. They lived just down the road from us. A few years later Howard came east to Ontario and visited the Simpsons. This Monteith was the Honourable Nelson Monteith, a Conservative politician and Minister of Agriculture and would be I believe an uncle to Waldo Monteith our Health Minister during the days of Prime Minister Diefenbaker. Mr Davis spoke well of the Monteith family and also of Mac Simpson of Motherwell.

Harry Bull's Farm (Oyen Alberta) 1952

Howard directed us to the Bull farm. This time I arrived not as a stranger, not even as a hired man, I actually felt more like a guest. Whenever some one dropped by, or when we visited a neighbour Mr. Bull would introduce me proudly as, the man from Ontario whom he works for. They had one son Wm. who married Alma McGowan Oct.15th 1949. He and Alma lived across the lane in a new house they had built. They eventually had three children Barbara, Karen and Brian. Wm and his dad farmed all this land together, each owning their own land but shared the cost of machinery. This worked well for both of them.

The McNee's, Uncle Frank and Aunt Rosena had by now sold the farm to Earl Regan a local lad whom I already knew, and moved into Oyen. They seemed very content and comfortable in their little cottage-like place, about three blocks east of Main Street. For once Aunt Rosena was able to tend a few flowerbeds and a wee garden with ease. I visited them some evenings and weekends Somehow though I wish I had understood better then what old age was like, and maybe I could have given them just a bit more of my time.

Both Bill and I settled in with ease at our place of work, Bill at the Sutherlands and me at Bulls. At the time neither Bill nor I knew just how much the Bulls and the Sutherlands would mean to us as the years rolled by as we both became a part of a family, Bill to the Sutherlands and I to the Bulls. Over fifty years later we still keep in touch, sadly now all of that older generation has by now passed away.

Harry Bull was an Englishman born in London, and he remained an Englishman all his life. He had that little bit of something that made him stand out in the crowd. At 18 years of age Harry left England for Canada in 1910 much to the disapproval of his family. They wanted him to stay and take his place in the family business, which was Tooke's manufacturer. Tooke's made some of the world's best men's shirts. Anyone who could afford a good shirt at that time owned at least one Tooke shirt. But Harry wanted adventure not necessarily wealth, so he left on a boat for Canada.

He met up with his older brother William in Ontario and together they headed to Western Canada. They got a job working on the grade for the CNR railway across Saskatchewan and on into the Oyen Alberta area. Although he did not come from farm stock Harry loved this new country of Canada and Alberta. He found himself scouting ahead of the grade work whenever he had time off to search for a homestead. About 12 miles southwest of Oyen he found what he was looking for. He quit his job with the railway and walked one hundred miles to Brooks to file a Homestead. He and his brother built a wood shack 10 ft. by 12 ft. and a stable for the stock out of sod that first year. Then with the help of three oxen and a mule they broke 20 acres before winter set in. They often travelled the 100 miles to

Brooks for farm supplies and food, and at times took a job in the Brook's area to earn some money. Trying to earn some extra money was how he met his wife Irene Snell. Harry took a job of picking rock off newly broken land for Mr. Snell.

Irene Snell was born in Seaforth Ontario and came west with her parents first to Saskatchewan and then in 1910 they took a homestead south west of Oyen. On January the 24th of 1917 Harry and Irene got married and moved into a new house Harry had built. They lived in that little house all of their lives until Harry passed away. It still stands proudly but empty on the old farm today.

Now in the year 1952 after such a modest start in 1910 they were farming about 1600 acres, half of which was summer fallow and the other half in crop. I was hired for five dollars a day rain or shine and twenty-five cents an acre. This meant if I stayed until the crop was all off I got a bonus of twenty-five cents an acre on the 800 acres of grain crop. As a rule it took about 6 weeks to get the crop off, as there were usually a few wet days or you might also have a few breaks on your combine.

One might visualize my pay if all turned out well something like this: If we worked six days a week for six weeks at five dollars a day I would earn 6x6=36 days x 5 dollars = $180.00

800 acres of grain x 25 cents an acre = $200.00. If I finished the harvest I would get $380.00

Wm. loved machinery and had about the best-equipped farm in the country. In 1952 he had a brand new Massey Harris combine and a Ford Truck with a lift box on it. The box held just about 200 bushels of wheat, which was thought a lot of grain at that time. The combine had a 14-foot straight cut header on it, and a storage bin that held 45 bushels of wheat. On a good day one might combine 60 to 65 acres. All this may not sound very impressive today but at that time in 1952 it was very much so.

Sutherland's Cattle, on the Range at Oyen

Over fifty years later I was back to visit on the Bull farm. Mr. Bull's grandson Brian is farming the land now. He has I believe nearly 3000 acres of land; his combine has a 30-foot header (they have them up to 45 foot now) and the combine grain bin has the capacity to hold 300-bushels. On a good day he could combine 200 acres of wheat. He has two huge grain hauling trucks the largest of which holds 600 bushels of grain. Now that is impressive!

The Sutherlands by choice were more ranchers than farmers; their first love was their white face cattle and their horses. They grew grain more because they needed the revenue from it than the love of field crops. In fact one of the Sutherland brothers told me once when I mentioned that his summer fallow was getting green,

"I will not sit on a tractor and eat dirt," thus weeds were taking valuable moisture out of his land while he spent his time watching his cows and calves and mending his fences. For many this was a way of life to which they had been born into. The world around them at this time was still afar off and the idea that change was inevitable was not always well received. Even I at that time was very much aware of the romance people had with this country. It was in the noonday

heat and the evening sunsets. It was in the clear starry sky at night or the early morning air full of promise, pure and exhilarating

Bill Snell's Dried Up Slough

This area was a broad flatland between ranges of rolling hill angling from the northwest to the southeast on either side. Down through the very centre was an off and on alkaline slough, which filled up on the run off of melted winter snow and the spring rains. In wet years the slough grew and in dry years it shrunk. If you happen to own some of both, flat land in the valley for your grain crops and some rolling hills for your cattle you have the best of two worlds You can be a grain farmer and a rancher. Having a hand in both was a great benefit to many in dry years as they had their cattle to fall back on when the grain crops failed.

Deke at the Windmill

Bill worked for Don and Olive Sutherland, a very proud Scottish couple whose parents on both sides came from Old Ontario. In the west you often heard people say Old Ontario. I would like to believe it was a sort of endearment much like I heard my grandfather speak of his, dear old England.

Don and Olive had three boys, Don Jr. (Deke) 15, Colin 14, and Neal about 5. Don Sr. was an easy guy to like. I enjoyed chatting with him immensely about cows and calves and horses the land and ranching. I would listen for endless hours to the stories he told about those early years in Alberta and how he remembered them. He was however very set in his western ways and ideas. He had been born and raised in the Oyen area of Alberta and had never been outside of the province in his entire life. He didn't think the outside world and especially Ontario had anything to offer. He was very much down on the Federal Government and the east in general yet he never met a person from Ontario he couldn't like. I would say this of him. I feel honoured to have had the chance to know him. I think fondly of him as a friend, but he was a man with a very set mind.

Olive Sutherland had been a schoolteacher for a number of years, and carried herself like a schoolteacher all her life. She took a few years off from teaching to raise her boys. Olive had a great head on her shoulders and flair about the way she looked and dressed. When you chatted with her you could talk about anything from books to cattle or politics and you were soon very much aware she had her homework done. Olive was more open to ideas and to change then Don was. She played the piano wonderfully well, filling the house with music. Don Sr. and Don Jr. both played the violin and Colin played the guitar and the piano. Neal eventually took a liking to the banjo. Each night the house overflowed with music.

About ten thirty Olive would disappear to the kitchen and Colin would take over the piano. In fifteen or twenty minutes we would smell the fresh coffee brewing. Soon Olive would call us to come to the kitchen for lunch. It would usually be something wholesome and good, perhaps home made bread or buns, or scones with Olive's own homemade jam or jellies, the kind of things you would expect to find on a ranch. One night at coffee time Don and Olive spoke of The Bad Lands, and of course a name like that draws attention. I had never heard of The Alberta Bad Lands. Olive was well informed so she set about to enlighten us. The Bad Lands are found along the Red Deer River, and one of the best places to see them was about fifty miles south of Hanna. At that time only the local people knew much about it. Today it is a provincial Park called Dinosaur Provincial Park. This is what Olive told us.

The Alberta Bad Lands are best described as a miniature version of the Grand Canyon. It is carved out of the prairie itself; every part of it is below the flat prairie land that surrounds it, thus you can not see it as you approach. Eighteen thousand years ago as the ice age retreated an immense amount of water was released and carved a drainage channel down through the soft rock on both sides of what is now the Red Deer River. This soft rock was left exposed to the wind and rains, which carved and moulded it into a kind of moonscape. There are walls to scale and caves and sinkholes to explore and endless miles of river to see.

Bill and I decided we should drive down to see The Bad Lands the following Sunday. The two Sutherland boys young Don and Colin would go along with us. They had been down there before so they would act as guides. Don Sr. advised us on some of the things we should take along to play safe, things like a flashlight each to explore caves and rope in case some one fell in a sinkhole, and an axe to cut firewood. We would also take a large container of water and matches to light a campfire to cook our supper. Olive would pack a box with some dishes and cutlery, a coffee pot and a frying pan. All this appealed to us as something adventurous and exciting to do. We decided on bacon and eggs and toast and coffee for supper. I was to bring the eggs. Now I feel a bit guilty telling you about this, but all week long I visited Mrs. Bull's hen house and sneaked off with a couple or three eggs a day and put them in my car. By the end of the week she was complaining that her reliable old hens were just not laying enough eggs. Whatever was she doing wrong.

Pin Cushion Cactus In The Badlands

Sunday eventually came. We packed the car with our strange gear and boxes of food and water and were off. At that time the roads going south from Sutherlands or Bulls were not great for cars, and especially for strangers to travel. When it was dry it would be a dusty trail and when wet, full of mud holes and wheel ruts. So we travelled the long way around, taking the number nine highway towards Hanna and then south on the thirty-six. I remember the drive south through dry flat prairie ranch land with the ranch buildings scattered far apart. There were not any signs giving us directions on how to reach the Bad Lands, so we followed young Don's directions when it came time to turn east off the highway and we arrived at our destination.

Just as Olive had told us, the prairie suddenly opened up, and before us was a very strange land " The Bad Lands." After spending weeks on the flat prairie it was awesome to see. We found a good place to park the car and set about to explore. We decided to stick close together for safety. Olive had warned us to watch out for snakes, rattlesnakes, and Don added a warning to also watch out for hoop snakes. I asked him how I would know a hoop snake when I saw one. He said you would always know one when you saw one as they put their tail in their mouth and roll towards you. At that point everyone laughed and I realized I was on the butt end of a very old western joke, which was sooner or later told to every green easterner.

Sandstone hills and coulees lined the walls on either sides of the river. Each coulee eventually ends at a wall of sandstone or a hole. We ventured into some of the larger caves-like holes always carrying our rope and we always left one person on the

outside in case of trouble. Most caves would end with holes in the ceiling where water from the flat prairie above poured down through the roof when it rained. Many had a pit or sink hole perhaps ten or twelve feet deep at the entrance of the cave where the rain water pours out of the cave churning up and washing away the sand stone. We found more then one cave with animal tracks on the well-packed floor, along with a few bones.

Sage Brush

There were many tall monuments like sand stones capped with a layer of shale lying flat on its top. They come in all shapes and sizes and are called Hoodoos, by the Indians and the locals. The shale on the top keeps the wind, the rain, and the snow from wearing the sand stone away. We climbed the tallest and took some pictures, which I still have today. Later we ventured down closer to the river and found yet another world of huge Cottonwood trees, which seemed entirely out of place away out here on the prairie. Along the river there was an oasis of grass and shrubs and vegetation for the pronghorn antelope and mule deer and all kinds of birds. The Red Deer River late in the fall looked lazy and cool as its quiet waters wound its way amid the walls of sand stone. All this added together made a strange and spectacular view.

Between the sandstone walls and the river are some open spaces, which are almost desert like. Here sparse grass grows amid the sagebrush and huge beds of the most beautiful pincushion cactus. There is also prickly pear cactus. There's a wealth of discoveries to be made in the Bad Lands but our time was getting short as the darkness descends early down below the horizon along the river. The evening sun sets on the prairie above and the eerie quietness descends. This quietness seems so very fitting for this strange land along the river. We gathered wood, which at that time was plentiful under the trees along the river. The wood was bone dry and eager to burn. We drove a stake on both sides of our fireplace and a piece across from stake to stake on which we hung our coffee pot. Soon we were frying bacon and eggs and along with home made bread and coffee we enjoyed a traditional campfire meal, which was fit for a king. This day was a lasting memory for us all; perhaps it was the food; perhaps it was the company of good friends, or perhaps it was the enchantment of the campfire and a meal by the Red Deer River in The Bad Lands.

With the grain harvest over and the good weather lingering on, life returned to a more leisurely pace. There were bundles (sheaves) of green cut oats to be brought in and stacked to supplement the bales of slough grass hay for the cows in the winter. I rather liked the job as it required skill and in the end you found great pride in building a good stack of green feed. Picking up potatoes though has never been high on my list of social activities for the year but like many other jobs on the farm someone has to do it, but why me? Mr. Bull manned the old hand-held horse plough, which was hitched behind the Ford tractor and Wm. tried to drive in a straight line down a row of his mom's big Red Plymouth potatoes. There was much shouting, and cussing and flaying of arms as it seemed no one was happy with this job.

The potatoes were picked in five-gallon pails and emptied into burlap sacks. When the job was done we loaded the potatoes onto the old steel wheel wagon and with the Ford tractor pulled up close to the kitchen door. A trap door in the kitchen floor led to a steep wood stairway down into the cellar. While I had seen the door open a number of times I had never been down there. It seemed like Mrs. Bull's private domain, and unless you were invited you had no business being down there. With a bag of potatoes in my arms I backed slowly down the narrow wooden steps into the dark coolness of the cellar. The single light bulb showed me that the house sat on a cement foundation about two or three feet into the ground. The basement though had been dug on down into the cool dry earth so that there was enough standing room. There were no windows and without the light bulb it would be absolutely dark. It smelled of earth and was so very, very cool.

Everything down there was stacked in neat rows on shelves in a showroom like condition. I felt privileged to have this chance to see all this canned food Mrs. Bull had preserved. It was her pride and joy, her entire year's hard work. There were jars of Saskatoon berries that were picked down by the river, strawberries and rhubarb from their very own garden. Huge half peaches and large whole crab apples from BC and all kinds of home made jam and jellies. As a rule they always raised a pig every year and killed it in the fall. Mrs. Bull made lots of canned pork meatballs, and also canned chicken. I would give anything to taste all of this once more. The potatoes were put in a wood plank bin. The carrots and parsnips were cut just so and stored in boxes of black earth so they would stay solid far into the winter. Later after a frost, the turnips would be put in a bin next to the potatoes. The onions were pulled with the tops on and spread on the floor of the old shed to dry. Later when dried they were braided by their tops one by one into binder twine until they hung down two feet or more long, the dried tops holding them firm. Later they too would be hung in the cellar. They learned a lot about survival in their pioneer days and then passed this on to their children.

I spent a number of days on the Oliver tractor pulling a Graham Plough around and around the field "eating dirt" while working the summer fallow. However with all this good weather Bill and I were anxious to leave on a holiday trip we had planned, first in Alberta then to the coast before heading home.

Mr. Bull said an early " Good Bye " and then went for a walk in the garden. I found out in time be hated goodbyes, thus he usually came to you well before your departure and then disappeared. As an Englishman he was not allowed to get all misty in front of friends or family. One had to be proper at all times.

Bill was packed and waiting for me, but before I left I got out my camera and took a picture of the Sutherland family- Don, Oliver and the three boys. It is not what some might call a beautiful picture, it has the bare packed dirt yard as a back ground and everyone was dressed for the day's work, but I cherish that picture because it is so honest. It is the way I found them - hard working, hard playing and their hospitality was only outdone by their honesty. Even now in my mind's eye I see them as a real model of a western ranch family at that time. Weathered by hard times, and nourished by their proud Scottish ancestry they survived many tough years and now stood proudly side-by-side as a family.

The day before we left there had been a prison break from a prison near Edmonton and everyone was concerned because we would be on the road travelling to Toefield, a small town south east of Edmonton. It seemed several members of the Boyd gang had escaped. They were bank robbers that had made quite a name for themselves. So we told everyone we would not pick up any hitchhikers and promised to be careful.

First we were to drive to Toefield to call on some friends of my mom's who came east and visited with us a number of times. They had asked me to come and see them after I finished the harvest at Bulls. My mom had gone to school with these people years ago in Ontario. It seems two Frances brothers had married two Skinner girls and then gone west to grain farms in the Toefield area. We found their farms without any trouble and spent a couple of enjoyable days with them. One thing of interest was our visit to a surface coalmine in the area. I also remember a conversation with one of the Frances boys about a lake of tar sand found in the wooded areas north of them. At that time no one knew much about the sand tars, or if they had any value, but we are hearing a lot about it today.

From Toefield we wandered west to the Edmonton / Calgary highway, then drove south. I well remember driving through Red Deer when it was just a small town stretched out along the gravel highway and railway track. Its grain elevators were its skyline. It was many years away from the beautiful and great city it is today. We drove on down to Calgary and then south to High River. In those years everyone who travelled afar came home with silk cushion tops for their mom it seemed, so I bought a cushion top in Red Deer and Calgary and one in High River. Many years later I got them all back when mom passed away and I still have them today. I understand they are now a collector's item.

It was late evening when we found ourselves on the road west of High River on the way out to Wib Duncan's ranch. We were driving into a setting sun beyond the mountains It was hard to see the road clearly, as it was just a dirt trail across open fields and in places not at all clear. I remember we came to a place where the road turned sharply to the right and a faint un-travelled looking trail went straight ahead. I was sure the path or trail straight ahead was the right way to go. I made a hurried decision and drove straight ahead with the dying sun in my eyes. Suddenly the car fell through the roadbed and stopped dead in its tracks leaving me spinning my tires. .

Bill looked at me in great despair and exclaimed with open hands,

"What do we do now!" almost as if at a time like this he expected a civil answer.

I was rather short with him right then, and I have always been sorry for that, I said,

"Just let me think!"

Darkness was coming on fast as it does when the sun goes down in the mountain country. We didn't have long to sit and think for out of the darkness, far away across the field we saw two headlights heading in our direction. In a few minutes a large tractor came roaring up and made a wide circle and backed up to us. A man with a broad smile on his face got off the tractor carrying a logging chain in his hands. He said,

" I thought you might need some help, I was working away over yonder when I saw you fall in. Where are you heading?" to which I said,

"Wib Duncans."

I don't think we were in there much more then five to seven minutes before this man was unhitching his logging chain and saying good bye to us. I said,

"Thank you, and how much do I owe you?" to which he replied.

"You owe me nothing, a friend of Wib Duncan is a friend of mine" and he jumped on his tractor and left. That was not the last time I was to hear, a friend of Wib Duncan is a friend of mine. What a wonderful way to be thought of and to be remembered.

As to the roadbed, it seems the area had always been part of an on and off slough. In the past year there had been more then the usual amount of snow and rainfall and it filled the area again with water. All summer people had just driven around it. Now while it had dried up on the surface, it was still very wet underneath.

Gateway to a Ranch in Southern Alberta

Wib, Nell and Charles, gave us a warm welcome, and we spent a couple of days looking at cattle, drinking coffee and chatting. Wib was familiar with the names of many of the older homesteaders in the Oyen country. He knew of the Sutherland family so he and Bill got along just fine. We found lots to chat about.

We had decided to take the backcountry road from High River through the Turner valley and on north to the Banff Highway. We arrived in Banff that day with lots of time to tour the park and walk the main street. The town of Banff is unreal as it is seems too picture perfect. One would think they built the town first and then placed the mountains around it. Banff Park was the first national park in Canada, set aside in 1885 right after the last spike was driven into the Continental Railway line. When you look at the Banff Springs Hotel it is hard to believe they finished building it in 1888, three years after the Park was made. Even in 1952 it was just amazing to see it sitting there in isolation amid the mountains. It reminds you that there were men and women with great vision, who looked afar into the future when Canada was very young. In 1952 the shops in Banff, where nearly all owned by the local people, who had opened their stores and watched them grow. Banff then was truly unique. Banff was then totally a different Canadian scene.

Late in the evening we checked out the motels and found them a bit too expensive for our taste. As we wanted to drive all the way to the coast we thought we might save some money if we slept in the car. We found an out of the way place well back off the road where we thought it would be safe to stay. Bill got in the back and I tried to sleep in the front. Late at night nature called me so I quietly opened the door and stepped out into the darkness, I know I hurried as I imagined all sorts of large and furry things might be close at hand. When I got back in the car I saw a movement out in front so I hastily turned on the headlights, and there right where I had been standing a few seconds ago was a massive bull elk with "totally" the biggest rack of horns I had ever seen.

We were settled down again when suddenly there was a rapping sound on our window. It was a park warden in uniform who wanted us out of there. However we pleaded as only boys know how, and he was forgiving, as he understood when we told him we found the motels too costly for us. He said he would ignore us and let us stay as long as no one reported us. Early the next morning we left for Lake Louise. The tall mountains along the way filled us with awe; never had we seen anything so wondrous before. It is a place that lifts the spirit and enriches the soul; as the mountains make you realize just how small man really is. That all the things man has done is nothing, when compared to the wonders and greatness of the mountains.

It was getting late in the fall and we found Lake Louise quiet and very cool, its great hotel "The Fairmont Chateau Lake Louise" looking empty and quite out of place so far from people. The lake itself was wind swept from its glacier source to the beach beneath our feet. Its beauty is in its cold aloofness cradled on all sides by majestic mountains.

Travelling westward through a high mountain pass just north of Lake Louise, we were now on our trip to the Pacific Coast in earnest - first to Golden then on to Revelstoke. In here somewhere we came across what I would call a semi-arid desert. There was no grass on the hardpan earth, but great clumps of silver green sagebrush that grew to great height, twisted and weathered and looking as tough as an old rail fence. The one thing I remember was that we came across two beautiful mules walking one behind the other along the north side of the road travelling west. We stopped and they stood still letting us pet them. They were well mannered and it was almost as if they felt the need of human contact. When we left I looked in the rear view mirror and they were again plodding on westward one behind the other. I hope they got home in time for supper, as there was nothing edible there for them.

We were now at the northern end of the Okanagan valley country. From here it's a beautiful drive south through Vernon, Kelowna, Penticton, and to Osoyoos. As we traveled southward we saw a great change in the countryside, as there were more and more garden products growing and orchards of apples and pears and plums. While today there are a lot of grapes growing throughout this area I don't remember seeing grapes there in 1952. Perhaps most of all I remember our arrival at Osoyoos the best. We arrived high above the town and the lake; below us were small square checkerboard patches in different shades of green. Each square was actually an apple orchard; an ever-winding road wind back and forth taking us down; down and soon the small patches took shape as rows and rows of fruit trees. Their fruit burdened branches propped up with stakes kept the laden branches from breaking down. This is one of the greatest fruit growing areas in BC and it is truly magnificent to view as you pass through.

Driving on to Princeton and Chilliwack we found ourselves following the Fraser River in the evening with a setting sun before us. The whole country had that peaceful, quiet yellow mellow look of fall. There were many dark skin people walking along the streets and roadway wearing strange clothing and turbans. I had the feeling that I had somehow been transplanted to another country as the scene was played out all about me. Somehow Bill and I just didn't fit in; it was as if we were the foreigners in a different land. There were a large number of people from India living here along the Fraser River.

We stayed over night just east of Vancouver and early the next morning I drove down Davie Street past my Aunt Becky's beautiful old white clapboard house. By now my uncle and dear aunt had both passed away. That was the last time I ever saw the great old house as along with many other houses it was torn down to make way for the many expensive high rises that rose along English Bay. We drove on into Stanley Park and to a special parking lot at the south end of the Lions Gate Bridge. Bill and I sat and watched great boats on the Burnard Inlet coming and going under the Lions Gate Bridge. We were in a happy mood as we had achieved our goal we had made it to the coast and now we were homeward bound.

We had decided to go home via the States, as it would be a faster route. I believe we crossed into Washington State at Blaine and then east on number 20 highway. At one point we could see Mt.Baker to the southwest of us. We drove east to Spokane and across Idaho to Butte Montana. As all this happened over fifty years ago and I can't remember where our days ended but I do remember the route. We turned southward into Yellowstone Park, Wyoming and yes we did see "Old Faithful" erupt. We spent most of a day driving about the park. It is beautiful and it is big. We filled up our gas tank and decided to drive out of the park onto a road going homeward.

Now things really got complicated. I had done well getting about ever since I left home, but somehow I got lost and we wandered about trying to get back onto a main road. It was dark and we could not get our bearings. We drove aimlessly about hoping to end up somewhere at a place with a name. But there were endless winding mountain road all the time driving southward with no roads going east. Finally a car with a spot light surprised us and pulled us over. It was a park warden and he was looking for guns. I guess he first thought we might be poaching in the park; he searched the car then told us we were really lost. He was good enough to draw us a map that would take us south to Rock Springs Wyoming east of Salt Lake City. We found a place to stay for a few hours' sleep, but were back on the road early the next morning on Highway 80 that crosses the country like an arrow all the way south of Chicago and on to Toledo, then followed a great expressway to Detroit.

The highway was straight and my foot was heavy and we were after all homeward bound. I opened the car up and we flew across the states. One could see ten or twenty miles in every direction so there was little chance of us getting a ticket. We only stopped for gas, food and the bathroom. But we drove from Rock Spring Wyoming to Detroit that day. Late that evening I pulled into my dad's sister's place on Alcoy St., Detroit Michigan. My uncle had a hard time believing we had driven from Rock Springs that day. We stayed over one more day resting and visiting with my aunt and uncle. The next night when my Uncle Guy came home from work he told me that the guys at work told him there was no way I could have driven from Rock Springs to Detroit in one day. I rest my case and you can ask Bill. From there Bill and I drove home.

Over the last fifty some years Bill and I have had many chats about this trip, the things we saw and the people we came to know. We have kept in touch with each other and also with the Bulls and Sutherlands. Bill married a very good friend of mine Anna May Thompson of Motherwell, who along with her brother Vernon and sister Helen use to walk to school with my sisters and me. Bill and Anna have visited and kept in touch with the Sutherland family over all these years. Harry and Irene Bull and Don and Olive Sutherland have all passed by away. However they are not forgotten.

" There is common ground that kindred walk, that forever binds the soul "

When one leaves the west in the late fall you have the feeling that winter is close at hand or knocking at the door. Upon arriving home in Ontario it seems you step back into fall again and you're given a gift of perhaps a month or more of good weather before snow flies. As always upon returning from the west it takes a few days or even weeks to get oriented again. Very soon the cattle will be in the barn for the winter and I will be back milking cows and cleaning stables. During the winter months the work is at a quieter but steady pace and very much the same from day to day. After the milking is done and breakfast over dad heads off to the village store and I head straight out to clean the stables. This is the way it will be every day. By now I know about how far on I should be with the chores by the time dad gets home so as to keep him happy.

Both dad and I were having great luck with our sows raising large litters of healthy little pigs. Dad usually kept his little pigs and raised them to fat hogs at 200 pounds or more I would sell mine as wieners or chunks to neighbours or friend or yes, to John G. Scott. I always raised great looking pigs and never had a problem selling them for top price. By now I had three or four sows and I would manage to average twelve little pigs a litter. To do that I practically had to live with them the first few days. To this day I love old sows and little pigs ...... especially the little pigs.

In the fall of 1952 I had three litters of little pigs ready to sell. At six weeks old we called them weaners. If you wean then from their mother and feed them a special pig feed for a few weeks they would get bigger and were then called chunks. That winter I cleared over four hundred dollars from my little pigs and in 1952 that was a nice bit of money. Of course this money was burning a hole in my pocket. By now my dad had sold his old 38Ford and was driving a black 46 Chev. I had been offered a good price for my 47 Chev and I was itching to sell and move up. I knew my mom would have a fit if she knew I was even thinking of doing this. Somehow I was sure it would be OK with dad.

The Henry J Kaiser Fraser

A number of young people I knew often stopped in for coffee at Sweetzir's Garage and coffee shop at Rannock at the south end of the Mitchell Road. Sweetzir's had taken on the agency for the Kaiser Fraser cars. Kaiser Fraser had made the original Jeep for the military during the Second World War and made a big name for them. They also made the "Willy" a sort of no nonsense ugly small car that looked like a box. After the war Kaiser opened a plant at Willow Run Michigan where they made the Kaiser Fraser, the Henry J and the Willy. The Kaiser itself was a head turning car, with fleeting lines. It was truly a luxury car and perhaps a bit ahead of its time. The real problem with it though was its huge price. On the other hand the Henry J Kaiser was a smaller version with a four-cylinder motor, one of the first truly mid size cars and it too was perhaps a bit ahead of its time.

One night when I dropped in for coffee there was a beautiful maroon Henry J Kaiser sitting in the show room. I was sold on it. The priced was $1,900.00, there was no special tax on cars at that time and GST and PST had not been invented yet.

I had been offered eleven hundred dollars for my 47 Chev, which was the same price I had paid for it. With the four hundred dollars from my pigs I would only owe a bank note of $400.00 on the new car.

When I told my dad about it he took it very well, and at the breakfast table he spoke to my mom about it, and naturally she got very angry with me and said,

" You don't need it, you just have a big head."

Dad said, " Let him have his new car, if he doesn't spend the money there it will dribble away on something else." Later, he told me that once I had a new car I should trade up every few years and avoid the car problems he always had This was the first of many new cars I have owned. Except for my first two cars I have had ten brand new ones, and I loved every one of them.

The Henry J was a great little car in many ways and I was very proud of it. Because of its mid size and new style it drew a lot of attention and favourable comments. All cars then were big monsters and every year it seemed they kept getting bigger. This car was a step in another direction from what the big three were building. However when winter came I found out I had a problem. The Willy

Jeep Overland four-cylinder motor was just too heavy on the front end. If you touched the brakes on a slippery surface the car would spin around, because of the weight up front. It seemed the front end stopped while the rear end spun around.

In the fifties every one put snow tires on their car in the winter. Most snow tires would be what we called re-caps. Places that sold new tires would save your old tires if the walls on them were good and send them in to a tire re-cap plant. In the winter these tires with huge grabbing treads did a good job of getting you wherever you wanted to go. All cars including my Henry J were rear wheel drive back in those days.

Many evenings when I left home to do up the town, I would have to drive out our snow filled lane onto the slippery snow packed road. To get to the road I would have to keep up a fair speed or I would be stuck before I got there. Then just when I thought I had made it I would sometimes feel the need to touch the brake so I could turn when I reached the road. With the Henry J the minute I touched the brake the rear end came around and I would slide across the road into the ditch backward with the front end facing the road.

Every time I went out on winter nights my dad would look at me in a painful way and say,

"Please don't go into the ditch tonight," and of course I said I would be careful, but chances are I would go into a spin as I hit the road and end up in the ditch. Standing beside my car down in the ditch I could see my dad watching from the little kitchen window, and I knew he would soon go out to start the tractor to pull me out. Now few people winterized their tractors at that time, so the first thing he had to do was to go to the hand pump on the well and get a couple of pails of water and carry them out to the tractor. You dare not put the water in until you found out if the tractor would start or not. Those old tractors had to be hand cranked and believe me they did not start easily for in the wintertime everything was frozen stiff. When or *if*, it started you quickly put the plug in the radiator drain hole at the bottom of the radiator and poured the water in.

Now I can't tell you how much I loved my dad for always being there when this kind of thing happened to me but I always hated this moment. Dad would come roaring out the lane on the tractor and make a U turn and back the tractor up to my car. I would stand there all dressed up and not wanting to get dirty and dad would have to crawl in under the front end of my car and hook the logging chain onto the car frame. He then got back on the tractor and pulled me out. Then back under my car to unhook the chain. Jumping back onto the tractor he roar back up the lane. He never said a word to me; I would have gladly taken a cussing. Just maybe I would have felt better as certainly it was not a happy outing for poor dad.

The next day it was never mentioned. Not until the next night when I headed out the door to do up the town, he would again look at me, oh so painfully, and say,

"Jack, pleeease don't go into the ditch tonight."

My winter was taken up with the usual farming chores and community activities. Then spring came with maple syrup time in the Morrison bush. Once spring came it seemed the work was endless until fall. Always just as you were about to finish one job another was already waiting on you. On top of all this, the cows were always reluctantly waiting to be milked morning and night. Pigpens were most often in need of cleaning and were often left for rainy days or Sunday mornings. I was sure if I ever farmed it would have to be a straight cattle ranch or a strictly cash crop farm in Alberta, thus ending all these never ending little jobs.

Jr. Farmers and Young Peoples and an active part in the Mitchell United Church, filled in much of my time off the farm. I also enjoyed doing some writing for the Mitchell Advocate on Jr. Farmer and Community news. The editor Mrs. Mounteer was always encouraging me to write.

When fall came again my dad and Ed Smith teamed up to thresh grain with my dad's threshing machine. Somewhere my dad had picked up a very old railway red Sawyer Massey wooden threshing machine. Other people prefer to call them a grain separator. We spent days inside it during the winter and spring making repairs. There were many tight places where dad sent me in to fix, as he just did not fit in there. I am not a mechanic and I hated being inside the machine working in tight quarters. I happen to like elbowroom. Actually I thought the machine was a kind of joke as it was so very old, huge and cumbersome and very hard to move. I was sure it might fall apart en-route to the Smiths when we took it down the road. Once there, getting it up the gang way and into the bank barn was a dangerous mission in itself. Westerners always find it hard to believe that in Ontario they actually thresh the sheaves on the barn floor right inside these huge hemlock board bank barns. We do this because we need as much of the straw as possible inside the barn for bedding and feed. Dad used a long extension tongue to push the machine up the gangway and into the barn on the front of his big Model L Case Tractor. Sometimes the tongue would jackknife so we always had to be ready to block the wheels on the threshing machine. It was a dangerous job. But once set up and made ready to go, there was a great feeling of success of a battle won.

In 1953 Jerry Baltesson Came East To Visit

Jerry Baltesson, the young schoolteacher and nephew of the Aubrys in Cypress River, had written me a letter to ask if it would be OK if he came to visit us the end of July into August of 1953. Of course dad and mom said yes. Jerry arrived on the bus in St Marys. He had just taken a one-way ticket to Ontario as he was hoping he could ride back with me if I drove out. He knew I had received word from Mr. Bull that they had yet another great crop in Alberta and that they needed help with the harvest. Ed and Joy's second son Ron wanted to go west with me. He was young but a good worker and I knew there was a good place for him to work at Joe Quain's who was Mrs. Bull's nephew.

Jerry made himself at home, and even pitched a few sheaves onto the wagon in the field when we were threshing, both at my folk's place and at the Smiths. My dad and mom liked him very much. A number of years later Jerry and his wife and two children were on holidays here in Ontario and mom and dad baby-sat their two children while they attended a play at the Stratford Shakespearian Festival.

Harvest time was a busy time for us to have company, but Jerry fitted in well and we all enjoyed him. On weekends I would take him out to see whatever I thought he might like to see. We spent a day at Niagara Falls, and visited at Queenston Heights, we even climbed Brock's monument. As a teacher he was very much familiar with history of this part of the country so to visit these places was a plus for him. Another weekend I took him up to Penetanguishene on Georgian Bay to visit the Martyr Shrine and then to Wasaga Beach to swim. Of course we also visited Ipperwash Beach and Grand Bend and he loved all of them. I took him down to Port Stanley to see Lake Erie, and we visited a tobacco farm.

One night I asked him what he would like for lunch before going off to bed. He asked if he could have a Denver Sandwich. I was not really into cooking in my younger years and my limit at that time was coffee and toast if you were not too fussy. So I had to tell Jerry I never even heard of a Denver Sandwich. He offered to make them for us. He asked for the frying pan, eggs and milk and onions He chopped some onions and beat the eggs then added milk and onions and beat it all again. It was of course what we call a Western Sandwich here in Ontario. I got educated that night as do you know that all three Prairie Provinces still call a Western Sandwich a Denver? Jerry was having a good time and it was about two weeks before he got around to writing a letter home to let his folks know he had arrived safely and all was well.

Ron Smith, Jerry Baltesson and I Drive West

Finally the day arrived when Ron and I were to leave for Alberta. Jerry would return home to Cypress River Manitoba with us. Ed and Joy, Ralph and Gordon Smith all came to our place to see us off. I remember the morning as if it was just a fall ago. It was such a wonderful sunny fall morning and ideal to start out on a trip. We followed the same route that Bill and I had taken and stopped to see Paul Bunyan.

Paul Bunyon and His Blue Ox / My 1960 Starliner Ford

I will always remember what happened when we arrived in Cypress River, Jerry's mom came flying out of the house taking Jerry in her arms and exclaimed,

"Oh, Jerry I just got your letter this week and I have been worried sick about you being down there in Ontario with all those English Protestants." Then I could see she realized she had said this out loud and was quite embarrassed. I remember telling her.

"It's OK, don't let it bother you as I understand. It was just a short time ago that I was out here all alone with all you French Catholics, and at first I was more than a wee bit concerned. I think this has done Jerry and me a lot of good, we are now friends and not going to dwell on English, French, Protestant, Catholic kind of stuff, ever again. We look forward to being friends for a long time, maybe forever."

We stayed over at Jerry's place for two days. We gave the Henry J a good cleaning as we had found lots of juicy bugs and dirty roads on the way out. Leaving Cypress early one morning we drove to Regina and on to Pasqua just east of Moose Jaw to Jim and Eva Howe's. By now we were seeing field after field of grain standing in water. It had been raining for days before we got there and it was still raining and even more was predicted. Jim and Eva advised us to not to continue on, as many roads were partly under water and all heavy trucks had been ordered off the highway. This did nothing to discourage Jack with his Willy Jeep motor in his Henry J. The luggage in the trunk was a plus as it added the extra weight for traction, and I had lots of power, but still I didn't know what lay ahead.

We took the road north to the Qu'Appelle Valley, then north again through Davidson to Kenaston, then west to Outlook, Rosetown and Kindersley. We crossed the Alberta border at Alsask and on to Oyen our destination.

All these roads at that time were made of upgraded earth from the ditch, capped with a small amount of gravel. They were getting soft and in many places holes and ruts and worse still, many places were under water. Every now and then we came upon a low stretch of road covered with water. A mile or so down the road we could see the other end of the road coming up again. We had no idea how deep the water might be. For miles on end I travelled in second gear. Truly my Henry J acted just like a jeep with its powerful four-cylinder engine, which behaved wonderfully in mud and water. Time after time I plunged into the water driving only by my mind's eye in "dead centre" of the road. Then once more we drove out of the water onto the roadbed ahead. We would pull into a gas station for gas and a crowd of people would venture over to look at this mud covered little car "that could." As there was literally no traffic on the road they marvelled that we could travel. All the hotels and motels were full with truckers and salesmen and travellers. No Vacancy signs were out all day and night. So we kept the gas tank well up and travelled on through the night.

We arrived in Oyen at dawn, just as the sun was coming up. To my horror I found the streets in town flooded with water. Not a foot of black top had been laid in Oyen at that time. The streets at their best were dirt in dry weather and mud when it was wet. I remembered then, I had been told they were installing gas lines on every street in Oyen that summer. Apparently they had dug up most of the town and after the digging was done along came the rain. Everything was like a bowl of soup. A deep trench was dug across the front of my Uncle Franks place so I could not drive in. I was afraid to stop the car in case I would be stuck. I wanted to park the car on solid ground and out of the water. At the end of a street near my Uncle Frank and Aunt Rosena's, I could see a great high mound or hill of sand, maybe twenty feet high. This was to be used to fill in over the gas lines. I aimed for the hill and drove up near the top. At last I was high and dry.

What a welcome to town. Ron and I donned our boots from the trunk and walked back to my uncle and aunt's place. We had been on the road now for almost 24 hours and in second gear most of the time. My Aunt Rosena gave us breakfast and then sent us off to bed. I don't remember how long we slept, but I think till almost noon. Uncle Frank came to tell us that we were the talk of the town. There was a great crowd down at the sand hill looking at this strange little car " that could. " It was of course plastered with mud. Everyone in town knew of it, but no one in town knew anything about it, whose it was or when it came or why it was left sitting there. " Me Thinks," I should have sold this story to Kaiser Fraser at that time.

The rain stopped that day and Ron and I were able to drive out to our place of work. Ron went to Joe Quains and I to Harry Bulls. Things dried up and the rest of the fall was good harvest weather. We worked hard all week and then went into town on Saturday night. First we would take in the movie; then after the movie was over they would push the chairs aside and hold a dance. They did this every Saturday night, and to this day the folks talk about the great and wonderful times they had at these dances. It was the ideal way to meet and get to know many people in the community. I found people were easy to get to know and eager to be a friend. By now I had made quite a number of friends from the previous years.

At that time the road east of the Quain farm ended at a barbed wire gate a half-mile beyond, at foot of a very high hill which overlooked the country side. The area around this hill and far beyond was hilly and rough and covered with natural prairie grass. A paradise for the heard of white face Herfords that claimed it as home. This high hill was called Buffalo Bird Hill. Atop the hill is an Indian grave beside a mammoth rock. Almost everyone I took out west climbed up there at least once. From here you could view the whole valley to the northwest Most of the taller hills throughout this area have Indian graves on them. It is sad that many of them have been disturbed.

The View From Blue Bird Hill

When the harvest was over and it was time to leave for home I thought it only fair that Ron should see the mountains. So we left for Calgary and up to Banff. We did the usual sight-seeing and then in late afternoon for some reason we decided to climb a small mountain. Well we though it was small until we were well up on it. You might ask why would we do a thing like that? I guess the only answer to a question like that is the usual one "Because it was there." Ron was young and nimble and got quite a ways ahead of me. When it started to get dark Ron thought it best to turn back, which was a smart idea, but somehow we passed each other. Ron went down and I continued up. I knew, as it was getting dark I should be going down, but I didn't want to leave Ron up there alone. I called for him but of course I would not hear him even if he did answer. Even now I remember how amazing Banff looked at night in the dark from above with its town lights coming on. It was just so dazzling. The air was cool and getting cold, but all about was calm and tranquil in my Silent World.

Jack in the Mountains 1953

Meanwhile Ron had returned to the car and blew the car horn until the battery was low hoping that I might hear it and realize he had gone back down. Of course from up on a mountainside I was too deaf to hear it. Somehow Ron contacted a Park Ranger and he sent out for a searching party. Meanwhile Ron and the ranger started back up the mountain, hoping to find me before I had an accident and fell and damaged my hair. While it was beautiful up there it was getting cold fast, and I was really worried about where Ron was.

I saw two flashlights coming up behind me so I found a place where I would be out of sight. I didn't really want to meet any strangers away up here on a mountain so late at night as I was sure it would not be the Avon Lady. When they were almost upon me I recognized Ron. So I said,

"Are you guys looking for someone?"

Ron said he almost jumped off the mountain that night as the Park Ranger had just been warning him about bears, and said,

"If you hear or see anything and think its a bear, go down the mountain as fast as he could as a bear rolls when he goes down too fast." When we got down, the searchers were ready to start up. We caught hell with a good talking to about just setting off to climb a mountain. We were told you must register before you start out to climb in the park, and never start out late in the day. One more lesson learned. I have learned a lot, the hard way. They say you learn from your mistakes so I knew that I was designated to become a very smart man. After a short trip to Lake Louise we turned around and headed homeward.

We drove south down to High River and stayed over a day at Wib Duncans. Driving south again we crossed the US border at Coutts into Montana. The number two highway goes all the way across the northern states, Montana, North

Dakota, Minnesota, Wisconsin to Northern Michigan and the Strait Of Mackinaw. Home again. Life went on for another year, but I was feeling very unsettled.

The following year Ron went back out west with me again, but only as far as a cousin's farm somewhere north of Outlook or Rosetown Saskatchewan. I left him there and drove on alone. I remember once back on the road I missed him. Ron had been good company.

That fall I spent a lot of my Sundays with Don and Olive Sutherland and family. I had met Don's brother Lorne and Isabel who lived just across the road and a younger brother Cameron who lived with his dad and mom on the old home place north of Don. Grandpa and Grandma Sutherland were more or less retired on the old homestead farm, and Cameron was working it. I found Grandpa Sutherland very distant, but he was very deaf, so maybe he sought sanctuary in the quietness and just felt safe getting away from it all.

Sutherland's Horses

On the other hand I found Grandma Sutherland a great personality and a joy to know. She talked about the early homesteading days in Alberta and of the Old Ontario she knew. She never forgot her Ontario roots and liked to chat with someone from back home. I remember more than once she invited young Don or Colin and me for a Sunday dinner. Her table was set for royalty with her best silver and linen and china. I felt it was an honour to dine at her table. There was one other member of the Sutherland family I would like to mention and that is her daughter Maxine who was a schoolteacher. In many ways Maxine was like her mother that is she liked nice things and had her very own flair in ways to dress. She is still living right now as I write this and is in her nineties. She lives now of all places, on the east coast instead of the prairies. I just cannot visualize her so far away from her western roots.

A few times I was to the local store in a local village of Lanfine. The store served as a post office as well as a place to buy basic groceries. There was a very nice young village girl behind the counter and her name was Lenora Robart. Everyone was made aware that she was Cameron Sutherland's girl friend. In those days it seemed that people thought it was great that a daughter of one old pioneer family and the son of another old pioneer family should marry. They sort of assumed things should proceed along this line and discouraged everyone else standing in line. Whether they were indifferent to each other was not to be questioned, not even by them. Their neighbours, their friends and family had already cut the deal.

Sutherland's Cattle on the Range

Cameron and Lenora were going to get married that fall of 1954 and Cameron was building a new house down the road north of his dad and mom's farm. Young Don (Deke) and I spent a few Sundays working on the house with him. I remember going over one morning and finding a skunk had fallen into the basement. Cameron was wondering what to do.

We decided not to do anything; just leave some planks down from the basement windows onto the floor hoping it would climb out by itself over night. The next morning it had left. Never mess with a skunk if it can be avoided.

Harvest was over and the fall work was winding up and soon I would be heading home. We decided to drive down to the Bad Lands in my Henry J. for one last special outing together.

Pinto Horses In The Bad Lands

There was Cameron, Lenora and young Don and Colin and myself. I still have a snapshot of us all gathered around a campfire eating our supper. Cameron is sitting on a small cream can in which we took down water, and the rest of us are kneeling about the fire. There are a couple of frying pans with bacon and eggs along with a coffee pot on the ground. Memories are made of special times with special friends, and good memories should last a lifetime.

I arrived home without much fanfare. Ron was already home and settled back to his usual farm work and social life. It always took a few weeks for me to adjust. It was as if my body was here but my head was still out west. Soon, hopefully they would get together again.

Amos Graver and Maple Island

Late that fall Amos Graver, a friend of my dad's and an uncle to my brother-in-law Arnold Graver asked if I would go north with him as company to deliver the hunting equipment to Maple Island for the Mitchell Hunting Club. Amos worked for Coveney Chicken Hatchery in Mitchell. Coveney donated the truck, and Amos his time after hours to do this delivery. It was plain good business on their part.

I always knew Arnold loved his Uncle Amos and I could see why. He was a friendly easygoing talkative guy, who had a way of making everyone feel at ease. This was the first time I was ever to Maple Island, but through a twist of fate I would return some day.

It would be in late November and very cool when we left Mitchell. At that time of the year the days are very short. I'm not sure the time of day it was when we got away. I just remember it was still daylight for a couple of hours or so. I could carry on a conversation with Amos as long as I could see to lip-read him. Once it got too dark I could no longer, as I always say, "see to hear." This must have been very hard on Amos as everyone knew he loved to Chat.

I was almost asleep when Amos reached over and shook me awake saying,

"Wake up Jack we are almost there."

In the distance I could see a bright white light bulb showing up a long white storefront. The ground stretching ahead of us was covered with a sift of white snow. Standing on the east side of the store was a team of horses and a wagon waiting for us. There were a few welcoming handshakes and then we unloaded the hunting equipment from the truck onto the wagon. It was dark and we travelled on a very rough trail. I remember it really shook me up and by the time I arrived at the clubhouse I was wide, wide, awake. I can never quite remember just where we ended up or how we got there, but it seemed to me we travelled east or northeast. I do remember though that when we arrived at the Hunting Club I recognized the long white building as one from an army base. After the war many of these military buildings were sold for all kinds of community purposes.

They fed us and the men started to talk. I think they talked well into the night and no doubt Arnold's Uncle Amos would be very happy. As for me I could hardly stay awake and they pointed out a bunk and I was asleep even as my head hit the pillow. It was the smell of coffee and bacon that awoke me in the morning. I had a great night's sleep. After breakfast we were ready for our return trip to Mitchell. I remember Amos telling me he was going to take a longer route home, as he wanted to show me something he thought I might like to see. That was Amos, and I was happy about this.

He drove to Burks Falls where he took some great pictures of me and the falls, then along the Magnetawan River. I have never forgotten that trip, but it was actually years later that I found out exactly where I had been. Amos passed away a number of years ago.

Years later Arnold and my sister Pearl bought a cottage up north on the Magnetawan River, and although they had told me it was at Maple Island. I didn't connect it up to the place Amos had taken me to visit or the Mitchell Hunt Club. But that's another story. I will take you there later.

The Henry J had performed so well on the trip west and back and I had all but forgotten about how it behaved on slippery winter roads. Then winter came again and I was faced with the same problem. I just could not keep that car out of the ditch. A friend of my dad's, Percy Laurence of Stratford sold cars for the Ford Dealer in Stratford and one day he dropped by with this almost brand new robin egg blue 1954 Ford Galaxie. It had white rear fenders and a matching white roof, it was fabulous. It seems a lady teacher had ordered it and a down payment made, but now she decided they should buy a house instead and wanted out of the deal. Percy offered me a very good deal on the Henry J and my dad thought I should take it, as he did not want to spend another winter pulling me out of the ditch. I have a soft spot in my heart for that Henry J because it never left me stranded in all that mud and water, but it just could not handle slippery roads because of that big heavy motor. The 1954 Galaxie Ford cost me $2,300.00.

July the 2nd 1955 my sister Jean married Bill Butler of Munro. (It was the best deal he ever got.)

Western Trip 1955
Earl Paulen, Glen Sykes, Bruce Eisler, Earl Foster

I made several other trips west at harvest time and I want to mention them briefly as these trips and the people involved are a part of my life story. In the fall of 1955, I got letters upon letters from the west telling me there was a great crop and they needed help so could I find a farm boy or a young man for them. While not everyone out west likes the east for some reason they all liked the Ontario farm boys. They found them to be of good character, honest and hard workers. The fall of 1955 several of my best friends wanted to go west with me. They were, Earl Paulen, Glen Sykes, Bruce Eisler and Earl Foster.

When I took a group of guys on a trip like this I knew there would have to be some road rules. So rule number one was. When we stop for gas everyone goes to the bathroom whether you need to or not, as we can not make time driving if we have to stop every half hour to let some one go to the bathroom. Rule number two. Everyone had a say in where or when we should stop to eat or where and when we should stop for the night, but in case of a dispute....the driver was always right. Rule number three was everyone had to help to keep the car clean. Litter went in a bag and your feet were always kept on the floor. I reminded them they were travelling in a good car and I wanted them to respect that. This was not a problem with these guys.

The boys wanted to see Winnipeg, so I drove into the city so we could cruise the Portage and Main area. Then we visited the Parliament Buildings and walked its well-tended lawns. I also took advantage of the opportunity to have a short visit with my Uncle Fred, perhaps a couple of hours. The time was all too short, but Uncle Fred understood the situation. We couldn't expect the boys to wait around for long while we visited. I will always remember that when we left he insisted on filling the gas tank on my car. That was such, an uncle sort of thing to do and I thought it was kind and generous of him. We travelled on to Regina and there again, we visited the parliament buildings.

Upon arriving in Oyen I drove all of the boys to their places of work We seldom saw each other all week but on Saturday night I would make a round trip picking them all up so they could go to town together. Then I would have to make the round trip again to take everyone home. I didn't mind this anyway as these were all my very best friends. Getting together like this gave us a good chance to compare our bosses, our working conditions and our wages, etc. We didn't have anything to really complain about as these were all fine people we were working for. They appreciated that these boys had come a long ways to help them and so they got the going wages. Perhaps the best was every home was super clean and the food was great, and the boys were treated kindly and with due respect.

Earl Foster, Glen Sykes, Earl Paulen and Bruce Eisler

On Sundays the boys were often invited to one home or another for dinner or supper. It was simply good western hospitality. The Bulls loved to have the boys come to their place, so it seemed we met there most often. Wm. Played a violin and a banjo. He preferred to play the banjo and Earl Paulen would play the piano and Bruce Eisler the violin and Glen Sykes and Earl Foster and I would sing. We knew just about every song that was out, so the music went on for hours. Then when it was time to go home, Earl always played, "Good Night Irene Good Night Irene," as Mrs. Bull's name was Irene. There were tears of appreciation in her eyes for the boys as she said good night. I would have to drive them all home to where they worked. Each would have personal problems to discuss before they left the car and it was often late when I got back to Bulls.

After a few days of rain, which held up the harvest, we were glad to be back in the fields working again. The weatherman was predicting more rain by the first of the week but Sunday was going to be sunny and dry. A few of the neighbours in other years had started to work on Sundays. However the Bulls and the Snells, the Quains, Harry Dell, the Whites the Robinsons the Parenteaus or Sutherlands all honoured and respected their Sunday. For the first time in 1955 it seemed all these people got together and decided they would ask their hired help to work on the Sunday. On Saturday we were all told by our bosses that they were going to work the next day, Sunday and they would need us to help.

Me and Ole Lizzie, 'er... I mean (Elizabeth)

We all went into town together that Saturday night as usual, so we had a chance to talk about the pros and cons of this. At home our parents would never even think of harvesting on a Sundays. While it was true, in Ontario we would do barn work on Sundays we looked upon it as caring work to keep our stock clean and comfortable. So we decided to all stick together and tell our bosses that working on Sundays was not the kind of thing we wanted to do, as it was against our Ontario upbringing. Mr. Bull and Wm. Both took this very well but they still put in a rather small, uncomfortable day combining. I do remember going out to help Mr. Bull several times when I saw the truck come in with a load of grain to unload, as I didn't want him shovelling grain and overdoing it. He was a wonderful man and I cared about him. I don't remember that they ever worked another Sunday that year, but that was a start and from then on everyone worked at combining seven days a week whenever it was dry and ready.

The Old Barn on the Fowler Farm

Good weather prevailed, the harvest was finished, and we were ready to move on.

Earl was a cousin to my friends the Skinners at Toefield, so when we finished the harvest at Oyen we drove to Toefield and called on them. A nephew, David Skinner from Mitchell was visiting and working for them at the harvest. He was naturally very happy to see his cousin Earl and friends from the Mitchell area. When he heard we were going to drive on to Jasper and down to Banff he wanted to go with us. With five guys in the car plus luggage we really were already feeling a bit crowded. I didn't want three in the front seat as I felt it unsafe for the driving. Earl however begged me to take his cousin and I knew it was a chance of a lifetime for him to do this with Earl Paulen and friends, so in the end I could not refuse him.

Driving west we skirted the southern end of Edmonton then took the number 16 highway west. This would be my very first visit to Jasper. The mountains were already capped with snow and looked cold and overpowering. The trees and vegetation were well advanced, and almost over their fall dress and colours. Most places of business were already closed down for the winter.. It seemed a very short season for Jasper in those days. We found a place to stay over and the next day after filling the gas tank found that the highway south to Lake Louise and Banff was already closed for the winter. What were we going to do? We realized we had come a long way to see this and at our age we were not going to give up so easily. We could see on our map that there were very few places where we might be able to stop for gas or food. We reasoned that with luck surely we would find at least one gas station happy to sell us some gas. If not we were sure we could make it to Lake Louise on our tank of gas. We had no idea of turning around and going home without seeing the Rockies. So we decided to drive around the road barrier and drive to Banff.

For a time we forgot everything, lost in the beauty that surrounded us. We stopped to view the mighty plummeting waters of the Athabasca Falls. Its roaring milky waters funnelling itself through deep cut lime stone gorges on its way to the Athabasca River. We saw the river and its milky white waters rushing north to its destination wild and free. Ice fields large and small clung between the mountains on the west side of the road.

Farther on the azure blue lakes lying at the foot of great mountains along the route to the west astounded us. We were captivated by a world of wonder such as we had never seen before. Its grandeur in size and beauty staggered the human mind and makes us ever mindful just how small and powerless we really are.

Far ahead there appeared to be a wall of mountains white with snow blocking our southern journey. It grew larger and larger as we drove south towards it. When we finally arrived we realized we were looking at the Columbia Ice Fields, huge, cold and foreboding. Tours of it were of course closed for the winter. As yet we had not seen any sign of life along the highway. We were apparently very much alone.

Our gas gauge was definitely getting low. The one thing we had not taken into consideration was that we now had one more passenger and this was mountain driving so we were using far more gas than when we were driving across the prairies. It was getting on in the day when we found a road crew just ending their day's work. They were naturally surprised to see us as the road was supposed to be closed. It was I believe actually unlawful for us to be on this road travelling. They had part of a gallon of gas, and offered it to us. I needed a funnel to get it into the tank, so we spilt much of the gas pouring it in. We drove on and on and it seemed our gas tank just kept on giving us gas, but at any minute we expected the motor to sputter to a stop. Then what would we do high in mountain country at night, hitchhike?

On the west side of the highway we saw a building and a Forest Ranger's truck. We drove in and it was a Park Warden's office. He was not happy to see us, but he must have been young once so I guess he understood that young people don't always make the right decisions. He told us that he was going for a walk and that he had forgotten to lock the gas pumps. If we should happen to fill out gas tank and he didn't know anything about it, he would not get into any trouble. We offered to pay for the gas, but he told us he could not sell the government gas. So he left to go for a walk and after a minute we drove over to the pumps and filled our gas tank up on the Canadian Government. Somehow I don't feel very guilty today about this.

We arrived at Lake Louise, and walked down to the shoreline of the cold sky blue lake. There is something so overwhelming about this place that words cannot begin to describe it. It is as if nature created something so beautiful then hid it here between the mountain ranges out of sight to be kept unspoiled, and now we have intruded. We stood for a long time facing the ice field with the Chateau behind us looking quiet and empty. On each side the tall mountains enclose this historic scene, an intact paradise. I think every Canadian at least once in their lifetime should stand here and witness this beauty and greatness.

It was late when we found a place to stay in Banff that night and everyone was very tired and I think a wee bit cranky from being in such cramped quarters for so many hours. The next morning we toured Banff the town and the surrounding area of the park.

We saw the Banff Springs Hotel overlooking the Bow Valley. In 1955 the hotel looked historic and entirely out of place in this fairytale setting. We stopped to see the Bow Falls on the Bow River not far from the Hotel. A few years later a movie was made there on the Bow River and at the falls with Marilyn Munro. We went up the mountain on a chairlift and had more or less a bird's eye view of Mount Rundle and a fantastic view of the town of Banff from high above. Soon we had to say farewell to the mountains, Banff and the park as we left for the Big City. …. Calgary.

In Calgary we found a huge McCloud Western Clothing Store, which sold everything from jeans, to shirts and cowboy boots. But it was a Stetson Cowboy Hat the boys wanted to buy before leaving for home. A hat cost us more than a week's wages, but that was the way true westerners were. They would spend a fortune on their hat and their boots and five bucks on a pair of Wrangler or Lee jeans.

It came time for Dave Skinner to part with us and go back to Toefield to his uncle and aunts. I was surprised to learn that Earl Paulen had decided not to go home with us but to go back to Toefield with Dave. So we parted in Calgary.

I drove south towards High River with the rest the guys, Bruce Eisler, Glen Sykes and Earl Foster. Now we had actually regained room for our elbows in the car, two in the back and two in the front.

A few years before when I visited Wib Duncan at High River he had taken me to see the Prince of Wales Ranch near Longview and told me all about its history.

It is straight west of High River towards the foothills and is also very close to Wib's own Ranch, just a few miles as the crow flies. So we decided to visit the E P Ranch.

In 1955 the Prince of Wales, or E. P. ranch was intact with hired workers and a few hundred head of magnificent white face Herefords. A beautiful log barn with a hip roof that extended out and over at its gable ends made an impressive setting within a fenced yard and topped by a white pole all the way around. A large low ranch house with two cape cod windows in the roof and vine covered verandas were set on well-tended lawns. An extension to the rear of the main house was a servant quarters we were told. There appeared to be no one around so we ventured onto the veranda and boldly looked into the living room and dining room windows. It appeared that everything was kept clean and ever so ready, ready for a Prince to come home someday and run this wonderful ranch. But that was never to happen.

Glen & my '54 Ford at the Prince of Wales Ranch

Wib believes this prime ranch country is perhaps the best in all North America, and I believe he is right.

The first breeding stock of 11 cows and a bull were brought in about 1873. It wasn't until 1881 that leases were made available for individuals and also large ranch companies. One could lease up to one hundred thousand acres for one cent an acre. In spite of what sounds like a great giveaway today it took 21 years to sell all the leases. You were only to put one cow per ten acres of grassland. So if you wanted to run one hundred cows you would need a thousand acres of ranch land.

In 1919 after the First World War, Prince Edward heir to the British throne was sent abroad on a world tour. When he travelled across Canada he spent most of his time visiting veteran's hospitals in large cities. While in Calgary he received an invitation to visit the Bar U Ranch at Longview. As a young man this must have appealed to him as a vigorous and challenging break from his royal duties. Like all of the royal family he loved stock, sheep, cattle and horses, so visiting a real ranch must have been a great adventure for him. Edward was very likeable and enjoyed being just one of the gang as he was when he fought in the trenches during the First World War. He rode a horse in the fall roundup and it is said he did very well herding the cattle. He was exhilarated by this life and sold on the romance of ranching. He arranged to buy a 4000 acre ranch near Longview. He kept the ranch until sometime in the 1960's when it was split up and sold.

Cattle Drive in Southern Alberta

The duchess was not at all the ranch type, and did not share his dream. He was a young man who could well afford to make his dreams come true but he gave it all up for his love of the duchess. One can't help but wonder what might have been if he had been free to live a normal life. Did he just while away his years in Paris living in luxury and boredom? Did he ever dare to dream again of his youth and his ranch in Alberta?

The trip home was made across Canada to Manitoba and then down into the US where we followed the same route we had come out on. All I do remember about the trip home was that the boys took up cigar smoking. While I might have enjoyed smoking one cigar, they kept on lighting up. I was sick from breathing in all the smoke and they were sick but too proud to admit it. I couldn't get them to stop so as punishment I drove late, late, after dark, listening to them whine about being tired and wanting to end the day and yet still smoking. Finally they got smart and quit or ran out and I found a place for the night.

Over the years we have reflected back to this trip many times. As far as I know only one of these boys, along with his wife (Glen and Jean Sykes) ever returned to Alberta. Each of them married and kept on farming and now brag about their grandkids. Sadly Glen passed away with cancer in the late fall of 2004.

Upon arriving home I was surprised to find out that my Dad had bought a brand new John Deere AR tractor. I was rather shocked to say the least, as I had no idea he was thinking of trading up. Also I was not really a fan of John Deere. Then again I felt hurt because he did this without saying a single word to me. I guess it was just that I could not shake the thought that as a son I was in some kind of partnership and a part of all this.

Jack on Dad's New John Deere
The John Deere proved to be a great tractor and I soon loved it.

Dad and Mom Take A Boat Trip To England in 1956

In 1956, my dad and mom decided to take a trip to England by boat as my mom would never fly. They hoped to sightsee in both England and Scotland and to visit my grandfather's family in Peterborough. My grandfather, born in 1866 was one of a very large family. His youngest brother, my Uncle Ted and wife Gussie had visited us several time on the Mitchell Road farm. Up until this trip to England dad and mom had scarcely ever, been away from home overnight since they were married. Such was the life of a farmer. After that trip to England they had only two other trips before they retired, both were trips to western Canada. This first trip was by themselves to England; the second to Western Canada with my mom's brother, my Uncle Roy and Aunt Myrtle Butson. Len Butson the son lent them his brand new Dodge car to take the trip. They were overjoyed about this. The third trip was again out west with mom's oldest brother my Uncle Loril and Aunt Pearl Butson. They would take these trips between seeding and haying time for about three weeks long; the trips could not be any longer, as the hay crops would be waiting on them upon their return. I managed to keep the farm going while they were away.

When they left for England in the early spring the cattle were still in the stable, calves were to be born, milking had to be done morning and night and stables to clean with the fork and wheel barrow and in my spare time I was to see that the land got worked and the grain crop put in. I also had to feed the hogs and watch the sows with little pigs, plus tend 500 baby chicks. Nothing went as planned mostly because it kept raining and raining all spring keeping me off the land and the cattle in the stable. The fields were too wet and soft to turn the cattle out, as they would ruin the pasture and turn it into a sea of mud. Calves that were supposed to be born outside in the pasture fields were born in the barn and were always under my feet. I had no space for them so I had white-face-calves tied up everywhere. They would grab hold of my shirttail or pants as I passed by them in the passageway. Nothing is as cute or more innocent than a white face calf.

I didn't see much of my sisters all the time my folks were away. I know they were busy but I could have used a helping hand and was sorely in need of a good meal. I do remember that Pearl dropped by one day and left Ron her oldest son who was three and a half years old with me. I appreciated the company but I just didn't have time to keep an eye on him. I remember telling him not to go near the 500 little chicks in the colony house. When he disappeared, I went looking for him.

I found him in the colony house playing with the little chicks. He never trampled any but they were piled a foot high in the corner and if I had not arrived just when I did they would soon have suffocated. I'm sad to say I gave him a real spanking that day, one that he remembers even though he was just three and a half years old.

He was the only one of my sister,s kids I ever laid a finger on. I have apologies to him as today they say spanking is not proper. Well Ron thinks it was the right thing to do as he was caught in the act and even at that age he says he knew he was not supposed to be there. Still he is my nephew and I feel sad that I did it. .

The crop went in very late, about the first of June and then grew like mad. I was very proud when I went to Stratford one evening to pick up my dad and mom at the train station. Everything was under control at home; the crop was in and looking good in spite of its lateness. All my calves and little pigs and even the baby chicks survived, but I myself lost over ten pounds of weight in two months. At that time I really could not afford to lose that many pounds. The neighbours told my dad that the lights were on in the barn when they got up in the morning and were still on when they went to bed at night. They didn't think I ever had time to sleep or feed myself, … and that was about the truth as the stock always came first.

That year the grain harvest in Ontario was very late and while the crop looked good in the field when threshed we found the grain seed had a lot of hull and very small kernels. We were thankful for what we had and although it was a big crop of many bushels the grain did not have the usual food value we were used to.

I should mention that mom was not going to get her usual flock of 500 baby chicks as she didn't think I had time to look after them and the other work too. She was very surprised and happy when she arrived home to find she had her chickens.

As the 1956 harvest was very late. There was no thought of a trip west for me that fall.

Everything was back to normal for the rest of the summer of 1956 and into the winter of 1956 to 57. My evenings were again taken up with the Young People Union and Jr. Farmer's activities; I also took a position on the Mitchell Federation of Agriculture Board. It seemed I enjoyed doing these things and found it hard to say no when offered a job. This would take me away from the farm work at times and my folks just didn't see any point in it. Thus there was always some conflict over what I did that took me off the farm, yet there was always time for dad to spend 2 hours at the village store every morning gossiping with the neighbours. Nearly all my time off the farm was in evenings for community work not just to gossip.

Both dad and I had enlarged the number of sows we kept to raise little pigs. Dad liked to have me handle his sows and little pigs as I got along better with them. Thus when a sow was having her litter I know it was a comfort to her to know I was there to help. Since it seemed this was something I was good at, I wondered if there was not a future in a sow farrowing business. I spent a year or more doing research and talking to people in the business. At that time there were not many real farrowing barns as there are today, but they were already on the way with many new ideas for mass production of little pigs.

I talked all this over with our agriculture representative for Perth County, and to Beaver Lumber Co. in Stratford and together we worked on a building plan for thirty sows. In fact they came to the farm and worked it out on the kitchen table. Then I talked to the Staceys who owned the Mitchell Feed Mill and they were enchanted with the idea. I had won a lot of friends through my Jr. Farmer and Church and Young People's work and they had confidence and faith in me. The Mitchell Feed Mill not only sold feed but also contracted out hundreds of little pigs to the local farmers at a said price. The farmers paid for the little pigs and the feed when they sold their fat hogs. Stacey offered to give me the feed in advance without having to pay for it until I had things up and running. This was a bonus. Then to top it off they would buy all my little pigs. This was a second bonus and a great thing. Now I had all the bases covered except one, the building?

I went to the bank and talked to Mr. McDougall the manager. I knew him because he belonged to the Mitchell United Church. He said the only way I was going to swing this whole thing was to get my dad to sign over the sixty-acre property to me. Then I would take a mortgage against the property to build the building. For several months now dad knew I was dreaming of building this sow farrowing business. He knew I drew up the plans on his kitchen table with the representative from Beaver Lumber yet he showed no interest in it. He didn't say no, and he had not said yes. When I told him that Mr. McDougall said I would have to have the sixty acres in my name so I could proceed he scoffed and said no. He would not even talk about it. I could sell it to everyone else but not to my dad.

So I had to go back to everyone involved, Stacy's, the bank and Beaver Lumber and explain to them all why I could not proceed. I realize now it was a good idea, but my dad was never going to change his ways.

Life was getting rather discouraging for me, as I also had a personal problem that I was alone with, one that is best not discussed here. I saw my friends getting married; taking over family farms or getting good jobs and for some reason I just didn't seem to fit in. When you are deaf you some times feel like a sparrow caught out in the rain on a sparse tree branch. You wonder if you should just sit still and weather it out or if you should take a chance and fly away. I was getting close to flying away.

Western Trip 1957

Jim Bearss, Ross Robinson, Keith Stevens and Ron Patterson

Fall came in 1957 and I had yet another letter from Mr. Bull asking if I could possibly make it out to help him and Wm. with the harvest. They also had requests from several neighbours wanting help. How they loved those Ontario farm boys.

Word got around that I was going west to help with the harvest again. Ross Robinson was the first to see me, then Jim Bearss and Keith Stevens all were friends and lived on farms near the village of Anderson just southwest of Motherwell. Then Ron Paterson from Munro asked to go. That made five of us. Ron's father Harold and my mother went to school together, so I was happy to have him along. As I don't like driving with three in the front seat I told everyone else that called I had a full load. We all agreed to take the U.S. route via Port Huron to Manitoba. I was still driving my Blue and white 1954 Ford Galaxie.

I took the usual route to the ferryboat at the Strait of Mackinaw as in 1957 the bridge across the straits was still not built. However the boats ride in itself was always something different and enjoyable. We had great weather for travelling. As three of the boys were old friends from the same community they had lots to chat about while I drove the winding highways through N. Michigan and Wisconsin. As for Ron he was a very likeable lad and found it quite easy to fit in.

They had a chance to see Paul Bunyan and his blue ox that I was by now looking at as an old friend. After crossing the border into Manitoba I drove on to Cypress River and called on my boss and friends Marius and Bertha Aubry and family. They welcomed me with great heart and I did wish I had more time to stay and visit, but the boys were anxious to get on to Alberta and at the harvest. That night we stayed at a hotel in the town of Moosomin Saskatchewan.

Our next stop was at the Parliament Bldgs. In Regina Saskatchewan. I have some nice pictures of the boys sitting on a ring-like railing inside the building and also standing by flowerbeds on the grounds with the parliament buildings in the background. Another spot we stopped that sticks out in my memory was on the long low bridge that crosses over the South Saskatchewan River west of Outlook. We also climbed the northwest bank and got some good pictures. All these memories and pictures I treasure.

We arrived in the town of Oyen for supper and then drove out to the Bull farm. As always I liked to arrive coming over the crest of the hill, to see the farm in the valley before me, its well-tilled fields, its bright red buildings, the windbreak of blue spruce and lower shrub trees stretching for the whole mile across the front of the farm. Taller trees surround the inner grounds around the two houses and gardens. I was proud to tell the guys that this was the place where I worked. A number of people were looking for help and some I knew and others I didn't. Mr. Bull however knew everyone for miles around and he was not going to let me place a boy at a bad place to work so the only problem was to try to fit the right boy at the right place. In the end everyone got a job and were happy with the people they worked for.

There was a great crop and a good year to harvest it. The boys worked hard all week and then on Saturday night I made the usual round and gathered them all up to go to town. On Sundays our bosses took turns having us all over for the afternoon and evening supper. The boys were given the respect they deserved and as always the hospitality they all received was beyond belief. To this day the guys all remember and remark about it. It gave us a lasting impression of the real west and its ties to its roots in the east and especially to " Old Ontario. "

I had told the boys about the Bad Lands and as the weeks went by they began to remind me as they hoped I had not forgotten about it. Eventually with the harvest well along the way and the promise of nice weather for the weekend we made our plans to go. We found out at the last minute that Jim Bearss had gone to visit a relative in Saskatchewan so he would not be with us.

Of course the Sutherland boys wanted to go along and be our guides. A friend of Colin, a Johnson boy also wanted to go. Colin went with the Johnson boy in his truck but (Deke) young Don came with us. I have some splendid pictures of everyone climbing and exploring about in the Bad Lands and also of our campfire supper that evening.

Late in the afternoon Wm. Bull arrived and managed to find us. I always wished he had told me earlier he would like to have gone along, as somehow we could have shuffled our load and found room for him. However he arrived in time to do a bit of climbing and sightseeing, then stayed to enjoy a real campfire supper with us. After supper William and Colin and I walked along the Red Deer watching its peaceful flow, taking in the quietness all about us. There are times in life when you share something beyond description with a friend or friends, a time when quietness reflects a mood, a time when quietness speaks and words fail us. Such was the time I spent that evening with William and Colin and my Ontario friends.

Top to Bottom: Ron Patterson, Keith Stephen,
Jack Cooke, Ross Robinson, Colin Sutherland

A few weeks later we were finished with the harvest and ready to go home. The boys all said their goodbyes and promised to someday return. As far as I know not one of them ever returned to Oyen. They all wanted to see Calgary before going home. As Jim Bearss had not seen the Bad Lands south of Hanna with us, he was fascinated with what he saw at Drumheller. The town was built right in the valley along the Red Deer River amid the towering hoodoos and hills. When you arrive in Drumheller you are greeted with huge life-like, man-made Dinosaurs in a small park setting. Soon we were back in the car again and off to the big city "Calgary." Even then Calgary was a fabulous city.

We toured the downtown area to give the boys a true feeling of Calgary, and then I took them to the McCloud Western Men's Clothing Store. The boys all bought their Western cowboy hats in multi colours and had them blocked in various design. Jim even went for a black and white leather jacket with a fringe hanging down the sleeves. They left the store looking like very classy dudes; they were now officially and finally honest-to-goodness……….cowboys.

We stayed at the old Hotel Empress at 219-6th $^{Ave.}$ S.W. overnight where I had stayed several times before. It was a rather modest historic but clean, older hotel full of cowboys, farmers and Indians so naturally it appealed to me. Polished brass spittoons graced the entrance sitting room along with a few real leather upholstered chairs. A room for two would cost about $6.00. That will sound cheap to you today but remember we had been working for $5.00 a day all fall.

The next morning the weather turned cold and windy with flurries. It appeared winter had finally arrived. We decided it was time to head for home. There was a real winter blizzard before we reached Lethbridge. I have some pictures of us stopping to fill up with gas at a Husky Station, my car looking a scornful mess with ice and snow hanging from the fenders and door pans. I remember we stopped for a very short time to let Keith Stephens have a visit with someone in Medicine Hat. We arrived home safe and sound and the very next day Keith Stevens started to work at the cement plant in St Marys. Ross went on to farm. Jim farmed for a number of years and then sold Real Estate, and Ron went on to teach school.

Knowing that I was not going to be able to proceed with the sow farrowing business, I needed to consider my options. I think my biggest problem was not just that I found it hard to get a job because of my hearing loss, but also my deep feelings that this was my grandfather's farm my only home, and that was where I belonged. Off it I had a feeling of being lost. It was the only home I had ever known.

I found out from the neighbours that the Mitchell Feed Mill was selling a great milk supplement powder for raising calves. It came in a bag with a small cup with measurements down the side. It was to be mixed with real warm water, not hot and certainly not too cool or your calves would get scours. I bought a hot water heater and some milk supplement and then I started going to auction sales barns to buy calves. There was one problem though; you see I could not hear the auctioneer.

However I would arrive early and pick out a calf or two I really liked and I was willing to out bid the competition for the calf. But sometimes I found the calf cost me a few more dollars than I thought I had bid. As a rule the calves would sell for some where between $35.00 and $42.00 so I nearly always came home with at least one calf.

Dad was rather fascinated with how well I managed to feed this supplement and do it just right. He knew other people who tried it and didn't have much luck with this stuff. I knew success was all in how you followed the directions, especially the temperature of the water and how well you mixed the supplement. Dad switched his calves from milk to the supplement but he insisted that I do the mixing while he did the feeding. I always double-checked the heat on my wrist the same as mothers do with baby bottles before I passed him the pail.

In any spare time I had I worked for Albert Norman painting. Then I rolled the money I made over into calves. For a while dad didn't say anything, but eventually, whenever he noticed that I put a bran sack in the trunk of the car he knew I was going to go to a sale and buy at least one more calf. So he started to warn me not to buy any more calves, as he did not have room for them. Then when I arrived home with yet another calf he would come out to the car looking annoyed, but as soon as I showed him a beautiful white face calf he seemed to fall in love with it. Then all was OK until the next time.

To bring a calf home in a car trunk, you put it in a large bran sack; first you pick the calf up with its back towards you and gather up its hind legs. Then with your free hand you slip the bran sack over the calf's rear end and pull it up while the calf slips down into the bag. Now if you quickly gather the top of the sack around the rear of the calf's neck and with pieces of twine tie it close, but not so close to effect it's breathing. The calf can lie comfortably but not stand. You can easily put two calves in the trunk this way then tie the trunk lid down against a small block of wood to let air in. Warning! … It is best to be sure the calf has already been to the bathroom before loading. Bathroom accidents are bound to happen sooner or later.

I bought more calves in the fall of 57. I would be crowding the barn that winter and the pasture fields the next summer and that was not good. I bought some beautiful clover hay from Joe Taylor for the calves that first winter. I didn't know just where this new venture was going to take me or if it might end. I knew dad was running out of patience with me and I could sympathize with him but I wanted so badly to do something to get a life of my own and to feel secure. I realize now that they had reason to be upset with me even much more than I'm willing to tell you here. Dad never set down with me for a heart to heart talk about my future. If I had no chance to farm, then what was I to do? I had more than once gone to plants and filled out applications for a job, but I actually knew when I walked out the door they were not going to hire me because I was deaf. When it comes to hiring, deaf people are not high on the list. Everyone wishes you well, but as they say, "Not in my back yard" as then they would have a problem too.

I was back working for Robinson's Lumber in Mitchell off and on, I worked on a few jobs with Ferg in the early fall, but spending most of time just working around the mill. This pleased me as I enjoyed working with wood and tools, but once we got into winter they gave me the sad news that there was not enough work coming in for them to keep me on. I knew it was true, but it really hurt me as I liked the job and the Robinsons were great people to work for. We were however left with a great respect for each other and a lasting friendship.

I had been getting up early doing chores before going in to work up until now, so I was back to a better schedule. I was able to get a few day's work in now and then with Albert Norman painting, but nothing steady. I did like Albert a lot; he had gone to public school with my mother so was actually an old family friend. I have always been thankful to Albert for teaching me the right way to paint. Most people do a very amateur job when they paint and all because they have never learned how to handle a paintbrush. One thing I really remember about Albert was how often he came home after work to find his supper on the table along with a note from his wife saying,

"I have gone to Wingham or Seaforth or Stratford to play Bingo," he would say.

"I work hard all day to make a profit and she will spend it tonight on Bingo."

As a rule Albert would contract the job and often things would go wrong and by the time he paid the wages it didn't leave him a lot of profit. Still if you wanted to look for Albert on a Saturday afternoon you would go to the local Pool Hall.

I still bought a few more calves whenever I had a chance but I knew dad had reached the limit of his endurance. In the spring of 1958 I found a wonderful grass farm at Prospect Hill to pasture the yearlings, which numbered about 15 or 20. I believe the guy who owned the grassland last was named Rundle. The grass was about the best I had ever seen on a grass farm. It also had an ever-flowing creek that crossed it. I felt good knowing the yearlings would be happy there and grow.

My Uncle Frank McNee of Oyen passed away in 1958 after a lengthy illness. Aunt Rosena, now in poor health was taken to a hospital in Turtleford Sask. by her niece, Mrs. Stanley (Hazel Butson) Scott where she passed away in 1959.

A great tragedy was going to happen to the cattle in Ontario that summer. We started to see a new fly, which went for the cattle's face. They later called them "Face Flies." The fly seemed to want the moisture from the nose and mouth and eyes. They gave the cattle no peace; often the cattle would run madly to try to rid themselves of flies. The flies crawled up inside the cattle's nose and lined the eyes lids with hungry sucking hordes. Some cattle which had rivers or ponds would spend hours submerged in the water systematically dipping their heads below water. The one thing the fly didn't like to do was to go into the barn. When you brought the cows in to milk they would be covered with flies, and as they approached the barn door the flies would fly up on the side of the barn and wait for the cows to come out. When the cows knew they could find solace inside the barn they would come up from the field in midday and bawl to be let inside.

The cows spent more time fighting flies then eating. Thus their milk production dropped. Small calves gave in and let the flies walk across their eyeballs and suck the moisture out of them. In the end the calves went blind. Their strength was sapped and they grew thin and many blind. I watched all my beautiful yearlings and calves being destroyed by these monstrous flies. I felt I was ruined as no matter what I had to pay for the pasture, the yearlings were losing weight not gaining.

I drove west by myself that fall of 1958 in a perilous mood. Feeling totally unravelled. I had no prospect for a steady job, nor could I proceed to farm and my life was in shambles. I had nothing going for myself that was for sure. Some how I always found solace in the west. That fall I worked at the harvest for Joe Quain as Bulls already had a man.

Joe Quain's cats washing up!

When the harvest was off I wrote home and told my dad that I was not going to come home and asked him to sell all my sows and cattle and pay my bills and then put what was left in my bank account. In a way I like to think that my dad and mom might have been glad it was finally over, as no doubt they didn't know what to do about me. They should never have had a son; it is better to have daughters, as then it is someone else's problem.

Bulls had a cousin helping them for the summer that year and he stayed on to help with the harvest. As soon as the crop was off the cousin was off to college.

Joe Quain never married and lived with his father Will and his step mom who was his Aunt Bell. To keep the story short two brothers married two sisters. Will lost his wife and Bell lost her husband. As they were both in-laws and neighbours and both had children they helped each other out as much as possible, and in the end Will and Bell were married. Joe though always called her Aunt Bell, never mother but no mother ever had a better son or son a better mother.

On the Quain farm, every morning started out the same way. We milked cows by hand as Joe had two or three Hereford cows to milk. Cows that lost their calves often ended up being milked for household use. Any milk left over went through the cream separator, and the skim milk was often used to raise a couple of pigs. One morning as I finished milking my cow, nature called me. I walked quickly to the little house, which was mid-way between the house and barn. Morning had not yet broken and the lights within the house looked warm and inviting. I could see

Aunt Bell in the small pantry window busying herself-getting our breakfast. She lifted her head and saw me cross the yard and gave me a cheery wave.

Everyone wore leather gloves on the ranch or farms in those days. That fall I had bought a brand new pair of what they called Kangaroo Tans from McLeod's. They were of beautiful soft leather with high tops and I was very proud of them. As I closed the outer house door I realized there was no light in there, in fact it was pitch black. I took off my gloves and slapped them down on the seat next to me. I realized too late the seat lid was up and I had tossed my new gloves down the toilet hole next to me. It was not a happy moment, however first things first. When I finished my business I quickly ran off to the barn and returned carrying two long handled pitchforks and re-entered the little house. Aunt Bell was at her window looking on with great interest. With the aid of two pitchforks I recovered my precious gloves, a little smelly but otherwise none the worse. Aunt Bell was standing at the window taking it all in and laughing her head off. At breakfast she had to know all the details. It was a long time before I lived that one down.

Joe Quain Combining in 1958

After harvest they wanted me to stay on for a while so they could take a trip to Calgary to shop and visit. They set up a list of things they wanted me to do while they were away. The first one was to paint the step's railing and landing outside the kitchen entranceway door. After that I was to put green cedar shingle stain on the roofs of several granaries. It was nice weather and I rather liked the job, I naturally thought of my old friend Albert Norman, and it was comforting as it was because of him I knew exactly how to do go about this and how to do a good job.

However disaster was about to strike! I had just returned up the ladder to the roof with a fresh bucket of shingle stain. As I stepped off the ladder onto the roof my foot slipped and I found myself descending to the ground. Even before I hit I had this vision of exactly what was going to happen. I landed on my rear unhurt with a whole can of green shingle stain on my head. The paint can did the neatest flip and landed directly on my head. I had on my favourite grey flannel shirts and my first thoughts were for it. So I tore it off but I could see it was much too late to worry about the shirt. So I started to mop myself with it. I could see the hair on my chest and arms was green as grass. So in desperation I ran to the shed and grabbed a small can of gasoline and washed myself in it. While it worked very well on my arms and chest and shoulders I hesitated to use gasoline it on my hair.

I remember seeing a fresh bottle of hair shampoo sitting by the sink in the little entranceway, so I though I had better try that first before I tried gasoline. I ran off to the house but I could not go up the kitchen steps as they were freshly painted that morning. So I ran around to the front door, which was seldom used, but found it open. I grabbed the bottle of shampoo and in great haste lathered my hair. I had lathered and rinsed it several times when I saw Mr. Bishop the mailman arrive. He always delivers groceries and mail right to the door. I did not want him to climb my freshly painted steps, so I open the door and caught him just in time. He stood there, stared at me and then started to laugh. He said I was the first guy he ever saw with pure green hair. Apparently he continued on his route telling everyone along the way that Joe Quain had a hired man with pure green hair. They still remind me about this happening out there today.

When I finished at Joe's I went to Bulls to help them with the fall work, doing the summer fallow and bring in the garden stuff etc. Wm. And Alma and kids would be leaving for Calgary soon as Wm. Had been teaching a course at the Calgary Tech College for several winters. I was getting my five dollars a day for helping with the fall work, but I didn't know what I would be doing next.

The day came when it was finished and I had to look for a job again. I had hoped to find something in the town of Oyen or close by. I answered an ad for a job on a dairy farm at Beiseker, which is between Drumheller, and Calgary and I guess I should have taken the job, but I hated milking cows and being deaf I hated to leave my friends in the Oyen area and start over again among strangers. Eventually my money from the sale of my stock back home was put in my bank account, about $3000.00. So I felt more comfortable. One weekend when I was visiting Don and Olive Sutherland, Olive sat down to chat. I guess she could see I needed to talk to someone and I guess you might say I unloaded on her.

She told me Deke was going to work for a Rancher down south of the river for the winter looking after cattle. She suggested that I spend the winter with them and decide what I wanted to do the next spring when jobs opened up. They really didn't need a man but as Don and the boys liked to curl it would give them more free time and could work out well for everyone. I would get free meals and board and just be one of the family in exchange for doing everyday chores the same as everyone else. Every winter they joined a square dance club down at a river at a place called Bindloss. Olive said they danced till dawn and I found out it was really so, they did dance till dawn and then came home and did the chores and went to bed. My dad would think that was just plum crazy and perhaps it was, but I remember it as fun. Perhaps there should be time in everyone's life to do something unusual just for fun. That just might be what living and life is all about, daring to do something a bit different and not falling into a rut. That was one of the best winters of my life. Young Don (Deke) was at home and Colin had just finished high school while Neil had just begun.

With the crop off and much of it already delivered to the elevators there was money in the banks and in the pocketbooks. This reflects well on the community, and especially the local town, everyone from the dry good stores to the car and truck dealers, wants a piece of it. So one day a beautiful lady from Calgary arrived in the area selling Mutual Stocks. She made her sales pitch mainly to the men in the family and she WOWED them all. First she called on them and warmed them up and then went on down the road doing like wise. Of course word travelled up and down the road neighbour to neighbour and it seemed everyone felt the need to invest, and everyone looked forward to another visit with this fabulous lady.

Wm. And Mr. Bull, Uncle George and Joe Quain all decided to make sizeable investments. She was pushing American Growth but also sold European Growth. I asked Mr. Bull if he thought I should invest my $3,000.00 in it. Well I know now he hated to advise me, but he said if I invested it might grow and if I left it in the bank I might just dribble away on it and lose it anyway. Well he didn't say no? So I invested $1,000.00 in American growth and $1,000.00 in European Growth.

This still left me with lots of money to tide me over the winter, as I had no need to spend a lot. Bulls were not exactly happy about my decision to spend the winter at the Sutherlands as they thought I should have taken the job on the dairy farm. When the time came to pack my suitcase to go I could feel the disapproval in the air. I though had a good feeling about it, so I made the move.

After a few days I started to fit in and was able to lighten everyone's workday and all the time enjoy it.

Every evening we gathered in the front room reading or making music. We all took turns playing the piano the violin, banjo or guitar or singing. Then finally Olive would go out to the kitchen and make coffee and find something for lunch. It was never anything fussy, but for some reason it was always wholesome and good because she had made it. I loved to sit and listen to Don talk of the things that happened in this country where he grew up. He was born in Saskatchewan but was raised in the Oyen country. He had a deep affection for this land and this community, and a special respect for the families of all the original homesteaders.

I often milked one of Don's cows out in the corral by hand sitting on an old pail as a stool. The lantern would be sitting on the ground nearby showing a mellow light over the area. I had my head against the cow deep in thought when suddenly the pail shot out from under me and the cow bolted. I didn't know what happened for a few minutes. But when I looked at the pail I could see a bullet hole right through the middle and I realized it had been shot at. From behind a shed near by came an Indian lad by the name of Willy Little Bear who was working for Don's brother Lorne across the road. He was laughing his head off as he thought it was very funny and no doubt it did look funny, as both the cow and I were in total shock. I tried not to make too much of it right then but later I told Don I was not amused. I didn't like being shot at. So he told his brother to make the bullets scarce over there. The following year Willy Little Bear, a reckless lad was killed in an accident at the Calgary Stampede.

It seemed that it was always Colin who went into town with me on Saturday nights, although Neil went with us in midweek to the movie house in Cereal where we went now and then. Cereal was a small town on the highway just west of Oyen and about half the size. I always remembered this place, as the floor in the old movie house sloped sharply to the left where you sat to watched the movie. I am sure the place should have been condemned. However, building codes and such things at that time were much less rigid than they are today. After all, even if the building did slip off its foundation it had only about 3 feet to fall. On the other hand one got a pain in the side sitting for a couple of hours defying gravity. Then when everyone left after the movie you would think everyone had one long leg and one short because they all leaned to the right as they walked out of the show.

Deke would be in his early twenties by now and he often turned up on weekends. He had his own truck when he left home and he came home to pick up a few of his buddies and then do up the town He would come to the dance after the movie was over in Oyen and usually he and his friends had too much to drink. He also got into a lot of scraps. He and I got along splendidly; he seemed to have a special respect for me, and I knew he would be there for me if I ever got into any trouble. I hesitated to say anything to his folks about his excessive drinking because of our friendship. To get the mail we had to drive to Lanfine, a small village on the old railway track. Sometimes when I was hoping to have a letter from home I would volunteer to drive there in my car. It was on such a morning after a stormy night, that I found myself on the road to Lanfine. Deke (young Don) had not come home from his last night's outing. I came across his truck a few miles down the road in a deep ditch. I stopped to be sure he was not in it or hurt. The truck was not damaged but in mud and he would need help to get it out. I opened the truck door and inside was several bottles of whisky and etc all open or as they say "broken on." I thought if the RCMP was to find this he might get into trouble. So I took all the bottles out and put them in my car and went on to Lanfine and picked up the mail.

When I got back to Sutherlands I wanted to hide the bottles and not let Don or Olive see them. So I pulled my car over close to the shed and went in the side door and was hiding the bottles when Don came in view and said.

"Well, well, tell me what is Jack Cooke doing hiding his whisky at 11 o'clock in the morning?" So I was caught, and I had to tell him how I had found Deke's truck in the ditch and these bottles on the seat, and I told him I was really worried about his son's excessive drinking. Don said,

"Don't worry about him Jack. A man will never be a man until he learns how to handle his drinking." I was a bit shocked. This was the first of a number of times I would be shocked by Don Sr. but you see this was his world, the world he grew up in, the world as he knew it from a child up, and he was a product of it.

With Christmas coming up I decided to treat myself to a special gift. I ordered an Underwood Typewriter typing course from the Eaton's catalogue. In due time it arrived. Colin had taken a typing course in high school and he was a great help getting me started. I do remember though how he wanted to cover the letters on the keys, as that was the way it was taught to him at school. However I would like to confess to Colin's now, I cheated.

Olive being a teacher undertook to see that I didn't waste my money, so she set aside an hour every day for me to spend on my typing course with Colin. No matter where I was, or what I was doing, I was to report to the house at 11 AM every morning. I can see her now outside the kitchen door waving her apron to get my attention.

I learned one does not argue with Olive. You made a commitment and she is going to see that you live up to it and she very well knows when she is right.

Do you believe that there are times in our lives that God is preparing us for something down the road? Something yet unknown to us, but what we learn today will fit into our future needs? For me I know there were many times and many things, and certainly one was the typewriter. First came the Bell Relay TTY phone machine, which has a typewriter keyboard on it to contact the operator and to send messages. Then many years later came the computer with its keyboard all like the one I learned on so many years ago. I could not possibly do what I am doing to day if it had not been for Colin and Olive and their persistence; I have thanked them so many times for this gift they helped me achieve.

Christmas, 1958 was a joyful time in the ranch house, a time when they opened their hearts and home to all the Sutherland family and to neighbours and friends near and afar. While I missed my sisters and dad and mom and home, I certainly was not lonely. The house was filled with good cheer, music laughter and food.

After New Years 1959 the Square Dance Club started up at Bindloss, every other Friday night all winter. The days get very short in Alberta in mid winter so about 4.30 pm it is quite dark. We had a nice covering of snow and thankfully it was not moving about. Did you know that the Jack Rabbits in the west turn white in the winter? They think it odd that ours don't. During the winter I spent on the Sutherland ranch there were thousands of jack rabbits in the country. Apparently their numbers seem to travel in a cycle, and certainly right then it was a high cycle. They surround the sloughs area where willow and buck bush grow and chew the tops off anything eatable. The roadsides were littered with dead rabbits. As they are white and hard to see they seem to jump out of nowhere into the head lights of a speeding car or truck and try to out run you. No mater, which way you swerve, they seem bent on self-destruction as they stay within the headlight beam until something bad happens.

We drove down to Bindloss dodging rabbits all the way. The crowd surprised me, as Bindloss is a very small town south of the Red Deer River far out in sparse country. These people all know each other. Most are old homestead family names from all over the country. After working hard all summer they enjoy being together again in the winter and mix with ease. It was true, they do dance till dawn, and then I could not believe it. They accepted an invitation for breakfast at a friends ranch nearby before heading home. Once home we did the chores up right away, as we knew if we hit the hay it would be painful to get back up. But this was how they did it in ranch country in the west and it worked for them. After we recovered and our vigour returned, we anxiously awaited the next Friday night when we would go dancing again.

One day Olive got a phone call that a Mormon piano tuner from Edmonton was in the neighbourhood and going from home to home tuning pianos. He was said to be very good so Olive asked him to call and tune her piano. He arrived one afternoon and it was suppertime when he finished. So Olive like a true westerner asked him to stay and have supper with us. After supper the wind came up and soon there was a real blizzard. In the west you never send anyone out on the road in a storm, it is almost a written law. So they asked him to stay overnight. We had our usual evening of music and talk and then coffee and off to bed. Don, and the boys and I were all up early and did the early chores and then came in for breakfast. The Mormon was very thankful to them so when we sat down to breakfast and were ready to eat, he spoke up and said,

"Do you mind if I say the blessing?" to which Don said,

"No not at all, but just say it for yourself not the rest of us, as we don't believe."

There was a silence and I was rather stunned, while I knew they didn't say grace at the table I knew them as good people and I just thought it was natural that they believed in God. The Mormon started to object but Don cut him short by saying.

"This is my home and I have fed you and kept you overnight because we like to feel we are good people not because we believe in God. If you insist on preaching God to us I will have to ask you to leave." Olive didn't have a word to say.

Perhaps it was something they had talked about and reached this conclusion. As for me I was still speechless. The Mormon looked incredibly helpless and sad as he left. I am sure his intent was golden, as he had enjoyed his stay, and hoped to affix a blessing upon this household.

Back in the horse barn an hour or so later, Don came to me and said,

"Jack you looked a bit shocked by what happened at the table this morning."

I confessed that I was, and Don said,

"You don't believe in that stuff too do you?"

"Yes, everyone in my family believes in God and so do all my neighbours and friends. I can't imagine thinking otherwise."

Don said "Drop it Jack as it will only hinder you in your life. You can't depend on God. You can only depend on your self and your family."

This frustrated me and I was deeply concerned about this, so I said to Don,

"How can you be so sure you can't put your trust in God if you don't let him into your life?."

Don said, "Believe me Jack I have tried it and it does not work."

So he told me this story.

In the thirties when it was so dry in central and Southern Alberta that the farms and ranches were being literally blown away, many left for the Peace River country because they heard that they were able to grow hay and crops up there. He had taken a homestead and built himself a shack. One clear and starry winter night he decided he just had to get out to town to fight boredom and pick up a few groceries. He left his shack walking northeast by the stars that guided him. He could also see the reflection of the town of Peace River against the night sky in the distance. It was cold but very calm and as long as he kept moving he stayed warm.

Later when he started out for home, he again took his bearings by the stars and walked southwest from town. He now was carrying groceries and along with a few other supplies, so walking home was heavier. After a few miles he noticed clouds coming in from the northwest and soon it started to snow. He could no longer see the stars to guide himself. Then the wind came up and visibility became zero. Soon he found himself stumbling over rocks and sagebrush and he lost much of what he had purchased in town. He became very aware that he had lost his sense of direction and would die out there in the open before daylight came.

So he said, "Jack I prayed, and I prayed and nothing happened. If I had not gathered my wits and used my head I would have died out there."

"Well what happened?"

To which he said, "What do you mean what happened?"

"Well obviously something happened or you would not be here today."

Don said he stumbled onto a barbwire fence and as there were literally no fences up there at that time, so he reasoned that if he followed the barbwire it might lead him somewhere. He came to a line shack which had a stove and wood and some supplies so he had saved himself."

I said, "Saved yourself Don! How can you say YOU saved yourself? God answered your prayer, it's plain to see." "What did you expect a limousine to come and pick you up?"

I remember seeing a strange reflection in his eyes, and then it was gone.

After chatting some time about it, he told me I could believe anything I wanted to believe but I was not to preach this to his boys. I asked him what I was to say if they asked me. He said that I could tell them what I believed but do not tell them what to believe.

Later Olive wanted to talk to me about it. I could see that it was a topic that troubled her but she didn't want to disagree with Don. She said they had decided that her boys didn't need religion as they had given their boys all that they needed. So I asked, "Just what is that?"

"You are what you are because of your ancestors, and it is up to you to live up to your ancestry and to your family name and that's all that is expected of you. "

I knew that in many ways what she said was true, they were so very proud of their family name and their true Scotch history on both sides. This they taught to the boys in all possible ways, yet I feared what might happen in the lives of these boys if they denied themselves God.

In January the days were bright and sunny and brittle cold with the temperature dropping down to – 40 F. The local elevator at Lanfine was open to receive grain so Colin and I started to haul some wheat to the elevator. On the third load just as we turned off the road to go into the elevator we felt a sudden shift in the load. On getting out we discovered that the axle had broken and the rear wheel and axle on one side was a foot out. We hastily put a jack in under the axle and then called Don to come and pick us up. The Sutherlands had many trucks and tractors and pieces of machinery over the years. Unfortunately most of it was "at rest" down by the slough, meaning it was not in working condition. There was a truck down there by the slough that had the same axle in it as the one sitting with the load of wheat on at the elevator in Lanfine.

Colin and I were off to the slough with tools to take the axle out and then take it to Lanfine and put it in the truck there. This was just like having to do the job twice, take two out and putting one back in. What made it worse was the intense cold. I was never a mechanic; in fact I have no liking for the job, but there I was lying on my back on a windswept road in the centre of Alberta with the temperature hovering at – 40 below handing Colin tools. I remember saying,

"My mother never told me about days like this." Through frozen breath and chattering teeth Colin said,

"Stay out in this country long enough and you're going to find out that there are a lot of things that your mother has never told you about." We did get the axle in and somehow I felt good about the whole experience in the end, as I had proved myself to Collin and to myself. Maybe I didn't like it but knew now I could take it if I had to when the going got tough.

Several times I would be invited down to Don's younger brother Cameron and Lenora's for dinner or supper. It was always an enjoyable time. Many times I had morning coffee across the road with Lorne and Isabelle Sutherland, Don's older brother and sister in law. All these people treated me as family; they were a joy to associate with and were my friends.

In the winter Curling was the name of the game. It seemed no one minded going out late at night at any unearthly hour, or in the pre-dawn to curl. You would find them standing around on frigid ice in a long, low, un-insulated shed at – 40 degrees below. These sheds were often built at some lonely spot away out in the middle of nowhere. They gathered together to hurl round rocks down a lane of ice to see who could keep the most rocks on the target at the end of the game. So many of the locals wanted to play that there was a great shortage of ice time. It was nothing for the boys or Don to be called in at any hour around the clock to play their scheduled game. Just inside the door at one end of the shed there was a small room with a pot bellied stove that was kept going around the clock. This little room was kept so hot, I am sure hell would bring one relief. The few who came to watch the game would look out from this little room through a dirty, hazy glass window, which people had forever forgotten to clean. The other poor souls had to go out on the ice to curl. I went out a couple of times, to try to understand the game and offer some support. I was not sure which was the more punishing, the heat in that little room or the cold on the ice. As you can guess I never did pursue the game, but they claim it's FUN?

Getting a letter from home always made my day, but in my letters mom often told me of how hard it was for dad to manage all the chores and farm work with out me. So once after reading my letter I guess Olive could see I was troubled so she asked me if there was any bad news. I told her it was just that mom says dad is having it hard doing all the work alone. Olive spoke quite sharply to me saying,

" Now Jack don't let them do this to you, as you have asked them to share the farm so you could work together and they flatly refuse you." " They had a choice."

When spring came I was back working for Bulls for the whole year from spring right through till fall. One of the great things I remember about that summer was, it seemed everyone in the community wanted to adopt me. Will and Bell Quain became my Uncle Will and Aunt Bell and Mrs. Bull's brother George Snell and his wife Lucy became Uncle George and Aunt Lucy. I got invited out almost every Sunday to someone's place for dinner or supper. During the week there were many evenings with the neighbours. Talk about good old western hospitality. The country was full and overflowing with it.

Deke was now herding cattle for Red Jacobson south of Bindloss and next door to the Old British Block (now called Suffield C. F. B.) The story goes Red came home after the war and took over his father's ranch. In late 50's he had reached the place where he had more cattle than he had pasture for. If he sold cattle to buy more land then he wouldn't need it, unless he bought more cattle All the time there was pasture galore over the fence in the British Block going to waste. So one day Red cut a hole in the fence and drove his cattle in. Right where he was there was a long valley, which broadened out as you travelled west. On the west end of the valley was a row of hills and far beyond the hills was the army base and training fields. There was also a long finger-like lake of water stretching down the centre of the valley on the east end. It was a near perfect place to run cattle and hire someone to herd them every day.

Deke On Ace

Deke was in seventh heaven; everyday he was out in the valley on his palomino horse Ace, herding white face cattle. It seemed the cattle worked their way west to the line of hills everyday and everyday Deke rode out to the line of hills and slowing drove the cattle to the east end of the valley. There were many coulees where the cattle would wander in to graze. He had to be sure to find them all and by evening you would find all of the cattle lying along the south side of the finger lake bedding themselves down for the night.

Late in the fall after most of my work was done at Bulls, Deke asked me to drive down south and spend a few days with him herding cattle in The British Block. I knew this was a chance of a lifetime for me to see the old west as it once was. So I accepted the invitation. Deke stayed at the ranch house and the Jacobsons, gave me a hearty welcome. They were akin to so many other ranchers I knew in Alberta, tanned, strong in character, warm and friendly and great hosts. All day we leisurely rode our horses down the valley finding the cattle hiding in the coulees and headed them east. We were to not actually rush them, as they were to more or less graze their way back to the lake area. All day we crisscrossed the valley, first doing one side and then the other Deke was thorough and none could escape him. Red felt that as long as he kept his cattle under control and in the valley the army would not complain about them. After all he was a veteran.

I found out there was another reason Deke wanted to see me. He had met Cathy Campbell, the daughter of Happy and Mary Campbell the owner of a huge ranch along the south side of the Red Deer River. All day it was Cathy this and Cathy that. "I tell you he had it bad!" Cathy could outride and Cathy could out rope everyone. She knew cattle and she knew horses, and he wanted me to meet her before I went back up to Oyen. So on the Sunday before going home I was invited to Happy Campbell's ranch for dinner. Deke was one happy young guy, he loved his horse Ace; he loved cattle and he loved is job and no doubt most of all he loved Cathy. He could not feel anything but good about life, and I was truly happy for him. I always appreciated that he cared enough to want to share this with me.

On our ride back to the east end of the valley I noticed four large round holes in the ground all spaced exactly the same distance apart. I knew just by looking it had to be man made, but why? It looked quite out of place away out there in the middle of the valley where there was nothing but grass to see. To satisfy my curiosity I asked Deke about it and he said,

"Maybe God put them there." I know he thought this a great joke.

I found out later from Mr. Bull that it was where the land surveyors had set up their equipment when they surveyed the land and if I had looked I might have found an iron stake in the very centre of the four holes with the section numbers on it. .

Every evening from a flat top hill on the south side of the valley overlooking this land locked lake there was a sight to behold below us. There were about a thousand cows with calves quietly, bedding down for the night along the lake below us.

We had seen a number of antelope but Deke kept telling me that there was a main herd here somewhere and he wanted me to see it before I went back to Bulls. On the last evening I was there we came over a rise and there before us was a herd of hundreds of pronghorn antelope. I remember thinking, "Gosh there are more antelope in here than cattle!" At that time we estimated there were a thousand in the herd before us. We startled them as we came upon them and they raced off down the valley going east. In a short time they noticed we were not giving chase so the ones on the rear stopped with their white tails held high. Slowly the whole herd stopped from the back to the front all with their white tails held high and their bodies facing east but their heads turned back looking at us. Never had I witnessed such a sight, with their white tails and the pronghorns and their face markings. It was picture perfect and I was without my camera.

We would arrive back at the ranch each evening to cheerful greeting and a wonderful meal. I remember enjoying what I thought was some of their very own beef for supper. After the meal Red asked me how I had enjoyed the meat we had for supper and I assured him it was very good. He asked if I realized it was antelope. I could not believe it, as I am not one to enjoy wild meat, not even venison, duck or geese. The antelope we had for supper was good, but they told me it was all in the way you cooked it. I think that goes for all wild meat but I think I'll stick to my beef!

On Sunday we arrived at the Campbell Ranch in Deke's truck for dinner. Greeting us was Happy and his wife Mary and eight attractive and very healthy and active children. It was easy to see that this was a happy home as there was much love and respect all around. This was the first time I met Cathy and one could tell that she too was as much in love with Deke as he was with her. Like Deke she was a bit on the short side and like Deke every fibre of her body spoke of strength and knowledge of her world and ranch country living. She was a petite and lovely girl and I liked her from the start. I had always been under the impression one cannot have a perfect life when you deny God. Yet here was Deke with everything going for him and mocking God. I could not help but wonder what life held for these two people. But that is another story.

Unfortunately many years later their marriage ended in disaster, which was followed by a tragedy and their family separated and was torn apart.

Happy took me on a tour to see his ranch buildings and then the boys wanted every one to follow them to a grove of poplar trees to see their invention, a bucking barrel. This was the first time I ever saw a bucking barrel. There were four old car or truck inner tubes placed high up in the poplar trees with four ropes dropping down and tied to rings welded onto the barrel. A saddle was placed on the barrel and when you got on and ready, four guys, one on each rope would heave up and down on the rope and at times jack-knifing it, while in motion to buck you off. They claimed if you could ride the barrel then you were ready for the Calgary Stampede. I remember it as a day of fun and interest and I was touched by the closeness and respect of all members of the Campbell family. The day rushed by all too soon. They expected us to stay on for supper, and after supper Happy told me he wanted to show me something.

We walked over to his open Jeep sitting in the yard; this would be my first ride in an open jeep vehicle. Happy drove on a well-worn path or trail going west from the ranch buildings up through some treed and rough and hilly areas. Then we came out atop in an open area high above the Red Deer River flats. He wanted to share this view with me at this time of the evening. The day was ending and long shadows were descending from the hills out onto the river flats below. In several coulees along the flats below small channels full of water crossed the flats flowing to the river. Happy explained that every once in a while they dammed the channels and flooded the flats and in that way they grew a lot of hay down there, but they also shared the coulees and flats with deer and other animals that he spoke of with interest and concern.

As he spoke he pointed out several deer emerging from the coulee out into the open. It was getting late in the evening and shadows deepen, and then darkness descends quickly and silently on the flats below. I have heard of Happy Campbell many times over the years from my friends but have never seen him since that day. I have always felt honoured to meet him and that he cared enough to share that evening with me.

In June 2003 I heard Happy Campbell celebrated his 90th birthday. Unfortunately Mary passed away a number of years ago. I heard 80 members of Happy and Mary's family sat down at his Birthday party, their own eight children and all the grandchildren and great grandchildren. What a wonderful "Happy" legacy.

In a letter from home I heard that Albert Norman had been inquiring about me as he had a couple of churches to paint that winter of 1959 over to 1960. So I thought I would venture home for the winter and paint for Albert. Certainly I could not afford to sit out two winters without pay, as when you work on farms or ranches you have no unemployment insurance when you get laid off.

There was not much of a welcome for me when I arrived home and I was very uncomfortable with that. I could feel that even my sisters felt that at my age now I should not have to depend on my dad and mom for anything. I don't think anyone of them ever looked at my deafness as a handicap that kept me from getting a job. Perhaps in some way they knew me even better then I knew myself as I proved later in life I could do well at most things if only I got a chance to prove it. The problem was how do you get your foot in the door when they won't open it for you? Albert was happy to see me and soon I was back painting again. We painted a large church in Stratford and a Catholic church on the 23 highway north of Mitchell.

Ron Smith had got a job working in a huge Box Plant in St Marys. They made corrugated cardboard boxes for everything from beer to vegetables and soup. Ron offered to help get me hired. This worked and soon I was getting a good pay check.

I found it a bit strange working inside and between four walls after being out on the prairie, but in a few weeks I started to enjoy it and of course earning a good pay check was wonderful They hired me as a part time employee. I know now that I would never have been hired if it had not been that Ron had gone to bat for me. As a part time worker my hours were 11.00 pm till 7.00 am. They were busy so they had me working a full shift every week for several months, thus I earned the name of, a full time part time worker and I was beginning to feel secure. I was sure very soon I would be re-classified as a full time worker. When you're a part time worker it always meant they could easily let you go when there was not enough work, but I was confident if I worked hard and did my job well, I would eventually get hired full time.

These hours were a bonus for my dad to as I arrived home from work in the morning just in time to milk the cows. Then I had my breakfast, after which I cleaned stables and fed the cattle at noon. After eating my dinner I went off to bed and slept till six when I got up for supper. At seven we milked the cows again and by eleven I was back to work at the plant. This was a tough schedule but I was actually happy as for the first time in my life and I felt I was earning my true worth with a real paycheck. That winter I saved a nice bit of money as I had little time to spend it.

In 1959 my Uncle Frank in Oyen Alberta died and in early 1960 Aunt Rosena passed away. That spring I received a check for $1,200.00 from their estate, I added this to my bank account. I still had my two thousand dollars plus some gain in my mutual stocks. I was feeling very good about things for the first time in my life as things were going very well for me.

My 1960 Starliner Ford

There was a most beautiful Ford car in the window of the Ford Dealership in St Marys. It was a special model and a bit more expensive then a standard Ford, but that was the car I wanted. So I thought I was now in good shape to trade. This was what they called a Sunliner Ford, actually a hard top with a sweeping roofline on the rear window with three round suns on it. The colour was called Orchard Grey a sort of soft lilac colour. When I drove the car home my mom had a real fit and said it was a funeral colour and never in all the years that I had that car would she ride in it. Dad on the other hand took it for a drive and liked it and thought it was a good idea to trade up before my old car got too old. Besides things were looking ok money-wise for me so I could afford it The car cost me $3,600.00 and that was a lot of money in 1960.

In June my dad's oldest sister my Aunt Bertha was up visiting us from Detroit We had just sat down for breakfast when two cars full of people drove into the yard. They all got out and looked around hesitantly as if unsure of themselves. They looked just a bit strange to us for the moment, but then we realized they were a very large Mennonite family. We had no clue as to why they came to visit us. It seemed a St Marys real estate agent had been chatting with a number of local older farmers in the area about retiring and selling their farms. For most of the neighbours the timing was about right, but dad was only 61 and had not seriously thought of retiring just yet. Still he wondered just how much money he could get for the farm. They asked for permission to walk back over the land to see what it was like. These Mennonites were from Steinbach Manitoba.

We found out later that there were about eight or ten Mennonite families doing the same thing right at that same moment, all over the community. They were all supposed to pick a farm they liked from a list and just walk over it that morning. Then they would walk away and think it over and come back at a later date. It was Mr. And Mrs. Aaron Penner and nine of their eleven children that visited us that morning. They stretched out evenly across the 100-acre farm walking from the road to the backfield and then into the bush. From there they crossed over to the sixty-two acres and came back stretched out walking across it back to the road. They chatted with us for a wee while and left as mysteriously as they had arrived.

My Aunt Bertha who loved to tell fortunes and to predict the future, told us the farm was sold.

For the first time _ever_ my dad asked me a serious and important question,

"If I get offered enough money for the farm do you think I should sell?" I realized by now at 61 years old he was facing retirement in a few years and he needed what ever he could get for the farm to live on. So I said,

" If you can get enough for it perhaps you should sell and I will try to get on full time at the box plant."

The very next week I went to the office and told them my dad was selling the farm and that I would like to get on full time with them. I didn't think there would be any problem over this as I got along well with everyone in the plant and I was confident I was doing my job well. In a few days I got a notice that I was laid off, without any explanation. It was a disaster and I could not believe it. Ron told me that it was not that they didn't have enough work it had to be something else.

Apparently there had been a rumour spread in the plant by someone with a great imagination that because I could not hear I almost got squashed in a big press machine while it was closing. That was not true, as I never worked on or anywhere near this press.

Almost every week I went back to the plant to check and see when they would take me back. Then one day my foreman whom I had liked came to me and said,

"Jack I hate to see you wasting your time coming back here every week as they are not going to hire you, you know."

"I thought I was getting along well and that they liked me," I said

"We did like you and you were doing a good job, but do you see that sign out side the front door, the one that says- "We Have Been So Many Days Without An Accident?" "Well they think more of that sign than they do about giving you a job." "They won't hire you full time because you're deaf and you may get in an accident and that would raise our compensation fees, in other word cost us money."

So this is my story and this was the way the deaf were treated when they went out looking for work in the real world. This was the part that my Dad and mom and sisters never seemed to understand. They didn't seem to realize that as far as the public was concerned I had a handicap. Perhaps it was because they knew me as a capable person they didn't see me that way, but slowly I was drifting into a lonely silent world, which I felt was all of my own.

First the deaf were more or less kept in the dark as far as a higher education and then we were expected to be satisfied doing odd jobs, to be on hand when needed and disappear when not needed. Somehow this did not appeal to me. I had to find a better way.

I continued to help dad until the harvest was off. Then I was able to work a few days now and then painting with Albert. Late that fall my brother-in-law who did some backhoe work asked if I would help him with some work in Thamesford a town east of London. He was putting some drains in for the town. It was getting quite late in the fall and very cold and wet and apparently his help he had left him. It was a muddy wet dirty job down in a ditch levelling the bottom and laying drains. As he was my brother-in-law I was willing to help him get the job done. One day when it was very miserable a man came to see him from the town and asked him if he would extend his job and clean out a number of catch basins before he left. Oliver hesitated and then agreed and the man came out with,

"Thanks, I don't expect you to do it yourself but have someone with a strong back and a weak mind do it." After saying that he chuckled as if he had said something smart. That was all I needed to make me jump out of that ditch, as there I was covered with mud, cold and wet, and this guy who was all dressed up warm and comfortable would made a statement like that. I said,

"Well I am the guy that will likely have to do it and I do have a very strong back but I also have a very good mind. I want an apology from you for that statement!"

He looked at Oliver and Oliver looked at me. Neither said anything.

I said, "I am serious, if I don't get an apology I will quit right now."

Neither Oliver nor the man said a thing so I walked off and drove home. To this day I feel it was the right thing to do. Never in my life have I let anyone talk down to me.

I feel Oliver should have told the man that he was sorry but he did not hire men like that and perhaps this man should consider doing the job himself. From that day forward things between Oliver and me were never the same. This I know caused some grief for my sister and her family, and I am sorry for that, but I accept no blame. That winter I painted for Albert off and on as he didn't have enough work to keep us both busy.

The Old Farm Was Sold In - 1961

In the spring of 1961 the Mennonites from Steinbach Manitoba were back and very serious about buying farms. It was now just a matter of price. We were told later that they were all to go out to the farm of their choice and told to close a deal that day so no one would be left holding a farm while others went back to Manitoba. They also were not to bid against each other only on the farm of their choice. My dad had decided to ask $32,000.00 for his 162 and half acres. Of course he didn't expect to get his asked price. They finally agreed on $28,000.00

After the farm was sold Aaron Penner came to me and asked how I felt about my dad selling the farm. I remember this conversation clearly as it really meant a lot to me. I said,

"Well I was not going to be able to farm it anyway and now I'm not sure that I really want to, but it is my home the only home I have ever known." Aaron said,

"Jack I wont take your home away from you." " I want you to know that you can come back home to visit or walk the fields any time you feel the need to."

I hope he knew how much that meant to me. I still like to go back at least once every year to sort of feel my roots. Aaron and his wife Elsie have both passed away now as I write this. Their sons have honoured their dad's words and I am always treated royally whenever I go home to visit.

When Bulls in Alberta found out my dad had sold the farm they asked if I would work for them that summer and if I could also find Joe Quain a man. Getting a farm lad in the spring was quite different than getting one in the fall when the work was all done up. So I put an ad in the Stratford paper. One day when mom was home alone a very young chap knocked on the door and asked if he could have the job. For some reason my mom liked him and took the liberty to say yes even though he was very young and I had not had a chance to meet him.

His name was Barry White and he gave his address as Stratford. Some friend drove him out to the farm and would bring him back the morning I was to leave.

Jack The Mighty Hunter

On the way out west I found him good company and easy to talk to, and I think he felt the same. He told me the truth about himself. His dad owned a gas station and garage in the village of Gads Hill a few miles north of Stratford. His mother had died and his father remarried. He and his brother could not get along with their new stepmother so they more or less left home and ended up on the streets in Stratford before being picked up and looked after by the Salvation Army. At that moment he was 16 and running away from the Salvation Army. This of course alarmed me, and he begged me not to report him. So I told him that then he had to remember that he never told me anything about this.

It was a long hot summer and because I was there to help, Bulls broke a quarter section of land they called the CP land (Canadian Pacific) and also another piece at the rear of the home farm. They had a new piece of machinery called a Graham Plough; it had interchangeable blades or heads on a heavy spring-like teeth and dug deep into the ground and rolled great rocks large and small to the surface. Today they have rock pickers but in those days they had Jack Cooke and I am sure there is a huge rock pile out there somewhere with my name on it as I know I picked half the rock in all Alberta.

    Every now and then in your life there will be a moment, an hour a day, a time a place when you will be so happy, or so low, so exhilarated or so afraid that you will remember that time and the place for the rest of your life. Such was one day when I was working picking rock in the huge field at the back of Bull's home farm. The newly broken land had been worked down deep with the Graham Plough to pull up rocks. The land and rocks themselves reflected the heat from the hot sun above. Every step I took I sunk to my boot tops, just walking alone wore one out, but picking up the endless crop of rocks tore the fibre of every muscle and your body ached from head to toe. The hot dry sun bore down on you with even more punishment than your mind and body could endure. I suddenly realized this was not the kind of work one wanted to do for a lifetime. I felt as if (pardon the pun) I had hit rock bottom. I wanted to find a place in life where I could work and enjoy my job and still make a decent living, I also wanted dad and mom and sisters to be proud of me.

Jack Picking Rock at Oyen

    That was the summer I first heard of, and saw Cattle Oilers, a gadget made by a small company in Medicine Hat to keep the flies off cattle. It actually worked very well. A five-gallon tank was set on top a wood post with a spring like feeder valve into a burlap wick surrounded by a curled steel coil. It was attached first to the top of the post and then to a lower iron stake that was driven into the ground. The idea was that cattle love to scratch and they soon found the steel cleats on the coil felt very good to scratch on. Then they realize that that strange smell they got from scratching on this thing kept the flies away. So soon they would arrive every time the flies took an interest in them. So I wondered how this would work on these face flies in Ontario. I wrote to the company McIntyre's, and he assured me it would work well and that no one was selling his Cattle Oilers in Ontario.

Barry White and Diane

Meanwhile my new friend Barry had been busy. He had found a very nice little girl in Oyen and spent all too many evenings and on into the night in town arriving back home at Bulls ill prepared for the days work. I loved hearing his boss tell me of how he went to check on Barry one day when he was supposed to be summer fallowing. After sitting at the road for a long time waiting for Barry on the tractor to make its round, he drove his truck into the field to look for him. He found Barry sound asleep under a tree by the slough. What could they do. It seemed Barry had stole their hearts as he was a likeable guy and they only saw the humour in this. I had told Barry I was thinking of going back east with a few of these Cattle Oilers in my trunk and see if they would sell. He told me not to go without him. I had met Diane and liked her and I rather hated to break up what looked like a good match. So when the time came for me to go home I decided to go without Barry.

To get to the highway I had to pass the farm where Barry worked and there he was in the front field summer fallowing. When he saw my car he waved at me frantically to stop. So I pulled over and waited for him to approach. He of course knew that I would not be going out onto the highway early in the morning unless I was going home. He wasn't happy that I would go back without telling him.

I said, "What about Diane? I just didn't want to hurt her by taking you back." He said, " I'm not running out on Diane, we have talked it over and I am going east to get a job and a place to live, and when she gets out of school she will come east."

He got his things and then we drove to the high school and asked for Diane. She told me that she trusted Barry and that this was what they had planned. I remember asking them if they were going to get married or just shack up. They said they would get married as soon as they found a minister, so I told them about my great friend and minister the Rev. Robert Watt.

We first drove down to Medicine Hat to the McIntyre's company and I was able to put a couple of Cattle Oilers in the trunk. He said if they sold he would ship any number I wanted to Mitchell where I could pick them up.

Cypress Hills in Saskatchewan

We drove east from Medicine Hat and then south through the Cypress Hills to Montana. I found the Cypress Hill country spectacular in its own kind of rugged beauty, around every bend and over every hill. I guess I kept on saying,

"Look at that. Look at that." So finally Barry said to me,

"Jack you keep saying, Look at that, Look at that, and I look but I don't see anything but hills and a bunch of damn trees."

So I thought to myself, "I may be deaf but God gave me the gift of eyes that really see beauty, and a mind with a sense of appreciation for nature, in my silent world." So perhaps in that way one might say "I am blessed."

We arrived home but neither of us had a place to go. Barry was not sure he was welcome at home and the Penner's were now on the old farm. Dad and mom were now staying at Bill and Jeans until they decided just what they should do. I think dad realized that he could not afford to retire until he was 65 and had his pension. Dad had spent his time that summer driving tractors for farmers out in the country and mom was left alone a lot in town and she was not very happy.

Barry got a job at the Durisol plant in Mitchell the same plant that I had applied for a job several times and didn't get hired. We also found him a huge empty dark apartment above Mert Pugh's poolroom and lunch counter. Mert, like my mom took a liking to Barry and was soon mothering him. I introduced Barry to Mr. Watt the main street United Church minister and he assured Barry he would marry him and Diane when she came east. Eventually Diane came east and Mr. Watt married them in the Mitchell Main Street United Church and I stood up for them.

About now I ran into my cousins Ivan and Betty Lou Norris and as they knew my folks had sold the farm they wondered just where I was going to stay. I told them that apparently my Dad and Mom and my sisters had all decided it was time I looked after myself and were not going to offer me a place to crash. I think at the time they considered it a sort of tough love. I didn't really blame them but I didn't know what to do about it. I hated applying for jobs when I already knew they were not going to hire me. Ivan and Betty Lou said to come and stay with them while I set up this Cattle Oilier sales business and then surely something would come up.

I set about trying to find people that were interested in selling the Cattle Oilers. I ran ads in all the local papers from Wingham, Strathroy, Aylmer to Woodstock and many others. I sold oilers and chemical to each one of these guys who wanted in on this to sell oilers for me on a commission. I thought if I got a large area set up in the fall it would be up and running when the flies came back the next year.

Needless to say McIntyre's were very happy with me and I got a letter from the company saying my future was safe with them. I was looking forward to cashing in on a big thing the next spring when the flies came back.

Fall turned to winter and now I was going to have to find a steady job as any money I had was tied up in Cattle Oilers, so I was about out of cash. I have never been able to thank Ivan and Betty Lou for their kindness, for being there for me.

It always seemed it was Albert I turned to for a job. He was willing to hire me part time, as it was the best he could offer. That of course saved me from chaos.

The Taylor Farm
Dad and Mom Buy The Taylor Farm

Mom had served dad an ultimatum, telling him if he was going to be out in the country working all the time then they would find a small place and move back out to the country for a few years. Late that fall they bought the Taylor farm on the Mitchell Road just south of Fullarton. This was one of the best things my dad ever did as he was a just 62 years old and could not afford to retire until he had his old age pension check coming in. In other words he needed an income and also a safe investment for the money from the sale of the old farm. He didn't know it then but all things were going to work out for the best for them. He paid $14,000.00 for about 90 acres, 17 of which were across the road and next to the Thames River. They made a good living off that farm. Dad bought feeder cattle in the spring with the extra money he had from the sale of the old farm and pastured them across the road on the 17 acres. He raised little pigs in the barn from several Landrace sows and he grew some cash crop. Mom of course had to have a few hens. They stayed on the farm from 1961 to 1969 eight years and sold it for $28,000.00 doubling their investment and all the while making a living on it over those years. I think those eight years were dad's most rewarding years.

But I am getting ahead of myself here….. I'm not sure just how it happened but mom asked me if I wanted to come and stay with them on the Taylor farm. Maybe they missed me after all. So I moved from Ivan and Betty Lou's, cattle oilers and all to the Taylor farm. I do remember mom telling me she wanted me to feel it was home. I appreciated that, but that place was not home to me. When spring came and the cattle were out on the pasture the first few flies arrived again and I started getting orders from all over the area for my Cattle Oilers. For a few weeks I was wiring The McKenzie Company in Medicine Hat from the Mitchell Railway station every few days. I needed many more Cattle Oilers. Then for some reason things started to quiet down and we suddenly realized there were very few flies around. As mysteriously as they came the flies vanished and I was left holding onto a number of oilers and no buyers, not to mention a very large number of disenchanted sales persons. All my work and plans were for not, as without flies there was not any need for Cattle Oilers.

Thankfully that summer Albert had a lot of painting to do. He even hired Dean Robinson, a Mitchell high school student and one of the lads who was in the Sunday school class that I taught. Dean's dad and Albert were good friends so we all worked well together. I had many long chats with Dean over the summer. He was a very likeable young lad and I will always think kindly of him. He later worked for the London Free Press and then the Stratford Beacon Herald. He married Judy Brown the daughter of one of my Motherwell friends, Roger Brown, and they continue to live in Stratford.

Fall came and Albert took a job of putting asphalt shingles on Dick Thorne's house in Mitchell. Dick owned the shoe store on Main Street in Mitchell and to all his friends he was Dickie Thorne. My grandfather, my dad and I all at one time or another bought shoes from Dick or his father before him. He was a good guy who knew his shoes and he was never lacking for words. It was very late in the year, possibly the end of November or even on into December when I found myself up on Dickie's house roof putting on shingles. Dick wanted to help but said he was afraid of heights. I told him to just sit at the top of the ladder for a while and get use to it. This seemed to work and soon he was working beside me.

Dick always had a sincere interest in young people so he was soon asking me about my work and my plans. When I told him that with my hearing as it was, I just could not seem to get a steady job anywhere and I needed something secure.

A new barber had just came to town and moved in across the street and not far from Dick's shoe store. He had gone over to welcome him to town. Dick was telling me all about the new barber and his shop. Then he said he remembered I had once told him about my grandfather's brother my Uncle Fred Butson, a barber in Winnipeg, and he asked me if I ever thought of barbering. I told him when I was with my Uncle Fred I had given it some thought.

Dick said," Jack it is darn cold up here on the roof and winter has not yet begun. Just think, in a barbershop you would be nice and warm all winter and you could work in air-condition all summer. It sure beats a job like this, and it might work out well with your hearing problem as you would be working more or less with one person at a time."

The seed was planted; and to this day I thank Dickie Thorne. Now I only wish I had started to barber ten years sooner. It would have saved others and myself a lot of pain. I came home thinking about it. I told dad and mom about this conversation with Dick. Dad seemed to think it might be a good idea but my mom didn't seem to think there was enough money in it to make a living. Right then people were working for about $1.25 an hour with a ten-hour day plus four hours on Saturday morning. Forty-four hours a week at a dollar twenty-five is $67.50 a week.

Haircuts were $1.00 for adults in Mitchell but $1.25 to $1.50 in cities like London.

I found out Droulard's Barber School was in London, so I wrote them a letter in which I explained to them about my hearing loss. In a short time I receiver a letter back from Mr. Droulard himself in Windsor. While he owned the schools in London he wanted me to come to the Windsor School if possible. He wanted to find out how he could best teach the deaf a barbering course. If he could succeed to do this he might then be able to get the government involved with deaf students and his school, and of course both would benefit. The school had an admission fee in which they included a small cardboard suitcase or satchel, with a haircloth and all the tools that were needed plus textbooks; there were also two beautiful white uniforms.

I had been teaching a boy's Sunday School Class right up until I departed for Windsor and Barber School. The last Sunday the boys gave me a set of silver cuff links and matching tie clip. I still have them today and every now and then I look at them and remember those guys. They all grew up and made me proud.

Albert was happy for me and he went along with my decision to go to barber school. He told me he would bring my unemployment insurance up to date and see if he could get me some help. I knew he was supposed to be paying money into (unemployment insurance) as they called it then but as I worked for him so off and on over a number of years I just never gave much thought to it. Whatever he did he managed to get me a few dollars a week for several months. I don't remember how much it was but I know it was a great help to me to pay my bills.

To start Barber School there was an upfront fee to be paid in advance; this fee covered your kit of tools a haircloth and two white uniforms and your textbooks. Then a monthly fee had to be paid on the first of each month until you graduated. I had gone to the manager at the Bank of Commerce in Mitchell, Mr. McDougall, and he gave me a thousand dollar loan against my Mutual stocks. I hoped this would see me through the course. A thousand dollars was a lot of money in 1962.

Everything was settled so January 1963, I was off to Windsor and Barber College.

Chapter 5
January the 7th 1963 " Off To Barber College "

I arrived at my cousin Dorothy Williams, 148 Bertha Street in Riverside (which is now a part of Windsor) for a short stay until the school found a boarding place for me. Dorothy's grandmother and my grandmother were sisters. She was married to George Williams and they had one son Mark who was twelve and Penny a beautiful, loving Collie dog. Dorothy's mom, my Aunt Em was living with them at that time and I soon found out that it was she to whom I had to answer. I had to learn to toe the line. For me a confirmed bachelor and coming from farm stock it was not the easiest thing to do, but like it or not I was about to be citified.

It is not easy for a barber or young barber students to find a boarding place because of their long working hours. The school hours are exactly like barber shop hours. That is they opened at 8.00 AM and you worked till the last customer goes out the door. My dad's sister, my Aunt Maude who was a hairdresser in Detroit said to me,

"Are you sure this is what you want to do Jack? Being a barber or hairdresser is a life of service and it's not for everyone. It means you often have to give up your noon hour or work late at night as busy men often want to get a hair cut, on their noon hour or after work. Then you have to keep your shop door open until closing time even if it means working very late. Service comes first before yourself. If you can't do this then do not think of being a barber."

At that time barbers did not cut by appointment, but always on the first come first served method. You do not give preference to anyone nor do you ever juggle customers, as it was unforgivable. This system had worked well for barbers for generations.

My thoughts were of my Uncle Fred and his shop in Winnipeg. I had seen the pride he took in his work and the mutual respect between him and his clientele. I was sure this was what I had wanted all along, a steady pay check, no more cows to milk or rocks to pick, no more hot summer sun, or winter cold weather to fight. True as my mom said there might not be a lot of money to be made at barbering but at least you didn't get laid off every winter and maybe I could someday be my own boss. Somewhere in the background I could hear my Aunt Becky in Vancouver saying,

"Remember Jack, it's not the money you make, but what you <u>DO</u> with the money you make."

The first day of school we were all taken to a classroom where we met Mr. Drouillard who owned the school. We were all given a small black cardboard kit about 16 in. long and 12 in. wide and 4 in. deep. In it we found all the necessary tools we would need to start out on our journey into the world of barbering.

Everything in the kit was of quality, and I think this was a part of our training, to always buy quality tools. Of course the first tool we were drawn to was the great and powerful-looking black Oster Clipper with two detachable blades. One was size #1 and the other #000. Later everyone bought a # 2 blade.

There was also one tube of clipper grease and a small can of clipper oil.

There were two sets of C Mon Cadillac shears

      One set of C Mon thinning shears

      Two black   C Mon Combs

      One large Wahl brush cut comb

      One white Chair cloth

      Two C Mon chair cloth neck clips

      One whisk

After the class Mr. Drouillard asked me to stay so he could have a talk with me. He wanted to know how he could best teach me this course, as he wanted it to succeed. I assured him I was here to learn and would not be fooling around, but I would appreciate it if the instructors didn't make a big thing out of my deafness and especially not to pop a question to me in front of the class as I might know the answer if I only knew what the question was. I told him they could help me a lot by using the black board when possible. Then if I didn't understand something I promised to ask. So we decided to try this approach and see what happens.

Over the next day or two I met the director and the teachers.

Director D Bannon.   Teachers' Ron Zatine and Stan Tofflemire.

There were about fifty some students in the school when I started. It seemed to be divided into three classes. Our first class was the largest, then the intermediate class was next and then the senior class the smallest, was on the second floor. As it might be expected a number of students would quit after a few weeks when they found out they just could not do a decent haircut. There was not a single person in school that I did not like; they were all great, and the director and teachers too.

Droulard Barber College and Jack's 1960 Starliner Ford

The school was purposely situated on University Ave. a few blocks from the Ambassador Bridge in an area where there were large French and Italian families whose children were in need of a good or not so good, low-priced haircut. They came in hordes after school, and on Saturday they would sit forever waiting on a 35-cent haircut. Adults however were 60 cents.

On the second day of school we were told we were going to do our very first haircut with hand clippers. We all wondered though just how we were going to get our first head of hair into our barber chair for that very first haircut.

Thus enters Mr. Drouillard who in a loud voice to a room full of longhaired kids says,

"Who of you would like a nice free hair cut?" about a dozen kids all put their hands up and shouted.

"Me."

"Go down the stairs and into the classroom."

We all followed the kids down the stairs into a long narrow basement room where a dozen empty barber chairs set waiting. The kids all scampered aboard anxious to save themselves 35 cents. Little did they know what was about to happen, as to the kids we all looked very much like real barbers in our freshly starched white uniforms. Mr. Drouillard went from chair to chair handing out hand clippers. Some of the children let out a moan. Mr. Drouillard put his hand on top of his hapless victims head bowing it and then started clipping up the back of the kids neck with his hand clippers. The hair fell in an orderly manner in great locks; first curling and then rolling down his clipper hand and finally fell silently to the floor. He quickly and expertly did the back and then both sides. Then he stood back admiring his work and then invited us to do the same; I must admit these kids were either very brave or foolish and all for 35 cents, as soon great clumps of hair were falling as clippers ran wild and deep. Sometimes too deep and some kid would shout, "OWW, that's my ear."

In the end it was not a pretty sight. There were buckets of not too clean hair and kids with scruffy haircuts and great red welts up and down their necks. Soon however the teachers came to the rescue and added a few personal touches so that the poor kid thought he got a decent haircut. The kids were let out the side door and rushed off to spend their money. Again Mr. Drouillard asked the crowded room,

"Who all wants a free hair cut?" "Go down the stars to the class room." We would go through it all again. According to government regulations the school had to start us off using hand clippers before we could use the electric clippers. I don't think any one of us ever did a decent haircut with the hand clippers and we were happy when they got us started with out electric Oster clippers. I stayed with Oster clippers all through my barbering career; they are a great, reliable clipper. On the other hand in all my years of barbering I never did do another haircut with hand clippers.

One of the guys on the second floor was Floyd "Bud" Hillman of Kirkland Lake one of four brothers who all player on National Hockey teams. That winter of 62/63 Bud left class to go to Europe with the Windsor Bull Dogs to play Olympic Hockey and the team brought home GOLD for Canada. Needless to say we were all very proud of the Windsor team and we at school were especially proud of our "Bud Hillman."

It was rumoured that the boys spent a lot of Canadian Tire money in Russia.

You might be asking yourself why a guy who had been playing National Hockey was going to Barber College. Well at that time there was no money in playing sports, even Joe Louis the famous boxer ended up poor. You played sports for the joy of it. Then when you got older you had to find yourself a real job. In Bud's case he hoped his hockey fame would bring him a lot of customers so he could make a decent living at barbering.

George, Dot, Mark, Aunt Em and Penny decide to "Keep Me"

After a couple weeks the school found a boarding place for me, but when I told George, Dot and Mark I had a place to go, they baulked at the idea as they wanted me to stay on with them. They claimed even Penny would miss me. As for Mark I am sure he enjoyed having me around as a sort of older brother. I also knew that he wanted to keep my 1960 Starliner Ford in the driveway. I couldn't help but notice how many times he looked at it with great affection. Then there was Aunt Em; she still had a lot of work to do on me before she had me totally housebroken. Would you believe it as everyone here worked or went to school they had a rule:

You had to make your own bed. I never made a bed at home because that's what we all have sisters for. I hauled the wood and I pumped the water, and I milked the cows but I did not do beds. My thoughts on this were as long as you were going to sleep there tonight why bother to make the bed. In spite of my common sense approach and all my protesting I learned how to make my bed along with many other things.

So it was decided that I was going to stay on with Dot and George until I either graduated from school or they kicked me out, which ever came first. Dot had no idea what she should charge me for room and board but we settled for a dollar a day. It was undoubtedly one of the best deals of my lifetime. As I got a clean unmade bed, lots of great food and late night snacks, and in the summer many back-yard BBQs.

My laundry was done to perfection and every morning I was greeted with a freshly starched white barber uniform. I tell you those were the days! I got a lot for my dollar.

Winters in Windsor and area are very much milder then the ones I was use to up at Mitchell. I drove my car to school for the first month but it became obvious I could not afford to spend a lot of money on gas. So I started to take the bus. As Dot lived mid-way down Bertha St. and a boat canal was behind the houses across the road, I had to first walk down to Riverside Drive at the river and then cross over the canal bridge and back up the street on the other side to catch my Wyandotte St. bus. It turned around there and went straight back up town. Every morning when I walked towards the river I would see a number of people walking the other way and crossing the ice, on the canal to get to the bus. It was much shorter so naturally I had to give it a try. My Aunt Em and Dot were not very happy about this, as they didn't think I should trust the ice. Weeks went by and all was OK. Then one night it turned very mild and that morning I debated the wisdom of crossing on the ice, however I did. Upon arriving home that night I found out about an hour after I crossed the canal a neighbour lady fell through the ice and almost drowned. That put an end to my short cut and I had to again take the long route.

School was going well for me and I was getting good marks in everything. Every night I would sit at my desk in the basement and study. I would go back over what we had taken that day and pre-read what we would take the next day. You would never believe the stuff they ask you to study to become a barber - things like bacteriology, sterilization, sanitation, personal hygiene, and the skin the scalp and the hair, and then comes shaving and haircutting, barber ethics and shop management and more. My year's average for all subjects was 98 percent or the second highest marks ever made in Droulard's Barber School.

Believe me when I say all this did not come easy to me as my sisters stole all the brains in the family, I had to do it with study. Mark had his desk across the room from me and he astonished his dad and mom by taking a renewed interest in his school work and keeping me company by studying every night. His grades improved so much his mother actually stopped worrying about him. She was afraid he was going to give her more then a few grey hairs. Mark and I liked to doodle in our spare time and we got a kick out of what each could do. I specialized in sketching horses and country and mountain scenes and Mark would be forever drawing cars.

Mark is now an artist for the Ford Motor Company. His huge murals cover the walls at Ford plants and the walls in Walkerville and the city of Windsor. He is also very talented in doing magnificent life-size bronze work for Ford and the City. Although he credits me for inspiring him, he alone deserves the recognition for his achievements.

Every night when I came home from school Penny the dog would be at the gate waiting on me. I would sit on the rear steps and listen to her lovingly whine to me. Every few weeks I drove up home to see the folks who were now comfortably settled on the Taylor farm. They talked to Dot on the phone regularly and I'm sure she gave them a rather glowing report. It was good to find that they were actually happy for me and I could see that dad was very proud. I was dong well in school. I think I was more settled and happy than I had been in my lifetime. When I drove back to Windsor it was usually quite late when I arrived at 148 Bertha St. and Penny would be at the gate patiently waiting for me. Because I had been away for two days she poured out her heart to me. While I could not hear I could feel her whimpering cries telling me how much she loved me and had missed me.

When spring arrives, Riverside Drive comes alive with flowering trees, shrubs and bulbs. The big boats are again heading up the river to the lakes leaving a wide wake behind them. While the rest of Ontario is still locked in winters clasp, spring has sprung in Windsor. Every now and then I afforded the luxury of driving my car to work just so I could take in the Flowering Crab and Flowering Cherry trees and the striking view of Riverside Drive, the Detroit River and the Detroit skyline, I was beginning to love this city.

When the warm weather arrived we took boat rides to Peche Island in the mouth of the Detroit River with the neighbours Norman and Elva Speirn. Once there we would dive off the boat into the shallow waters off the Island. At that time the river was very clean and we could see the clean sand at our feet. It was like visiting a little paradise Island all of our own. When we arrived back home we would have a BBQ out in the back yard and eat out there at a table under an umbrella. I tell you for a buck a day I was living very well indeed.

Dot has a sister Bae who worked with the Red Cross in Windsor; she married Bill Stoddard. That summer as cousins we all grew very close, visiting back and forth a lot. Bill asked me early in my Barbering Career if I would cut his hair. Well in all truths Bill didn't have much hair to cut. He was the kind of customer that keeps the barbers very happy. Anyway Bill wanted to be my very first paying customer so I cut his hair in the kitchen at Dot's. He gave me a whole one-dollar bill. Later I framed it and hung it on the wall in my first shop but one night I had a break-in and it was stolen.

George and Dot and Mark and Aunt Em always ate an early supper and I would arrive home later or whenever I got off work at the school. If I were lucky catching the bus it would be sometime between six thirty and seven but sometimes even later. However every once in a while someone at the school would want me to do something or go somewhere with them after school and I would get home very late for supper. This was a no no as Aunt Em would be keeping my supper warm in the oven. Micro ovens had not been invented yet. Aunt Em would meet me at the door looking very stern and very much like my mother and I knew I was in trouble.

She would say, "If you think for one minute I am going to keep your supper warm for you all night while you gad about, you had better think again?"

Then she would say, "Now sit down and eat your supper, it's getting cold." She would then fuss over me making sure everything was just so. I knew she loved me so while she gave me a tongue lashing her anger could not last long against me.

Mark got a kick out of this and told me I got away with all sorts of things he would never even dare to try.

Everything was going along fine until one day I got a letter that my unemployment insurance had run out. I went to their office and talked to them but there was nothing they would do. A few weeks later I got a letter from my bank in Mitchell and it seemed my Mutual stocks had lost a lot of its value and would not cover my loan, so they could not give me any more money. I was in dire straits.

I talked it over with Mr. Drouillard and he begged me to find a way to finish my course as he said I was going to make a good barber. He wrote a letter for me to give to the bank manager Mr. McDougall telling him I was one of the best students in the school and to please help me finish the course. Dot even offered to help by cutting her board money to six dollars a week.

That weekend I went home not knowing for sure if I would be back to school or not as I was out of funds. On the Monday I went to the bank in Mitchell and gave Mr. McDougall the letter from Mr.Drouillard. I am sure I put him between a rock and a hard place. My only hope hung on that letter from Mr.Drouillard. In those days the bank manager had much more say about who got money and who didn't. After reading the letter Mr. McDougall said he would see me through my course by extending my loan to cover.

Before you can graduate from Barber College you must put in so many hours behind the chair cutting hair, I had never missed a day in school since I started in January so in a few weeks I would have my time in. My timing was going to work out very well for me as the very next government exams were to be held at Droulard's School in Windsor. The exams were held every six months at different locations from one end of the province to the other.

I enjoyed everything about that year in Windsor, the city itself, the school and above all my boarding place, which was more like an extended visit. It cemented my love and friendship with Dot and family and Bill and Bae "cousins forever."

Sometimes Mark came down to the school on the bus to have me cut his hair. I would give him the royal treatment, a scalp massage and hair treatment, shampoo and haircut and facial all for 35 cents. He was pampered and spoiled rotten for a couple of hours but I didn't hear him complain. I think he was a happy camper.

One of the things as a senior student you were expected to do was at times become a guinea pig for the younger students. When a class was going to give its first shave you might find your name on the list to be shaved the next morning so you would be asked to arrive at school unshaved. Getting a first time shave from a student barber is not exactly prime-time entertainment. Just the thought of lying in a chair with an unskilled student looming overhead with a straight razor is enough to send chills up some people's spine. It was on such a morning that Bud Hillman the hockey player found himself in my chair talking to me reassuringly. I remember him saying,

"Now Jack just stay cool and c-c-calm down, -d-don't be afraid."

I remember saying, "Eh Bud I'm calm and I'm cool, but you are the guy who should be afraid." All went well. Bud Hillman was a very brave man and he survived my very first shave. I didn't even nick him.

Sometime near the end of August the day arrived for the government exams and thirty some barbers from all over the province turned up. I was really scared stiff as I knew I had to pass this the first time and some of these guys were telling me they were back for the second and third time. Things went very well and when it was over I had the feeling it was going to be OK.

The next day Mr.Drouillard told us that only two out of the thirty barbers that tried the exams, passed. That was a guy called Ken Rowly from Ottawa and Jack

Cooke from the Windsor school. It was a great relief to know I had made it, and now I really was an Honest to Goodness Barber.

. One of the guys in my class Bill Kells had left school two weeks before the exams to take over a shop in South London at 873 Wellington Road. Since he had not passed the government exams he could not operate a shop so he had to give it up. He came to me and told me he wanted me to take a look at it and take it over from him. He felt since I was the only one in the Windsor school from up north it should be mine if I wanted it.

I made the trip up to London and found the shop closed as Bill had already left. It was just a small flat-topped shop made of cement blocks with an angel stone front. A big sign hung on two posts calling it "Southbreeze Barber Shop" While it sported two chairs, the previous owners Ozzie Aubin had only worked the one. He and his wife Kay a hairdresser who operated a beauty shop in the basement of the house behind the shop had left London for Orlando Florida. They sold the house, shop and business to his brother and sister in law Joe and Janette Tipping.

My First Barber Shop

The new owners Joe and Jeanette Tipping with a son Brian who was less then a year old lived in the house and were in dire need to get the two shops up and running. They had a hairdresser hired to operate the beauty shop while Jeanette herself was attending hairdressing school. As soon as she graduated she would run the beauty shop herself. They spoke of Bill Kells very fondly even though he had only been there for a short time; I had the feeling that while they desperately needed someone to run the barbershop I was second choice.

While they were showing me the shop a high school boy who lived close by came in. His name was Scott Barber and he asked if I would cut his hair. I had my tool kit in the car. While cutting his hair he convinced me that everyone out in this veteran's sub division wanted this shop to succeed. This was the southern end of the city and the last barbershop out and the bus service to go up town from there was not at all good. So I decided I would take the shop.

The Tipping offered the shop to me for seventy five percent of the daily proceeds, and I was to charge $1.25 a haircut. They would pay all the bills. That is they got 25 cents out of every dollar I took in and they paid for the hydro and the gas heat and the business and property taxes. They even offered me the London Free Press delivered to the shop each day. I felt it was a very good deal. However they told me they did not want to give me a lease as they looked at the property as real estate and if the time ever came they wanted to sell they didn't want to have to be concerned about a lease. Truly at that time I didn't know what benefit a lease could be to me or if I should have one. Actually I was afraid it would only mean that if I didn't make a go of it I was tied to it anyway, so I readily agreed to no lease. Then they wanted to know where I would stay when I came to London. I said I would have to look for a place. They told me that Bill had stayed with them as they had one extra bedroom so if I wanted to do that they would give me room and board. This seemed a good idea, as here I was right at work so it was agreed.

Joe had a large white sign about six feet long and a foot high with bright red letters on ready to hang out in front above the window that said "OPEN. Soon customers came flocking in, actually more then I could handle. The worst was that this area had been township until just recently when the city expanded and took it over. Ozzie Aubin had cut hair, free of any city regulations as far as price hours or days were concerned. I had a hard time to close the door at six o'clock, as they were use to coming in any time that they found Ozzie in the shop. I would turn the sign in the window at six PM to close, but it was as if they could not read. They just came in and sat down. I tried pulling the blind and locking the door and they would knock and become angry if I turned them away as Ozzie always let them in. It was not that I didn't want to cut their hair; it was because the city by law said I had to close the door at six o'clock, and I didn't want to get into trouble so soon.

I would find customers at the door at eight o'clock in the morning waiting on me to open up, and at noon they came in on their lunch hour. I would have to wait until I had a break then dash to the house and eat whatever Jeanette left for me. When I got back to the shop twenty minutes later it might be 2 o'clock and some one would ask me,

"Why don't you eat your dinner at noon as the shop should not be closed at 2 o clock." Well I learned there was no way you can operate a one chair shop to please the public so you just smile and cut hair and do the best you can.

A student barber from Windsor dropped by one evening to see how things were going for me. His name was Eric Kehl and as yet he was not working. Joe wanted me to let him have the other chair in the shop and cut hair along with me. I didn't really want to do this but, as I didn't have a lease or any kind of written agreement, I had to accept it. While I knew there were more heads of hair than I could handle right now I was sure it was just because the shop had been closed for a while. In the end I agreed that he could cut hair when there were extra customers waiting and right now he needed a job. For a few weeks we cut hair together, but true to what I had thought things started to slow down after a few weeks and Eric was not happy with his share of the haircuts. There was an ad in the Free Press for a barber needed at Wolsley Barracks the army base here in London. Eric left to cut hair there and I have never heard from him since. I do hope things worked out for him.

Jeanette (Mrs. Tipping) did not like house cleaning. At home her mother had kept a spotless house and had forced Jeanette and her sisters to do house cleaning as they grew up. Jeanette swore that once she had a home of her own no one would tell her how or when to house clean. Her mom though had different ideas and would arrive most weekends with a bucket in hand and nothing could stop her from cleaning the house from top to bottom. Her mother was a very short little Scotch lady not much over five feet high with a sharp tongue and the ambition of a whole Scotch Regiment. She picked up, she scrubbed, she dusted and when she left everything would be clean and in its place. Then in a week's time it would be a mess again as the Tippings had many friends and liked to party. One night when they were out I decided to wash the kitchen floor, as it was very dirty. When I pulled the drapes away from the wall there was puke on the floor behind them. Joe and Jeanette came in just as I was finishing up and instead of saying a <u>thank you</u> they told me,

"It was not that bad, don't ever do that again."

I said, "Well I had to do something about that puke behind the drapes," Jeanette said she had been sick on the weekend and did it and then forgot to clean it up.

I had been very spoiled in Windsor with everything spotless around me at all times, and do you know what? I grew to like it that way. So I thought I should start to look for a small place of my own sometime soon when I was more secure.

Joe Tipping had helped his kid brother to open a Skin Diving business at the back end of his brothers Harold's TV cable business on Adelaide Street. This was away back when James Bond was making his first movies, flouting skin diving wet suits and equipment and the teens were enchanted with it. The kid brother was doing well giving night courses at high schools and selling equipment and air from his shop. He also took groups of young chaps out to a site and showed them how to do it right. On such an outing one summer's day in the early sixties he met his fate in a quarry near Woodstock and drowned. Joe, having an investment in his kid brother's business automatically inherited it. For a year or more he tried to keep his welding job at Canadian Pittsburgh and run the Aqua Shop on Adelaide St. after hours and on weekends. In about 1965 he built a small extension onto the Barber Shop and opened the Aqua Shop there. This proved a good idea. I believe it was the first shop of its kind in London. It was actually good for my business too as it drew more attention to the lot. So we co-existed happily.

One day I was shopping in Eaton's when a young chap approached me and asked if I came from up north and of course I said yes. It seems his father had owned a small grocery store and gas station in the village of Ruseldale and he had put gas in my car a few times. His name was Robert Scott and he had a job working at Simpson's and lived in a rooming house on Wellington Street. After a few weeks he came to the shop and told me he had found a nice small apartment and wondered if I would share it with him. It was in the uptown area so he could walk to work, but there was a parking place for one car, so I went to look at it, and while it was small it was very clean and tidy and the rent was right. So I decided we should take it, as I did want a more private place then I had at Tippings.

Most of my first furniture was bought at Sayvette's and Kmart. I remember one of the very first things I bought was a black and white 17 inch Westinghouse TV. Regardless of its quality I think everyone remembers their very first, house or apartment. It didn't take a lot to make you happy, as it was all your very own.

I had been making payments on the loan for my barbering course quite regularly. However everyday I was watching the stock market plummet down and down and my mutuals slipped lower in value. This had been my first venture onto mutual stocks and I was afraid of losing it all. If I had known then what I know today I would have ridden it out as when you miss selling on the high market, never sell good stock when it bottoms out. You still own all your shares and someday their value will return and go on to make you more money. This is especially so when you're young as time is on your side. However I decided to sell and take what I could get. I got a little over $800.00 for the $2,000.00 I had invested. If only I had just walked away for thirty and forty years that $2000.00 would have made me a lot of money in the American Growth Fund, possibly several hundred thousand dollars. I took the money and paid off my bank loan.

Once free of the loan and the shop doing very well I decided to trade my car in for a new 1964 Ford Galaxie 500 convertible in a robin egg blue and black powered top. It had a powerful V 8 motor with 352-horse power. It was also the first car I owned with bucket seats and console and powered windows and locks.

Yes, I know <u>now</u>, I did everything wrong about this, but that is the great thing about being young, you can actually live with and enjoy your mistakes, as long as you feel it is worth it to get what you want. It's one of life's blessings or curses?

Things quieted down a lot at the shop but it was still fairly steady. Like all Barber Shops I would have my early birds waiting at the door when I arrived in the morning, then once I got caught up I might not have anyone in for some time. You could never leave the shop during the noon hour, as men like to sneak in to get a haircut on their noon hour and they expected to find you there. There is usually a lull in mid afternoon and then after school the kids would come in followed by men coming in on their way home from work.

On several occasions I noticed a car sitting just beyond my entranceway with a man sitting in it. He appeared to be watching my shop. One reason I noticed it was because no one is supposed to park on the shoulder of Wellington Road. Then one morning a man walked into the shop wearing blue Jacket with the seal of City of London on it. He said there had been a complaint so he had been watching my shop and found that I was flouting with the city by-laws in regards to the closing hours of six o'clock in the evening.

I explained to him how I had just taken the shop over that fall and that this area was recently township with no such by-laws. My customers were not yet use to the change and kept coming in after hours. They got very upset and angry when they found the door locked and as I was just out of Barber School I couldn't afford to lose them as customers. He told me that he was going to let me off this time with a warning but next time I would get a fine. It took a long time for my customers to come to terms with this. I am sure many just walked away in anger never to return. Rural people do not like to accept change or city bi-laws.

During the war brush cuts, bush cuts and crew cuts were the hairstyle. The army, the navy and the airmen brought this style home with them and they wanted their kids to accept the same style of haircuts. When I started cutting hair I would say well over half of the cuts were brush cuts or bush cuts. Brush cuts were flat on the top with the front standing straight up and longer at the crown. Bush cuts followed the shape of the head; a crew cut was sort of in-between. However change was on the way and not for the best. Kids started to reject their father's short hairstyle and I had many a father-son disputes in the shop, usually ending with the father pushing his son into the chair telling him to,

"Shut up and get in the chair You're getting a haircut."

I would sometimes ask them to settle this dispute before they came into the shop, as it was not a pretty picture. More than once I cut Scott Barber's hair the way he asked me to and when he got home his father would send him back to the shop to get more off. I remember Scott holding back tears and saying he would be glad when he was out of school and on his own as then he would have his hair cut the way he liked it. I was caught in between and I could not take sides or I would lose a customer one or the other.

I remember Cliff Inch, who's father owned "Roy Inch and Son" heating and cooling and appliance dealership next door coming in to me telling me his son was coming home from University on the week end. He would be in for a haircut in the morning and he asked me to cut the son's hair very short. I knew there was an on-going problem between father and son over the son's hair. So I told Cliff he had to talk this over with his son before he came to the shop. Then I would give his son the haircut he asked for. I reminded him that his son was in university and both he and I should treat him as an adult not as a kid.

Jack and Bob Go West 1954

In 1964 Bob Scott and I took a trip west to Alberta in my 64 Ford convertible. First we visited the town of Oyen and then all my friends, the Bulls and the Sutherlands, the Snells and the Quains. The harvest was long off and the good weather prevailed on into fall so it seemed everyone had time for a visit.

I was rather shocked to find that Cameron Sutherland's wife Lenora had left him and was now in Calgary training to be a nurse. No one wanted to talk about it so I thought it best not to ask too many questions. In this country everyone one way or another was related so they were very careful and kind with their words. Sometimes they know and understand more than what meets the eye.

From there we went up to Edmonton where for some reason we each went our separate ways. I was to pick Bob up at the Greyhound Bus Station at 4 o'clock. I remember him saying that if at any time we ever got separated, the person without the car should go directly to the Grey Hound Bus Station and wait for the other to turn up. Little did I know the value of that little conversation as it came in handy later on in the trip.

We travelled west to Jasper Park, wild in its rugged beauty, then south to the Athabasca Falls and on to the Columbia ice fields where we took a trip out onto the ice on one of their track vehicles. We stopped at Lake Louise and then drove on down to Banff. A mountain trip in a convertible gives you a wondrous view from up front and behind and up and down. I believe we had planned the trip to last two weeks and three days so we would not to lose too much business at the shop. When I told the Tippings I was going to take this trip they had flatly said,

"No there would be no holidays the first year." This attitude irked me so I decided to go anyway. Now on the way home I was not sure how I would be greeted when I returned to work. Would I find someone else behind my chair? While I felt pretty secure it did worry me a bit. The last few days coming home were of long days driving and we hoped to make Chicago that night. I remember driving into Chicago with its wide boulevards, signs and bulletins all around me but I was watching the highway number and traffic. In a strange city that alone kept one busy.

We needed a place for the night and as it was late. There were a lot of no vacancy signs out. I spotted an older hotel and pulled in and jumped out of the car to check it out. As I walked past a dark alleyway a man in shirtsleeves came out and put his hand on my shoulder and said,

"Come with me." and tried to drag me towards the alley.

I threw his hand off my shoulder saying,

"Get your hands off me"

After getting a good look at him I realized he was a cop, but without a hat or jacked on he looked very scruffy, but then this was the sixties and cops and postal workers all looked that way. Bob went to get out of the car to come to my aid and the cop pointed his finger at him and said,

"Get out of that car and I will throw you in jail too"

I realized it was all a bad mistake of some kind, but the cop did not want to talk about it. There was a paddy wagon parked in the dark alley way out of sight and another cop waiting to open the rear door. I was pushed in even though it was already about full with a mixture of black, white and Indians of all descriptions. The paddy wagon was soon on the road and after a short drive arrived at a police station. We were all made to stand in line and wait our turn to approach a window.

When I finally got there they asked me to empty my pockets, and they took my name down. If I tried to talk they hushed me up short. They were in no way interested in what I might have to say. It was like having your worst nightmare only this one was for real.

Apparently Bob had followed the paddy wagon to this station and he was on the other side of the glass asking to see me, but they would not let him in to talk to me. I spoke to him through the glass, but there was a lot of shouting and noise and he had trouble hearing me. I lip-read him as best I could. Then I told him to find a place for the night and come back in the morning and see what we could do.

We were taken deeper into the building through several great barred doors. Each had to be unlocked and then clanged shut behind us with much vigour so as to vibrate off the walls and dull our senses of any hope. There was an inner feeling of panic and despair that goes with the loss of one's personal freedom and also a loss of respect for law.

I was put in a cell with perhaps ten or more people. The cell had a bunk bed on either side so I would guess it was meant for two people. The best one could do was to sit down on the bed beside someone else and try not to take up too much space, as there was not enough sitting room for everyone. There was one black with the rest and us, a mixture, which included several Indians. A couple of the guys were rather brutish towards the Indians and the black guy. All night long there were fights in our cell and the cells about us. Several guys got beaten up very badly and the blood flowed. At times someone shouted for the guards but no one came to stop it. I realized I was in a dangerous situation. Everyone had a bit of a story to tell. When I told them I was a Canadian on the way home from Western Canada they were very disgusted that this had happened to me in their country. They said the police should have understood the situation and sent us on our way. I am sure just being a Canadian that night saved me from getting beaten up.

You see in 1964 there were race riots in the streets of all major cities in the United States, re the plight and treatment of the black people who were fighting for equal rights. We had entered an area of Chicago that was under curfew. You could drive through but don't get out of your car. It is sad to think though that the police would not use the head the good Lord gave them so as not to do an injustice to innocent people who were passing through. .

Early in the morning we were taken out of our cell and told we were to be leg cuffed in two's. I noticed no one seemed to want to be cuffed with the black guy so I said to him,

"Do you want to be cuffed to me?" I could see the appreciation reflected in his face. We were all put back in the wagon and drove for miles to a courthouse. Once there the wagon backed up to a door and we were let out and asked to climb a long flight of stairs to a courtroom. One by one we were hauled before a judge that told us something to the effect that we had been found in an area where we should not have been and how do we plead. I remember simply saying,

"Not guilty" and the judge said,

"Case dismissed."

I stood there not believing what I thought he had said. Why go through all this trouble for this? The judge looked at me sternly and pointed to the stairway and said,

"Well go."

I went down the stairway and there was a cop at the door, and I said to him,

"What do I do now?" he said,

"Well if they let you come this far go out the door."

I replied, "Well that might seem ok to you, but they took my wallet away on me and now I have no money and no identification and I don't have a clue as to where I am."

He said, "That's your problem. Out the door."

I went out the door and it seemed about half the guys that had been before me had already disappeared. A taxi was sitting there so I went over to talk with the driver, I told him I had to get back to where I stayed over night to get my wallet and what ever had been in my pockets.

He said, "No cash no ride." I was beginning to love Chicago. He did point to a tall building afar off and said,

"The police station where you stayed over night is in the basement of that building" So I began to walk keeping the building in sight. In two or more hours I arrived back at the station. Already a line had formed at the window where they had relieved me of my wallet. People that had been picked up the night before were now asking for their things back. After some time I reached the window, and the man says,

"Identification"

I said, "Please sir, I need my wallet back."

He said, "Identification".

I said, "How can I give you my identification, as you took it away from me last night."

"Well you can't expect us to just hand over a wallet to you without identification. Why didn't you at least bring someone down here to identify you."

"I am a Canadian just travelling through when I got picked up and I don't know anyone in Chicago except my friend who is out there in my car no doubt looking for me."

The man looked beyond me and said, "Next"

So I walked out empty handed, with no money and no identification. I was wondering where Bob was with my car. I was thinking that he would probably find out that I was taken to that courthouse and would go there looking for me. So I started walking back to the courthouse. A couple of hours later I arrived back at the court house but no Bob. I talked to another taxi driver and he was sympathetic and said he thought I should go back to the police station again and try to talk them into giving me my wallet. He offered to drive me back, saying if I got my wallet I could pay him if not it would be OK. At last I found a civil minded man in Chicago.

By now the line had gone and I walked up to the window and the man said,

"You again"

I said, "Please sir, I have to have my wallet as there is a taxi outside waiting on his money, if I don't pay him are you going to throw me back in jail? Look I can tell you every thing that there is in that wallet, there is even a picture of me in it."

Reluctantly he got my wallet and piece-by-piece I told him what to look for in it and of course it was all there. So he handed it to me and as much as told me to,

"Go and sin no more." I have never had any urge to go back to Chicago.

I paid the taxi driver and thanked him. Then I saw a young policeman standing beside his car so I walked over and told him my story. He said it made him angry, as it seemed the different police stations looked at the curfew as a contest to see which area could round up the most people and throw them in jail. He admitted that they should have explained the situation to me and just put me back in my car and sent me on my way.

I told him my friend would be out there looking for me but Chicago was a big place. He said, "If I wanted to say the car was stolen they could probably pick it up in minutes, but your friend would have to go to jail over night and appear before a judge tomorrow to get it straightened out"

I didn't want to do that so he told me he would radio a couple of his buddies and see if they could help keep an eye out for him. Then he asked where I would be so they could contact me. A sudden thought came to me and I said,

"At the Greyhound Bus Station"

So I went to the Greyhound Bus Station and sat near the main entrance, I noticed a Burns Guard watching me, and finally after a few hours he came over and asked me why I was hanging around. I told him what had happened and that I hoped my friend would think of coming here to find me and if not that the police might find him and send him here. He told me it was his job to keep people from loitering so asked me to move around a bit and he would ignore me.

An hour or two later he came to me and said, "Are you Jack Cooke?"

"Yes"

"Your friend is waiting for you at the foot of the escalator."

Never in a lifetime was I so happy to see anyone. Apparently Bob had found a place to stay over night and then over slept in the morning. He arrived at the police station after we had been taken to the courthouse. Then he had trouble finding the courthouse and arrived after I had left. Later in the day he had remembered the conversation we had in Edmonton about if we ever got separated to go to the Bus station and wait, so there he was.

I had not slept a wink all that night in jail, as I was afraid of being mugged. Then I had been under terrific strain all day and I had walked for miles. Letting Bob drive I climbed into the back seat of my car and I went right off to sleep. To this day I do not remember one mile of that trip from Chicago to Port Huron where Bob woke me to tell me we were at the border. After crossing the border I went right back to sleep and Bob woke me up again when we arrive back in London.

We arrived home in the wee hours of the morning and the next day we both were supposed to be at work. We had planned it so we would have a day of rest before going back to work, but as they say, "The best laid plans of men and mice."

The Tippings, while glad to see me back from my holidays were quite upset with me. To make matters worse I had taken my barbering tools home for safety so they were not at all sure if I was coming back to work in their shop.

It was that morning that Jeanette told me that she was expecting their second child Allen and that she didn't need this kind of thing happening to upset her.

Everything settled down, and my customers were glad the shop was open again.

"The Crazy, Crazy Colourful 60's"

1964 over into 1965 saw haircuts getting much longer and a lot less clean. Teens and twenties everywhere wanted to distance themselves from everything adult and from parental authority, army haircuts and standard clothing. They started wearing snugger jeans with sleeveless tops or brightly pattern shirts. Teens rebelled against haircuts! They dropped out of school and church and many left their home. The downtown streets of London were packed with hundreds of young people from the city itself, and from the towns and cities near and far and even out of province. Nighttimes would find the entranceways of stores crowded with overnighters. Soon they became known as Hippies. Few homes were left untouched by this new craze and culture. The Gypsies of the sixties were colourful, defiant and above all free.

This of course was not good for the hair industry, for as the teens won their battle to grow hair the barber's income took a fast dive. I remember a father bringing in his youngest son of four boys. This one had been my paperboy and I had learned to like him long hair and all. The father pointed to the chair as the boy stood back defiantly. The father said firmly,

"Get in the chair."

" I don't want a hair cut."

"Shut up and get in the chair. You're going to get a haircut," the father said.

This kind of situation makes for giving a very hard haircut, as a person who does not want a haircut does not help you by working with you, in fact they work against you. That is you push the head slightly aside so you can see to work better and it snaps right back at you. When I finally finished cutting I was going to hand him the mirror so he could have a close up look at himself. But he ripped off the chair cloth and tossed it in the chair and turned to me and said,

"Here's your money. That's the last damn haircut I am ever going to get."

I was really hurt, as I had given him a good haircut and he did look so much better. Of course this was not so in his eyesight or the eyes of his longhaired friends. His father looked beat and said,

"Don't let it bother you Jack. He is going to be 16 next week and he has this idea that after he is 16 he can do whatever he pleases legally."

The boy quit high school and worked the pumps at a local gas station for several years. I often stopped there for gas but he never let on he knew me. His full head of unkempt hair grew down well below his shoulder blades. He had won his battle.

Bob had a sister Jigs who married Mike Chubak of Dorchester. Mike delivered Milk for Bordens Dairy throughout South East London and to the Tippings. One day he dropped by the shop for a haircut. He knew of me and exactly where the shop was through Bob. Thus began a long and lasting friendship, which I have to this day. Until then I had never met his wife Jigs. I was invited out for a Sunday dinner and I found her to be a wonderful happy-go-lucky type of person who loved life and people. We became great friends, the type of friend you will never forget.

Bob and Jigs had a brother Randy who worked at Kelvinator the electrical appliance manufacturer of fridge and stoves on Dundas East here in London.

The Executive House 362 Dundas

In the mid sixties the Executive House apartment building was built at 362 Dundas Street just east of Waterloo in downtown London. Bob and I decided to move in there. It was a very prestigious building and the first high-rise in the downtown area. It had underground parking and a roof garden. The old city hall was less than a block and a half away and the library about the same. Beautiful Victoria Park was within walking distance and the city Garden Market close at hand. There was no doubt about it Jack Cooke had arrived. About a year or so later an elderly couple across the hall moved out and we moved across the hall to a larger and more expensive Apt. on which we signed a lease.

My friend Mike came to see me one day in the spring of 1965. They had found a nice piece of property near Fonthill in the Welland area, which they would like to buy. It had a rather new, very nice looking red brick house and a small acreage of garden soil, about ten acres. About half of it was broken and the other half in willows or brush. They were asking $18,000 for it. Mike had just bought a brand new 1965 Plymouth Barracuda in the fall of '64 using up most of his credit and he needed a ten percent down payment to close the deal on this property. Now I did something, which I have never regretted, however it is something which one should not do except perhaps someone within your family. My credit was in the clear so I went to a loan company and took out a loan for the money Mike needed, and left him to make the payments on this. Mike had found a job at a near-by pulp wood plant. He not only never missed a payment but he paid off the loan well before the year was out. This was the first of many places Mike bought, fixed up and sold for a profit.

It seemed if Mike touched anything, it made him money.

Every year Jigs would make home-made strawberry and raspberry jam, preserves, pickles and chilli sauce and load my car up with it when I visited them in the fall, then thank me once again for helping them out when no one else would. Needless to say Mike is a wealthy man today and still one of my closest friends. Unfortunately Jigs passed away a few years ago with cancer. Mike and Jigs had three children, Shelly, Connie and Joe.

Hairstyles got longer, much longer. A lot of teens just grew hair thinking it was beautiful the way it was and that they would never have to get another hair cut in their lifetime. Many mocked the barbers by saying with a smirk,

"Eh! Mr. Barber how's business?" and walked away laughing as if it were a joke. I always wondered what was so funny about having your income reduced to half of what you needed to live on. It hurt me deeply that they were so thoughtless and unkind for little did they know about how hard I as a deaf person had struggles to get this far. All I wanted was a place in life where I could earn a decent and honest living.

Help was on the way. Some say when a door closes on you the good Lord will open a window. All you have to do is accept it and for me it always seemed to be so true.

Regina Mundi College

In my clientele I had several priests from the Regina Mundi Residential College on Wellington Road just out over the 401 south of the city. All schools at that time found the long hair troublesome. One might only look to the army and note that they always insist on short hair, because it is easier to discipline men with short hair. The first thing they do to prisoners in jail or a prisoner of war is to cut the hair off because it humbles and subdues them. Hair in the sixties grew long in defiance of an older generation. Young people looking at the big picture, saw their parents, their teachers and their school along with all the rules and regulations a part that older generation which sought to mould them in their image. The hair problem would not go away easily. They would resist.

Regina Mundi however was a live-in school for boys and the school had almost parental control over the students. Rules and regulations governed the student's behaviour and their dress at all times while on the school grounds. Hair was to be no longer than to the collar at the back and no longer then the bottom of the ears on the side. While this sounds liberal enough to us today the students did not think so in the sixties.

Father Mellon, a School Director for Regina Mundi College came to the shop one day for his usual haircut. He asked me a few questions about how I felt about people from other countries, places like Mexico, Hong Kong, The Barbados, Chile and others.

At that time this school for boys took students from all over the world and gave them a good education. They left the school more worldly, moulded into gentlemen who had learned the basics to succeed in life. I myself witnessed some very crude and uncultured lads turn into clean well-dressed, well-mannered gentlemen. I knew this school worked.

The school wanted to know if I would cut hair two nights a week, at the school.

This was heaven sent to me at a time when I was getting fewer and fewer haircuts and finding it hard to pay shop rent and my share of the apartment cost.

During those years I remember watched many barber shops close all over London for want of more business. I wondered how much longer I was going to be able to hang on. Sadly the public did not seem to share our grief; after all we were just barbers. I am sure if it had been the postal workers or the teachers or hospital workers there would have been a public outcry, but no tears for the barber. In fact it almost seemed as if they looked upon it with humour; after all we just cut hair.

I remember looking at the want ads in the Free Press many times wondering if there was some other kind of job out there for a deaf guy but nothing seemed to fit. In the end I thought it best to hang in there, "In my Silent World" and wait it out.

So this was a window God opened for me and I was truly thankful as it arrived just in time. The school had a two-chair barbershop in the basement. It had been closed for a number of years, but now it seemed an AT HOME answer to their long hair problem: SIMPLY reopen the barbershop on the premises. So every Wednesday and Thursday Father Mellon walked through the school with a pad in his hand and whenever he saw boys with hair he thought too long he would say,

"You and you are getting a haircut to night. Report to the barber shop 7:PM."

The boys were not always happy when it came their turn to get in the chair but after a number of haircuts they at least liked me. They came to know that no amount of bickering or grumbling changed the fact that the hair would be cut at the bottom of the ear and at the collar. Most of the boys returned to Regina Mundi year after year until they graduated. Over the years I watched those boys grow up and mature, and change from awkward, insecure and sometimes uncultured boys into young men we could be proud of. I have nothing but great things to say about The Regina Mundi College and its staff.

Mrs. Murdock And Her Christmas Cake

Bob's father had been in the Army and while his father was stationed in some places like Camp Borden Bob came to know his dad's army buddies and their families. The army women often baby-sat each other's children to help each other out. Quite often this formed a life-long bond between families. Bob wanted me to visit Jack and Phyllis Murdock who lived in the old army section north of Oxford near Highbury Ave. Usually it was just Phyllis who was home with several kids as her husband Jack was still in the army. The two Murdock children I remember the best were Jim and Bonnie. Bonnie sometimes called on us at the Executive House Apartments when she was uptown. At this time she would only be about sixteen and I suppose like all teens she had problems she needed to share with someone she knew, so Bonnie and Bob would sit and talk at the dining room table for hours. I always enjoyed going over to Murdock's, as Phyllis was easy to chat with and was a wonderful cook. It seemed every time we went to visit she had just baked something great, and I would sit down and demolish it.

I must tell you about Mrs. Murdock's Christmas cake. Every year she made Christmas cake for all of their army friends. In fact the recipe she used came right from the army's barracks camp kitchen. It was so good that I was determined to make some for myself, so I asked for her recipe. She forgot to tell me to cut the recipe down for just a few cakes. It was just a few cakes I had in mind; I did not intend to feed the army. I had never shopped for anything like this before so I decided to follow through buying everything pound for pound and ounce for ounce. I soon realized that this cake was going to cost me a lot of money. Oh well never mind, it was something I wanted to do for the sake of doing. Perhaps I just wanted to prove I could. While mixing I had to change bowls several times as the batter or mixture grew and grew getting bigger and bigger. When I saw all this mixture I realized I was going to have to go out and beg and borrow or buy many more cake pans to put it in.

I was greatly relieved once all the pans were filled and in the hot oven. It was then though that I found out I had forgotten to ad the baking powder, so I called Phyllis and asked her if it mattered. She nearly had a fit, and she said,

" Yes, yes, it matters. Get it right out of the oven and mix the baking powder in it as fast as you can." It was a messy job but thankfully we were able to do that without too much trouble.

When it was done there was enough cake for a whole army I kid you not, but it was about the best Christmas cake I ever ate. I gave it away as a Christmas gift, to my neighbours and friends and sisters, everyone. No one escaped. But because of the cost and the work involved it was a one-time thing. Now if anyone of you is interested I still have that recipe. Just ask.

Some Strange Encounters

One evening near closing time at the shop a rather rough looking chap came in wanting a haircut. While I cut his hair he told me he was working for a certain man who had a brick cleaning business. I knew the man and also his two sons. When I finished the haircut he told me he could not pay me until payday the end of the week. Well we all know you can't get blood from a stone. So I told him, he should have told me that before he got in the chair, and that I expected to see him at the end of the week. I realized by now he never intended to pay for his haircut anyway, so I was not surprised that he never came in to pay.

Several months later he walked in the door, again near closing time. He looked even rougher and tougher then before. I said,

"I suppose you want a hair cut?"

"Yes"

"You never came back to pay me for your last one did you?"

"No" he said, " I have been out of work for a while." I noted a pack of cigarettes in his shirt pocket so I said,

"Well I note you still have money for cigarettes." He was embarrassed, so I said,

"Well do you have the money for today's haircut?" to which he sputtered and said,

"Oh yea, I have the money for today's haircut."

These were hard times for many people and while I am compassionate I don't like dishonesty. So I said,

" Well you can pay me for today's haircut and I am willing to forget about the other one under the circumstances."

When I finished his haircut he got out of the chair and made a big thing of reaching for his hip pocket. Then with a great show patted down the front pockets of his jeans and exclaimed,

"You wont believe this but my wallet is missing." He headed for the door saying, "I had it at the store just before I came here. It has to be somewhere between here and the store. I will be right back." Naturally he didn't come back.

Six or more months passed, then in the fall when it gets dark early, he walked into the shop along with another very rough looking character, and again right at closing time. Late in the fall when it gets dark early shop owners are very wary when strange rough looking people walk into your shop just before closing time. This is the time of year that there are many robberies. I had been going to the gym four times a week for some time now and I was looking very fit and muscular, but even then I felt this just might be trouble. I decided to meet it head on and not let them feel they had an advantage just because there were two of them.

I reminded him he had never come back to pay for his last haircut and he now owed me for two.

He said, "No just one, as you forgave me for the first haircut, don't you remember?"

I said, "I made you a great deal if you paid for the second haircut I would forget about the first, but you ran out on the deal so now you owe me for two haircuts," "Do you have the money for today's hair cut?"

"Yes"

"Then give me the money and get in the chair," He handed me a ten-dollar bill, at that time I think haircuts were five dollars. I put the ten dollars in the till and locked it. He looked at me and said,

"Well what about my change?"

I said, "There is no change. Hair cuts here will cost you ten dollars every time until you get caught up." I knew I was on top of them and they never said another word. He never came back to the shop for another hair cut. They say it takes all kinds, but sometimes I wonder why there has to be …….his kind?

Now in all my barbering years I have never refused to cut a head of hair if that person needed a haircut for a good reason. It might be, to get a job or for the school prom or many other reasons. But I always feel an honest person will tell you before he gets in the chair that while he really needs his haircut today he does not have the money to pay for it right now. I have cut many teens this way and they always came back to pay me, all except for one Italian family who really pushed it, ha ha! That is worth telling.

This very great looking Italian lad about 16 came in and told me he needed a hair cut so he could apply for a summer job at a local inn, but right now he didn't have any money to pay for the haircut. I liked this approach so I said it was not a problem. I will cut your hair now and you can come back in after you get the job and pay me, and if you don't get the job just forget about it for now.

A few days later a second Italian boy came in. He was a dead ringer of the first boy but about a year or so younger. He said to me,

"Mr Barber I need a haircut to get a summer job but right now I have no money to pay for the hair cut. Will you cut me now and I will pay you later?" I was suspicious but as I said I like this approach and the kid was so darn cute about it, so I said,

"No problem, you can pay me after you get your job and if by chance you don't get the job you can forget about the hair cut." Now you can't beat this kind o deal.

About a week later a very young Italian kid comes in about 13. I knew right away he was another brother as they were all dark, handsome kids and sort of like peas in a pod.

He says," Mr. Barber I don't have any money but could you please cut my hair so I can get a job?"

I told him, "Look son I don't think you are looking for a job but I do think you are looking for a free haircut. I tell you what I will do. If you can get your two brothers to come back in and pay for theirs hair cuts I will cut yours for free." Of course I never saw the brothers at the shop nor the money for those haircuts, but I have no regrets. You live and learn and sometimes its worth it.

Of Friends and Friendships

One night Bob brought home a neighbourhood lad for a cup o coffee. He lived just a little over a block away on Queens Ave. His name was Nevol Huddleston. It seems that during your lifetime you will meet many people who will become just a passing friend and then there are those special few who will become friends for a lifetime. Such was the friendship I found with Nevol. Now after all these years we have a great friendship and make an effort to get out for lunch together at least once a month and also work in a visit.

Nevol's mother had a cottage on the waterfront at Port Stanley and during the summer when it was hot in the city Nevol often drove to work from the cottage. Many times I was invited down in the evening to visit and we would sit out at the rear of the cottage and chat till late. Then Nevol and I would go for a long walk down the now cool sand on the beach, to the pier and all the way to the lighthouse. The waters of lake Erie are sometimes calm and sometimes rough with huge waves slapping the pier and spraying us and adding coolness to the night air. When we came back to the cottage we would see the glow of lights in the cottage window comforting and beckoning us, and we knew Nevol's mom would have a pot of tea and some of her home made cookies waiting for us. I have many kind thoughts and memories of Mrs. Huddleston and my visits to the cottage at Port Stanley.

One hot summer day I stopped at an ice cream store just a few doors west towards downtown from the apartment building. A big sign over the door said Jumbo Ice Cream. Generations of local high school students from Beal and Catholic Central had frequented this place. Everyday at noon hour they stood in line waiting on their treat. Jumbo made there own ice cream right there on the premises and they gave you a great size cone of wonderful ice cream for your money. I walked out of the store with a huge triple deck, one any ice cream lover would die for. It was a beautiful sunny day and my day off. So carrying the cone well out in front of me I headed for uptown.

Just as I reached Waterloo Street the light changed and I stopped rather abruptly causing the whole triple deck to do a fancy flip flop and then a cur-plump at my feet. I was totally embarrassed left holding onto an empty cone out in front of me. A young man standing next to me started to laugh hilariously. At first I was angry, then perhaps provoked and then I guess I saw myself as he saw me standing there with an empty cone out in front of me and all that great ice cream at my feet. So I started to laugh too. We introduced ourselves to each other. His name was

Rick Deluca and he lived in an apartment close by. Rick's mom worked at 3M and had a house on Bond Street with a fantastic back yard. It included a deck and a large in-ground pool. Along the east side of the lot was a beautiful new 6ft. stonewall with a Lion atop on either end. There was some lawn at the rear and many colourful flowerbeds and flowerboxes. On a hot summer day it was an amazing retreat from the heat.

Rick invited me to go swimming many times that summer in his mom's pool, and his mom and I became good friend. She invited me to stop in on the way home from work anytime for a cool dip and that was great especially in those hot dog days of summer when the steady heat gets you down. I would then go home refreshed. Rick eventually moved to Toronto but his mom who is now retired, lives in a plush apartment building in Old North London We remain good friends, always ready to help each other out whenever needed

I have made many long and lasting friendships within my clientele, and it is enjoyable to be able to meet and greet them where ever I wander throughout the city. I often run across them at the most unexpected times and places. At the car wash, at McDonalds, at the bank or in the malls, the parks or on the city streets. By their warm smiles and friendly hand shakes I know they are happy to see me because over the years we have developed a lasting friendship. It was not just because they felt good about their hair-cut, all this simply brightens my day. However for the most it seemed I always thought it best to kept my personal life and my shop and clientele separate. Thus it seems most but of course not all, of my closes friends are neighbours or people I have met by chance..

When I came to the shop in 1963 there was just wild grass and weeds growing out in front of it. Let us say it was very much in the rough, or its own natural state. I put in six-foot long cement curb stones from the shop to the edge of the roadside, for the cars to pull up to, then a flowerbed behind the curb stone and lawn beyond that. I also cut the roadside ditch to make the place look attractive colourful and neat. At first I used Tipping's lawn mower to cut the grass but it was always out of gas or gave me too much trouble. In the end I bought my own green Lawn-boy lawn mower and ended the problem. It was a good lawn mower. I used it for years.

I decided to change the name of the shop from Southbreeze to Southdale Barber Shop as the shop was just south of Southdale Road. I thought that was good for business, as people would then know the location. I hung a new sign from two square cedar four-by-four posts. Under the sign I dug a large flowerbed about eight-foot square surrounded by large rocks. Things were looking up. While my neighbours, Roy Inch and Don Brown didn't believe in cutting grass or tending flowerbeds they did keep their lots clean and neat.

Jack's First Barber Shop and Brian, Allan and Tracy

The two tipping boys spent a lot of time visiting me in the barber shop. I could depend on a visit from Allan every night. If truth be told, I would have missed them if they did not come in. Jeanette was now a hairdresser and working and managing her shop in the basement of the house. This, along with looking after two boys kept her very busy. She dearly wanted a little girl but knew that along with the shop a baby now would be a handful. The answer seemed to be, to adopt. So in the mid sixties they adopted a little girl "Tracy." The two boys were happy to have a sister.

"Jack and Allan have a Bad Day"

Early one Saturday morning I arrived at work well before my first customer of the day. I had my car trunk loaded with annual flowers that I had bought the night before at Mr. Wilson's on Southdale Rd. Mr. Wilson worked at the old veterans hospital. He had his own home green house in his back yard and he grew great plants.

The flowerbed had been prepared the night before and Allan was waiting on me when I arrived. I remembered how my grandparents and mom had taken the time to show me how to plant things so they would grow. So I had Allan down beside me planting flowers. He seemed happy to help and took pride in the bed when it was done.

At noon I went out to Ritchies my favourite lunch counter for lunch. Two Greek brothers Jim and Louis Lathouris own it. When I returned from lunch I found my flowers pulled out and strewed all over the bed and dying in the hot sun. I felt very sad that anyone would do that to me. I quickly replanted and watered them as fast as I could and then covered them with newspaper to keep the hot sun off them for the rest of the day.

That after noon a young chap came in for a haircut and he told me he had come in while I was out to lunch and saw Allan pulling out my flowers. He had left without Allan seeing him, but he thought I should know about it. I was really hurt that Allan would do this. That night when I took the money to the house, I told Jeanette what had happened. She said she would deal with it. For about two weeks Allan never came near the shop and whenever I saw him I never looked at him or spoke to him. Then one night he came in at closing time in tears and asked me if I could forgive him.

I said, "Yes Allan I can forgive you because I love you but I thought you loved me too?"

Allan said, "I do love you Jack, but NOW I know it."

The good part was I never lost a plant. That's the beauty of having a green thumb.

"Unpleasant Encounters"

There was a local restaurant called, "The California." A huge Greek man who drove a huge car and smoked huge cigars owned it. Whenever he came in to get a haircut he sat reading the newspaper and filled my little shop with cigar smoke while waiting his turn for the chair. When he finally did get in my chair he continued to smoke his huge smelly old cigar practically under my nose and held the newspaper up in front of himself thus guiding the smoke upward. If at any time I tried to carry on a conversation with him he would point his fat finger to his head and move his fat hand back and forth as much as to say,

"Just cut my hair." When you operate a shop you have to understand that a city license is a privilege to own and you must serve all people unless you have a very good reason not to. This man came dangerously close to crossing the line. He was a man who had little respect for others except for his own. Many times mothers with young children would also be waiting and when a small child came near him he would flutter a huge hands at the child and utter,

"Go way, Go way." At other times he brought in his own little over weight and spoiled grand children for a haircut and continuously fawned over them as if they were royalty. Thankfully I have kind thoughts of the most of my clientele. There were some people who didn't know how to cope with a deaf person.

I remember a number of men, who walked in the door already talking as they entered and upon finding out I was deaf backed out the door saying,

"Oh you're deaf, well fine fine, ok, bye." and leave. I don't feel for a minute that they wished me ill. In fact they probably wished me well. But somehow they had the feeling if they chose to give me their business they would somehow involve themselves with my problem, and more problems they did not need. So rather than help a deaf person to earn a living they chose not to get involved.

Mr. and Mrs Bull's 50th Wedding Anniversary

In January of 1967 I flew to Calgary to celebrate Mr. and Mrs. Bull's, Fiftieth Wedding Anniversary held on Saturday January 21st. at the Legion Hall in Oyen. The ticket to fly out was a Christmas gift from my friend Bob Scott. He had also arranged to have Wm. Bull come to the airport to pick me up. There was a lot of snow and it was very cold that winter but it did nothing to dampen the celebration.

A turkey dinner was held for all of the family, which somehow included yours truly, Jack Cooke. Certainly I did feel very much as if I belonged to this family. Later at the legion hall there was a program with many of their many friends taking part, one being an old Scottish friend Bobby McCallum singing and also a song by myself, How Great Thou Art, with Olive Sutherland playing the piano. There were greetings from Prime Minister Pearson and leader of the opposition John Diefenbaker and also Premier of Alberta, E C Manning.

Barry and Diane White are Doing Well

Barry and Diane White were living in Oyen and by now they had two children. It seemed they were doing very well. Barry at that time was building a huge bridge over the Red Deer River south of Oyen. I found it hard to believe how it was that I had taken a fifteen-year-old boy out west, who was running away from the Salvation Army and now he was building bridges, not a small bridge, mind you, but a large one. Barry asked me if I would go down to the river with him one night, as a man from the government was to meet him there. At that time the Alberta government helped small Alberta contractors expand by helping them along financially as their project proceeded. This man was to inspect the work and see that it was proceeding as planned. I remember seeing giant pumps at work pumping river water out of forms where the abutments were to go. Great blocks of ice lay on the frozen river, some with fish frozen in them.

Barry continued to build and expand, build and expand, building all sorts of buildings from Grand Prairie to Calgary. Everywhere you went people knew of Barry, the kid who came west from Ontario and made good. Somehow I felt good about that.

When I arrived home the end of January I was amazed to find the snow all gone and the weather sunny and warm. Bob met me at the Airport with the top down on my 64 Ford convertible. Good times come to an end and I was back to work at earning a living.

By the fall of 67 the mileage on my 64 Ford was getting quite high so I thought it was time to trade again. This time I bought a 1968 Fury three Plymouth convertible with a dark red body and black top. It was a great looking car with a good ride and I was thankful it used a lot less gas then the huge motor in the 64 Ford. My dad was thrilled about my new car but my mother warned me I was going to loose all my hair riding around in convertibles. I guess I should have listened to my mother, but I kid myself. It was acid rain!

Two Hockey Greats "Sittler and Ciccerelli"

One morning two very vibrant young boys walked into my shop. They introduced themselves as Darryl Sittler and Dino Ciccerelli. They were both playing hockey for the London Knights. I have always felt honoured for being able to spend time with these two guys. I followed their careers over the years and every time their names came up I sense happiness for the contact I once had with them. In 1969 Darryl was first pick for the Toronto Maple Leafs

"A Fateful Tragedy"

Often, a friend and buddy of Joe's, who was interested in skin diving, helped Joe on weekends in the Aqua Shop. His name was Mike Hatch. In the summer holidays Mark Moxham ran the shop for Joe during the day until Joe got home from work. Mark was a kid brother of Richard Moxham a long time buddy of Joe's. In August of 1968 Joe and Jeanette and kids left for a few days' holidays and Mike and Mark were to look after the Aqua shop. The last thing the Tippings did before they left was to tell me to keep a good eye on the back yard gates leading to the swimming pool; they didn't want the neighbourhood kids to swim in the pool alone.

It was late in the afternoon near closing time and I was just finishing a hair cut when I saw the flashing lights of an ambulance making a U-turn at the end of the boulevard in front of the shop and turn in on our lot. My first thoughts were, "Did I check those gates this afternoon?" I was sure some kid had drowned in the pool.

When I rounded the corner of the Aqua shop I could see Mike lying face down on the grass with people standing around him. There were the two ambulance attendances and Mark, Richard and his girl friend. Apparently Richard had been barbequing supper and had called Mike who wanted to take a hurried dip in the pool to refresh himself before eating. Working in the Aqua shop was hot when the pump for the air tanks was working. When Mike dove into the shallow pool, he somehow broke his neck, vertebra and spinal cord. I watched as the attendant ran a sharp instrument from Mike's neck all the way down his back, down the back of his legs, down his calves then down the bottom of his feet to his toes. Mike never flinched. I looked at the attendant and said,

"That's bad, uh?" He looked at me and shook his head and said,

"That's bad."

I remember going up to the hospital a few times to cut his hair. I found him with steel pins holding his head straight, and strapped to a board. What a difficult haircut to perform, I cut part of it with him facing the floor then spun the board over and did the front part with him facing the ceiling. Mike went on and took a few courses at Western University to further his education. He got himself a computer a long time ago and keeps in touch with his family and friends.

Many times when I am feeling a bit down because of my hearing loss, or when something had happened that hurt me, I would pop in and have a coffee with Mike. He was always "up beat" and when I left I would think to myself, "If Mike can do it with his problem then I should be able to do it with mine." Life goes on, but Mike and I know life is not always fair. Hopefully down the road, when God takes us home, Mike will walk and I will hear again.

"Time For Dad and Mom To Retire"

In 1969 my dad was 70 and my mom 68 years old so they decided it was time to give up the second farm and move into town. They had been on this farm for 8 years from 1961 to 1969. They bought it for $14,000 and sold it for $28,000. It had served their purpose well giving them a good investment and also a living.

Coveney, who had owned the chicken hatchery had closed down his business and torn down the many huge wood frame hatchery buildings. From this lumber he built himself a new home and a number of other houses on Arthur Street in Mitchell. My Dad and Mom purchased one of these homes for just under $12,000.00 in 1969. They also bought a 21 ft motor home and planned to do some travelling. While my mom loved her little house she was always ready to travel in the motor home.

Before they moved into their new home in Mitchell they came to London and I took them out to the Leon's Furniture Store where they bought the new furniture for the house, kitchen table and chairs, chesterfield and chairs end tables and coffee tables, lamps and then new bedroom furniture. It was all delivered at once.

Much of their old furniture they gave away and lots of old things were burned in a huge bonfire down on the bank of the Thames River. Unfortunately unknown to me a lot of my stuff ended up there too. Sheets music and pictures I had taken over the years out west and boxes of stuff I had received from Uncle Fred and my Aunt Rosena all disappeared.

My sisters and I bought dad and mom all new everyday dishes and cutlery. It was good to see them so happy. That winter I painted every room in the house over in the colours they chose. Over the years they lived in that house I painted the outside twice. I put in flowerbeds all around the house and every spring I would arrive with my car packed full of Mr. Wilson's flowers ready to plant. Dad would have the beds all dug over by the time I arrived. Then he would spend a lot of time grumbling about too many flowers, too many flowers to plant. But once they were in, they took great care of them and the little place was a showcase to all who drove by. No one took more pride in showing off the flowerbeds then my dad did. Whenever someone came to visit them they were taken on a tour by, yours truly, my father. I got a kick out of this because then I knew in spite of all his grumbling about too many flowers he did appreciate it. Those were good years for me and my dad and mom and it just seemed that finally things were going right for us as family.

"Bob Takes Leave"

For some time I had known that my friend Bob who shared the apartment was disenchanted with things here in London. I came home from work one night to find all of his things gone. There was a note saying he would write and explain things to me sometime later. Later turned out to be a couple of years when I got a post card from New Orleans. This left me with more rent to pay than I could afford as I had the shop rent to pay as well as the apartment. About then Randy Scott, Bob's brother had a car accident on Springbank drive. The steering wheel of his car had punctured his chest. He came to see me and asked if I could do the work at the Victoria Order of Nurse Building for him until he recovered.

Little did I know that God was opening another door for me? For almost two months I looked after the VON building cleaning the offices every night and on week ends cutting the grass and doing whatever had to be done while Randy was recovering. When I did this I met all of the staff and they seemed to like me and were satisfied with my work.

Randy recovered and was back to work at the Kelvinator's plant during the day and did the VON work at night and weekends. But Kelvinator had been plagued with strikes for some time and they suddenly decided to close down the plant here in London and move to Quebec and end their problems with their workers. Practically over night Randy found himself without a job so he decided to move to Niagara Falls to take a job there. He came to tell me he thought that if I wanted the apartment and job at the VON they would give it to me. I could not afford to stay on at The Executive House by myself so I put in a tender for the job. I was still cutting hair at the Regina Mundi College two nights a week so I knew I was going to be very busy.

A few weeks later the VON called me over to their office to let me know I had the job. We discussed the work and the free apartment and utilities and also the wages. When I asked about any benefits I thought I blew it. The lady in charge informed me very sternly that this was indeed the VICTORIAN ORDER OF NURSES, and no men were allowed to be more then casual outside workers. I didn't even get paid holidays. If I wanted a holiday at anytime I had to find someone to fill in for me and pay them. However it was a good steady job, which I learned to appreciate as it paid me money and at the same time cut my cost of living at a time in my life when I really needed it. Many times I have heard people say they could not get the job because they were over qualified. I was never over qualified and I was only too happy to do whatever it took to earn an honest buck.

I rented a truck and Randy Scott and Rick Deluca helped to move me from The Executive House to the VON in the fall of 1969.

I remember the first thing Randy Scott did was to back the truck wheel right over top the neighbours little lilac bush and squash it flat, what a way to start off with new neighbour's. Lilac's though are very hardy and sometimes seem to thrive on abuse. It flourished into a mighty bush and grew many flowers. I always remember my Grandma Butson saying her lilac by the gate never grew up until her youngest son, my uncle Bob grew up and left home. It seems grandma cut many switches off the lilac to keep uncle Bob in line.

Chapter 6
LIFE AT THE *VON* HOUSE

The VON House
362 Dufferin Ave. London

The Victoria Order Of Nurse Building (VON) in London sits on the north side of Dufferin Ave. just three buildings east of Waterloo Street. It was a magnificent huge old pale yellow brick house that still had its original slate roof. Four great round cement pillars abutted out in front, two on either side of the cement staircase. On the east and west ends of the veranda was a huge square bulwark of angel stone that held up a sturdy veranda with an elaborated roof. The house was built by an army officer who also built the next two houses to the east for his daughters. Something told me that even then the government leaked a lot of money to people in the right position. There were five outside entranceways on the ground floor and one on the third floor above the veranda. On the first and second floor there were many huge square windows with a half moon window on top of church-like coloured leaded glass, all still in perfect shape.

At the base of each of these windows was a large windowsill with a built-in door embedded in the sill. The drop-in doors had a drop-in brass oval type ring.

Inside these doors were three sets of pull up wooden sunshades connected to ropes, pulleys and weights, ingeniously placed inside the window frame. The downstairs floor was the original, made of solid oak cut into small pieces and set to a design. Never had I seen such a stunning floor. It was a thing of beauty.

There were two fireplaces, one on the first floor and one on the second floor.

Across the rear of the lot one could see the foundation of what was once the carriage shop and horse barns. The driveway and rear lot was gravel when I arrived there but was later hard-topped. One thing I loved was a majestic great old horse chestnut tree about thirty feet out onto the lot from the rear door. Once a year it was covered with the most beautiful white blossoms, which was something to behold. But very late in the fall a ton of leaves and leaf stems came down to be bagged and carried to the curb. I never complained, though as I loved that old tree.

To get to my apartment on the third floor you entered through the front door, which was made of thick oak planks surrounded by an oak doorframe. Outside of this doorframe were narrow windows built in on either side, and then a large heavy oak casing surrounded all this on either side and above.

This front door entered into a large hall with an open wide staircase, a full size banister post and railing facing you, going to the second floor. Mid way the stairs did a sharp left turn. Then you walked down a long hall and turned right and there beside you was a door to a second staircase going up to my apartment on the third floor.

Being an attic apartment, the ceilings on all sides slanted down with the roofline to the walls on all sides, giving the place a rustic loft look. I backed my chesterfields against the wall and it worked out well. There was an open kitchen and living room with the railed-in staircase coming up in the centre. There was a huge walk-in closet and a bathroom along the living room wall then two bedrooms overlooking Dufferin Ave. at the front. The one bedroom I turned into a den or TV room. The whole place was warm and cozy all winter and easy to air condition in the summer

One of my biggest expenses was a new Moffat fridge and stove in avocado green for my kitchen from Don Brown appliances next door to my Barbershop. The two cost me $500.00. They lasted me for many years and in the end I got my money back, but I will tell you about that later.

My agreement with the VON was that while I could have friends come to visit me I was not to have any parties. I was to walk down to the front door and escort my company in and out of the building. If at any time someone came to stay longer than over night they had to be registered. This would be something not everyone could live with but it worked fine for me. The VON nurses came and went 24 hours a day so while they would be happy to know a custodian was in the building they would not appreciate meeting a stranger in the building alone late at night. Every night I was to check the premises before I retired to be sure it was secure.

For a short while I wondered if I had bitten off more then I could chew. While I wished I were busier at the barbershop I still had to stay and put in the time and always be there. The waiting on business to come in is something one never gets use to, and especially so when you knew there was work you could be doing elsewhere. Then there were the two nights I cut hair at Regina Mundi Residential School. It just seemed I was always on the run trying to catch up and was not making enough money for all the hours I put in. The answer of course was that I had to get myself organized and make better use of my time.

First I decided that since I could not do all things one might normally do because of my three jobs, I would eat a full dinner out at mid-day everyday at a restaurant, and more or less lunch every evening for supper. This set me free from making lunch to take to work and that in itself was a blessing. It also made it so I didn't have to spend a lot of time cooking a supper as I had my lunch then, thus I was able to start my VON work earlier.

Soon I was organized and able to do the work in the office building in far less time. I would start the nightly office cleaning at the same place every night and end up at the same way. Gradually things started to work smoothly as I set up a schedule and time to do every thing. This made it hard for people to visit me as my work always had to come first. Luckily I was a night person to start with.

I also wanted to get into a gym and work out, as the sitting in a barbershop was not good for my health. I joined the downtown Y, leaving home at seven thirty each evening and I was back home again by nine. I worked out four nights a week really seriously. The brand new Y, was about two and a half blocks away so I walked down and I walked home. I always showered at the Y before I left as it saved me time. I tried to put one whole hour working out in the gym. Time was the name of the game. If I didn't handle my time efficiently I would have to give some things up and I didn't feel I could afford to do that.

First thing every morning I would have to go down and turn off the VON outside lights. In the winter there might be snow to shovel from the driveway entrance before going in to the shop. As a rule I shovelled the sidewalk and cleared the doorways and entrance to the drive the night before, usually about eleven PM or later. Many mornings a plough would drive by and dump a gift of snow in the drive before I got up. Overall the VON job was a good thing for me, but only because I didn't mind the hours and extra work. If I had worked for Ford or 3 M I would have made more money in an eight-hour shift. I was actually always on duty at one place or another from seven thirty in the morning till near midnight seven days a week with no benefits, or holiday pay. For the most I was self-employed because certainly as a man I could not belong to the VON. Everyone thinks it's great to be self-employed. Everyone should give it a try.

There was a well kept 23 unit apartment building next door to the VON House, and after a few weeks of coming and going I was aware that an older couple living on the third floor overlooking our parking lot watched my every move. He always sat on the north side of the window and she sat on the south side. Some time later I met him down on the lot. His name was Clark Buchanan and he owned the building. His wife's name was Vera. To me, they were always Mr. and Mrs. Buchanan, the same as Mr. and Mrs. Bull had always been, Mr. and Mrs. Bull.

Mr. Buchanan came from Kincardine up the lake north of Goderich. He came home after the war and married and took over the family farm. His wife died a few years later and he decided to sell the farm and buy a 36-unit apartment building in Goderich. Some time later he met Vera who came from Whitechurch west of Wingham. Vera though was a nurse here in London. Clark took a mortgage on the Goderich apartment building and bought this 23 unit building next door to the VON House on Dufferin Ave. It is called The Berkeley Apartments.

Clark also got the job as custodian at the Catholic School around the corner on Waterloo Street. He was a very hard working little man, and a proud Scotchman. He had hired someone to do the everyday work at the Goderich building, but he drove up every week to do the big jobs such as painting, repairs and plumbing.

I found a wealth of knowledge in Mr. Buchanan, which helped me to become a better custodian. Whenever I had a problem with old plumbing, doors or locks he was happy to rescue me. We both took pride in our work, be it cutting the grass or tending our flowerbeds. The neighbour on the other side of the VON house, a Mr. McGregor joined us, keeping his place neat and well kept and soon we had the best-kept ground area on Dufferin Street.

I remember years later talking to a chap who told me that he never could think of the VON property without thinking of it as the place where the snow was shovelled a little wider in the wintertime and the grass was a bit greener in the summer time. That was the kind of comment one likes to be remembered by.

Mrs. Buchanan was a great conversationalist and I enjoyed chatting with her, but she was of a curious nature and just had to know everything. If I was out too late at night she always had to ask where I had been and what I was doing. Lots of times I really didn't want to tell her. So I would say,

" Let's not talk about it."

" But I want to know."

"Ruff."

Mr. Buchanan would be sitting in his chair chuckling as he got a kick out of it. We became wonderful friends. Many times when I came home from work, she would hold a plate of homemade goodies at the window and beckon me to come on over. They waved me off to work every morning and were there to welcome me home each night. On Sundays I would go over for morning coffee.

During the first few years I was there the head office of the Canadian Girl Guides and an organization called Friendship In Action and the John Howard Society all shared the second floor in the building. It came to an end a few years later when the government told the VON it was going to have to expand its Home Care and take over a lot of different kinds of homecare work. So they asked the tenants on the second floor to vacate. The VON borrowed a lot of money to buy office equipment and more new cars so it would be ready for this new work.

Then the government changed hands and the extra workload never came. The VON was left with a huge loan to pay off and there was no way they could do it. They complained to the government and asked them to rescue them from this debt. The government sent an auditor to their office to go over their books. While doing the books they found out the custodian on the third floor received a free apartment and paid utilities. Apparently this was a no no. The VON had been declaring my wages but not the value of the apartment or utilities. So they came calling on me.

At first they told me that they were going to value my apartment rent at the same value as an apartment in Mr. Buchanan's 23-unit apartment building next door. Then they would go back five years and ask me to pay income tax on this.

I told the guy if they did that, the VON would have to either give me more money in wages or I would leave. I explained to him that as a deaf person my chances of getting one good job that paid me a good living wages was nil. That, with all the hours I put in with three jobs I still did not make the kind of money that would please him or most people working for the government. I also pointed out that the VON could not rent an apartment like this out to just anyone, as few people could live with all the restrictions they placed on it.

He was actually very reasonable and in the end they only went back three years and they valued my rent at one half of what an apartment in the building next door cost. There were however no winners as I had to pay extra income tax. Then the VON offered me more money if I would stay. They wanted to keep me on as over the years they had all too many custodians come and go.

When I started working at the VON I made a pack with myself that I would stick this out for five years, with hopes that by then the barbershop would carry me so I would not have to work so many hours. At the end of five year I had bought a new car and some new furniture but for some reason I was not exactly happy with myself, as I didn't really have one cent more saved to show for all this extra work.

About that time The Registered Retirement Saving Plan came into being, so from that very first year I began to put money into the RRSP. At first it was just the cash I received from the VON each month, then I decided to match it from my other income. Somewhere deep inside my head I would often hear my great aunt Becky's voice saying,

"Jack its not the money you make, but what you do with the money you make."

After a few years I decided on another more definite plan. You were allowed to put 20 percent of your net income into the RRSP each year, so in January at the beginning of the tax year I would go to the bank and borrow what I thought would be that 20 percent. The bankers were only too happy to loan you the money, as you would then invest it back in their RRSP. I always borrowed for only one year making twelve even monthly payments. Then when the loan was paid off I would borrow again the following January, always a year before I needed it. This way I always got the cost of the loan back plus some interest on that very first year. Best of all no mater what kind of year I had financially as long as I somehow made the payments on the loan at the end of every year I knew I was ahead as I owned my RRSP.

I was sure my little ole Aunt Becky was up there smiling down on me.

By now all my sisters had children, Laurine had six, Pearl had five and Jean three. As I was growing up I had two Uncles, which stood out, as examples of what I thought an uncle should be. That was my Uncle Loril Butson (mom's brother) and Uncle Guy Starch (my dad's sister's husband). I wanted to be a good uncle to my sister's kids. I wanted them to love me, but I soon found out it was not going to be an easy task. Some things you cannot beg, buy or demand, you had to earn it by being ever-patient and ever-loving and hopeful and in the end, win it. Once won it is a gift of love for a lifetime, which you will treasure for the rest of your life. Years or miles will only add to its endearment. I feel I have won all but one of my nieces and nephews. I miss that one, and I wish I could win her, but life is a two way street and you can't go where you're not wanted or not needed.

When I first arrived at the Barber Shop on Wellington Road there was a farm across the road with a huge red L-shaped barn and a two story white brick house set among tall maples. Every morning the sun rose, shining down on the barn and lot and it looking for the entire world a picture postcard. Far back on the farm there were clumps of trees dotting the countryside and I would often see deer travelling from one clump of trees to another or pasturing on the fields of winter wheat. When I looked southward I could see for miles all the way to 135 or Exeter Road. During the seventies all this was to change. Within a few short years the entire area was built up with houses, schools banks and plazas.

Kentucky Fried Chicken moved in next door to me, with a Restaurant and a carry-out service. They were the first of many more eating-places to come.

One year a few days before Christmas I got a word from Barry White in Alberta asking if I could meet his flight at the London Airport. When he left this country he was not on good terms with his dad or stepmother and now he was not sure how they would welcome him home, but he wanted to see his family at Christmas. I met the flight and he stayed overnight at my place and rented a car to drive up to Stratford and Gads Hill the next morning. I gave him a key to my apartment and told him that if things didn't work out he was welcome to come back and to have Christmas with my folks and me. He never came back and never did return my key.

In October a few years later I flew out to Calgary on a late Saturday night flight to visit my friends at Oyen. I found myself on the bus going east out from Calgary in the early morning as the sun appeared on the eastern skyline. To the west the mountains greeted me, reflecting a mirror of colours on the first new fallen snow. There is always something good about watching a country come awake in the early morning hours that makes you feel a kindred spirit, at peace and at home.

When we arrived in Drumheller we were to have time for our breakfast. In those days most of the towns served you from behind a long counter. It saved them a lot of running around. I ordered coffee and my oatmeal cereal and there on the counter within easy reach was a large cream pitcher full of fresh thick cream. When I went to pour it I could not help but think of my dear old Mrs. Bull, as it was so thick you had to encourage it to pour with your spoon. In my mind I could <u>see</u> Mrs. Bull shouting at me faster, faster as I turned her cream separator in the little entryway of the old farmhouse. She always wanted the cream very thick. It probably tested at least 40 BF.

I had a visit with everyone, catching up on all the news as to how their grain crops turned out and how many spring calves were born and also everyone's family news. I was more and more aware that forever I was going to be a part of these people's lives. They had opened their hearts to me long ago and I was now very close to being called "family."

Barry and Diane were now living in Red Deer and when they heard I was out they wanted me to come and visit them. To get to Red Deer from Oyen by bus you have to take a long trip around. Either you go back to Calgary or up to Edmonton. So I went back down to Calgary and then up to Red Deer. Barry had a grand new large home and two cars, and several trucks for his concrete forming company.

He was surprised that I was travelling by bus as he thought I would have rented a car. At that time I didn't have any money to waste, and I knew I could drive one of Bull's trucks while I was there.

Barry said, " I will have one of my trucks cleaned up and waiting at the door for you in the morning."

I replied. "Oh I can't let you do that."

"Why not? "

"Well its just because I don't usually drive other people's vehicles."

Barry said, "Jack, when I had nothing you were good to me. When I arrived in London not knowing if my folks would let me in, you took me in and gave me the key to your place, and told me to come back if things didn't work out. I still have the key to your apartment. Now I can help you so please take the truck and go wherever you want It's yours for as long as you can stay." What could I say?

Everywhere I went people would see Barry's name on the truck and ask me if I worked for him. It seemed everyone knew how he came west from Ontario with nothing and made good. Whenever they asked me about him I would proudly say,

"I'm the guy that brought him out here in the first place." He made me proud.

Meanwhile hair in the late sixties and the early seventies was getting longer and longer. Styles had gone from the brush cut, the bush cuts and the crew cut, to longer style pompadour styles and weird flat top boogies with side burns and duck-tails Soon the hair cascaded over the ears and down on the collar. I had not been trained in Barber college to cut long hair, so when I heard there was a night course in men's hair styling at Fanshaw College being taught in January 1971 I enrolled. The course was a big help in many ways but I have always felt it was a friend called Fred, a hair dresser who helped me more than any one by teaching me a better technique, one which I chose to follow.

Dad and Mom and Nancy Go West

In the summer of 1972 dad and mom hitched onto their trailer and headed west. They took my sister Jean's daughter Nancy along. She was 15 turning 16 that fall. They visited my friends the Bulls at Oyen Alberta, where Nancy was able to practice driving a car and also my much-loved old Lizzie the truck in the field. The fields are awfully big out there, in fact several hundreds of acres and I have it on a very good report that she did not take out any fences while she practiced her driving. Still she has never been back for a visit and I keep on wondering why.

Elizabeth

They visited the Skinners at Toefield who were old school friends of my mom's. Then they drove to Jasper and down to Athabasca Falls and on to The Columbia Ice Field, then to Lake Louise and Banff. From there they were on the way to Waterton Park, which is on the Canadian side of the Montana border.

While passing through Pincher Creek they remembered I had a friend Lenora living there who was now married to Ron Oddie. They called Lenora on the phone from Pincher Creek and were invited out. That was the beginning of many years of great friendship between Dad and Mom and the Oddies.

Photos of the Canadian Rockies by my father, John W. Cooke

Nancy says she only remembers the trip in part. She remembers being at Bulls and driving the car and truck and of being in the mountains with grandpa and grandma. She is forever happy to have shared this with them. I keep thinking she was exactly the same age I was when I first took off on my first trip west on the Harvest Train all alone. I was fifteen coming 16 in October and all grown up.

The craze in the early Seventies was a razor cut. Everyone wanted you to razor cut his hair. Now some people's hair looks great razor cut, especially the first time. But if you razor cut it every time you end up with split ends in your hair and many, many different lengths in your haircut. The short ends tend to be much stronger than the longer ends and it is a bit like combing your hair over a brush cut beneath. Sooner or later you need a good shear or scissors cut to get control over your hair again. But this kind of talk was a hard sell to kids wanting a razor cut.

The course also taught us to style hair with a brush and the use of gel and a hand held blow dryer. If you have a problem with unruly hair and you can't handle it with a brush by stretching and turning it, then throw a wet net over it and blow-dry it through the net with hot air. The heat turns all the curls and rude ends under. When you take the net off spray the hair with hair spray. The hair is cushioning like, but hard. Do this too often and your hair will look and feel like sun-bleached hay. However the customer goes home looking great but after a day of sweaty labour and a shower he finds out he can do nothing with his hair himself. So in a short time he is back in to see his barber for another razor cut or he blames his barber for a bad haircut. I would try to sell him a scissor cut, telling him it will take two shear haircuts to outgrow the damage, which the razor cutting has done to his hair. But no, all his friends swear by razor cuts, so he will get another razor cut and blow dry and again he leaves the shop looking great and he feels good. But I know that tomorrow he is going to be cussing his barber, as he is sure it is entirely the barber's fault.

The afro-hair-cut was a great hit with teens, especially those with kinky or curly hard to manage hair. The hair was pulled and combed straight out from the head with a wide comb called a pick and then cut to the shape of the head and sprayed with hair spray to hold it there. Some kids went for huge heads of hair. They spent hours picking their hair in front of a mirror and patting it with their hands to halo perfection. Then as if all this was not enough to get attention, bell-bottom trousers and outlandish loud pattern shirts and platform shoes came in style. It was like a crazy cross between a zoo and a sideshow, but somehow we all survived it.

Towards the end of the seventies some sanity returned to men's hairstyles. It is the younger guys that always want change which lead the way to a different style. Each generation just does not want clothes or a haircut like dads. The guys that have the worst haircuts in the world today are those Johnny-come-late guys of the late sixties over into the seventies. They finally gave in and let their hair grow longer just as shorter hair came back into style. They think the Pierre Burton look of the 70's is going to look good on them forever. They walk into a barbershop scared to death of getting into a chair and say, " Just a trim." They sit stiff as a dead man in your chair ...   praying you wont let their ears show. You know before you start that you can't please them. It's hopeless as anything off is too much. They can't seem to see themselves as others see them. They just want to go on looking like Pierre Berton.

There are many stories I could tell you connected to the people I came to know through the Barber Shop. Some people become your friend just because you do a good haircut, and others because you took an interest in what they do for a living or their way of life. For a number of people though it is because they are New Canadians and everyone who they come in contact with on a regular basis is a familiar face among a mass of strangers. They are indeed in need of a friend.

The Sad Tale Of My Friend " A New Canadian "

One morning a very muscular well-built powerful looking man with a great head or salt and pepper hair walked into the shop. He had a warm smile and as he reached out to shake my hand, he said,

"My name is …….. I am Macedonian, I no speak much English."

I said, "You're Greek then are you?"

"No Macedonian"

"That's would be something like people in our province of Quebec saying they are Quebecois and not Canadians" I replied.

"I suppose so, do you like Greek people?"

"Well you're in Canada now. We don't look at things that way. You treat me right and I treat you right and we will get along. Anyway I am stone deaf so we should get along just fine." He saw the humour in this and quickly reached out his hand again to shake hands and said.

"We be friends."

That was the beginning of a long time friendship, in which he shared many ups and downs in his life with me.

Mr. …. came to Canada in the 1970's and went to work for his uncle at a lunch counter business on the southeast corner of Dundas and Maitland here in London. When he felt established he sent for his girl friend in Macedonia to come to Canada and marry him. She worked alongside him at the lunch counter for a few years. Soon they saved enough money to make a down payment on a house in Westminster Park in south London. Over the years they worked and saved to pay off their mortgage. They also had two children a boy and a girl. Mr. … opened one of the first sub shops in the heart of down town London on Richmond Street near Dundas, and it soon became a family enterprise. The family worked it in shifts keeping it open from early morning till 1 and 2 A.M.

This story took place over a number of years, but I would like to enter it all here.

One morning he came to the shop for a haircut and he was exceedingly happy. He told me he had just sold the house in Westminster Park and bought two forty-unit apartment buildings in the north end of London. When he told me where, I knew it was not the best part of town to own Real Estate, as you didn't always get the best tenants. However the price was right and I didn't want to damper his enthusiasm. He moved into one of his own apartments so he could do his own custodian work. He and his wife also put in long hours at the sub shop. Later as the two children grew up they to helped in the sub shop and all seemed to be going well for them so he opened a second shop on Dundas street east. I remember once when he was in for a haircut how he told me he planned someday to retire to Florida on the income he would make from his two apartment buildings. He said,

"Jack, I am on the way to somewhere, but whatever," he reached out to shake my hand, "We be friends." I could not help but like the guy.

Then his dreams all came tumbling down. This is what happened.

The boat people from China arrived by the hundred to Canada's west coast. They staggered up on the beach half dead from hunger and seasickness. They told sad stories about what would happen to them now if they were sent back to China. Our government asked the cities across Canada to open their hearts and wallets and accept them. The city of London volunteered to take some of them. Of course they had to find a place for them to stay. Certainly they were not going to put then in expensive or even mid-priced apartments. The cheapest rent they could find was on the north end of the city. When they found there were a few vacancies at my friend's apartment buildings they asked him to take in some of these boat people and this was the beginning of what destroyed his Canadian dream.

Several families were put into each one or two bedroom apartment. For a number of years more and more boat people arrived in the city and each time the city turned to him to accept more and more of these people. Mr. ... did not want this number of these kinds of tenants. He wanted to be able to chose his own. After all, this was his investment not the city's, nor the Province nor the countries.

It was he who had to keep the building clean and in good repair. These people were not use to counter tops in the kitchen, so they hacked on them and damaged them. They were not use to inside plumbing and with several families in one apartments the toilets were clogged and over flowed. The washing machines were broken down from too many clothes being washed at once. More and more children were born each year and only added to the problem. Kids fixed bikes on the tiled area at the front and side of the building and broke it up. They took their bikes up the staircase and down the halls marking the walls. Mr. ... could not keep up with the damage and the problems. The city tried to enforce repairs and sanitation, but as quickly as he fixed things they soon broke down again. When in his broken English he tried to express his personal stand on all this, the city and the press took advantage of his limited English. He made the statement that these tenants behaved like pigs and of course the CFPL, the Free Press and one of the cities most prominent human rights personnel set out to chastise him.

Together they contributed to his downfall. It seemed the story they tried to get across to the public was that here was a wealthy man who owned two forty unit apartment buildings and he was a racist and didn't want these people in his building. The truth was he was willing to help, but he didn't want the full load.

When all this erupted on TV and the newspaper some people even went to his sub shop to cause him trouble and it affected his business causing it to dry up. All this happened because the general public was kept ignorant of the real problem.

Certainly the city dumped a huge problem on him, and it was the city's problem to solve, not his. No private citizen should be forced to do what was asked of him. In the end he had to walk away from everything, his two apartment buildings and his sub shops. He offered his property, the apartment buildings to the city, but of course the city knew very well the problems they would inherit if they took on the building with these tenants. Mr. …. Came in for a haircut and told me about his loss, in tears.

He said, "I came to this country with intentions of being a good citizen. We have worked hard to get ahead and to have something of our own and see what happened. If this is democracy then I might as well go back to Macedonia."

A few months later Macedonia became a country of its own separating from Greece. Mr. …. Came in to tell me that this would be his last haircut that he was leaving with his family for Macedonia. I remember asking him if he was sure he wanted to do this. He assured me that it had been his dream all his life that one day Macedonia would become its own country free of Greece, so we said goodbye.

A few months later he was back to the shop. He told me that while he and his wife would like to live in Macedonia, his two grown up children who were born here would not stay. They said they were Canadians. He and his wife of course would not stay without the two children as someday they hoped to watch their grand children grow up.

The last I heard of him was that he was driving a huge transport truck to and fro from California to make a living. I feel ashamed and sad that our Great Canadian System was allowed to do this to a good man and his family. Shame shame.

Just before Christmas in December of 1979 I received the shock of my life when Tippings came into the shop one Saturday morning serving me with a letter. The letter told me they had sold the property to Kentucky Fried Chicken next door and I had sixty days to vacate the shop. They tried to ease the situation by telling me they had not sold it as a business but just as Real Estate. I suddenly realized the value of a lease and Joe's words came back to haunt me when he had said,

" Now Jack if you don't trust me, I will give you a lease."

They had bought this property on Wellington Road in 1963 for $23,000.00 and sold it in 1979 sixteen years later for $170,000.00. This was a lot of money at that time. Word soon got out about the sale and some of my customers came in to congratulate me thinking I would have been able to sell my business to Kentucky Fried Chicken for a good thing. They were shocked when I told them I couldn't because I didn't have a lease. So the Tippings sold my business along with the house and the beauty shop and the Aqua Shop all together and called it real estate.

Some local businessmen suggested I threw away perhaps $25,000.00, which I might have got from Kentucky Fried Chicken if I had owned a lease and had been allowed to deal with them myself. It is interesting to note that in January 1980 I got 17% for the money I put in RRSP. That money would have more than doubled if compounded in those five years. I really knew I had missed the boat all because I wanted Joe to feel I trusted him. If I had said I wanted a lease I would be a much wealthier man now about twenty-five years later. The oldest Tipping boy was now 16 and he came in for his last free haircut. He was concerned about what was going to happen to me. He was only 16 but had his own ideas about what was right and wrong.

He said, "Jack it is not right. I told dad and mom they should have given you a lease and let you deal with Kentucky Fried Chicken on your own."

Jack Loses His Shop and Starts Out New

After searching all over the south end of London for a place to locate my barbershop, I settled for a space in a new Plaza at the corner of Jalna Blvd. and Meg. At that time all the money I had was tied up in RRS and the government will not let you use Registered Retirement Savings money as a collateral for a loan. To put in the new shop I needed about three thousand dollars cash. The banks at that time wanted 23% interest on a loan, so I thought surely after what had happened re my business I could just ask Joe and Jeanette for a three thousand dollar loan at a lower rate. They owed me at least that.

They hated to just come right out and say no, so they put me off for several weeks and then when I could wait no longer as I had to have an answer they said no. I found it hard to forgive them as I had given them no reason not to trust me. Well my credit was good at the bank so I took a loan of $3000.00 at 23% and somehow I managed to pay it off along with my RRSP loan.

Regina Mundi had two barber chairs in their shop and I was only using the one. I asked if I could buy the second chair for my new shop. They sold me the chair for fifty dollars, which was a very great buy.

The new shop was to open on the Tuesday of the first week of March 1980. I worked in the old shop right up until the Saturday night the weekend before. Nothing was going right over at the plaza it seemed. I just could not get the management to partition off my shop early so I could start to paint and decorate. The shop area then had to be partitioned off again to build a hallway back to the bathroom. Only when this got done could I proceed to paint and paper. I remember that on the Saturday I slipped over on my noon hour to see what was going on. I found them putting up the wall in the wrong place, giving me more space than I had leased. I called the owner and he said it was too late to change things now and that they would just let me have the extras space.

That after noon Arnold and Pearl dropped into my old shop to ask me how things were going in the new shop. I told Arnold that I had not been able to get them to proceed and get things done so I could start to decorate. There was no way I could get it all done, move in and open the new shop the next week.

Arnold said, "Then you could use a hand."

"I could use a half dozen hands."

Arnold told me he would see what he could do.

Jack In His New Barber Shop On Jalna Blvd.

The next morning, Arnold and Pearl and Bill and Jean came down to help me. I was never so happy to see them in my whole life as I was truly up against the wall. Time was not on my side. You could not imagine the work we managed to do that day. Bill and Arnold first put the oak panelling on the south wall of my shop, while Jean painted the front and rear wall, and I papered the north wall. Pearl papered the hallway and the bathroom, which even included the piping. Then Bill and Arnold put my bathroom vanity stand in and hooked up the plumbing. They also hooked up a basin in the shop area as required by law within six feet of the chair. At noon I took them all down the road to Ritchie's lunch counter at the northeast corner of Wellington and Exeter Road for dinner. The Ritchie brothers fed them well knowing they were my sisters and brothers-in-laws When Sunday night came we had made amazing headway and things were well along the way so I could move out of the old shop and into the new one on Monday.

Bright and early on Monday morning my work crew arrived back in London. They also brought Jean and Bill's son Wayne to help me. Jean and Pearl tackled the big front windows, which were filthy with both dirt and four letter words. Then we washed and waxed the floors before bringing in my new furniture from the vacant area next door where I had stored it. We hung my Glen Loate's animal pictures in a grouping on the oak paneling south sidewall where they stood out beautifully. I remember Pearl and I went over to the mall to buy a clock to put on the rear wall. We found a beautiful one with an oak frame. Bill admired it right away when I brought it back to the shop. Looking at the rear wall I found that Arnold already had a screw in the wall waiting for it. I have that same clock hanging in my kitchen today, a pleasant reminder of time spent in my barbershop.

For My Grand Opening March 4th 1980

My good friend Olga Filko wanted to come to my opening and look after coffee and donuts; she also brought a great looking arrangement of artificial flowers with a masculine touch to go on my cupboard They were just perfect for a men's shop. I received several other potted flowers which I placed in the window along with a huge professional paper sign which said, Village Corner Barber Shop, Grand Opening Tuesday March 4th, 1980. When I had arrived that morning to open the shop I just could not believe it. Not only had everything got done, but also it was done to perfection. The guy who owned the plaza dropped in to congratulate me, and he said, "Tell me where can I hire a work crew like yours? I find all this hard to believe."

I will never forget my family for being there for me when I needed them the most.

The Sign Over My Shop Door

In September 1963, I cut hair in my first shop for $1.25 for adults and $1.00 for children. In 1980 when I opened the new shop at Jalna and Meg I charged $5.00 for adults standard cuts and $6.00 for full cut with styling and $5.00 for children.

One day Joe Tipping's sister came to the shop, partly to see the shop and partly out of curiosity to find out if what she heard about her brother was true. She wanted to know if it was true that Joe and Jeanette had more or less kicked me out without giving me a thing for my business. I told her that since I did not have a lease they didn't have to give me anything.

She said, "Jack, I can't believe it as they always made such a fuss over you. You helped raise those kids by always being there for them everyday. If it were not for you they would never have been able to hang onto that place. You literally paid the mortgage for them each month."

All this may be true but it was not to be, so now I had to realize this and move on. I had never charged Joe for a haircut at the old shop, so now he only came in when his hair was very long for a much needed hair cut, and I could feel that things were not the same between us. Eventually he stopped coming in. In spite of everything that had happened I will always have a place in my heart for the Tipping family as we had many great times together. I was included in many backyards barbecues after work and also Christmas and New Years parties. However one never really knows anyone until the money comes into the picture.

For All of Us, "Life Moves On"

Mr. Buchanan was getting older and his hip gave him a lot of trouble. Caring for the property was getting hard on him. I tried to help out by cutting his grass when I did mine and shovelling snow from his sidewalk and entranceway along with mine. Later when I dropped up for a visit or a cup of coffee, he would say,

"Jack I polished your halo last night, thanks for cutting the grass." I would tell him that that was good, as my halo could stand a lot of polishing.

When someone vacated an apartment, he would have to paint it before it could be rented out again. He would ask me if I would do the painting for him. He would pay me $6.00 an hour, which was above the government rate at that time. Over a number of years I painted just about every apartment in his building. Then he asked me if I could paint the whole inside of the building, meaning the halls, stairways and front and rear entrance ways. I said I could as long as he was not in a hurry. I would paint evenings and weekends. Now that I didn't have the Regina Mundi haircuts to do I liked the extra work. Today I cannot imagine doing it.

I dug his flowerbeds and put in the flowers and flower boxes. I took off the storm windows and cleaned all the apartment windows in the springtime and again in the fall. I cleaned all the apartment windows and then cleaned the storm windows and put them on. It was a big and tiring job especially when I had the same work to do at the VON building too. Today I have no idea how I got it done. Somewhere along the way over the years my get up and go, got up and left me.

In the late seventies my dad and mom traded the trailer for a 21 ft. motor home. They were both in seventh heaven, as they just loved to travel on weekends or take short trips up and down the lake, to Algonquin Park or into Northern Ontario. They even spent a few winters with it in Florida. Mom told me once as much as she loved to go away in the motor home she loved even more getting back to her little home in Mitchell. Indeed it was a showcase with the house surrounded by shrubs and flowerbeds and a lawn that was always kept neatly cut.

They had been west several times over the years with the trailer and the motor home, but when dad announced they were leaving on yet another trip west in the summer of 1982 we hardly knew what to say. Dad was 82 in Oct. the fall before, and we did not want to destroy the faith he had in himself, yet we could not help but worry about them out on the road so far from home. We also knew that once dad made up his mind to do something he was not going to back down. So we sent them off with our best wishes for a safe journey, and begged them to be careful and to keep in touch with us. They made it all the way to Waterton Park Alberta and also visited with Ron and Lenora Oddie in Pincher Creek, then drove on to Oyen to visit with the Bulls. After several weeks they returned home safely. That was the last of their big long trips.

The Dream Car

The 1983 Z 28 Chev Camaro

In late fall of 1982 I thought it was time for a new car again. Like ever so many guys at that time I liked the Chev Camaro Z 28. After searching and comparing prices at many places I ordered a new black 1983 Z28 Camaro from the dealer in Aylmer, a small town southeast of London. I still have the bill of sale; it cost me $15,192.00 with tax. I sold my Dodge Magnum privately to one of my customers only a few blocks from my shop. I told them they could have the car in 6 weeks. That was when the car I ordered was to be delivered. Six weeks came and went and no car and my buyer wanted the car. I had to take the bus to work for two or three weeks until my car arrived and by now it was mid-winter. I can tell you if you're used to riding in your own car to and fro from work it is no fun riding on a bus. When the Camaro finally arrived my friend Nevol drove me down to Aylmer to pick it up. Man! I was one proud guy driving my Camaro back to London that night. I remember stopping at the Wellington Rd. Southdale light and a kid in the car next to me looking over at my brand new black Z28. He inhaled and exhaled deeply and shook his head as if in a sort of dreamy daze and then smiled at me.

My 1983 Z28 Camaro

My Friend John

There are many people who come into our life's temporarily, we call them acquaintances. Others come into our lives and stay. They are your friends.

The London YMCA Burned Down Jan. 1981

The old London YMCA on Wellington Street in downtown London burned down one terrible cold and stormy winter's night in January 1981 and the new one opened the fall of 1982 on Waterloo Street at King. With all the new equipment and plush surroundings at the new Y. I was inclined to work out even more seriously. The great thing about the YMCA was that you became acquainted with many good people young and old and of all nationalities. There was one young guy there who worked out most nights with great energy. He stood out in the crowd. His name was John. As a rule he worked out with an older person who worked at London Life. We had chatted casually but I didn't get to know him very well as with only a little over the hour to work out I didn't have a lot of time to socialize. John was always there when I arrived for my workout and while his friend usually went home early, John himself was still there working hard when I left for home.

One day John came to me and told me his friend was going on a month long holiday out of town and he wondered if I would work out with him for a month. Well as he was only 17 at the time, so very much younger then I was. I was a bit flattered to say the least. However I told him that I noticed he was already working out when I arrived at the gym and he was still working out when I left and I didn't have that kind of time to work out. Naturally he asked me why I had so little time. I told him about my second job as custodian at the VON. Building. He seemed to understand but he was not about to give up. He asked me if he was to give me a hand at night and on weekends, then, could I work out with him? I found it hard to resist, as he was so earnest I told him we could give it a try and see how it worked.

Over that month we became great friends and we are still friends today. John went on to take a sheet metal course at Beal, and after working for someone else a few years he started his own business on Hamilton Road called "Home Comfort." It seemed he put the same energy into his work as he did to his workouts at the gym. I am proud to say while John is only 38 yrs old he is a multi-millionaire today. However to me he is still the young lad I remember meeting at the Y.

Barber Shop Tales

I had a great looking "V" billboard sign made and professionally hand painted advertising my shop and haircuts to put out by the curb. I carried it out every day and every night at 6 o'clock I carried it back to the shop so it would not get vandalized. A little kid called Johnny who lived in a townhouse across from the plaza watched for me at six o'clock and every night he would come running out across the street to help me carry the sign in. Actually if he let me do it by myself I could balance it by the middle to carry much easier. But who am I to spoil a little kid's thoughtfulness? One night his kid brother who was carrying a peanut butter sandwich followed him on the run. As he approached us he stumbled and his sandwich fell apart on the asphalt parking lot, peanut butter side down. The kid stopped and looked and then with two fingers and great care he turned the one slice of bread over on the lot, then carefully picked up the other slice with two fingers, one on either side placed it exactly on top of the slice he had turned over.

He then raised it to his mouth and took another bite. Johnny and I watched with humour, but when I saw him raise it to his mouth.

I said, "No! No! Don't eat that" but Johnny spoke up and said,

"Don't worry about him…. nothing can kill him."   So much for brothers.

For many years it seemed when you didn't know what to buy your dear brother or uncle for Christmas you could always solve the problem by buying him yet another good lambswool sweater. For some reason I never could wear wool and every year I got more and more of these beautiful wool sweaters. My drawers were full, and no room for anything else. So one year just before Christmas I thought I would put up a table at the rear of the shop and sell them. I divided them into three groups and put a stick-on price on each sweater. I also had a few sweaters from a friend to sell. He was asking several dollars more for his sweaters so he put the price he wanted on each of his sweaters. This way even if I was busy with a haircut I could handle the sale. On a Saturday morning when I was very busy a dark man who looked as if he came from the Middle East looked at the sweaters after he had his haircut. He put a sweater in a bag and handed me a price tag, along with the money. After he went out the door the next guy that got in the chair told me that he saw the guy switch the price tags on the sweater he bought. I checked and sure enough he had taken one of my friend's best sweaters and it was ten dollars more then I was charging for mine.

I waited for him to come back for his next haircut; he was always a very fussy customer and frankly I was going to be glad to be rid of him. Finally one day he came in and got into the chair, I put the chair cloth on him and gave him his usual haircut. I think he would know I was not my usual self. When I finished his hair cut I put the clippers in the centre of his head and I told him I knew he had switched the price tag on the sweater he took as one of my customers had told me that day right after he walked out the door. I told him it had cost me five dollars to pay to my friend as he entrusted his sweaters to me. I advised him to reach for his wallet very carefully and give me the ten dollars plus the price of his haircut or I would run the clippers down through his hair. Then I told him he was never to come back to my shop again. At that time I was all muscle from my work out at the gym so he didn't argue with me. In fact he never uttered a word and I never saw him again.

There were many special times I have wished I could hear, as being a barber gives you a lot of insight into life and other people's problems. While I manage to understand a lot, I only get a fraction of what is said. A lot of people just need a deaf ear to lean on, to shed their pain and sorrows or share their joy and happiness. Some little guys came in for a haircut with their daddies, brimming full of great and important news. They had so much to tell me. While daddy had tried to explain to them the barber was deaf, they didn't quite understand, so they just kept on jabbering away while daddy rolled his eyes.

At times like this I try to fit in the right answer with,

"Oh! Is that so and right, right, and you don't tell me" I keep hoping I get it all in the right place. If I get an odd look I quickly cover myself by changing my mind.

I remember this one little chap who was so very earnest in his conversation that I just had to ask his dad if he could explain to me what this was about. His dad said,

"No no, believe me it is best you can't hear him."

Thus I miss quality conversations with children, because I live in a Silent World.

"Break-ins" plague all small shops, and insurance rates climbed out of sight. All those years I had the barbershop I didn't feel I could afford insurance on my apartment and contents and insure the shop too. So I just carried insurance on the shop. This might not have been a very wise decision as I had a lot of collectables, but it worked for me, as I was fortunate not to have had any great need for it.

We always felt that the "break-ins" were done by local kids, and it was petty stuff, as who with a brain in their head would break into a barbershop, especially so if they did not want your barbering tools. One good Oyster Clipper with tax is worth about two hundred dollars, the blades are worth about $50.00 each, and you must keep two large clippers and two smaller trimmers on hand at all times in case one stopped working in the middle of a haircut. A good pair of shears today can cost you $45.00 to $85.00.

However they came looking for money, so usually we left a small bit of change in the till with the hope it would satisfy them and thus they would not vandalize the shop. So they overlook almost a thousand dollars worth of tools and take home a few dollars worth of change. The first times it happens, you feel it is personal, but after a few years and a number of break-ins you know it is just some local kid whose parents have lost control and don't know where he is late at night. If he is looking for excitement and cash, he could hardly take your clippers and barbering tools home to mother. He could easily vandalize your shop but doesn't do it as he most likely knows you quite well and perhaps even likes you, but at this time in his life he would steal from almost anyone, even his parents.

There was a deaf lad about 17 who came in for haircuts and sometimes just dropped by to chat. I had heard he was trouble but I felt because we were both deaf we had a common bond between us. At six every night I would go out to bring my billboard sign in from the curb. One night when I went out I noticed him and two other chaps hanging out around the plaza, but I just didn't give it much thought as I had often seen him on the plaza lot. To me he had a right to be there as he was one of the local kids. On returning to the shop with the billboard I noted only one kid was now visible. The other two had disappeared. The boy walked away as I approached the shop. On entering I saw the till had been pried open and damaged. My day's proceeds were gone and the shop's back door was now open.

I looked out on the lot and none of the boys were in sight. I knew the deaf boy hung out with another boy who lived directly across the street from the plaza. So I hurried over there and the mother answered the door. I told her what had happened and she called her son to the door and had him tell me where this deaf boy lived. I went directly to his home and his father (whose hair I cut) and mother were home. They were very upset as he was already on probation for theft and break-ins.

They were happy I had not gone to the police and said he would go directly to the mall to spend the money so in great haste they left for the mall to try to catch him before he spent it. They promised me they would be at the shop first thing in the morning with the boy and my cash.

True to their word they were at the shop the next morning and I got an apology from the boy and all of my money back. That may sound good, but I still lost in the long run as neither the father nor the boy ever came back to the shop for another haircut, so in the end I lost more money than I gained. However I think I handled it right, as I just didn't want to have a deaf local boy locked up over me. I do feel the dad should have come back to me for haircuts as I had done right by that family, but I guess they didn't know how to handle the shame and that is sad.

Mr. Buchanan next door was failing and needed more and more help each year. I was always there and ready to help him whenever he asked. I actually had a busy enough schedule keeping the VON work up but I wanted to be a neighbour. I painted whole apartments at nights and over weekends. I really didn't enjoy doing the painting, as it was just too many hours work for me on a weekend. I would go back to work a little wealthier but tired from my weekend work.

In the spring and fall I went up on the roof and greased the ventilators. I cut grass or shovelled snow and all the time he would polish my halo. He had family up north near Kincardine but they never came near him to offer any help. I suppose they felt he could hire it done.

They had me over for Sunday dinners and many times for coffee, especially Sunday mornings. It was a great place for me to go to when I had a problem or when I wanted a second opinion. I knew I would always get the right answer but perhaps not always just what I wanted to hear. I felt more and more like a son to them.

Life through the mid eighties was more or less, more of the same. God never meant for me to get wealthy but I dare not complain as some how at the end of every month the bills got paid and my monthly loan payment for my RRSP made.

In 1986 my dear old friend and second mom Mrs. Bull passed away at 92.

Dad and Mom Sell and Move to Ritz Villa

Dad and mom were not getting along very well at home. My mom was diabetic and her memory was getting very bad and she was confused. It was hard for them to sell that little house as they had a happy retirement life there.

Dad and Mom Seeing Me Off

From Their House on Arthur Street Mitchell

I was up to see them on a Sunday, and dad said he was going to put a for sale sign out on the lawn the next day and he was going to see if he could get $50,000.00 for the place. The place had been well kept up inside and out.

I told him I thought it was worth more and that he should ask $60,000.

He put his sign out and it was sold within a couple days for $60,000.00. Dad was so proud of this and kidded every one he was going to start selling real estate. They bought the house in 1969 for $12,000.00 and sold it 15 years later for $60,000.00.

It's called inflation and it is supposed to be bad for us. It was hard to see all their treasures sold off in an auction sale, but they held nothing back. I had bought dad all kinds of tools over the years for his birthday, Christmas or fathers day. I had often said,

"Oh well I can't lose, I will get it all back some day as I am the only son."

How very wrong I was as every tool was put in the sale, nothing held back.

They moved into Ritz Villa, one of Mitchell's finest retirement homes. It took a while to adjust and settle in, but they seemed to make the best of it. Dad still had his wheels and that alone meant a lot to him. There was a bad winter or two and dad just let the car sit on the lot all winter. He was good about not driving at night as his eyesight was failing him. If he went out to visit he arrived home before dark.

I am sorry to say we sort of tricked him out of his driving license in the end, as we wanted him off the road before something bad happened. His birthday was Oct. 21st and his driver's license was due for renewal on that date. We said,

"Well since you don't care about driving on winter roads why don't you take a six month licence and save money?" That appealed to dad. He thought that might be a good idea. However the next spring when he wanted to renew his license, he could not drive the car to Stratford to renew and that was just as we had planned it.

My sisters had told me not to give in to him if he asked me to drive him to Stratford. Sure enough one fine spring day he asked and he was very angry with me when I said I could not do it. He left the room in a huff and did not come back until I was ready to go home. As I walked out the door of their apartment I said,

"I will see you in a couple weeks."

Dad said, "Well we will be here, where else would we be? We can't go anywhere" It wasn't funny for him, but I have chuckled over that many times over the years.

He got a fair price for his Grand Fury Plymouth car selling it right off the Ritz Villa lot and this seemed to help him to forget the pain of being without his wheels.

Wm. Bull Passed Away

March the 8th 1987 I got the sad news that my dear friend Wm Bull whom I had worked for so many years ago had passed away suddenly in the Red Deer Hospital of a heart attack. He and Alma had been visiting Alma's brother near Delburne when Wm. had pains, so they rushed him to the Red Deer hospital where he spent the night. The next morning they were ready to release him but he suddenly took a massive heart attack and passed away. I grieved for Wm; he was a good man a good husband and father and had been a good friend to me.

My Friend Mike Returns To The West
In Search of His Roots

In the spring of 1987 my good friends Mike and Jigs took a trip west, to see the country and to visit Mike's many uncles, aunts and cousins in the area far to the north west of Peace River, a place called Worsley. Mike, like all of us wanted to return to his roots, and to visit the old farm on which he was born and lived for the first few years of his life. When his dad and mom left Worsley with him in tow for Ontario, he remembers vowing he would return, and return he did, but many, many years later. Mike and Jigs had three children by now, Shelly the oldest then Connie and Joe. Connie was now living in Prince Albert BC, so after they finished the visit at Worsley they drove south into the interior of BC into the picturesque country of Prince George. It seems Connie had just recently moved there from the town of Creston a fruit and vegetable area at the south end of the Kookenay Lakes, and only ten miles north of the Idaho Border. She wanted her Dad and Mom to drive down there to see that area as she thought it would make a great place for them to retire to, when the time came.

When they reached the Creston valley it was love at first sight, and before they left they bought an empty piece of land out in the country south of the town and 6 miles north of the Idaho border. It was a bit less then 50 acres and a mixture of level alfalfa fields, bush, swamp and an ever running fresh water creek that winds it way down from the mountains. One day they would return to build here.

One Of Many Fruit and Vegetable Stands
In Creston BC

Lenora and Grace Travel East

September the 10th, 1987 my friend Lenora Oddie left Pincher Creek Alberta with a friend Grace Snell for a trip east to Ontario. They ended up visiting my dad and mom the evening of Sept. 19th. A few days later on a Monday they came to London and I took them on a royal trip down to Niagara Falls and area. Neither of them will ever forget the great effort it takes to get in and out of the back seat of a Camaro Z 28. They took turns grumbling as to whose turn it was sit up front and whose turn to sit in the back. I have never heard so much grumbling and grunting and groaning in my life and I was never been able to live it down.

While driving around Southern Ontario I have never felt a great need to consult a road map. They were constantly worried that I was lost. Actually I did get lost once when I took a short cut but men never admit getting lost to lady friends; it is not manly and it's very unbecoming. These two women should never travel together as each one has a mind of her own. Once out of the car they walk off each in her own direction. Neither one will follow the other. There was a huge crowd at the falls and Lenore went east and Grace went west, I stood half way in between them calling, beckoning, pleading for everyone to stay together or someone would get lost. But they paid me no heed. I would hate to have to act as a guide for a busload of western women as unlike cattle they won't follow the leader.

Lenore and Grace went back to Ritz Villa in Mitchell to say good-bye to my dad and mom, and that was the last time they had a chance to visit While Lenore was there, dad complained that he was not feeling well and was in pain. The ambulance was called and took him to the Stratford hospital. They found he had to have surgery for tumours in his bowels. The operation went well but a day or two after the operation he had a mild stroke. This seemed to rob him of his strength and will to get better. He pleaded with us to make them stop the recovery program, as he just had no strength to endure it. We told him it would mean the wheel chair if we did this. But he reasoned that a lot of people spent most of their lives in a wheel chair and he didn't feel he had that many more years left to live. Right then all he wanted to do was rest and be left alone. So we gave in and let him do this.

When he came out of the hospital Ritz Villa was not prepared to handle people permanently in a wheel chair. So in a short time he and mom were separated when he went to Smiths Nursing Home in Mitchell. Mom began to fail a few months later and she was moved to the same nursing home as dad, but because of various problems they thought it best to keep them separated. This always made it difficult for us when we went to visit. Each wanted more of our time, as they were lonely.

My Mom Passes Away

June the 4th 1988 mom had a massive stroke first thing in the morning and passed away. Dad in his wheel chair was not well enough to attend her funeral. Mom's funeral service was held at the Lockhart Funeral home in Mitchell.

I don't think anyone is ever quite ready to see his or her parents pass away. They may be old, weak and frail but while they are with us our lives and the lives of the family circles around about them. They give balance to the family they represent. They are the rock, the glue that holds us all together. When they pass away we find ourselves thrust forward to fill that vacuum and that is somewhat scary.

I remember that morning as I travelled north on the 23 Highway south of Mitchell on the way to the funeral home. I felt numb and still in shock. Then suddenly the smell of new mowed clover hay wafer into the car. In that instant my mind was set at ease, as it seemed my mom was saying to me, "Jack do not weep for me, for I was ready to go. Smell that new mowed hay, it is ready for the harvest. To each and all living things there comes a time that we must go. I am now at peace."

Mike and Jigs Chubak Pull Up Stakes and Go West

All winter long my friends Mike and Jigs Chubak's only thoughts were of Creston BC and the piece of land they had bought out in the valley. In the spring they ended up selling everything here in the Ontario and moving west to Creston BC. They found a place to rent while they investigated the cost of building a house out on the land they had bought. For one thing Mike wanted to build the house near the back end of the property in front of the bush. He loves nature and that is where he wanted to be. There was a road line all down the west side of his land but as yet no road, and for one person they were not going to move yet to build it. So he would have to upgrade a lane the full length of his property from the existing road. Then he would also have to bring in the electric power, which would cost him a fortune; also he needed a well for water. Upon checking on all these costs it seemed just too much. What they actually needed were other new neighbours to move into the valley and share the cost.

Upon checking the cost of houses in town they were amazed to find that you could buy a nice clapboard house for $36,000 to $42,000, and therein lies a story.

Creston was full of nice little vacant houses all with weathered wood siding in need of repairs, paint or recovered with new vinyl siding. It seemed that during the eighties the Japanese flocked to BC with a lot of money to invest in many things. Lumber and surface coal mining were high on the list. There were few good year-round paying jobs to be had in the Creston area. So anyone who wanted a good pay check had to go north to where the jobs were, places like Kamloops, Williams Lake or Prince George. Many just locked the door on the house and went north thinking that in time they would come back. However places like Prince George became a big city of 75,000 people and it offered all the benefits of big city life where Creston was strictly a beautiful but small mountain town. So the houses in Creston were for sale..........cheap.

During the eighties many second world war veterans who retuned to Alberta after the war were turning 65 and tired of a lifetime of hard winters. They dreamt of a little home in the BC interior where it was not so cold, a place where they could enjoy a rose garden and some fruit trees and free of shovelling snow. Creston is just a day's drive from Calgary, Lethbridge or Fort McLeod and all of Southern Alberta. Mike started to buy up some of these homes, remodel and cover them with vinyl siding. As fast as he could fix them up he sold them.

Over the next few years I flew out to Calgary and visited the Oddies at Pincher Creek then rented a car and drove out to see Mike and Jigs, Now I don't want to get ahead of my story here as I will be writing more about my ventures into BC.

Meanwhile back in Ontario Jack is still cutting hair at his shop "The Village Corner Barber Shop" at Jalna and Meg. My business was stable but never quite what I wanted it to be. I know all about watching the end of the month come up and having to meet rent and utility bills. Still I had always managed to keep a kitty for a new car when the time came so I didn't have to go into debt.

Jack in the Barber Shop

I Trade My Z 28 for a Grand AM

I was getting a lot of miles on my Camaro Z 28 by the fall of 1989 and my mechanic said it was time to let it go. He told me a number of things he felt were going to go wrong with it. So he offered me $4,000.00 for it, and I was a bit shocked. I had paid just over $16,000.00 for it in 1983 and I had the feeling a Camaro would hold its price better than that. The motor had always leaked oil at the gaskets and he made a big thing of that saying the motor would have to come out to do this work and it would cost me a lot of money. A friend of mine told me once he never saw a General Motors car that didn't leak some oil at the gaskets and not to worry too much about it. So I took the risk of taking the car to the car wash and using a degreaser and then washing the motor up clean. It looked really super and didn't show any real leaks. The car itself was without any rust and looking like new. It drew a lot of great comments, and every kid on the block wanted it, but didn't have the money.

I put it out on the lot with a 4 sale sign on it with an asking price of $8,000.00.

I had a lot of offers but not quite what I wanted. Then one day at noon a man came in and asked about the car. He said that his son was looking for a black Z 28 with the same bottom lines I had on mine and that his son would come to see the car the next morning.

The next morning the boy and his mother were on the lot waiting on me when I arrived. The boy's eyes were shining bright as he walked across the lot to look at the car. He could hardly contain himself. After walking around the car a couple of times he got in behind the steering wheel and looked out over the dash and at the upholstering that was spotless. I can see him now; he hit the steering wheel twice with the palms of his hands and said,

"Mom, this is it, this is it, this is the car I want." This poor boy was in love, and I was sure I was going to sell him this car.

We went into the shop to talk about the deal and the mother offered me $7,000.00 and I said no the price is firm at $8,000.00. She offered me $7,250.00 and again I declined. The poor boy said,

"Mom" in a pitiful and pleading voice.

The mother offered me $7,500.00. Again I reminded her that the price was firm.

The poor boy again looked at his mom in desperation and wailed,

"Mom"

She offered me $7,750.00 but I held firm. The boy and his mom went back out on the lot to look at the car again and I wondered if I was pushing my luck. But in ten minutes they came back in and said they would take the car at $8,000.00, and she gave me a down payment. They let me drive the car for a week so I would have transportation to go to dealers to buy my new one. I knew they lived just off Trafalgar Street and one day a year later I happened to be driving by and I saw the car sitting in the drive spotlessly clean, so I stopped to ask them how it had turned out. They were happy with it and had no real problems. I noted it now had tinted dark window glass and sporting new wheels. They showed it to me with pride and somehow it made me happy that it had found a good home.

I finally settled for a 1989 two door black Pontiac Grand AM SE which cost me $22,260.20. I arranged for the buyer of my old car to buy it from the dealer, as at that time there was only a Provincial Tax on the difference, which you had to pay between your old and the new car. The federal government collected a hidden tax, which the dealer paid when he ordered the car. This was the last car I was able to buy where we didn't have to pay a Federal Tax. The new way was supposed to be better for us as it lowered the cost of the car when you went to buy. However today you must pay the whole tax on the value of a new car and not on the difference. By changing the rules the government always wins.

My New 89 Pontiac Grand AM SE

The VON Decides To Move

About this time there was much talk going on in the VON building about moving to a new location. They had outgrown the facilities and especially the parking lot. Also the people living in Mr. Buchanan's apartment building were constantly complaining about the traffic under their windows and at all hours.

On the other hand Mr. Buchanan was getting older and found the work a bit more then he could handle. One day as I was chatting with the Buchanans about the possibility of losing my job if the VON moved out and he asked me if I would consider taking on the custodian work in his building. He asked me what I was paid at the VON and I told him $150.00 plus a free apartment and utilities. He said he would offer me the same deal except that I would have to pay for my hydro and cable TV. Then he added,

" I promise you it will be a whole lot less work than looking after the VON building."

It was late fall 1989 and he wanted me to start right away as he was going in for a hip replacement sometime soon. First I felt I should talk to the VON, as after 19 years of being their custodian I'm sure they looked at me as being just a part of the environment, or perhaps a permanent fixture to their property. They told me they were close to closing a deal on property on York Street. I suggested that I would stay on for awhile and do the work for both of them as best I could while I cleaned and redecorated the apartment at Mr. Buchanan's before I moved in. My friend John was a big help to me at that time taking the cupboard doors off and sanding them of the many layers of paint over the years, then repainting the cupboard inside and out and putting on new Amerock handles and hinges.

One thing that bothered me greatly was that the previous tenant had watered plants in huge pots sitting right on the carpet and rotted a huge hole in two places.

When you vacuumed over the spots you grabbed the carpet and ripped up more. This was the original carpet that was put down in the building. It was old and well worn. I wanted a new one, but Mr. Buchanan said no to that. So I ordered new carpet on my own and told Mr. Buchanan I would just lay it down on top of his and not fasten it down so if I was to leave I could take it with me.

Mr. Buchanan came to me with a deal. If I removed the old carpet and took it to the curb he would pay for a new under pad and the installing of the new carpet. If I left before three years he would pay me for the carpet but if I stayed longer then three years the carpet was his for free. I said OK; in the end he got a cheap carpet. I moved my own Fridge and stove in from the VON House, as they looked better.

A short time later one of the VON office workers took the custodian work over. I was finished working for the VON and I was rather sad to see this come to an end.

Bill and Jean and Arnold and Pearl and Laurine and her daughter Karen (my niece) came to help me move next door. My Friend John McMahon and Nevol and a few others helped form a chain from my apartment at the VON down the stairs across the lawn and to my apartment next door. As fast as Laurine, Karen and I could pick things up they disappeared down the stairway on the way next door.

I never dreamed I had so much stuff. 19 years in one place is far too long.

I will always think of the VON kindly. I love that old house, and the apartment that I had there. The job I had there helped me greatly to set up a savings plan that worked for me, at a time when interest rates and Mutual stocks made you good money. Now many years later I often go out of my way to drive by and look.

I still remember my first night after moving into Mr. Buchanan's apartment building. It was the first time I ever experienced a panic attack. I had felt very secure at the VON building and for some reason I had the idea this was not a good move. Have you ever heard the expression used?

"He is a great guy for a friend, but I would not want to work for him."

Chapter 7
The Berkeley Apartment Bldg

350 Dufferin Ave. London

The first few weeks I had trouble sleeping, I was working all sorts of hours, trying to please everyone and then I also had to unpack my things to get settled in. The strange thing was it seemed, as if Mr. Buchanan was now a very different person. When he saw me from afar he didn't know me, and many times he would turn and walk away instead of towards me. Suddenly our relationship had cooled. It donned on me now that he was my boss and he was no longer my friend. I knew there were people like that out there but this was actually my first encounter.

However I was sure it would pass as I was bound to please. I set up a working schedule so I would be sure to get everything done. I was to vacuum the three flights of halls floors and staircases twice a week, Wednesday and Saturday nights. This worked well for me, as I would put my laundry in the coin operated washer and dryer in the laundry room while I vacuumed. When I finished the vacuuming, I walked up and down the halls with a bottle of spray cleaner looking for finger marks or marks of any kind on the walls, door and glass. The front and rear entryways were to be cleaned every night. The garbage barrel in the furnace room under the garbage chute was to be emptied every night and carried outside. When the snow came the sidewalk was shovelled across the front and up to the front steps. I felt nothing was left undone. Yet I could not shake the feeling something was wrong. For one thing I was no longer invited to the Buchanans for coffee anymore, and if bi-chance we met in the halls we never had a comfortable conversation like we had before.

Often my friend John walked home with me from the Y to chat and stayed for coffee before going home. It was on such a night I first went straight to the furnace room so I could put the garbage outside before going up to my apartment. Mr. Buchanan suddenly appeared in the furnace room doorway and said,

"Where have you been?"

"To the Y"

"What are you going to do tonight?"

"Well just empty the garbage barrel and put the garbage out"

"That's all you're going to do," he asked?

To which I said, "What do you want me to do? Tell me and I will do it."

"I just wanted to know what you are going to do tonight, that is all"

I said, "Look, your hall carpets are clean, the entrance ways are clean, there are no marks on your walls and the snow is all cleared away, now tell me what it is you want me to do and I will do it?" He spread his hands out at his sides and walked away, as he didn't really have an answer. Right then I made a mistake that I regretted later. I told him I could tell for some reason he was not happy, and when he was not happy I was not happy either. I would stay until spring and then I will go if that was what he wanted. Little did I know, I had handed him exactly what he had wanted, a way out of his deal with me.

Carol and Nell Millar had moved into a two-bed room apartment on the second floor on the east side just inside the door. One night quite by chance I walked home from the YMCA with him. He told me he had worked at custodian work with Clark (Mr. Buchanan) at the Catholic Central High School and that he had just retired. Mr. Buchanan had just hired him to do the custodian work at the apt. bldg. He was to start the first of March. I was of course a bit shocked as this was news to me. I had all but forgotten about that conversation with Mr. Buchanan.

Carol had just moved in a few days ago and we had not met until just now. He didn't know I was the present custodian just yet. So I asked him how much money he got for doing a job like that. He said he was to get a free two-bed room apt. in exchange for looking after the property. So now I knew what had been bothering Mr. Buchanan all along, In order to get me to work for him he offered me the same deal I was getting at the VON which was a free apartment and $150.00 a month. Then later he found out his old friend whom he had worked with was soon retiring and would do the work for less money than he had offered me. This wore heavily on him and bothered him night and day, until I had handed him a way out.

This was a chance for him to break his deal with me. If I would leave in the spring, he would save over one hundred dollars a month.

One night about the end of December 1989 Mr. Buchanan came to my door to say,

"You said you would stay till spring and then leave, so I will set the date for the first of March and then you will be done here." I was expecting it so I was not at all surprised. He told me if I wanted to stay on, I could rent the apartment from him.

As I knew most of the tenants by now, I decided to stay on, as there is no fun in moving if you don't have to. Besides who would help all these little old ladies put in their air conditioners and take them out, or hang venetians and blinds and fix their taps, if I left them. I also painted and hung wallpaper, I could never say no.

I loved and respected this area of London, the huge beautiful old homes, the tall maple trees and the city centre skyline always present as a backdrop in the south and west growing ever taller each year. After living all these years in this area it seemed home to me. There was only one thing that bothered me here and that was the air quality. Every morning and evening thousands of cars spewed out carbon dioxide into the air coming and going and sitting at stoplights. On quiet nights it lingered long below the great forest of trees leaving us gasping for air.

This older part of the London city with its tall trees and historic homes is known as "Woodfield." The Woodfield Area has a very active committee of local residents set up to protect its historic homes trees and property. Before making any changes to your property, house or driveway you have to get it past this committee and then city hall. That is not always easy. You cannot just buy an old house and turn it into apartments or blacktop your lawn to extend your parking.

City hall and this committee work together to preserve the area and that is good. I loved to go for long walks late after dark past these old estates, some dark and spooky and others flooded with the warmth of light from within. In the daytime you see and admire only the outside, but at night you see a different dimension and you are more aware this is not just a house but also a special heritage home showing all its warmth and loving care. Passing by you will glimpse coloured windowpanes and old staircases and wonderful old chandeliers. Attic lights on the third floor show beams and sloping ceilings, all this rich in yesterday's culture and beauty safely protected for us now and hopefully well into the future.

With the help of the Woodfield committee and city hall it will be there for a long, long time.

A TV Caption Machine

It was while living in this area during the 1980's that the Canadian Hearing Society and Rogers Cable made TV Caption Machines available to the deaf and hard of hearing. No other one thing made my Silent World more enjoyable. then TV caption.

How many times have you heard a person say they stayed home and watched TV? They were lucky as they also heard it. I watched TV for many years and never heard it and I found it almost impossible to lip-read TV. It's sort of like trying to read writing by looking in a mirror. It appears to be backwards. The captions machines were a wonderful gift to the deaf, and a gift they actually were. To get one you had to go to your family doctor and get a letter to give to the Canadian Hearing Society telling them you were <u>legally</u> deaf. Then you became a member of the CHS (Canadian Hearing Society) and they issued you a form to take to Rogers Cable where you could pick up your TV caption machine free of charge. Not only that, if you had any problem with them you just returned them to Rogers where they would exchange it for another, <u>free</u>. I still have and use my caption machine on my RCA TV that I bought in the fall of 1989.

At that time RCA did not have the caption in their TV. I found out later a few other models did. It is only since the 1990's that most TV came with close caption within the set. While all late model TV today have the caption within them sadly very few people know how to turn it on. When I go to visit people, very few think of turning it on for me. If you ask them to turn it on they spend the whole evening trying to turn on the caption and the evening is spoiled for everyone.

At 92 My Dad's Health Was Failing

During this time my dad's health was failing fast. Life in a wheel chair was very much different from what he was use to. I found myself visiting him each weekend, as I knew our time together was not going to be too long now. For the first time in our lives we looked forward to seeing each other as father and son. My dad talked to me, and told me many things he would never have spoken of years ago. His greatest wish was that he could live his life all over again, for as he said,

"Jack, things would be so much different between us if I could do it over again."

I knew then that I loved him, and he loved me. It is sad that sometimes life takes us on such a long journey before we find ourselves, and what we were looking for. Those last few months we shared together healed a lifetime of misunderstanding.

By Christmas dad was just a shadow of the man he use to be. His last thoughts were of his family, so he had us all together in a place that use to be the old Plaza Theatre on Main Street in Mitchell for a Christmas dinner on him. He himself was not able to be there. This would be our first Christmas without our mom and dad. This was in itself sad. On Jan. 4th.1990 a little over a week later dad passed away.

Dad's funeral service was held at The Lockhart Funeral Home in Mitchell. On the evening of visitation I stood for hours with my sisters and family greeting the hundreds of people who came to pay their respects. They came in a never-ending line and I found it hard to believe that my dad's life had touched all these people.

It was sad that it took my dad and me a lifetime to find each other, but as I said away back in the beginning of this story, it seemed as if dad was able to talk to everyone but his son. He had made no attempt to talk to me, or be close to me. I always had the feeling that perhaps he never really wanted a son, until late in his life. Perhaps I could share the blame, as I know I had too many personal problems. I guess we will never know, " What might have been," as we do not get that second chance.

I remember my sister Jean saying to me that night after the funeral,

My Dad and Mom and My Grave Stone In Mitchell

"Now that both dad and mom have both passed away we don't want you going back to London and not coming up to Mitchell to visit us anymore." I appreciated that very much, but to this day it just seems that because I had always done the driving to Mitchell to visit dad and mom they don't feel they need to drive to London to visit me. So we don't see each other near as much.

Soon it was March the 1st. and I had to give up my custodian work at the Apt. Bldg. I found myself for the first time in years with only one income, and frankly it worried me.

There is little profit in running a one chair Barber Shop because of all the expenses. One has to pay not only the rent for the shop but also the shared cost of the plaza. Then there is insurance, heat and hydro and both property and business tax. Then I must have money for rent for my apartment and the utilities there.

For a couple of years I had to manage everything very close. Then at income tax time one spring I happened to have a chat with a very nice older lady at the income tax office downtown. She had some very good advice for me; she encouraged me to start taking my Canada Pension out a year early. She showed me the figures on what would happen and while it made only a small difference in what I would receive monthly for the rest of my life, it would solve my financial difficulties right now. Then too, the bonus was just because you received it did not mean you had to spend it. At that time you could put money into your RRSP up until your 71st. birthday so I rolled half of this money back into my RRSP. This gave me a better return on the money than I would have got inside my CPP.

Carol Quits As Custodian

Mr. Buchanan lost Carol as his custodian within six months. It seemed they could not work together. So he hired another younger tenant who lived on the first floor. This did not seem to please him either so one night he came knocking at my door and after a few minutes of difficult conversation he asked me a question which I did not really understand and I have pondered it ever since. He asked me.

"How much time do you really have?"

I said. "What do you mean?"

He said, "To look after a place like this. How much time would you have?"

I pondered this as I was not at all sure just what he was getting to, so I remember saying,

"Well experience has told me we all have the same amount of time, and we all have to put first things first and then make the most of the time that we have left. With me the Barber Shop comes first and then whatever else works in after that."

He did not like the answer, and as he turned to go I could make out him saying,

"I'm talking about this place and that is not good enough. This place has to come first." again he turned to leave.

I said, "I don't want the job because I cannot please you."

"Yes you can, but you have to put this place first."

"As long as I have the Barber Shop it will always come first." He was not happy.

A few days later Mrs. Brown who lived across the hall stopped me and said.

"What ever did you say to Mr. Buchanan to make him so angry at you?"

I said, "I don't know, what did he say to you."

She said, " He is going to have to sell this place now and it was all because of that damn Jack Cooke." I told her about the conversation I had with him, and that he wanted me to take the custodian work back on. She thought it was actually more than that and that it might have been that he wanted me to take the property over from him somehow. So that was why he has said the property had to come first. It was left like that and Mr.Buchanan never mentioned it to me again.

Selling the apartment building was not an easy task, as like so many other older buildings it had got caught in the government rent control trap. That is when rent controls were put into effect. Mr. Buchanan's rent was modest and locked in and ever after that he could only raise the rent by the guideline set by the government each year. Well-kept lawns and great flowerbeds and a clean well-maintained building did not count. Your rent could only go up perhaps 1 to 3 percent a year. At that time the rent there was about $300.00 a month so it would go up three to nine dollars a month. It would take years to get the rent up to $500.00 a month.

Thus people interested in buying an apartment building with little money down had to buy it cheap in order to make it pay for itself from this low rent. However there are people out there who know how to work the field and turn a profit.

Stranger The Fiction
Or How the Government Gives Money To The Rich

I won't use any names here but after a time the building was sold to a foreign family of brothers and uncles who were into Real Estate. This is what happened.

An older Uncle bought the place from Mr. Buchanan for a very modest price. Within a short time he resold it to his nephew for fifty thousand more then he paid for it. Now I don't know but I doubt very much that this fifty thousand ever changed hands. It was just a way to increase the market value of the property on paper to get a loan later. He then approached City Hall for a free $100,000 government grant to make improvements on this as a an older city apt. building.

The city asked that he put up one third of this money or $50,000 and then he would get this $100,000.00 forgivable government grant. He went to the bank and extended his mortgage by $50, 000.00 and used this money to obtain the loan at city hall. Then when the work on the building was finished he would apply to the rent control board for a larger rent increase explaining that he has just made $150,000.00 worth of improvements to the building. They will allow him to jack the rent away up beyond the government set rate for the year. Yes it stinks to the far heavens that our government would promote this, as he actually using our tax money to improve this building. Then the kicker is the rent control board allows him to raise his rent Its like asking us to pay back his $50,000.00 in higher rent.

In this case the owner lived in the building and spent most of his own money, the $50,000.00 in his own apartment. He tore out the kitchen and the bathroom and replaced it all new - far beyond what the rest of us had. Inside his entrance door was a new marble-like tile floor. He raised his dining area floor and even put in a great round post for décor. He put in a new chandelier and all new lights then carpeted the whole apartment, and then added new doors with new hardware and all new moulding and baseboard. Its easy to see where most of his $50,000 went.

You might ask how do I know all this? Well when he raised our rent we were allowed to go to the rent control office here in London and go over all his business and make copies. It is all there for us to see, while we might object it was all legal.

Mr. and Mrs. Buchanan moved out before the new owner took over. They moved into a beautiful new high- rise not too far away and life went on for us all.

That winter the new owner put two huge steel bins on the front lawn and started the improvements. First they replaced the windows one apartment at a time. Never again were they going to have to put storm windows on in the fall and take them off in the spring, and never again were the tenants going to get their windows cleaned for free twice a year. Next they replaced the rough plaster in the halls and added moulding. For years the plaster had been popping off in the humidity of the summer. New chandeliers were hung in the entranceways front and back. Most of this work was what one would call exterior work. What the tenants got was a very small cheap vanity and basin with taps for the bathroom, and new cheap melamine doors but good hardware on the kitchen cupboards. Therein lies my story.

If you remember away back I told you when I moved in to this apartment I had replaced the kitchen cupboard hardware, with Amerock handles and hinges. I had asked that they let me know when they would be ready to do my place so that I could have the hardware off before they arrived. I came home from work one night to find my new doors hung with Amerock hardware exactly the same as what I already had. I asked them about this and where were my handles and hinges. They said they had no time to take off the old hardware and that my doors and hardware were in the bottom of the bin out in front. That weekend I went to the bin and I could not see my doors, I threw everything out piece by piece onto the lawn and as they had said there were my doors on the very bottom.

But not one door or drawer had any hardware on them. So I left my doors out and threw everything else back in. On the Monday morning I confronted them about their dishonesty. I gave them a box to put the new hardware in. Begrudgingly they did. The moral of the story is "Don't mess with Jack Cooke."

Jack Takes On A Garden

Spring came, trees leafed out, the grass turned green, the spring flowers bloomed and the weeds grew high. It was on such a morning as I went to my car to leave for work I saw my neighbour on the rear of his lot next door behind the old VON Bldg. With his hands on his hips he was surveying a weed and grassy area that adjoined the two lots. For years it had been overgrown with tall grass and weeds. I stopped to chat with him. He told me he just had to do something about this plot of weeds and was considering covering it over with black top. It was an area the width of the lot and perhaps sixteen foot deep. I told him that I knew what I would do with it if I were in his place. He asked me what that would be?

I said, "Give it to me and let me plant a garden."

He said, " Do you have a green thumb?"

"I have the greenest thumb in all London," I confessed.

"OK you got yourself a garden," he said.

Within a day or two my customer and long time friend John Futcher from south of town came in for a haircut. I mentioned to him about my new garden enterprise. He offered me his garden roto-tiller to work it up. A day or so later he delivered it to the apartment building. The ground worked up great as it was good garden soil.

Getting Taken

The landlord saw the great way the soil had worked up on this garden patch and his crafty mind began to churn. He had removed the huge steel bins from the front lawn leaving behind a deep depression and an area of dead grass where the bins had sat. The lawn was also deep in ruts where trucks had parked over the winter while they were doing the repairs. The lawn was sorely in need. He approached me to see if I would use this roto-tiller on his lawn. I should have known better than to get involved with this man, but the truth was I lived there and I wanted the place to look nice and all my life I have loved to work with lawns and flowerbeds.

So I called John and asked him if I could do this work with his tiller. He said yes it would be OK. I found out working an old lawn down proved to be a real chore, but after working it over many times, in the end it turned out well.

The landlord came to me now and asked if I would put the lawn in for him and get it started, as he had no idea how to go about it. I really didn't want to get too involved in this with him, but I said that on the weekend I would help him. He said OK to that. When the weekend came he told me he had to go out of town on business and asked if I would proceed and get whatever I needed for the lawn and he would pay me. I told him if he would let me have water for my garden and pay me for my labour and whatever I needed I would proceed and do it myself. He agreed to this. Where I came from when you make a deal you keep your word.

I went to the Royal Purple Store on the bottom end of King Street and got the grass seed and fertilizer. They loaned me an over the shoulder hand turned grass seed spreader. I also got the loan of a good lawn roller from a neighbour and I owned my own fertilizer spreader. I worked very hard all day raking, picking up a lot of rock, then fertilizing and sewing the grass seed. The last thing I did was to roll it down well and soak it with water. Then I went to a lumber place and bought some wood stakes and drove them in the lawn and put my own nylon rope all around it to keep people from walking on it. In a few days the grass sprung up with wild abandon, and the ground turned green. Everyone watched it grow in amazement and wonder. I watched over it like a mother hen with baby chicks and I watered it each night when I got home from work.

I had saved the bills from Royal Purple and the lumberyard for the stakes and I added to it my labour, a modest amount of time at the government rate of about six to seven dollars an hour. I think the total bill was about $140.00 some dollars.

I knocked on his door a number of times and no one would answer even though his car was on the lot and I knew he was at home. After a few weeks I sent him a registered letter along with the bills. A number of days later the post office sent me a message that there was a letter there for me to pick up. It was my own registered letter, which I had mailed the landlord. It had come back to me. The post office told me that no one has to pick up a registered letter, and people that are dishonest know this so never do.

The weather in June was very hot and by now the grass was ready to be cut. I did not have my own lawn mower anymore and I was not the custodian here anyway.

I told the guy that was the custodian that he would have to take this over and look after it as I was done with it. He cut it off all too short for a new lawn and then never watered it so the grass started to die. As much as I hated to see all my good work wasted I just did not want to do anything more for this man as I still was not paid for the grass seed, fertilizer or for my labour.

I had one more option, which I knew was not quite legal, but heck when you are dealing with a dishonest person who cares as long as it works. I deducted the money he owed me from my monthly rent. This got his attention; he had his custodian serve me with an eviction notice. I had 60 or 90 days to pay up or they would take me to court and evict me. I laughed at his custodian and told him to tell the landlord I would love to talk to him in court in front of a judge as I am an honest Canadian and he is a rogue a scoundrel and a thief.

However in spite of knowing this I lived with the anxiety for the 60 or 90 days wondering what might happen. Of course nothing ever came of it, as he knew very well he would not fare well in a Canadian court of law because of his dishonesty. .

My Garden was a great success. I had planted all the basic things my mom would have had in her garden, red and green leaf lettuce, white and red radishes, carrots and green and yellow beans. There were sweet corn and tomato plants and even a cucumber patch. Of course the weeds vetoed hard for space in my garden too, but as I was practically born with a hoe in my hand the poor things really never had a chance. The first problem that drew my attention was some bicycle tire marks that crossed the garden every day. I realized that for years this lot and the VON lot were used as a short cut for kids going up town and back. I decided to make a 16-inch wide pathway across the garden with two sixteen-foot long 2X4 imbedded in the soil one on each side. The kids seem to respect this idea stayed on the path and there was no further problem with bicycle or foot traffic.

My thought turned to my dear old Mrs. Bulls and her garden in Alberta, and how she liked to plant a few rows of annual flowers in her garden. So I planted a row of giant Zinnias all around the outer edge of my garden and then down each side of the garden path that I had made for the bikes. Everything was producing and blooming and of course I was in seventh heaven.

Soon I had more garden products then I could possibly eat and I told a few tenants and an elderly neighbour to help themselves, but just take what they needed for the day and there would be lots for everyone.

I had been watering the garden from the tap on the wall to the rear of the apartment building; this was in the agreement I had made with the landlord when I put his grass in for him. A few nights after I had been served with the eviction I found that there was no water at the tap. It had been turned off from the inside. I asked the custodian to turn it on and explained my agreement with the landlord. He said he had been told to turn it off and I could not have any more water. The garden soon began to dry up and things began to die. The tenants in the building of course were aware what had happened but my old friend and neighbour on the street behind did not. So he came to me and asked why I had lost interest in my beautiful garden. I told him what had happened. He said he would solve the problem. He ran a garden hose from his place through a rear window of his garage into my garden. That ended my water problem. I imagine when the landlord saw this he had a fit as he felt he could hurt me by cutting off the water.

Retiring to the garden in the evening after work with a hoe and a basket can be very relaxing to those that love the earth and gardening. There was a cement slab in the northwest corner of my garden where a small tool shed had once been. A few times I would take my folding down lawn chair out there and lie in the sun. One Sunday I was lying there with my thought a few thousand miles away, when through my almost closed eyes I saw a movement, I lay still but opened my eyes slowly. Down the garden path walked the biggest daddy coon I ever saw in my life. He was standing walking towards me on his hind legs with his front leg across his chest; much like an arm and it was full of my tomatoes. I set up and we each stared at each other, and I could read his expression. He wanted to know just what the heck I was doing, lying there in the middle of his garden. Begrudgingly he backed off carrying his load of green tomatoes into the treed lot to the east of the VON. I never did get many tomatoes as he took them before they ever ripened.

Mandy My Manx Cat

About this time my friend Olga had been to the humane society and brought home a beautiful big calico cat. Mr. Buchanan would not have a cat in his building but now that he no longer was the owner I wondered if I should have one for company. I was sure it would be cheaper then a wife. So one day I decided to drop in at the Clark Road Humane Society and see what they had. When I entered the area where the cats were that were available, there was a Manx kitten in the first cage inside the door. Manx cats have no tail and usually look a bit like a lynx and are a bit of a novelty. I took it out of the cage for a minute and petted it. Then I went on down the row to look further. Every time I look back that little Manx kitten had its paws out through the cage and was mewing pitifully for me to come back, I almost thought I could hear him say,

"Take me, take me, I will be a good kitty." The lady attendant said,

" I think that cat wants to go home with you." So that was what happened. I owned a cat. No! No! No one owns a cat, a cat takes your place over and lets you stay on and serve it. It was Mrs. Buchanan who thought of calling it Mandy since it was a Manx cat. At first I wondered if it had got crossed with a rabbit as it would run and then sit upright as rabbits do. They are a novelty but not as graceful as most other cats. Mandy was a good cat and I had her for many years. Like most Manx cats though she was a one-person cat and would not let anyone but me touch her; if they tried she slashed out viciously.

Mr Buchanan Comes Around

Mr. Buchanan had not been coming out to the shop for his usual hair cut for some time, so I was both surprised and pleased when he turned up there one day. Of course at first we both were a bit uncomfortable. Then as if he recaptured his voice he asked me if I could let bygones be bygones and be friends again. I assured him that it would please me very much as I had missed them too.

He said, "Well Vera (his wife) asked if you would drop over for coffee sometime soon. We both really missed your visits?" So I promised I would be over very soon. That made my day as I had cared a lot for these two people as for many years they had been a very important part of my life. This whole thing had been eating away at me. It seems I am a person that needs to have things right between me and those I love or care for.

Visiting the Buchanans was once again a pleasure; they oozed with hospitality and kindness. Their new place was much larger then their old apt. on Dufferin Ave It was more like a condo or a house, but truly they needed new, larger furniture to do the place justice. They had a lot of glass windows in their living room facing the northeast, the centre glass being sliding doors out onto a huge balcony. The lower half of the balcony itself was fronted with Plexiglas in an aluminium frame.

This made it so you were able to see the city from within the living room; the view however to the northeast was not great.

There were several high-rise towers on this corner of Colborne and York Street and it seems a southwest wind laden with dust and dirt funnelled in between. Thus this glass needed to be cleaned every few weeks. They were already tired of cleaning it. Mrs. Buchanan asked me if I wanted the job of cleaning the balcony and the glass for them periodically as it had to be done and she might as well pay me if I wanted the job. Of course as I was always trying to make an honest buck I said yes. So for a couple or more years I looked after this for them. They also had me go to the market and buy flowers for their balcony flower boxes and pots. I enjoyed doing it as they looked after the plants diligently but gave me all the credit. Every time I went over they took me out to the balcony and proudly showed off their flowers, then happily gave me all the credit.

Soon I could see they were not very happy here, as without his Apt. Building and something to do and to care for Mr. Buchanan was bored to death. One night they both confessed this to me and I suggested that maybe they just needed a change and should go south for the winter. They both scoffed at that idea. They did not want to go south.

Then I said, "Maybe you just need new surroundings, something that would make a change in your everyday life."

They said, "What do you mean?" I looked over at their small TV set that had been put inside an old stereo set. This might be ok if you could not afford anything better so I said,   " Well for one thing you might enjoy a large new TV set as that one is very old and very small."

"But what would we do with the stereo set then?" he said.

"Well either sell it or give it to Sally Ann,"

"But that wall would look empty without the stereo sitting there." he said.

"Then why not buy a nice new wall unit for that wall and put the TV in it?"

They could not see any sense in this. It was sad to see that while they had no real problems and were sitting on a small fortune they were not happy with their retired life.

One night when I arrived to visit, Mrs. Buchanan came waltzing to the door in a happy mood; I could see something great had happened. So I said to her,

"Now what happened to make you so happy tonight?"

She said, "Well you would be happy too, if you had what I have."

"Pray tell me what is that?" I said.

"How many Millionaires do you know?"

"Actually just a couple," I confessed.

"Well now you know a couple more," she said and continued, "We just sold the 36 unit apartment building in Goderich and dad (she often referred to Mr. Buchanan as dad) put half the money into my bank account for income tax purposes. Now we both have over a million and a half dollars in our bank accounts."

Of course in a way I always knew that they were well off, but in real estate. I had never given it much thought, as they did not act at all like people that had a lot of money. So now I wondered if they would be happy and perhaps spend a little money on themselves. I continued to visit with them and everything seemed to be going ok.

Mr Buchanan Has a Stroke

Then one day I got word that Mr. Buchanan had a stroke and was taken to the old Victoria Hospital by ambulance. For a number of weeks we were very concerned about him. He seemed to need visits from those he was close to. His wife Vera had never driven a car so her sister Mrs. McDonald from Glencoe south of London came into the city and stayed with Vera for a few weeks. Together they drove up to the hospital every day. I started the routine of visiting every Wednesday evening on the way home from work and then again on Sunday afternoons. After a time Mrs. McDonald went home and Vera took a taxi to the hospital everyday. For some reason she complained to Mr. Buchanan she was not feeling well. Then the next day a Wednesday she called to say she could not make the trip as she had a very bad stomach pain. I went as usual to visit on the way home and Mr. Buchanan asked me if I would go to the apartment and check on Vera.

Mrs Buchanan Passes Away

She answered the intercom and let me in. When she met me at their apt. door I could tell she was in a lot of pain and I wanted her to call a doctor or let me take her to the hospital. She said she thought it was just from over exertion and anxiety and all the extra things she had to do since Mr. Buchanan had this stroke. She promised me she would call the Dr. in the morning if it were not any better.

That night the pain got so severe that she called an ambulance. She died on the way to the hospital. They found that she had a ruptured bowel and the poison went through her system and killed her. Three days later a funeral service was held for her in London. With great difficulty Mr. Buchanan managed to get there and sat in a wheel chair looking very much at loss and alone.

Vera was buried in her old home community in a very old cemetery just outside the village of Whitechurch next to her first husband. I felt very sorry for Mr. Buchanan. His life now was going to be in for a great change.

It didn't seem as if anyone from his side of the family would step forward to assist him when he needed it the most. His side of the family all lived up in the Kincardine area on Lake Huron north of Goderich. At no time did they ever offer to help him out around his apartment building. They left him on his own. It was Mrs. McDonald, Vera's sister and her family who packed up Buchanan's thing and closed down his apartment in London. They even took his car out to Glencoe and put a for-sale sign on it and managed to sell it. When he was finally able to leave the hospital Vera's sister Mrs. McDonald got him into a private room in a nice new home in the small town of Wardsville south of London. It was only a short distance from Glencoe where she and her family lived. He never recovered from his stroke so he spent the rest of his life in the wheel chair.

After a few weeks in Wardsville Mr. Buchanan called a friend in the old Apt. Building and asked if she would deliver a message to me. He wondered if I would drive down to the Wardsville and cut his hair. Well I didn't mind really, not at all, as it was time I visited him anyway. But it was a long drive from my place to drive for a haircut, about 40 miles or more. So I packed my tools on a Sunday and drove down. It was a pleasant drive and a good excuse to get out in the country. When I arrived I found him and Mrs. McDonald deep in conversation. I felt a bit as if I were intruding on them, but I am sure he had a lot of things on his mind, between settling up Vera's estate and managing his own business, he was not longer mobile except from a wheel chair.

Mrs. McDonald left us to ourselves and I finally got around to cutting his hair. When it was done he thanked me and gave me a twenty-dollar bill. At first I said no as I didn't want to take his money. But he told me that since his stroke he realized more then ever, he was never going to be able to spend all of his money. So as it cost me money to drive down to Wardsville he thought I should take it. I realized he was right but I have this odd feeling about cutting family or friend's hair outside the shop. I feel better if I don't take money. I did want to stay in contact with him, partly because I valued him as an old friend and partly because I knew he needed me. I was now very conscious that he was a wealthy man with millions of dollars. I felt guilty to even think about it, but perhaps, perhaps, as a close friend who had always been there for him he just might leave me a little bit of it. Let me say $25,000 or $50,000 from his millions, I am sure no one would miss it, yet it would be a lot of money to a person like me. These kinds of thoughts bothered me as I thought it was wrong for me to even think like that.

I remember talking this over with my sister Jean once and Jean said,

"Jack you just do what you feel is right, stick by him if he needs you, then in the end if he does leave you something you will feel good about it, as in a way you earned it, and if he doesn't leave you anything, then you will at least have a clear conscious because you stuck by him as a true friend when he needed you and you did your duty to him."

For a couple of years I drove down every two or three weeks to see him and he was always ready for a visit. I was aware he felt out of his own territory in Wardsville and I was his link to his London home and his past. I continued to cut his hair and he would pay me the $20.00.

My Aunt Maude

A few weeks before Christmas 1999, Jean and Bill in Mitchell, had Arnold and Pearl, Oliver and Laurine and myself come for a Christmas dinner in mid December. As the families started to grow up marry and have children we started to do this so we could have a quiet time together. Someone at the table mentioned that my Aunt Maude (my dad's youngest sister) would celebrate her 90th birthday June 4th, 1992 so we should all fly down to California to celebrate.

My sister Jean said, "Well if you don't plan ahead to do things nothing ever comes of it." Right then we all said we would give it serious thought and make plans to go.

Aunt Maude was born on the old farm on the Mitchell Road on June 4th, 1902. She was a one and only. I have never met anyone quite like her. She wore her heart on her sleeve, and she loved us all equally. We knew that without a doubt. Her visits to the farm were the highlight of the year, she walked with us, she talked to us and above all showed us love, and life on the old farm was never more joyful. then it was at the time of her visit. We waited on her visits with great anticipation.

When I was a kid up on the farm, I remember looking out the highest south side window watching for a cloud of dust away down the long gravel Mitchell Road. Sometimes my sisters and I watched for what seemed like hours, but we knew that sooner or later out of a cloud of dust would come a little green 1935 Ford car with my Uncle Guy and Aunt Maude to spend a week's holiday with us. There are no words to describe our happiness.

For a whole week my sisters and I would sit on her lap, cling to her and follow her everywhere. As she said years later we literally loved her to death, but as you and I know, one can never get too much of a good thing.

Then in turn, we would go to Detroit to spend a whole weekend. At night her living room floor was wall-to-wall kids. Aunt Maude was a great cook and if you have never tasted her lemon meringue or apple pies then you have never lived.

All during those hard times of the thirties she would arrived at the old farm with the car loaded with box after box of clothing she managed to come by. As she had two fast growing sons I got all their best clothes as they outgrew them. There was everything from shoes, pants shirts and jackets. I was a well-dressed lucky boy.

I remember once when we visited her in the 1940's she gave her daughter-in-law Wanda some money to take us all to an amusement park to go on rides. Up until then about the only thing I had ever had a ride on was a wheelbarrow. Years later when I had some American money saved from the shop I happened to think of what she had done for us that day. I wrote her a letter reminding her and I enclosed the American money telling her to go out and have some fun on me.

She always insists that I was the letter writer in the family so she expected letters regular and on time. At times when I got lazy or neglectful she was not afraid to lay down the law with a pep talk. For some reason my sisters were exempted; it was my duty, one that I kept up until she passed away. No one knew me better than my Aunt Maude, I shared all my thoughts, my dreams, my joys and sorrows and even my sins with her, yet she still loved me, of that I was very sure.

Uncle Guy and Aunt Maude retired to California to be close to their daughter Shirlyan and Dan Hurt and family. Even in her eighties and on into her nineties she flew home to Detroit where I would pick her up and bring her north to visit the family. I guess what I remember most about her was that she was never afraid to show her love for you and to say, "I love you," or to praise God for all her blessings every day. We will always remember her. Everyone should have an Aunt Maude.

The California Holiday Trip

Late in May 1992 we started to check on the cost of flights to California. We had decided not to travel all together as a "Just In Case" for family security. I got my ticket, and then I had a phone call from sister Pearl. When she went to buy their ticket Arnold backed out. We all knew he had never been on a plane and for some reason had a great fear of travelling on a plane. So Pearl wanted to know if she could go with me.

I said, "Yes of course you can." So I took my ticket back to the London airport and exchanged it for a ticket with two side-by-side seats.

A few days later we got word that aunt Maude's daughter Shirlyan had decided the party should be held in Detroit so the family there would not have to fly to California.

It was too late for Pearl and me, because we could not take our tickets back. As the party in Detroit was going to be later in the month, Pearl and I decided we should go anyway and see California and then celebrate this 90th birthday on June the 4th with Aunt Maude.

I had not told Pearl before we left that when I bought our flight tickets I had also arranged for a three day's stay at the Desert Inn in Anaheim, directly across from the main entrance to Disneyland so we could go there. This was a gift from me to her.

We flew from London to Toronto and from Toronto to Los Angeles. We picked up our luggage then we found a car rental service, which took us in a small bus to a car rental lot some distance from the airport. We rented a very nice blue four door 92 Pontiac Grand Prix. It proved a great car for us to travel in, and we really liked it.

I remember getting in behind the wheel on the car lot; I seemed to freeze, or panic, as I had no sense of direction. I looked at the map, but I didn't know which way was north or south, east or west. Pearl on the other hand didn't seem to understand what my problem was, and she looked at me with frustration and said,

"Well let's go, we wont get anywhere just sitting here." I could not explain to her my problem very easily, as here we were two deaf people in a Silent World travelling together pen in hand, ha ha!

Regardless, and against my every feeling, I started to drive across the lot, the wrong way. We soon found out there was just one-way off this lot. On all four sides there were entrances, which had these huge sloping steal spikes in a steel plate. If you drove over towards them you had four very punctured tires. You could drive in however with the slope without a problem. This was to stop people from stealing their cars. At the one entrance that you could exit I asked the attendant which direction to turn to go to Anaheim and he said to turn left, and then go straight ahead. Once I finally got my direction I had no further problem and it was happy driving.

We found "The Desert Inn" quite easily and were able to park the car in front of our suite. This in itself was good, as then we didn't have to carry our baggage very far and we felt we could keep an eye on our car. We unpacked some things and both had a shower and a short rest. It had been a long day for us, but we were happy, tired and hungry. We left in search of a place to eat. Outside our door we admired the huge flowerbeds in bloom and this alone made Pearl and me happy.

The closes place to eat was "Denny's" which became out favourite eating-place.

A lady there sort of adopted us when she found we were both deaf and Canadians. Every time we walked in the door she came and escorted us to her section and waited on us as if we were family. That night we were very excited but slept fittingly. The next day we were going to Disneyland. We felt like two kids up on the old farm again.

After breakfast at Denny's we arrived at the gates of Disneyland and bought our pass for the day. I don't suppose anyone is prepared for all that there is to see and do at Disneyland; it is a happy world within itself. Pretty soon all your worries and cares and negative thoughts disappear as you join the throng, the ever-happy jungle of people under the California sun and find delight in a world of make-believe. Pearl is excellent company and more adventurous then I am. Can you imagine diving down a mountain in a Redwood log canoe from a great height into a pond and then wanting to do it again? Pearl did. For me it was a once in a lifetime thing.

This one particular ride called, "Splash Mountain" will remain with me always. We climbed into the rear of this Red Wood log boat with a Japanese couple and two small children in front of us. We entered into the side of the mountain following a river. Along the bank was dense virgin forest. Then through a clearing we saw a bonfire and Indians dressed, as they were when the first white men came to this country. It was spooky as they moved about the bonfire and everything looked so real.

We could almost feel the need to glide by undetected, as we were indeed the intruder here. We encountered black bears by a stream and beyond the stream a huge buck deer stood alone as if on guard. Farther on was timid looking doe with a small fawn. Wolves were there in packs and the beaver were busy building dams. Every now and then our log boat entered a ramp, which took it up to another level, with a different scene. Log cabins with a few acres of cleared land, a white man and family had arrived looking ill equipped for this vast and dangerous land, into which he had intruded.

There was one scene that I must tell you about. When we neared the top of the mountain our log came to a waterfall, and slowly we were swept towards the brink. I was aware of the mist and water spray falling back onto us as we were caught up in the current and drawn ever nearer to the brink and then a plunge. Suddenly we could hear a great boom of a cannon and feel the concussion. A great and wondrous scene was being played out before us, one I can still see clearly even to this day.

It was night and the sky above us was the blackest of blue. We could see to great heights and as far as the eye could see the sky was full of brilliant and wondrous stars. Below us there appeared to be a great bay of water lit up because of a great fire. There was a large fort built of logs built into the cliff across the bay. A pirate ship, with full masks was in the centre of the bay firing its cannons upon the fort. The fort was ablaze with fire; reflecting upon the water. There was flame and smoke rising all over the fort. The men were still manning their cannons and bravely firing back on the ship. Cannon balls were constantly landing in the water sending a great amount of water high into the air.

It was into this wild scene we went as our log boat was caught up and swept over the falls. We hit the water sending out waves and then glided forth into the line of fire. All around us cannonballs exploded in the water wetting us thoroughly. Those guys in the fort must have been the world's worst shots or else they thought we were the enemy too. We glided across the bay through all this chaos undetected by the pirates. As we neared the far shore we were swept in and under the burning fort. Huge timbers were aglow with flame and embers and hot looking charcoal. Even the smoke looked and smelled real. Soon we left it all behind and our log climbed to the very top of the mountain. Now I was really in trouble as I could see a little pond far below, and we were going into a free fall and nosedive into that puddle. I would have paid anything for a way out. The log paused at the edge while the nose turned down and the rear end came up. An overhead camera takes your picture just as you go over. I still have that picture. Horrors, it's a good thing I didn't have any hair to stand up. We arrived at the bottom intact, and as we got out of the boat, Pearl says, "Lets do it again."

We met a nice young lad from New Zealand who was there all alone. Both Pearl and I wore a small Canadian flag. He noticed it so came over to chat with us. He was a university graduate and had been offered a job in California. I think he was just a bit homesick. He tagged along with us for a number of rides. I think he felt closer to us Canadians with our historic British ties than to the Americans.

We returned to Denny's for our supper and our friend there met us and took us under her wing. What a wonderful and exciting day. We were both tired out.

The next morning we were back to Denny's for breakfast and we asked our great hostess if there was a shopping centre close by. We explained we were on the way to San Juan Capistrano to see the mission. Was there one along the route which we would be taking? She wrote the directions down on our place mat. Following the directions we came to a four way stop with buildings on all corners.

The buildings cut off our view around all corners. According to her map we were to turn left here and the plaza was within our view just around the corner but there was nothing in sight. So I turned left again, not wanting to stray too far from the main highway we came in on. There was a wide median here with a strip of grass running down the middle of it. A very well dressed older lady perhaps in her mid to late eighties was crossing the grass coming towards us. White gloves in hand, she knew how to dress and she was what one would call, elegant.

I stopped and got her attention and she came to the car,

I said, "My sister and I are Canadian and I am afraid we are lost."

She asked us where we wanted to go; I showed her the map and pointed out the plaza. At that moment a car started down the street toward us and she was standing in the traffic lane talking to me.

She said, "Quick open the door and let me in." so I let her in the back seat.

I was a bit shocked, as there she was what one might call a little old lady and perhaps almost as old as my dear Aunt Maude who was ninety and she would get into a car with perfect strangers.

She set us straight and I told her how much we appreciated it.

She said, " Well I use to live in Sault Ste. Marie Michigan, and we loved you Canadians, so I just had to help you out." She was not only elegant on the outside she was a real lady on the inside and a real ambassador for the USA.

We drove back to the corner and turned the other way and found the plaza.

After a short shopping spree we continued on our way to The Mission. Juan Capistrano is a quaint little town located above the shores of the Pacific midway between Los Angeles and San Diego. I had been there once before when I visited my friends Bob and Judy Scott many years before and I wanted Pearl to experience it. Once you visit the Mission you will always remember it. Most people my age remember the old song, "When the Swallows Come Back To San Juan Capistrano." Visiting this place, seeing its beauty, and feeling its place in the history of America will be a memorable event in your life.

This mission is called, "The Jewel of California Missions." The Spanish founded it in 1776 and sent Father Junipero Serra to educate and convert the Indians who lived along the coast. Until he arrived their diet was chiefly fish from the ocean. He established the mission with workshops where the Indians learned how to make furniture and make brick to build with. There were loom rooms and tallow vats and perhaps most important to its founders a church where they were called to worship each day. Spain controlled California until 1821 when Mexico won its independence.

The disastrous earthquake of 1812 did a lot of damaged to the mission. The church itself was damaged beyond repair, and it is in these walls the swallows found a home. Every year like clock work they return from the south to nest in the walls. People from all over the world go there to witness the event and feel it is a holy event. "When The Swallows Come Home To San Juan Capistrano"

We returned to the Desert Inn in Anaheim by following the Pacific Coast Highway that winds north high above the scenic pacific shore. Somewhere along the way it became suppertime and we went into a village store and bought food more fit for a picnic. We had found a dead end street that ran off the highway west. It came to a dead-end high above the pacific shore. A wondrous sandy beach stretched out north and south far below us. Here there was a little circle of gravel with some lawn and a few picnic tables. We watched the sun go down over the Pacific, one of those things you like to share with a friend or loved one. Pearl and I will always remember this. Far to the north a single figure emerged walking towards us. We noted that he was walking to and fro on the beach as if searching for whatever he could find. He passed below us; he had long blonde sun bleached hair, and looked much like a displaced hippy of the sixties. He disappeared to the south leaving us wondering about him. Who was he, where was he going, did he have a home to go to or was he a lost soul, just wandering the beach in California?

We arrived back to our room at the Desert Inn for our last night. We were both very tired after a big day on the road. In the morning we would be off to visit my dear Aunt Maude in Oxnard where she lived with her daughter, Shirlyan and Dan Hurt, 2013 Spyglas Trail. Our plans were to find a motel close by from where we could visit them. When we went to check out in the morning they told us there was E Mail for us from Shirlyan telling us to come straight to their house and not to take a motel room They wanted us to stay with them. To get to Oxnard we had to bi-pass Los Angeles and Hollywood and Beverly Hills, then along the Santa Monica Mountains to Oxnard. The driving was hectic to say the least and I was relying on Pearl to read the map. It seemed as if every one else knew where they were going but me. I found out that my sister turns the map every time I turn a corner, thus she would have the map on her lap upside down and when I asked her,

"Do I turn left or right here?" She could not give me a quick answer and by then of course it was too late as I had gone on through or turned the wrong way. However!

We arrived at Dan and Shirlyan's place and spent two or three memorable days with them. During the day we had Aunt Maude all to ourselves and we chatted endlessly. It was a wonderful visit and at ninety she had a wonderful mind. She was spry and always cheerful, witty and loved to joke. There will never be another like my Aunt Maude and we loved her dearly. After talking to Dan and Shirlyan we outlined a trip, which we thought we could handle and be back to Dan and Shirlyan's in time to celebrate Aunt Maude's Birthday on June the 4th.

My Cousin Dan & Shirlyan Hurt's Home in California

Up The Coast and Into the Interior

Early one morning Pearl and I left on our trip to see more of California. First we drove north up the coast to see the famous old Santa Barbara Mission. The Spanish started the mission there in 1786. The Santa Barbara Mission is beautiful to say the least and is called the Queen of Missions. There were several churches built on this location before these present Mission buildings. The earthquake of 1812 destroyed the third church on this site and this present mission was fifty years in the process of being built from 1820 to 1870.

It is very much Spanish with its white plaster walls, its many arches and red tile roof, and is surrounded by tall palm trees, green lawns and flowers beds which are full of strange plants, a lot of which are cactus.

From Santa Barbara we travelled north again and then inland to the town or city of Solvang. It is a Danish place and the downtown has been renovated over into blocks and blocks of new looking craft shops, stores and shops and eating places of all kinds with a Danish flair and design. We enjoyed several hours of browsing and buying gifts. Late in the afternoon we left the town behind and travelled back towards the coast. Tomorrow we planned to visit the famous Hearst Castle at San Simeon. The evening retreated, and the sun grew low on the Pacific as we arrived in a place just south of our destination called Grover City. It is actually a coastal town but more like a village on which the surrounding mountainous country seems to have encroached.

A brand new Inn or hotel called Oak Park Resort Hotel was on our left, and we decided this was it. Pearl always took a look at the rooms before she would say yes. I told her in a nice place like this they didn't keep bed bugs, but in spite of that she still had to take a look. I went in the office and got a key, then drove the car closer to the part of the building our room would be in. We sat in the car for a few minutes discussing the day. Then we got out to go and check on our room. The minute I shut the door I realized I had not taken the key out of the ignition. I think it was because I was holding a set of keys in my hand, keys that belonged to the room we were renting for the night. I didn't say anything right then to Pearl, but my head was working on the problem of how to open that door. Sadly when you rent a car they only let you have one key and that is fixed so you can't make yourself a second even if you wanted to. I wondered if they might have a wire clothes hanger in the office. I was well aware it that it is very hard to get into today's cars unless you call a professional.

Pearl OK'd the room and we walked back to the car.

I said, "Pearl I have some bad news to tell you, I locked the keys in the car."

She said, "Oh Jack you couldn't do a thing like that?" Of course I assured her I was quite capable of doing things like that. I left her standing there beside the car while I walked back to the office to ask if they had a wire clothes hanger. They searched the Hotel and as it was brand new all they had were plastic ones. However they said they would send someone out in search of one.

I didn't like to leave Pearl standing outside alone, as it was late in the evening by now. As I walked towards the car I could see Pearl talking to a young guy maybe in his late teens. As Pearl has three boys of her own she was quite comfortable talking with him. I guess he had noticed her distress and wanted to find out what the problem was and if he could help. When I walked up he said,

"Mr. I can get into that car for you It will take me about five minutes."

I said, "How will you do it?"

To which he said, "I will be right back."

Off he ran to an old souped up car parked across the lot, its rear end jacked up high on springs or shocks or whatever kids do to cars to get it up there. I remember how upon opening his trunk he had to lift up high to get his toolbox out. Soon he came running back across the lot, tools in hand and without a word he started to take the radio aerial off. I remember feeling a bit alarmed by this, as I didn't want to take a stripped car back to the rental place.

He had noticed that one of the rear windows was down just a wee bit. He turned the aerial up side down and then down inside the window, to the door button. It was a kind of door rocker button so when he touched it the door opened. I could not believe our luck.

I reached for my wallet as I felt I should give him something, but he put his hand up to stop me and said he would not take anything and that he was happy to be able to help us. Then he ran off, back to his car and we were never to see him again. By now a couple other lads were at his car and I could see him going through the motions of what he had done, taking the aerial off and sticking it down into the car. What can one say, except some dad and mother raised a good kid? Another good ambassador for the USA.

The next morning when we returned the key they were serving free Danish buns and coffee. We obliged them by staying for breakfast, as so far nothing much had been "For Free." Soon we were again on the road to the Hearst San Simeon Castle.

One might expect something more at the highway entrance where you arrive at the Hearst property other than a parking lot. Perhaps a good idea would be a Tim Horton's (Sorry I could not resist that,) but all that's there is a parking lot where people wait for the mini shuttle bus. There are four tours a day, the first one starting at 8:20 am. Each tour is supposed to take about two hours. We arrived for the second tour of the day perhaps 10:30 AM on a glorious sunny spring morning. One can see a narrow winding black top road going east far into the distance where it disappears in the endless hills. High on the hillside afar off you can see something shining white in the sun against the skyline. This is the castle.

I doubt if there is anything in North America that compares to what you will see here at the Hearst Castle. It is well known William Randolph Hearst made his fortune in the Newspapers world. Therefore if there was anything out there anywhere he wanted, he had the money to buy it. From all over the world he gathered artefacts of the best for his castle. He bought everything from lumber to marble, furniture, plants and even animals for a zoo. Endless roads were travelled all over the world for his needs for his castle.

The castle was built between 1919 and 1947during a time when all of Canada and the United States had little money for the necessities of life, a time when they faced depression and then a war. All of which was news, and news on paper sold.

I cannot begin to tell you here all of what we saw, and only by seeing it yourself could you understand its outrageous size and its grandeur and beauty beyond belief.

I remember a dining room larger then some town halls, great carpet like tapestries hanging on the walls between great wooden hand carved arches, twenty-five foot or more ceilings with gigantic size chandeliers, plus tables and chairs of massive size fit for Vikings or kings of yesteryears. There were two great swimming pools; the outside one, which is called Neptune Pool and is 104 ft. long, is made of marble from Vermont. On one end is a temple facade with ancient like Roman columns on either side. The pool holds 345,000 gallons of fresh mountain spring water. The second pool is inside and called a Roman Pool. It is of Olympic size, and is a flat bottom pool ten feet deep. It is surrounded by gold leaf fused with glass tile, made in Venice. The pool interior is designed to suggest the atmosphere of the Roman Bath. On the sides are oversize reproductions of classic Roman figures.

Hearst himself was a motion movie picture producer for several years, mainly in the newsreel end of it. Thus he had his very own theatre in his castle, which we visited.

It seemed the guides were timed and they kept us on the move, on tour one you only see about a quarter of the castle. I believe there are four tours. If I ever go back to California I would definitely want to go back to see more of this man-made wonder. Before Hearst died he realized he wanted to preserve all of this and keep it together. It was a lifetime of gathered treasures intact. In the end he left it to the State of California.

We gathered together ready for the return trip to our cars. Far to the west the blue Pacific glistened under the noonday sun. We left hoping to return some day.

The next part of our trip was to take us to the Sequoia National Park about 200 miles northwest of where we were as the crow flies, but many more miles by road.

First we had to drive through some scenic coastal hill and valley country, some of which was fenced and farmed and all of which looked rather dry and infertile. Then we drove through some rather mountainous-like country, before we drove out of the hills onto a great broad irrigated valley. This valley is called the "San Joaquin Valley" It stretches from San Francisco almost as far south as Los Angeles. Here they grew many different kinds of crops, everything from walnuts from walnut trees to vineyards of grapes. There were fields of garden products, lettuce, celery, carrots and onions, and oh yes strawberries.

There were even fields of irrigated hay, and many long stacks of bailed hay covered with tarp and weighted down with old car tires. Hundreds of dairy cows stood in feedlots where they got room service as hay and feed and water were brought to them.

Since seeing this valley and its incredible productivity I have had many thoughts about it and its future need for more and more water. What will happen if the irrigation system continues to expand or if the weather turns dry as it has in the past and the need of water gets urgent? This valley supplies much of America and Canada also with fresh food year round. We are dependent on it during the winter months. If there is need for more water, can we afford to turn our backs while water in BC flows west into the Pacific Ocean, or if the Americans want more water will they not use trade with us to get what they need?

Pearl did have a problem with me, as I liked to drive late into the evening and she was always anxious to find an inn, have supper and settle down and enjoy it. Women just love to play house. However in June the days are long and the most beautiful time to drive is when the sun is low in the western sky and behind us. It is easier on the eyes as things take on a soft and mellow, friendly look. We arrived late in the evening at Visalla a nice little town and just a short drive to the Sequoia Park the next day. We had been staying at Days Inns and found them to be constant in hospitality, cleanliness, quality and price. In spite of this, Pearl always had to check the room out first. You can't go wrong when you have your sister travelling along and looking out for you.

Pearl had taken her TTY phone machine along with her and she was anxious to call Arnold (her husband) from the phone in our room, but for some reason she could not contact a Bell Relay System. So I went down to the office to talk with someone. I was rather surprised to find out that the state of California did not have this kind of service for their deaf. People outside the state could call in and the operators would take the call but you could not call out from California. So I asked them if they would call Arnold in Stratford Ontario and have him call the phone in our room so Pearl could talk to him. They said sure they would do that for us.

I went back up to our room and told Pearl to connect her phone to the room service phone and wait on a call. She was very happy.

Arnold called and I think it made the day for both of them. Later when I was checking out the bill I realized they did not bill us for the call to Stratford.

In the morning we were soon driving in mountainous country again. As we neared the Sequoia Park entrance a giant Redwood log stood on end with a second huge hand carved slab attached across it. An Indian head was carved into one end of it facing towards the park, big letters written across it read, "Sequoia National Park." Just beyond the entrance the highway went under a huge bolder sitting above it. This boulder stretched all the way across the highway dwarfing the cars that drove under it. The highway continued to climb up and up from the valley.

The park is at a very high altitude. There were many grand views of smoky looking mountains afar off through valleys which opened to us. Soon we began to see huge trees along our route. We stopped at one where the centre had been burnt out. Pearl stood in the burnt out area while I took her picture. It was big enough to drive the car in. The road we were travelling on was what is called The General Sherman's Trail, and it would take us to the "Giant Forest Village."

Entrance to Sequoia National Park

We arrived in the village at noon. All around us were these great giants of trees over 3000 year old. Around the base of the tree is a red powder that comes off the bark and is both a fire retardant and it also kills insects, - natures own protection.

We had our lunch in the village restaurant and then wandered out among the trees. Pearl and I have always loved the woods, but this kind of woods was something else.

When we were on the trail again we came to what they call, "The General Sherman Tree." It is the daddy of all trees. It is said to be over 3,500 years old, and is 272 feet high, and 36 feet wide. Now that is a big daddy and a lot of wood! Driving on we came to a grove of these huge trees and as there was a place to park we decided to take a break and stretch out legs.

Look!   I Found a BIG Tree

I don't know just how this happened, but I walked one way to look at something and Pearl walked another. When I turned around she had disappeared. Naturally I called out her name even though I really knew she was deaf and wouldn't hear me. I walked here and I walked there and there was no Pearl in sight, somehow she had got swallowed up in this vast Silent World and I was getting a bit upset. Then suddenly a head appeared up over a steep ridge in the mountainside and there was Pearl climbing on her hands and knees all covered with dirt mud and stain. She had seen some giant pinecones away down below and wanted to pick them up to take home. Up here on the mountainside with all the great trees and rocks in such massive dimensions, one looses his sense of size. The side of the mountain was much steeper than she imagined and so once she started to slide she rolled and slid all the way to the bottom among the pinecones. It was a wonder she was not hurt, but that was Pearl. She always could take her tumbles. She was not going to go through all that and not get her cones. So there she was coming towards me with her arm full of these huge pinecones and looking as if she had been wallowing with a bunch of wart hogs. She went to the car to clean up and change her clothes. We laugh about it now but it was not very funny right then.

We followed the road to the north end of The Sequoia Park; from here if you turn west you go out of the park back into the valley and out towards Fresno. If you continue north you go into Kings Canyon National Park. Sitting there in the car we wanted desperately to drive on farther north and see more of this wondrous park. Pearl and I were fascinated with all the things we had seen. We wished we had more time so we could travel on into Kings Canyon but we knew we had to turn back as we were about two days drive north of Oxnard and my cousins. Besides that, Pearl was anxious to get to an inn or motel where she could have a shower and change of clothes after her tumble down the mountainside.

So we drove west towards Fresno. This was a place that I had heard of all my life and wanted to see. My grandmother Butson's sister, my Aunt Tish (Mrs. William Piper) lived here most of her life before she passed away. Tish was also a sister to my dear old Aunt Becky in Vancouver whom I wrote about in the first part of my story. I remember my mom getting letters from Aunt Tish somewhere in California. Somehow I had always pictured Fresno as being closer to the coast. But it is away inland nearer to the mountains in a very fertile irrigated country. Fresno is very much a big city now.

Horrors! It was late by the time we arrived and as this is the very first city out from the park all the smart people had left the park earlier and now were comfortably settled down in their rooms for the night. We faced rows and rows of "No Vacancy" signs. Poor Pearl was miserable, tired sore and grumpy. She didn't want to go into a place to eat or be seen until she had a shower and got prettied up.

We were told that there were no vacancies to be found in Fresno, as it was June and tourist time. Our best bet was to drive on to Hanford a town west of Visalla where we had stayed the night before. Looking at the map there was a shortcut down a secondary lonely road of ill repute, so I took that as it cut off miles. There were no towns or villages nor any signs on this stretch of road. We drove and drove and we began to fear we might be lost. All this added to poor Pearl's misery. Then when we arrived at Hanford there was no vacancy. They phoned the Days Inn in Visalla and they had one room left which they said they would hold for us. So we were back on the road, backtracking to Visalla. Pearl slept most of the way. When we got there I asked her if she wanted to inspect the room. She told me I was not funny. She stayed in the car until I opened the door to the room and then she sneaked in. After a shower we found a nice place for supper and things got better.

Visalla is situated just east of # 99 freeway going south. So in the morning we were on it knowing that we could make it back to Dan and Shirlyan's by night. In spite of what had happened last evening we both realized we had a great trip and saw some of the great wonders of California. Again we were driving through irrigated farm country. Nowhere else does one see so many acres of garden products mile after mile. In spite of all that the most impressive thing I remember on that return trip was a huge dairy outside Bakersfield. Never have I seen such a herd of Holstein cows standing in one place. The milk from places like this ends up on the shelves of stores in LA.

In early evening we reached the place on the freeway where we had to turn off at a town called Saugua. From there we drove west on highway 126 which would take us back onto the coastal highway just north of Oxnard. This meant too that we would be driving out of the flat valley country into the mountainous coastal area. This area was made for beautiful driving in the late evening with the sun lowering itself in the west. We drove up and down and around the rugged mountains with breathtaking views beyond each bend. As we neared the coast the valleys showed smog from the late evening traffic on the freeways of this great populous area, which stretches for miles along the coast.

I'm not sure just what time it was when we arrived back in Oxnard, but everyone was looking for us to arrive home that evening. While we had a trip of a lifetime we were glad to get back to my cousins, to be with our loved ones.

The next day Pearl and I drove to a large shopping centre to do some shopping. I don't really remember buying anything, but if women don't go shopping then they haven't been there. We were inside a store going up on one of several escalators when I looked across and saw my next-door neighbour who lived one apartment down the hall from me. Well you know things like that do not happen. I saw him look my way but there didn't seem to be any recognition. I mentioned this to Peal saying,

"That chap over there is the spitting image of Chris Potter my next door neighbour." Pearl said. "Oh I suppose there are a lot of look-alike in the world." So I just let it go.

I first met Chris Potter at the "Y" a few years ago. He was a guy who worked out in the gym real serious, as I did too, and I think because of this we became friends. He was going to Western University at this time and had a room on Waterloo Street not far from me. Besides university he had a great interest in acting. He had played parts in the London Little Theatre. I remember him as a friendly sort of guy easy to chat with and he liked dogs. Chris's father who lives in a village just north of London raises German Shepherds just for the love of dogs.

Chris was looking for an apartment and he just happened to find one down the hall from me. I often saw Chris sneak a puppy into his apartment. The management didn't take kindly to dogs in the building. Some nights when I went for a walk I would meet Chris out on the sidewalk and we walked together and chatted. He was teaching the puppies how to behave on city streets. While Chris lived in the building he landed his first movie part in a weekly TV show called 'Material World' filmed in Toronto. He played the boy friend of a dizzy gal who owned a material and dress making business. Right at this time in my story, 1992 he was on TV every Wed. night in Material World.

However as Pearl said there are probably a lot of look-alikes in this world, all this was soon forgotten.

The next day we celebrated Aunt Maude's birthday with a BBQ in Dan and Shirlyan's, well-groomed back yard. Dan and Shirlyan's son Scott and his wife, and daughter Michele and husband came too. We had our last evening visit with us all together. Come morning, after our night's sleep we would be going home.

I was more than a bit concerned about getting our car back on time to the rental place. My problem was --- I was unsure if I could find the rental place in such a huge place as Los Angeles. Dan was a big help as he sent us on a coastal route on which there was less traffic. It was also close to where we had to go to return the car.

I think it was mostly luck that we found the place without getting lost. After paying our bill we rode their mini bus back to the airport. Soon we were in the air and flying home to Toronto. We both slept most of the way. After we landed we had to change airports to fly home to London. Pearl was getting very tired by now and found the walking difficult. So I asked an aid for a wheelchair. It came with a very courteous and helpful lady. She told me to follow her and she got behind the wheel chair and soon we were swishing down long passages and places I would have never found on my own and through the final doors into the right airport.

She left us and as I turned around Chris Potter came rushing up to me and greeted me with a big hug. He was very excited and happy to see me.

He said, "Then that was you I saw back in California? I just couldn't believe a thing like that could possibly happen, and then again I didn't know who the lady was with you."

I introduced him to Pearl. He was very excited; he took my pen and pad from my shirt pocket and began to write me a few notes, (notes I kept and still have today.) He had gone to LA for an audition for a new movie called, "The Legend Continues" with a lead roll playing opposite to David Carradine. He got the part and he considered it his first big break into the world as an actor.

I was the first person he knew that he was able to share it with. Naturally I was very happy for him. He won Pearl as a fan for a lifetime as he took the time to write things down on paper for her so she would understand everything too. I might add that Chris is doing well in the movies industry. Right now I watch him every Monday and Wednesday evening in a weekly series called 'Wild Card.'

Thus ends one of the best holiday trips I ever took, and I was really happy to be able to share it with someone I loved, my sister Pearl.

Chapter 8
Coasting Thru My 60's In The 90's

The first weekend after getting home from California I thought I had better drive down to Wardsville to see Mr. Buchanan as it was now over a month since I last saw him. I took my barbering tools along, as by now I was sure he would need a haircut. Upon arriving I walked straight to his room. Can you imagine my surprise when I found someone else there who knew nothing of a Mr. Buchanan?

I went to the desk and asked where Mr. Buchanan was. It seems they were not at all happy about what had happened either. Mr. Buchanan's brother and family who were lawyers in Kincardine had come down and talked to him and convinced him into moving north to Kincardine to be closer to them They had brought an ambulance down with them and in great haste they removed him to the Trillium Court Retirement Community Centre in Kincardine.

I knew where Mrs. McDonald lived near Glencoe so I drove to her home to see what she could tell me about all this. She said it had been a surprise to her also, to find him gone when she went in to visit. I could see she was hurt at the way it had been handled. The least they could have done was to inform her in advance of their plans. After all she was a sister in law and she had done right for him when everyone else stood back and left him on his own. However knowing all about lawyers I guess we should not have been surprised, especially when the lawyers were all in the family. After all there was a few million of dollars involved.

On a nice day a few weeks later I felt the urge to get out of the city and re change my batteries. I am a country boy at heart and every now and then I seem to have the need to get out in the open and away from the city. So I decided I should drive up to Kincardine and see how Mr. Buchanan was making out in his new residence. I have always loved driving north through country roads north of the old Huron Track Highway #8, and then west, into picturesque hill and valley country along the Maitland River. Somehow by luck more then by design I would end up in Benmiller, one of Ontario's more captivating villages with historic beauty and natural charm…it looks and smells, …of old "Canadian Country."

It is a quiet little out of the way village in a tranquil setting along the banks of Sharpe's creek. A place once found is hard to forget. Then I travelled north through Carlow and Nile, going every which way north by northwest until I ended up in the town of Kincardine. Seldom do I go up, and come home the same way. This is a picturesque country that holds many great delights for those who like to wander.

I found, Trillium Court, retirement community on Philips Place without much trouble. It was a new red brick three floor mammoth ultra clean residence, with the air of a hospital. I found Mr. Buchanan in his room asleep in his wheel chair. I called his name quietly and he awoke. It was good to see the reflection of joy come into his sleepy face when he saw me. It was a Sunday and no doubt he was hoping someone would come to visit him. It was sad to see that life was slowly ebbing from his tired body. While he had always been a man of few words, what he had to say was always worth listening to. Though he was a little man he could sometimes do the work of two. He had always been very energetic, tireless and capable.

I did have some difficulty understanding what he said, but he was persistent and in the end we managed to understand each other. At times I find it goes better if I sort of guide the conversation. That way I know if we are talking about the elephant or the peanut. Naturally he wanted to hear all about the people he knew locally in and around his old apartment building. How was their health and what were they doing? He would ask how the building was being kept up and if the lawn was kept cut and about his rose bushes outside the entrance doors. I often snitched a rose and took it up to him. He loved the lilacs in the back alleyway so when they were in bloom I would take a bunch of them to him. I knew no one else but me would understand what these things meant to him. They were a part of where he had been for so many years and it was where his heart was. I had worked in those flowerbeds along side him and I knew how much he cared for them, and how even now from afar it was a touch of home for him.

He insisted that I go for supper with him in the cafeteria. It was nice as we sat at our own table and he introduced me to several of his new friends around us.

When we finished I wheeled him back to his room and I told him it was time for me to go. I will always remember what he said right then,

He said, "Jack don't go away and leave me." It was more like a plea, and for a minute I didn't know just what he meant.

I said, "I have to go home Mr. Buchanan, it's getting late and I should be on the road."

"Jack, I mean don't go back to London and never come back to see me. Please come back again soon as I need to see you."

So we chatted about this and I told him I knew it was difficult for him, and that I would keep in touch with him and see him through this. I would write him a nice letter every two weeks and drive up to see him on the fourth week. We agreed to this. It seemed I was committed to seeing him through these last years of his life.

Ever after, when I visited him I would see my letters propped up on his dresser and many of the staff would make comments to me on my letter writing ability. It seems half the hospital had read those letters, and he was very proud of them. As time went by he seemed to lose interest in watching TV or life beyond his four walls. He did enjoy visits, his letters and his meals. His world had become very small. I would talk to him and sometimes he didn't seem to respond, but I think he just took comfort in the fact that I was there.

On Reaching 65 in 1993

In the fall of 1993 I would be sixty-five Oct.17th so I decided to fly to Calgary and visit friends and perhaps see a bit of BC. As I still had the shop I was not free to keep it closed too long as that is bad for business. Most of the holidays I took were for ten days so I could be back to work by the middle of the second week. The rent had to be paid, but as this was for my 65th birthday I splurged and took two whole weeks plus 2 days.

My friends Ron and Lenora Oddie of Pincher Creek insisted on driving to the Calgary Airport to pick me up. While visiting them they gave me a whirlwind tour of places such as Head Smashed In Buffalo Jump, Writing On Stone National Park, the Oldman River Dam and a visit to Waterton Park, for my birthday dinner.

Soon it was time to move on so I rented a car from a place in Lethbridge, and left early one morning to drive to Creston BC for a visit with Mike and Jigs. It is a picturesque drive from Pincher Creek through the Crows Nest Pass and then south along the Elk River to Fernie and Elko where the highway turns sharply northwest and then south again to Cranbrook where I stopped for a late dinner. While I was not yet retired I was just a few days short of my 65th birthday and I had many hidden thoughts going round and round in my head about the future. I had worked and planned for retirement for many years but was still not sure if I was ready for it. Old people retire. Right? I had always worked all my life. Was <u>nothing</u>, what I really wanted to do?

I arrive at Yahk 15 miles north of the Idaho border where the highway turns due west. One drives for miles and nothing much changes, then suddenly as you round the corner near Creston you see apple orchards, and I mean beautiful apples of all kinds. Then there are pears, and plums and peaches. Soon you will see huge fruit and vegetable stands such as one would only expect to see farther west near the coast.

By now Mike and Jigs were building their dream home out on the farmland in the valley south of town. Jigs had written me and sent directions and a hand drawn map. I still have those directions and the map today. Lenora had phoned ahead to let them know I was on the way. They were watching for me late in the afternoon when I arrived. The new home was something right out of a book, and everything Jigs and Mike had always dreamed about. The house was built on a slope to the south, which ran off in lawn toward the bush. There was a southern deck built high all across the south side of the house and below this deck a patio and sliding doors into a basement apartment on the lower lawn level, a great place for guests or for family members. We talked late into the night and I got up late the next morning and found that Mike had already gone into town. So after Breakfast with Jigs, I took my camera out and wandered about the property. There was an area set aside for a garden although the soil right there was not good as it was heavy clay. I found a well-worn pathway leading off into the bush and down a winding lane to the creek. There I saw the new well, which they had dug a few feet from the creek bed from which the water would seep. All along the way I took pictures. There was the greatest selection of evergreen trees I ever saw in one place, many of evergreen trees I was not familiar with at all.

Mike came home with the truck box piled high with green stuff, which turned out to be Alfalfa leaf dust. There was a plant in the valley that made alfalfa into pelts for pet food. All around this pelt machine was alfalfa dust and as any farmer knows this is a great source of nitrogen and good for the soil. He also had several bags of peat moss. Now don't expect for one minute that Mike planned it this way. However there I was all afternoon wheeling, wheelbarrow loads of alfalfa and peat moss out into the garden while Mike mixed it into the soil with the tiller. Somehow it was good to be working and doing something I also liked to do. As we finished up the garden and put our tools away, I happened to mention something to Mike about taking pictures and walking down to the well.

He said, "Oh I meant to say something about not going down there alone" so he picked up a baseball bat and asked me to go for a walk with him. We took the path down through the bush leading to the creek and the well. Mike walked to the fresh earth packed all around the well and pointed out some tracks, which he said, were bear tracks. So no one walks down here alone and even then always carries a big stick. That night we planned a day trip for the next day.

My friend Mike has this thing about early mornings, so before anyone else is up he has half a day's work done. What he needs is a big barn and ten milk cows.

I decided to let Mike drive the rental car as he knows this country, and besides he always accused me of having a heavy foot, whatever that means. Soon we were off driving west across the Creston Valley flats that grows many kinds of crops. These crops are irrigated from the Kootenay Lake to the north. Once west of the Kootenay Lakes the winding road rises over the Nelson Range steadily higher and higher until it crosses the Mile High Pass over the great divide. Then we took the route north at Salmo to Nelson.

We arrived high above the town of Nelson and it was an amazing sight. I just found it hard to believe such a town existed in this part of BC. It is a town built of brick and limestone and would be more at home in the heart of old Ontario than away up here in this mountainous area of BC. The BC government has refurbished the buildings to preserve the town and attract tourists. North of Nelson we drove the car aboard a large double deck-ferry with an enclosed lounging room above and cruised north on the lake for the most of two hours before docking at Kootenay Bay on the east side. There was an ice cream store high on the shore to the north fronted with a long curved sandy beach and a few tables outside their door. I bought us all banana splits and we sat outside enjoying the sun and the view of the bay. From here we returned home to Creston on the east side of the lake. This is a torturous winding road that hangs tight to the mountainside above the lake, and certainly not a good route for a guy with a heavy foot like me to drive, so we let Mike continue to guide us.

We stopped along the way to see "The House of Glass." It is a house that some retired funeral parlour man built in his retired years. Over many years he visited funeral parlours all over the prairies and BC collecting empty embalming oil bottles to build his house. He first set them together in blocks and then built the block into the house. It is completely fire proof and has natural light; it is not a dollhouse but a full size home built as a castle. However I am not sure that everyone would sleep well in a house built of embalming oil bottles. It was a big day's drive and we all arrived back a bit tired but happy to be home.

The weekend was coming up and I had told my nephew Wayne Butler (Bill and Jean's son) in Red Deer Alberta to expect me. So on the third day I left early in the morning for Red Deer. It was one of those perfect warm sunny October days when the leaves on the trees were in full colour, and the air had that tang of fall to it. First I backtracked the way I had come to just beyond Cranbrook, where I took the road north to Kimberly. Then the road swings north east to join the 95 Highway, which goes north to Golden where it ends at the Trans Canada Highway. By noon I found myself in paradise cruising alongside a small southern branch of the mighty Columbia River through places with strange names like, Ta Ta Creek, Skookumchuck and Canal Flats. Now how can you not love a country with names like this? When lunchtime came I could see a rather nice eating-place straight ahead of me with a great body of water just beyond it. This is a small Columbia Lake and the highway swings left over a bridge on the river to follow the lake along its western shoreline.

I could not have found a better place to stop for lunch, as the food and service was excellent. My table was in front of a large picture window looking out to the forest in its blaze of colour on the far side of the lake. The sun was high and to the southwest just beyond a colourful mountain. All colours of mountain and trees reflected like a silhouette onto the lake. It was quiet, one could feel it, and oh so peaceful. My thoughts at that time were, if this is a part of my retirement then I am all for it. Perhaps at that time it gave me food for thought, that there was a time for everything, even retirement. There was certainly more to life then just work. I stayed on the 95 all the way to Golden where it ends at the Trans Canada Highway. From there I travelled east to Banff National Park through the Kicking Horse Pass.

Mountain Beauty on the Yellowhead Hwy.

The beauty was majestic and breath taking. This put me on the Banff to Jasper Highway just north of Lake Louise. One can't be this close and not take one more look at such an historic and beautiful place as Lake Louise. It was late in the afternoon and in the mountains it gets dark early. The season ends early here and even though there is much splendour to see it is a cool or even cold splendour indeed.

Now I should have turned south from here and found a gas station, but my journey was to take me north about mid way between Banff and Jasper and take the number 11 highway to Rocky Mountain House and from there on to Red Deer. So I turned north from Lake Louise and drove on. There is simply nothing along this stretch of highway, not a gas station for over 50 miles. Darkness came on and my gas gauge said zero for miles and miles. I know I must have had a guardian angel along with me or perhaps like that rabbit on TV, I had the right batteries. When I finally arrived at the #11 highway there was a huge new gas station and motel. I drove on to Rocky Mountain House and stopped for a late supper. I had a waitress phone Wayne, as I was sure by now he would be worried about me. So I asked him if I should stay at Rocky Mountain House overnight or drive on to Red Deer. He said to drive on to Red Deer and he would be up waiting for me when I got there. It was many years ago that Deke (young Don) Sutherland and I drove up this way to look at a ranch. At that time Rocky Mountain House was just a village with a large village store with Elk horns hung all across its front. Today it is an all-new large modern town with everything from great looking new motels to Tim Horton's.

Wayne was at this time working for Fracmaster, an international company in the business of sealing new oil wells and recovering oil from old wells. Wayne was working in Russian Siberia and was home for his holidays. He worked for so many days and then they flew him home for so many days off. He had been doing this for a number of years. He actually seemed to like the job or perhaps the money it paid.

I had visited Wayne before in the fall and I don't know how come my visit always coincided with digging potatoes but strangely enough it always did. After a couple of day's visit with Wayne I left Red Deer to drive east to Oyen, where I had spent much time in my youth. A part of me will always belong to that country.

When I pulled out on the freeway to drive south from Red Deer I felt in a good mood. Perhaps it was because I was out of the mountain with a wide-open highway in front of me, or maybe as Mike says I do have a heavy foot. But I stepped on the gas to hurry the car up to the point where I could turn on the speed control. About a quarter mile down the highway there was a growth of trees and an off-the-highway parking area. In there out of sight the Mounties had set up a radar trap. I got flagged off and it cost me big money. In mid afternoon I arrived at the turn off on highway #9 where you drive into the town of Oyen. Every time I return to Oyen so many memories of so many old friends and good times, flood my mind. Many of these friends are by now passed on. A half-mile down this road is the old cemetery where my dear old Aunt Rosena and Uncle Frank are buried. I had not gone far when I noticed a police car ahead. They flagged me to stop. I thought. "Not again!"

However it was just a routine check it seemed.

Their first question was, " Where are you going?"

I said, "Do you see that cemetery ahead, well I'm from Ontario out on holidays. Right now I'm going to that cemetery to have a little visit with my aunt and uncle."

Uncle Frank & Aunt Rosena's Grave Memorial Plaques

He shook his head and said, "Well I can't top that, go ahead and have a nice visit."

After a few days' visit with my many friends in and about Oyen I drove back to Lethbridge to return the car. My good friends Ron and Lenora were there waiting for me at the car rental place. I was to spend a couple more days with them. The next day they wanted to treat me to supper in an all-new plush restaurant at the golf course. I didn't feel it was at all necessary but they insisted. We arrived donned in our country best, and inside the door there was a large message board on which they would usually write down their special of the day. However in big bold writing was, "The New Waitress has nice big boobs" WOW! The Oddies were in shock. What a reception! However neither Ron nor I thought they were worth bragging about.

Now Ron and Lenora begged me to try the rainbow trout as they had it before and said it was the best they ever tasted. On the whole I am not a fish eater. While I love haddock as my fish and chips that is about it. Salmon steak is great if it is cooked thoroughly. As I wanted to please them I let them order me rainbow trout. The place was all new and very beautiful; they put us away over yonder behind some tall palm like plants. It appeared that the management was off and the young staffers were doing more then a little bit of joking around. It took us a long time to get service and then even longer to get served. Then when I went to cut into my trout I think it squirmed. It was raw, very raw. There was no way I was going to be able to eat this fish. I didn't know what to do as I deeply appreciated what they were doing for me and I wanted to be polite. Ron and Lenora were eating theirs so I started to eat around mine without touching it. They noticed this and asked what was the matter?

I said, " My fish is raw, I can not eat it."

We tried forever to wave down a server, but with no luck. Part of the reason was because this damn palm plant hid us. All this was sad as I lost my appetite looking at this raw fish on my platter. The Oddies paid the bill and we left. I checked out the bulletin board as we walked out the door and it still advertised the boobs and not the trout.

Early the next morning they drove me back to the Calgary Airport and saw me off home. Once back in London my friend Olga Filko met my flight and drove me home. The next day I was back to work cutting hair, but my mind was still away out there in the heart of BC, amid the towering mountains and tumbling creeks and rivers. So much was taken in, in all too short a time; it staggers the mind and takes time to accept.

My First Old Age Pension Check
November 1993 Woooopeee

Hurray! It was the end of November 1993 and my first Old Age Pension Check arrived. I had been taking my Canada Pension for a year now, so along with the shop income things suddenly felt a lot more comfortable. As yet I had no idea of stopping work as I enjoyed my clientele and cutting hair. I just could not see quitting.

Over the winter I continued to drive up to see Mr Buchanan, and thankfully the weather and roads remained good. It became harder to communicate with him and I can remember feeling relieved when the time came to leave for home as the visit had been taxing; yet I knew he looked forward to spending this time with me.

Thursday April 6th 1995 at the age of 88 years my dear old neighbour Joy Smith passed away at the Ritz Villa in Mitchell. As I mentioned earlier Ed died in 1978. These two people were a cherished part of my life and close to my heart.

Mr Buchanan Passes Away
Sept. 15th. 1995

I came home from work Sept. 15 1995 to find a letter taped to my apartment door. It was from Mr. Buchanan's niece Wendy Dale who lived here in London. She herself was a lawyer and the daughter of Mr Buchanan's brother, a lawyer too. Mr. Buchanan had passed away in the afternoon of the day before, which was Sept 14. There was information about visitation at 1 PM until 2 PM before the funeral. The funeral service would be held in the Davey Linkletter funeral home in Kincardine at 2PM the following Sunday. Interment was at the Tiverton Cemetery north of Kincardine, so it was over and I could not help but feel relieved for Mr. Buchanan and for myself but I could not help but wonder what would happen now. While I knew no one had done more for him then I had over the last twenty some years, I still felt it wrong to expect anything. Then again I reminded myself that he had several million dollars involved here so it did not seem at all impossible he might have thought of me and left me something.

However I never did hear anything about his will or whatever happened to his money to this day. I expect his family of lawyers saw to it that the money stayed close to home and in the family. Now years later I have no regrets, for as a friend I followed through and did what I knew was right.

The next few years went by very smoothly, '95, '96. I was more relaxed as I had fewer financial worries with my pension checks and my shop income. I started to think about buying a condo as the rent for the apartment was going up every year and the owner was not looking after the property. It was a joke to see as many as three men come with a lawn mower to cut the grass. They left it until it was a foot high, and by then the mower would balk at so much grass. They cut it in every direction blowing it out onto the sidewalk, the street and onto the driveway. One guy would work at it for one minute stalling the motor and having to re start it, as he fought to get from one end to the other and back again. Then a second guy would grab it from him and do the same. When it was finished it looked as if the aliens had landed. When I came home at night from work or on weekends this unmaintained look bothered me to no end. I did not enjoy living like that. I was determine to do something about it, but not sure just what.

I Think About Buying A Condo

I asked Olga to come with me to take a look at some Condos on Deveron Crescent in southeast London. I found the price was right and they were well maintained and also had good funds in the Condo's shared cost, balance on hand. One does not want to move into a place that is short on funding for upkeep and maintenance.

Other things I liked about it were the many conveniences near by. A big box Grocery Store, (its Basic's now) a Home Hardware a Zeller's, two gas stations and a Burger King. Then there was a long strip plaza with all conveniences one needs from a library to pizza shops, sub shops, a dry cleaner and variety stores, even a One Dollar Store and a Canada Trust. To top that was a brand new Shoppers Drug Store a new super car wash has been added as of late. Every thing was within walking distance and all relatively new. My thoughts were that if I ever had to give up my wheels this would be a good place to be. It was about one block off Highbury Ave and so a direct route across town to drive north to Mitchell, St.Marys or Stratford and also a direct route to the 401.

It was time to do some serious thinking about the future. I had thoughts of buying all new furniture. Although much of what I had at this time was in really good condition it was nearing forty years old, and now with hopefully many years of retirement ahead of me I wanted a change for the sake of change. I felt it would be good for me health-wise to sort of start anew. I was also wondering just what I was going to do with the old stuff. My first thoughts were of course "garage sales" so I had a number of garage sales. Although it seems many people don't like doing them, I actually enjoy garage sales and I really made out very well with them. At the first few I would ask a fair price on things and then later on have a fire sale. Then I packed up what was left and took it to the Salvation Army Store. One of the things I took was an under-the-arm crutch, which was in like-new condition. It had been in the closet of my apartment when I moved in and thankfully I never needed it. A week after I gave it to the Salvation Army a close friend had a bad fall and phoned me to ask if they could borrow it. I drove down to the SA Store and bought it back for $10.00. I will just consider it a donation. Now isn't that life!

I shopped all over London for months searching for the perfect Chesterfield and chairs, end tables and wall units. I looked at most furniture today as being rather bulky and too big for condo living. Then one Sunday as I was returning from out of town I decided to stop at "Partridges Furniture" a well-known furniture store for its quality, far out on the #22 Highway west of town. It was closed right then but I knew you could walk across the front and down the sides and view into its huge showcases windows.

In the one window I saw exactly what I was looking for and it was love at first sight. It had nice flat oak armrests, square oak legs and the end framed with slats. The end tables matched the design with the same oak legs and slat sides. I thought this part of my search was now over until I went back later to check on the price. The price was beyond what I thought I should afford. So my search continued.

This search took me to what use to be Patton Brothers on Wharncliffe Road South where a second cousin Wayne Butson worked. He showed me everything they had in the store but there wasn't anything I really wanted. I finally told him I knew exactly what I wanted but I could not afford it.

He said, "Jack tell me what it is you want and I will give you a cousin deal?"

I said, " Pray tell me what is a cousin deal?"

"It's a whole lot less then you would have to pay anywhere else," he said

I told him it was La-z-Boy furniture I wanted, so he got out the catalogue and we found the furniture I wanted. We worked on the price and true to his word I could not afford not to buy exactly what I wanted from him. The set I had seen in the window at Partridges Furniture had two love seats and a La-z-Boy chair along with two end tables, so that was what I ordered.

I returned over the months and bought much more furniture, three sections of wall units and a dining room set and buffet, then a beautiful oak hall table and mirror for my hall, two Queen Ann chairs for the bedroom, and a La-z-Boy bed chesterfield, which was to go in the den. I can't thank my cousin enough for what he did for me. "Happiness is new furniture paid for." I was buying the furniture and paying cash for it as I went along. I could do this as I was cutting hair and collecting my pension. At the same time I was selling off, or giving away my old furniture.

In the summer of 1996 I decided to try to sell the shop before fall so I would not have to drive to work five days a week the next winter. I put an ad in the London Free Press and ran it for a several weeks. A number of barbers came to enquire about the business, but no serious buyers. Everyone wanted to rent it from me or make some kind of weird deal. Right then in 1996 all business in general was not good and people were afraid to step out and take over the shop or start any kind of new business.

By fall I was getting a bit discouraged and my lease was coming up for renewal by the end of the year. Soon I had to make up my mind as to whether I was going to close the shop down or continue to work. I was more inclined to continue to work.

Yvonne Has A Deal

Then one day Yvonne Enright, who owned "Reflections" a unisex shop in the same plaza, dropped by to see me. We had always got along well and as a rule we never visited each other unless it was for plaza business. I think we both felt the same way. We were aware our shops competed for business in the same area but we respected one another and neither of us would bad-mouth each other. Yvonne asked me how I was making out re selling the business. I told her it looked as if I was going to have to stay working until things got better business-wise.

She asked, "Do you want to quit work Jack or maybe just work shorter hours?"

I admitted that while I didn't want to come in to work five days a week anymore I enjoyed cutting hair, so I would consider a job cutting hair a couple of days a week.

Yvonne said, "So why don't you just close the shop down and come and work for me a couple of days a week? In the end you might make more out of it than if you sold too cheap." Now I had not thought of this option and it was right in front of my nose. I told her I would give it serious thought and get back to her.

Over the next few weeks I managed to sell or give away everything in the shop. My chair went to a shop on Clark Side Road here in London and my beautiful oak barber cupboard went to Bill Kells in Strathroy. Bill had the chair next to me in barber school. My couch and end tables went to my niece in Stratford, and my old oak desk to my niece in Mitchell, as it was her mother, my sister Jean, who had given it to me. Just walking away from the shop was very hard. It was mine and I was proud of it.

The first week of December 1996, I started to work with Yvonne. At first I believe I sometimes shocked her with what I might say, but in time she came to know that sometimes she had to take what I said with a grain of salt. By the end of the next year we were very good friends and have remained friends until this day. The two days a week suited me just fine and while I lost a number of weekend customers it still was a good thing for me and it was also extra money for Yvonne.

A Friend " Olive Sutherland Passes Away "
Aug.31st. 1996

It is always sad when those who were an important part of your life at one time pass away. Olive Sutherland died August 31/1997. I cannot visualize her for less than she really was, a well dressed, educated women, sharp and witty with so much love and pride for life, her family, her friends and of course her music.

During the summer of 1997, I receiver the sad news Jigs had cancer. She would have to go in for radiation treatments in Vancouver some time soon. Jigs and Mike had friends in Edmonton, Dave and Kathy Laing who had moved there from Creston BC to manage a huge storage company. Dave and Cathy invited them to come and stay with them and take the treatments in Edmonton. This was good as staying in Vancouver for several weeks would have cost them a lot of money.

I decided to take another trip west to see all my old friends once more and I also could visit with Jigs while she was taking her treatments in Edmonton. Perhaps I could cheer her, but secretly I was also afraid it might be the last chance I would have to visit with her.

I flew to Calgary where Ron and Lenora Oddie met my flight. We drove back to Pincher Creek for a few days where we could unwind together over many cups of coffee and endless chatter. It was always a great way to start off my holiday trip as I am with old friends tried and trusted. I get all the local news on the many people we both know. Then I get a pep talk on Alberta's many woes with Ontario and also an incriminating disclosure of our dear old Ottawa. Of course the best part of it is, it is all for free. It does not cost me a cent unless of course I open my mouth.

Lenora took me to the Ford Dealer, the only place that rents cars in Pincher Creek. I rented a brand new small Ford model, an Escort. At the time I was not impressed, but I learned to love the car. It had wheels that served me well, and in the mountains it amazed me with its response, and the deal was very good.

My plans were to drive across country to Oyen where I would visit the Bull family and see all my friends there once more. Even then in the back on my mind was the hope that if I went by the town of Brooks I might visit with my old friend Deke Sutherland. He was now living there in a Senior Citizen Home.

Deke and Cathy

Away back in the first part of my book I introduced you to a family, "The Sutherlands" Don, Olive and their three sons Deke, Colin and Neil, a ranch family near the village of Lanfine south west of Oyen Alberta.

I ended that part of my story with the oldest Sutherland son Deke and Cathy Campbell seemingly a happy couple who would marry that fall after the harvest was off and I had returned home to the east. While I was very happy for them I was yet concerned, as I have always been under the impression one cannot expect to have a full and satisfied life without God's blessings. You cannot openly or even secretly defy or deny God and have a full life.

Young Deke had shared his innermost thought with me and I knew basically he was a great person. He was fast to learn, quick to move and always had to be the best man on the job. Although short in stature he was strong in body and will, he was perhaps more like his father, very set and stubborn with his own convictions. Perhaps his greatest problem was that of his stature as he felt the need to always prove himself. In some ways we were alike and in other ways we were far apart. In spite of our differences we respected each other and were the best of friends. He had made me very much aware of his love for, "His way of life," which included first horses, then white face cattle and of course ranch lands of all Alberta. At that time I knew all this was dwarfed by his love for Cathy. Cathy was his everything.

Yet I was troubled by his open defiance and his seemingly lack of any religious acknowledgement, and I feared what might happen to this great pair of young people who were at that time very close to me. I myself was certainly no angel but still I knew God and I always felt that God was with me even though I may not have always measured up. The question I asked then was what does life hold for this young couple that I thought so much of…….Deke and Cathy?

I will continue with that story now.

Late in the summer of 1961 well before the harvest was ready at Bulls I drove down south of the Red Deer River to visit Deke and Cathy. They were renting a small ranch near Bindloss. While it had a very nice barn and coral and fencing, the house itself left much to be desired. It was a small square unpainted frame clapboard house seemingly lost in a huge spacious yard on the flat empty prairie. The packed dirt earth expanded all the way from the corals to the front door. Only a true westerner could learn to live like that. An easterner would have planted a tree, dug a flowerbed and grown a lawn, but I knew the best Cathy could ever hope for was a vegetable garden.

Deke was working off the ranch to supplement his ranch income. He worked for other ranchers and tried to get his own work done on the side. There had never been a lazy bone in his body. He was obviously a very happy and satisfied man. Cathy was by now heavy with child. She was only about five foot seven and small in frame, but now mid summer and it did not look as if she could wait much longer, but the baby was not due for perhaps a month yet. Cathy glowed and wore her maternity with pride.

The house consisted of one large room with an enclosed staircase going to a sole upper bedroom. Against the staircase wall was a large wood cook stove, which heated the whole downstairs and the stovepipe warming the bedroom above. To the rear of the stove and under the stairs was Cathy's pantry. While it wasn't much it was theirs and they happily shared it with me. I truly felt welcome, and the warmth of their hearts.

I stayed overnight sleeping on a couch. The only thing that bothered me was the stack of empty beer boxes in the kitchen. It made me very aware that while dollars might be short, beer was still very much in demand and a solid part of Deke's life. Cathy was as good in the kitchen as she was on a horse and always every inch a gracious ranch lady.

That was the very last visit I had with them. Deke's mom Olive wrote me many long wonderful letters over the years keeping me informed on the weather, the crops, and community activity and on Don and herself and the Sutherland family. In the end I came to realize her proud Scottish family pride would not allow her to acknowledge a bad situation if she saw one. In her mind she was sure if she willed herself not to see or believe some things, then all would turn out alright in the end.

Two beautiful healthy twin boys were born to Cathy late that summer. The Campbell and the Sutherland families rejoiced with pride. Of course Olive wrote to tell me the news.

When Christmas came, Deke wanted to party to celebrate his first year of marriage and his good fortune. He asked his many young drinking friends to come and party. The night of the party the temperature outside the little house dropped very low to perhaps 36 or 38 F below. The cook stove was fed wood and the house would grow very hot and then someone opened the door and it was suddenly cold again. The little house rocked with music and loud voices and free beer flowed.

As always when people drink heavily they have to relieve themselves and this little house had no inside plumbing. Every few minutes someone opened the door to go out and as it was so cold out there they were soon back in again. The two babies were in a crib in the same room and I don't suppose the loud music shouting and laugher and cold and hot air was at all good for them.

At that time almost one hundred percent of Alberta ranchers smoked, so these two babies were also struggling to breath in a house full of smoke. I remember how at the tender age of fifteen, Deke could roll a cigarette with one hand. It was a skill he had perfected. I know he had practiced long and now did it with ease and pride. It was a part of his ranch life, his personal cowboy make up. He had long practiced doing all the things he felt a rancher or cowboy should know or do..

A day after the party, Olive got word the two small children were both sick. She was very concerned so she made a hurried trip down to see them. In a short time they were taken to the hospital, as both were very ill. A day or two later one died and the other came home.

There was much talk in the community as to why they chose to party in such cold weather when they had two very small children in the house. The Sutherlands and Campbells were sad and in distress, but they hesitated to openly lay blame.

By now I was running my own barbershop here in London and as we sometimes say, "Life moves on" and for a number of years I did not hear much about Deke and Cathy.

I often thought of them and through Olive's letters I did know that several more children were born, I believe another boy and two or three girls.

Then one winter I heard shocking news of a second death in the family, a boy in his young teens. The story saddened me and I understand there was an inquest into his death as he died from a broken neck.

At this time Deke was butchering his own cattle and selling the beef to customers he had made in the town of Brooks. The children now were now old enough to be left alone. Cathy sometimes went into town with him to help deliver the meat and perhaps to shop, as Brooks even at that time was a large town.

The Sutherland family had always liked to work with their very own leather. Thus they all had a tack shop somewhere on the property. It was a nice place to spend a quiet winter afternoon, a place where they could make or mend their own saddles or fix a bridle or halter, or do repairs to a horse harness from their very own leather. Because of the butcher business Deke had lots of cattle rawhide which is what they call new leather. They sometimes cut long strips of leather which was hung in the basement to dry. In this case a strip of leather had been strung along the front of the boy's bunk in the basement to dry.

Cathy who was helping Deke to deliver meat in Brooks made a phone call home to tell her daughter Maryann they were on the way home. She was to start supper and to tell her brother to start the evening barn choirs. Maryann went to the basement door and told her brother mom had called and they were on the way home. He was to start the evening chores.

Perhaps they will never know exactly what happened but what they are inclined to believe is that the boy quickly slid off the top bunk under the strip of leather rawhide, and as he did the strip of raw hide came up under his chin snapping his head back quickly breaking his neck. After a time when he didn't come up his sister went to the basement and found him dead hanging from the rawhide under the chin with the back of his head against the bunk bed. We suppose that after his neck snapped he was unable to move. Again tragedy had struck this little family and many people were again in shock. Some thought while it was a tragedy it should not have happened and could have been prevented. We can all, always benefit from hindsight; however such was the way of life in those days of yesteryears. Bad things happened and few questions were asked. It would be many years before I heard much about Deke and Cathy again, not until a further tragedy.

It is hard to remember exactly when but I would say sometime in the mid-eighties I received a message from a friend that Deke was in extensive care in the Foothill Hospital in Calgary and that something very bad had happened to him.

They said they would keep me informed but asked me not to contact the family just yet until things were a bit more clear. I received more word from others but there was nothing very clear to help me to understand what had happened.

Sometime in the mid eighties I decided to fly out to Calgary and see all my friends again. I was advised not to ask Don or Olive any questions, as it was too painful. I think I have explained to you somewhere in my book that old families out there hesitate to speak too openly about neighbours as it seems somewhere down the line everyone is related.

However before I left for home I did find out what happened and it was hard to believe. It seems that Deke's drinking had consumed him and he often came home drunk and beat up Cathy and his kids. It was after one such beating Cathy left him. By now the last of the children had left home and Cathy had a very good job working at a huge sale and auction barns south of Calgary. She was on her own.

When Deke finally realized what he had done to his life and to his family he was in a sorry state of mind. He realized Cathy was serious and was not going to once again forgive him and come home. In spite of all he had done, in his heart he still loved Cathy and did not want to live without her. He took an old revolver out and put it to the centre of his forehead and pulled the trigger. No one will ever understand why it did not kill him outright. At that range the bullet should have gone right through his head but for some reason it lodged in his brain. I don't know who it was that found him or how he got to the hospital. They managed to get the bullet out but at some expense to his brain. He lingered near death for weeks and I suppose he had every reason to want to die. After all as far as he was concerned it would then be over, no heaven to think about, no God to answer to. It would be over and he would be free.

When he left the Calgary hospital he was taken to a 'Home For The Seniors' in Brooks. It was a home for elderly and people with problems like him. My friend Lenora Oddie in Pincher Creek was by her first marriage an Aunt to Deke. She was also a life-long friend. Naturally she was concerned about him and his welfare and she wanted to help. She called him on the phone at times and sometimes visited him when she drove from Pincher north to her hometown of Oyen.

Several times when I was west to visit I asked Lenora to ask him if I could have a visit with him, but he declined. Then on a trip west in the year 1997 I was driving a rented car from Pincher Creek to Oyen and I had to pass through the town of Brooks. I decided to visit Deke at the home as I longed to see him once more. I knew it was risky, as he did not allow many people to visit.

There was an intercom just inside the doorway. I hate all intercoms as in my Silent World I never know if anyone is there or not. I didn't feel I could handle it with Deke, not knowing how well he was or if he would remember me.

I beckoned to a lady within and she came to the door. I explained the situation to her as best I could. She said it would be no problem, to just take the elevator to the third floor then go to his door and walk in.

I found his door and knocked but he didn't answer. After knocking a few times the neighbour across the hall looked out and told me to just open the door and walk in. So that was what I did. I saw a perfect stranger seated at the far end of a long table. He was watching a TV on the other end of the same table. I noticed that the channel was blank. In front of him was an assortment of coffee mugs, dirty dishes and jars of jam and a loaf of bread. He looked at me without any sign of recognition.

I said, "Are you Deke Sutherland?"
He said. "Yes."
I said. "Do you know me?"
"No, I have never met you before."
"You mean to tell me you don't remember Jack Cooke from Ontario?"
A look of recognition came to his troubled face and he said,
"Oh yes I remember you now Jack, but it has been a long, long time."

It was hard to look at his face, as it seemed the bullet must have exploded inside the head bursting the entire skull outward. His head was so very large with a hole clearly visible in the very centre of the forehead. Never would he be able to look in the bathroom mirror and forget what he had done to himself. All the problems in his life surrounded that hole the size of a pencil and as deep as you could see in.

Now that I was here I was not at all sure it was a good idea. It seemed with his lack of memory and my lack of hearing it was hard to keep a conversation rolling. I soon found out though that his thoughts were a constant hit and miss. He thought he still had a truck and a ranch to go to. On his refrigerator I could see a few family pictures. Several of his son Cameron riding a bull with a story telling about his Alberta Bull Riding Championship. I left sooner then I had planned as time started to get heavy on our hands. I think I did right to go to see him, - perhaps more for him then for me, as now he might know I didn't just walk away and desert him. Deep within myself I grieve for Deke and Cathy for I know what could have been. Forever now when I think of Deke, in my mind's eye I will never be totally free of that hole in the centre of his forehead.

Cathy was working for a man by the name of John Scott who supplied horses and wagons for the movie industry. She also worked part time at the sales barns.

A few years later good fortune smiled on Cathy and her son Cameron when an American movie maker came to Southern Alberta to shoot the movie "Lonesome Dove." They needed all kinds of help to find the right horse to match to the right riders and someone who knew how to hitch wagons and buggies up properly.

Have you ever given thought to the fact that while some of those handsome dudes look great seated on a horse or wagon in the movie, most could not harness or even saddle their own horse? They would not know a whipple tree from a double tree nor neck yoke from the hames. All this was right down Cathy and her son's lane as they grew up on a ranch with all this in her everyday life. I am not sure but I think Cameron the son still works in this field today on movie sets in Alberta and BC. Don died in the home a few years ago, thus ending his life.

I sometimes wonder why one way or another I could not have made a difference in the lives of the Sutherland boys as at one time I shared much with them. I cared about them and I had foreseen the trouble brewing, but as Don had said, I could tell them what I believes, but I was not to tell them what they should believe.

At one time while working at Bulls I started to write a story on my troubled thought based on Don and Olive and what they thought they had given their children to protect them from the knocks of life. This basically was "You are what you are because of your ancestors and it is up to you to live up to your family name and not let them down."

It troubled me that I was forbidden to talk to the Sutherland boys about God or Faith, and they openly tried to bait me. Perhaps in my feeling of defeat I wrote down my thoughts for a book. Then after a time I realized I didn't want to or could not finish it so I put it away in my suitcase in my room. I think Mrs. Bull went looking for clothes to wash and she ran across the story. As it was based on her niece and family it troubled her, so she told Mr. Bull about it.

Some time later he came to me and asked me about it. It was the title that bothered them the most. I had chosen for the title, "The Bitter Fruits Of Empty People."

I told Mr. Bull someday I might finish the story; ---- this is the story that you have just read. I have finally finished it, as I had expected it has a sad ending.

Back to my visit with Deke, - I left Deke behind knowing in my heart I would never see him again. As I drove on to Oyen I had mixed feelings as to whether this visit had served any purpose or not. I think up until then I had found the whole thing bizarre and hard to believe. Perhaps I was looking for something I'm not sure just what, an excuse or perhaps for me, closure. I had once known Deke as a healthy vibrant and active young man, and now he was not only old but also a different person. How could all this be true? How could something so terrible happen to someone you grew up with, someone you had admired and cared for?

A Return Visit to Oyen

The Oyen country was still under a severe drought condition and I could see that no one had harvested a grain crop. Those that had cattle were already feeding their stock to keep them alive. Dust entered my car and did not agree with me.

I found my friend Alma and son Brian Bull home waiting supper for me. I had actually planned to stay for a few days there, as this at one time had been my home away from home. Then I would drive on to my nephew Wayne in Red Deer. By now I had a pounding headache caused by the endless prairie dust. There was no way you could escape it, as it is so fine. It was on every breath of air you breathe. After the second day I knew I had to get away from this dry and dusty country or I was going to be very sick.

I felt rather sad to leave Alma and Brian so soon. I felt my visit was interrupted.

I drove on towards Red Deer to visit with Wayne my nephew and his family. As I left the dry and dusty country behind my headache started to clear and by the time I arrived in at Wayne's in Red Deer I was feeling fine again.

Wayne knew I was coming so he had taken a few days off so we could be together. Before I knew it we were out in the garden digging up Yukon Gold potatoes again. No one grows monster potatoes like Wayne, but I am beginning to think what I hear is true. They say he relies totally on eastern help to harvest his potato crop.

When I left Wayne, I drove on to Edmonton. Upon approaching Edmonton I found the traffic backed up for miles. It seems the Rolling Stones were in town and all of Alberta was on the road. Eventually I was able to get away from the traffic and found the place where Mike and Jigs were staying. Because of the Rolling Stones being in town all the inns and hotels were already full when I arrived. Dave and Kathy said not to worry, as they would set up a cot in the laundry room for me. This worked out excellent, as I could stay with Mike and Jigs all the time. I rewarded the Laing's by going out and buying the hugest steaks I ever bought for everyone for supper the next night and Mike did the barbequing.

I also got to know the Laings. Since then they have come to London to visit me.

I had arrived about 5 PM and Dave and Cathy had to work late every evening as that was when people wanted to get into their lockers. So the first night I treated Mike and Jigs to supper at a restaurant plaza across the street. I paid for the supper with my master card. We chatted as old friends do, and while walking back across the lot towards the street a man came up behind me and said,

"I think you dropped this." In his hand was my master card. I am getting older and I am sure God has given me a Guardian Angel to watch over me as several things happened to me on this trip that could have been very bad.

Shelly, Mike and Jig's daughter had come down to Edmonton with her boyfriend from Grand Prairie to the Rolling Stone Concert and then had come by to see her mom. Shelly begged me to drive to Grand Prairie to see the city and have a visit with her.

As I had long wanted to see more of Alberta and BC interior I said yes.

I made plans to leave early in the morning and drive first to Peace River and then back down to Grand Prairie, a distance of over 700 km. or roughly 450 to 500 miles. This is a nice day's drive as long as you don't sit still too long in one place.

Mike assured me that with my heavy foot I was quite capable of doing it. I asked Shelly if she could arrange a place for me to stay in Grand Prairie the next night so I would not have to worry about lodging when I arrived. They said they would look after it as soon as they arrived back in Grand Prairie and then phone me. I got their phone call before midnight and the address of an inn not too far from where Shelly lived.

My little 4-cylinder Ford rental car took the trip with ease, and mile after mile flew by. All my life I had heard of these far away places. Now here I found myself looking down at the Peace River and all about me was this flat wonderful rich prairie farmland. I know I should have taken more time, as who knows if ever again will I stand there and view that historic place, a proud part of Canadian heritage. I arrived in Grand Prairie late that evening and found my inn. It was a bit more plush than I needed but Shelly seemed to think I had money to spend and she wanted me to spend it.

The next morning when I went down to the office Shelly was there waiting for me. We went to a Pancake House for breakfast and then she showed me a bit of the town. We also went to a Price Costco Store that was not far from my inn.

By early afternoon I was anxious to get on my way to Dawson Creek and hopefully on to Prince George by night. Shelly on the other hand was trying to get me to stay one more day. She was very sad when I left, as I was to her a touch of home. I had known her since she was a baby and she always called me Uncle Jack.

I was impressed with the newness of the country between Dawson Creek and Chetwynd, and then somewhere far beyond I was back into real mountain country again. Suddenly a blinding snowstorm came up and for miles I drove close behind a huge logging truck. I knew as long as I kept his taillights in sight I was fairly safe. This however slowed my driving down to a crawl. Then suddenly I rounded a bend at Pine Pass and as if by magic the storm had passed and it was calm and over. I remember pulling off the road to clean off my windshield and being amazed at the pure whiteness of the country all around me after this flash snowstorm. It was a ghostly sight as the mountains and trees, shrubs and weeds near and far were all pure white. It was all so quiet, so still, it was almost reverent.

The storm had put me hours behind in my planned arrival in Prince George and I was thinking I should pull into the first place I could find. But finding lodging in this country is not easy when you leave it too late. There is a stretch north of Prince George where there is no lodging, gas station or a store for over a hundred miles. Then if you come to a small place late in the evening there is "No Vacancy." So I knew I was going to have to drive on to Prince George. I had my CAA book along with me and I had picked out a place where I hoped to stay. The driving was now good and I was making good time again. I was aware one should slow down driving in the mountains at night and especially so when you're in strange territory.

I was driving down a steep hill with a rocky ditch on my left, and forest on the right. My headlight showed only downward until I came to the bottom of the hill, then the lights suddenly shone up and ahead. Caught in my headlights was a huge bull moose. I kid you - not, - the daddy of all moose. He was standing broadsided to me snorting vapour into the cool night air. He was taking up oh ... so much highway and I was driving oh... so fast. I doubted very much that I could stop in time. I had to make an instant decision. What was the best thing for me to do?

I realized my headlights had blinded him. I could not pass behind him as the shoulder dropped all too fast onto big rocks, but if I tried to swerve around in front of him would he stand still and let me pass, or as soon as the lights were off him would he continue to cross the highway? I was sure my only way out of this was to swerve and pass in front of him, but I had wasted precious seconds thinking about it so.... Is there still time? I swerved sharply to the left and as if by magic the great moose seemed to turn, smoothly as if on a lazy Susan towards me so he faced me and I glided by him, his huge body within a hair length of my far side window.

I found I was shaking from head to toe, as I realized I just escaped from having a terrible accident, and then I thanked my God for sending me that guardian angel. I slowed down; oh <u>yes I did</u>, as I continued on the way and neared Prince George. Truly I was not expecting much of Prince George, perhaps a lumber town with all too many huge trucks and rough truck stops, ill kept restaurants and tumbled down bars in old hotels.

Imagine my surprise to enter the city on a wide expressway that would put my London to shame. The traffic was heavy and as I was still shaken from my near accident. I got in the outside lane so I could drive slower and watch the highway signs and also for a motel. I already noted many NO VACANCY signs along the way. Suddenly I noted that the right lane had to exit, and the inside lane was full and would not let me over. I had to exit to the right. The ramp took me up and then to the left and soon I was driving over top of the highway below the one I had just come in on. Naturally I was worried about getting lost at this time of night, about 10 pm.

Oh well I thought, I will look for an inn or hotel and worry about the highway in the morning. To my left far down were bright lights, which turned out to be a huge gas bar along with a variety store. I filled up with gas and then went in to pay for it.

The store was busy and I had to get in line for the till. I wanted to ask about an inn or motel, a place to stay that night and about directions. When I asked the lady behind the counter she looked at me in despair, and shouted,

"Stephen come here." She explained to him that I was deaf, lost, and needed help.

I told him about my narrow escape with the moose out on the highway, and he told me it was rutting season and very dangerous to drive in the country at night.

Stephen said there was a nice motel close by and he knew the owner. He asked me to follow him and off he drove around the corner and down a side street. Soon a nice big motel came in view all lit up, looking warm and inviting in the cool night. I was in shock as it was the place I had hoped to find, - the one in my CAA book I had been looking for. Now what were my chances of getting totally lost and yet ending up here? However a big "No Vacancy" sign was showing and my heart sunk to a new low.

Stephen came over to my car and said to me,

"You wait here while I go in and talk to them."

I could see them from my car windshield talking in earnest. I had little hopes, but soon Stephen came to the motel door and beckoned me to come in.

The lady behind the counter looked me in the eye and said,

"Do you smoke?"

"No. I don't smoke." I said.

"Well I have one single left which I always keep back for emergencies and it is yours for tonight."

Stephen helped me carry my luggage to my room and then he drew me a map to show me how to get from the motel back onto the highway towards Kamloops. Then he gave me his card and phone number and said.

"If you have any trouble at all in the morning have someone call this number and I will come and put you on the right road." How could I thank him enough?

Now I ask you again, "Do you believe in Guardian Angels?"

The next day I wandered south down through Williams Lake country where Lenora's father owned a ranch for many years before he passed away. He and a son moved there and homesteaded about 50 years ago when there was only a trail in. It is great ranch country; the kind people like you and I have forever dreamed about. It is also the home of a large Jehovah Witness community. I drove on to Kamloops where I stopped for supper and then on again to Vernon on the northern end of the Okanagan Lake and valley where I stayed for the night.

In the morning I drove east through rather empty spacious country to Needles on the main branch of the Columbia River. Here you board a ferry and cross the river to Fauquier. I might add here that the ferries are government owned so free to travel on. Once across the river and back on the road again I found it hard to believe I had to travel over sixty miles due north around a mountainous part of the country before I could drive east again. So I drove north to Nakusp and then mainly southeast, then east to Nelson. That evening I was back in familiar territory again at Creston, but as Mike and Jigs were in Edmonton I had no reason to stay there.

I stopped at one of the larger fruit and vegetable stands and bought two half bushels of apples for Ron and Lenora, one of Spartan and one of McIntosh and also a large basket of plums. Driving on the smell of apples wafted in the car.

It was late when I decided to stop in Cranbrook for supper and perhaps the night. The waitress serving me was talkative and offered to call Ron and Lenora and let them know where I was and that all was OK.

Lenora was upset, as there was a bad snowstorm on the way. It would hit the Crows Nest Pass that night and Pincher Creek before morning.

She said, " Jack get out of the mountains tonight with that small car. You are about a two-hour drive from Pincher Creek. Have your supper and then drive on. You can be here shortly after eleven and I will have your bed ready and the coffee on."

I felt refreshed after my supper and actually eager to drive on to Pincher Creek to be with my old friends Ron and Lenora again. By the time I reached the Crows Nest Pass I could see it had snowed for some time, and was still snowing. As if by magic my world was suddenly white and much like a Christmas card. The driving though was good and shortly after eleven I was in Pincher Creek. Very soon I was driving east out of Pincher to the Oddie ranch. I could see the lights in the living room window and I knew the coffee was on and a warm welcome awaited me.

I arrived amid a few lonely snowflakes, which had followed me all the way out of the mountains. Certainly it felt great to find myself back inside under a friendly roof. I was sure that by morning I would wake up to a different world. Somehow I didn't mind the change of weather, as there is a certain comfort to be found within the home of friends on a wintry night.

Wood Carving and Photography

For many years Lenora had taken two hobbies very seriously, photography and woodcarving. Every wall in their house reflects her interest. I marvel at how she manages to shuffle everything and still find room for yet one more picture or carving. Her photography even found a place on the cover of the American Appaloosa magazine a number of years ago. Many livestock breeders call on her to go to their ranch or farm to take professional pictures of their stock for advertisement or sales purpose. Wherever she goes her camera is always close at hand and ready for a by-chance picture. So often a bi chance picture is the very best

In August of 2004 she exhibited her carving at the Cultural Centre Gallery in Medicine Hat along with other Canadian artist and sculptures.

"Lenora's Carving "Zips Top Crop"

"Walk On"
Bull of the year 1999
Lenora's Carving

Lenora's Appaloosa Horses

The next morning the snow had reached Pincher Creek and everything was under a blanket of heavy snow from the kitchen window to the far-off mountains.

I spent a couple of great days with Ron and Lenora and then flew back home to London. Wednesday and Thursday found me back in the shop behind the barber chair, cutting hair along with Yvonne. Hair was falling on the floor but my mind was still out there somewhere, lost in the mountains.

My Friend - Don Sutherland Sr.
Passes away Dec. 27th, 1997

December 27, 1997 I received word that my friend Don Sutherland Sr. in Alberta passed away at the age of 87. I feel an empty place in my heart for Don and Olive as they were there for me at a time in my life when I needed them. Don was born at Govan Saskatchewan, the third of six children. He came to Lanfine of the Oyen district in the spring of 1913 with his father and mother. In 1936 he married Olive Partridge and bought the farm south of Lanfine. Neil the youngest son now runs the farm.

We received a notice of yet another yearly rent increase on our apartments and I thought it was time to get serious about buying a condo. I had Bill and Jean come down to London and go with me to see the condos at 735 Deveron Cres. They too liked what they saw, and Bill mentioned that nearly all of the cars parked on the lot were late models so this would tell you a bit about the average tenant living here. These condos came in one, two, or three bedroom units. I decided on a two-bedroom, and I would turn the one into a den with a sofa bed for company.

So I started the paper work to proceed to buy a condo in early August 1998.

I had my choice of several condos, and I ended up picking this one. I also could pick out the paint and carpet. Everything was to be ready for me by Oct. 1st, 1998.

Bill and Jean and Jack Fly West Aug. 1998

About this same time in August of 1998 my sister Jean and Bill decided to fly west to visit their son Wayne and family in Red Deer Alberta. They asked me if I would like to fly out with them and show them some of the interior part of BC. They thought I would make a good guide as they were not at all sure how to pick a scenic route. I thought that it might be fun to share the trip with them so I went along. The good thing about three or four people travelling together is they can all share the cost and make things more affordable. Lets say the Inn in Grand Prairie cost me about $100.00 for one night which I really couldn't afford, but with three it would cost us only $33.33 each, so is very affordable.

Wayne and Alana met Bill and Jean at the Calgary Airport and took them back to Red Deer to visit for a few days. Ron and Lenora met me and took me back to Pincher Creek to visit with them. About three or four days later Lenora drove me north to the Banff highway where Wayne met us and took me back to Red Deer so I could have a visit with them.

I won't go into this trip in detail as it pretty well follows the same route I took the year before except in reverse. That is, we drove to Drumheller to see the Royal Tyrell Dinosaur Museum and then down to Pincher Creek to the Oddies before heading off into BC and then north in the interior. This was Bill and Jean's first visit to Pincher Creek and the Oddies. Ron and Lenore took us down to Waterton Park, to Head Smashed In Buffalo Jump and to see the Oldman River Dam. We also went out to see the windmills at Crowley.

Our trip continued from Pincher Creek driving past the historic Frank Slide, then through the Crows Nest Pass and on down to Creston, then into the interior of BC to Kamloops and Prince George and north to Grand Prairie, then all the way to Peace River and back through Jasper Park to Red Deer. Truly it was a wonderful trip. One of the things that surprised me was that I always visualized my brother-in-law Bill as a slow driver, but I found out he had a much heavier foot then I do. His grand kids would never believe how speedy grandpa is in the mountains.

Buying A Condo

When I arrived home there was much work to do, meeting with the lawyer and the bank and the condo corporation, signing ever so many forms and papers.

One of the perks the condo people were offering right then to get you to sign was a one thousand dollar coupon on furniture at Martins Furniture on Dundas E.

I had all new furniture by now except for a bedroom suite. I had been looking at them with my cousin Wayne Butson at Patons Place so I knew exactly what I wanted which was an oak Palliser suite made in Winnipeg. I also knew the best price on every piece of furniture that I wanted. So I drove a hard bargain at Martins and got everything at the right price, and then I used the coupon from the condo corporation and got a thousand dollars off that best price. Jack was a happy boy.

I had to order venetians and valances for the windows and borders for each room. I decided on a better bathroom vanity of oak with basin and matching oak cabinet above with three glass door mirrors. Then too I had to pack things at the apartment and find a mover. More "Garage Sales," oh yes-several, all in a row on weekends on the front lawn. Then there was still my two-days of cutting hair. I tell you there was never a dull moment, but truly I loved it. After all these years of renting and living in an apartment I was finally going to have my very own home to retire to. This meant a lot to me.

When it came time to move, my two nieces Nancy and Lori and husbands Martin and Grant came with their vans to move the packaged stuff. There was also a wonderful little ole lady with a new hatchback that made more than one trip for me from the apartment building to my condo. Her name was Vera Hewitt. I had done some paper hanging for her and she thought she owed me some help. When all the packaged stuff was unloaded and in my condo Nancy and I went down to the local Pizza shop and bought two large pizzas and some chicken wings and cold pop for supper before everyone left for home.

I went back to the old apartment to sleep that night for the last time. In the morning a mover truck and two men would come to move the larger things. Every thing was to go except for the fridge and stove. I had made a deal with the landlord for him to keep the two appliances in exchange for my last month's rent, which was about $500.00. I had bought both the fridge and stove from Don Brown Appliance next door to my old shop on Wellington road in 1969 for $500.00. They had been good to me all these years. Now in 1998 twenty nine years later I was getting my money back out of them in the way of rent.

The movers arrived early in the morning and soon everything was loaded and on the way to my condo. They charged by the hour, which I thought was a good, enough idea. However they both smoked, and took time off to smoke while they were being paid to work. To add to this they stopped at Tim Horton's on the way to my condo for thirty minutes. I was not impressed as I was paying them $60.00 an hour, which is a dollar a minute. When they billed me I reminded them about their 30-minute stop en route at Tim Horton's. They said it was legal for them to charge for time off to eat en route. Their donut and coffee or whatever cost me thirty dollars.

That afternoon Yvonne arrived to help me, and I was glad to see her as I was sitting there amid all those boxes and furniture, with nothing yet in its right place. I felt overwhelmed by it all. After a few minutes Yvonne got me to my feet saying,

"Lets get started?" Truly I didn't know where to begin.

Yvonne said, "We should start in the kitchen first," so that was what we did and by evening things were actually taking shape. I will always be thankful for her help.

That afternoon Martin's Furniture truck arrived with my bedroom furniture; we quickly pushed many boxes aside to make a pathway in. The bedroom furniture came in huge cardboard boxes, which they put in the centre of the room and then they were going to leave. Yvonne though was right onto them and had them un-crate the furniture before they left shaming them for not respecting a senior my age. Hmm? That night I slept in the condo for the first time and I felt good about it. I remembered thinking back to the first night I had spent in the old apartment building and the bad feeling of despair and panic. This time it was different and I felt something good would come of this move.

Yvonne returned to help me put up a border in every room; I have always loved this wide border I used on my living room, hall and den walls. It is of thundering Mustang horses all galloping off in the same direction.

My sisters warned me about putting too much stuff on my walls, and about clutter, but it seems I have many treasures. When I go into other people's homes the first thing I always notice are their empty walls and tables. I always feel your home should speak volumes of you personally and of the things in life that are important or dear to you.

Over the years I have collected many beautiful things among them thirty some Beswick horses. There are also Llandro figurines, small and large Staffordshire floral arrangements and a large G. Armani horse and colt figurine, a real treasure.

I have a collection of about one hundred plates, half of which are in oak frames made close to home in St Marys. The plates are by such great artists as Kevin Daniels, Fred Stone, James L Keirstead, and Lena Liu, puppy plates by Lynn Kaatz and five beautiful Royal Doulton plates by artist Nigel Hemming of Labrador Dogs. I have four of Ken Danby's famous Reflection of Youth Plates, framed two together in a frame. Perhaps some of the more favourite plates in my collections might be the seven plates I have of Peter Snyder's who depicts the Amish and Mennonites countryside scenes of rural southern Ontario. In spite of all this, one of my more treasured things might be a hand-made oak clock made by my brother-in-law Bill Butler. The clock is made of special cuts made in oak grain then fitted together so they accent each other in the face of the clock. The hours are told by Canadian, provincial coins, truly, - a great conversational piece.

Piece by piece, one by one my beloved stuff found a home on wall and shelf. I guess it is what one might call organized clutter. My sisters still joke about my clutter, and I still dislike looking at empty walls.

One of the first things I had to do after I arrived at my condo was to contact the Canadian Hearing Society to see what could be done about connecting something to the intercom to let me know when someone was at the door. The condo corporation would not let me use the old apparatus I had been using at my apartment and truly it was very outdated. Up until then I really didn't know what was available. I found out that there are some great new things available now. I will try to explain to you how it works.

They have what they call an Alert Master AM 6000, an all-in-one wireless system. It sounds impressive eh? Well it really is. First there is a master box, which sits on the nightstand beside my bed. On the front of it is a digital alarm clock with auto snooze. There is a round pad bed shaker which is placed between the two mattresses, which when set to the clock will awaken you with a powerful shaking motion. An in-line amplifier inside a small box is placed next to the intercom. When someone pushes the intercom button down stairs the buzz goes to the intercom as usual. Then this small boxlike amplifier picks it up and sends it to the Alert Master in the bedroom, which in turn, turns on the condo lights.

I wired every room in my condo to matching brass coach lights, which the Alert Master turns on when called upon for any reason. It can be the door, the telephone or a fire or carbon monoxide alarm. It also lights up for a strange noise such as a vacuum cleaner or a power drill. I also have a button on my condo door so people inside the building do not have to walk down stairs to the intercom to contact me. This is also hooked up to my TTY phone machine. However nothing is fool proof. There is nothing like being wakened up in the middle of the night with your bed shaking and every light in the condo flashing on and off, because some joker has pushed the wrong intercom button downstairs and set off the system. I have it so red lights come on for the phone and white lights for the door.

Summer of 1999 was very hot and I still had my old 8000 BTU AC, which I had used in my old apartment on Dufferin Ave. I put it in the box for an AC high in the bedroom wall. This of course is not a good idea as a window AC vents from the side, so you're venting into the box and then in-taking the hot air, making your AC very hot and drying it out. In the end I took the one bedroom window out and put the AC in there using Plexiglas above. This however was not good enough to cool the whole condo, so I bought a second 8000 BTU from Sears and put in the den window.

Then I bought some great looking ceiling fans; two were Honeywell with wall control buttons. So there I was with two AC and four fans, one in the living room one in the den one in the bedroom and one in the kitchen. My hydro bill took off.

People were friendly throughout the building but as yet I didn't have any close neighbours. There was no one living above me, and no one across the hall from me, and there was no one on either side of me. I longed for some real neighbours. One day when I was returning from a long walk two people were walking on the sidewalk towards me. I recognized them as tenants in my building, so I stopped to chat. When I left the lady told her husband that she was sure she knew me from somewhere. A couple of nights later the lady pushed the button on my door and when I answered she held up a large wedding picture in her hands and said,

"Do you know these people?"

I looked and said, "That's Jack and Phyllis Murdock."

She looked at me and said, "My dad and mom."

I looked at her in question, and said, "Bonnie?"

"Yes, I am Bonnie."

It seems she was chatting with a lady called Carrie. Carrie had a little dog that she used to bring over to a pet grooming shop in the plaza where my barbershop was. I had talked to her a few times when she was there with her dog. When Bonnie was out walking her dog she mentioned to Carrie that she had met me and somehow felt she should know me.

Carrie said, "Oh, that's Jack the barber."

Then of course Bonnie remembered me, and told Carrie I use to visit her dad and mom years ago when she was about sixteen. She remembered how I loved her mother's home-made cooking, and she claimed I ate them out of house and home. (Now really does that sound like me?) Bonnie used to drop by the Executive House to visit with Bob Scott who shared my first apartment with me here in London. Bob's father and Bonnie's father were in the army together thus the family kept in touch. It was good to feel I had an old acquaintance in this building to be an even closer friend and my neighbour too.

Finally in March of 1999 new neighbours moved in on the south side of me. I was really happy to see them. I remember going down the hall to their door to welcome them. I introduced myself and I told them I really needed a neighbour. They said they were the kind that needed a neighbour too. They were Fred and Muriel Halle.

My 1999 Rio Red Special Edition Ford Mustang

In the spring of 1999 my 89 Grand AM Pontiac was now ten years old, and still looked in good condition. Its beautiful shiny paint showed no outward sign of visible rust but I knew though once a car gets to a certain place the body starts to fall apart and with or without care, and it is going to start costing you money.

The Grand AM had been a good car and so I was tempted to buy another. But since they had stuck so close to the same body design for all to many years I felt I wanted something altogether new and different. So I went shopping for a car. I have never liked a four-door family type car; it simply does nothing for me. I want something I can drive with pride, something that makes a statement, as to me a car is more then just transportation - it's a lifestyle.

Bill and Jean came down to help me make up my mind about which car I should buy and the colour. I told them there were two or three cars I liked but the new 99 Ford Mustang was my pick, but unfortunately it was more money then I should pay for a car. It seems that Bill and Jean feel differently about my money and so encouraged me to go for the Mustang. For many years I have driven black cars, but Jean put down her foot. " No more black cars." All these years she had wanted to tell me she did not like black cars, so this time I had to pick something else. It was between the Rio Red and a Dove Grey; in the end I picked the Rio Red.

I have always managed to sell my car privately. It seems if you look after your car, have pride in it, and keep them clean, people do notice. This in turn helps to sell your car when the time comes. I put a 4-sale sign on it and the two days that I cut hair with Yvonne it was parked on the plaza lot. Soon people were asking me about it. In the end I sold the car to a lady across the street from the plaza for $3,650.00 I was fortunate enough to have the rest of the money in cash. So on April 15 1999 I was the proud owner of a Rio Red Special Edition Ford Mustang.

About three weeks after I bought the car I had a bad accident on Horton Street, here in London. It was one of those head tail head tail kind. A van up front darted across the street causing everyone up front to brake fast. The farther back you are it seems, the less time you have to brake. I hit the rear end of the car in front of me causing damage to the rear end and damaged the front of mine. I was really sick.

The damage to the front of my Mustang was just in the bumper, grill and hood, and not back as far as the radiator nor did it damage either of my front fenders. However as it was almost brand new, and the whole front, bumper grill and hood was replaced and cost over $7,000.00.

I had a 5 star rating on my car insurance. Which is the very best. However in the following October when I renewed my car insurance I found that it had jumped on a first accident from about $1,400.00 to well over $2,000.00 for the year. A mustang is recognized as a sport car; thus the insurance is high to start with, but this was a bit much. So I lost my 5 star rating and will have to wait and be five years accident free to get it back. Touch wood, it will be five years this spring that I have been accident free.

After I had been accident free for three years my broker allowed me to change companies which saves me about $600.00 a year.

In September George and Betty Vezeau, cousins of Fred and Muriel moved in two condos south of me and Elaine moved into the condo on the north, - all good neighbours. There are 51 condos in this building. By late 1999 all of the condos had been sold. It seems at least one is always "For Sale" as people move, leave town or move up to a house. The good thing is that the sales price has increased each year.

A Big Step Forward – "I Bought a Computer"

Older people, (That's not me), I mean OLDER people; think a long time about buying a computer before they take the leap. My sister Pearl had bought one some time ago and was doing well. She put us all to shame and we envied her. For her, being deaf did not seem to be a great disadvantage. She of course had members of her family who had computers and could help her. They were also used to her deafness and managed to help her to understand. By that I don't mean it was easy.

My neighbour Fred had a computer and urged me to go for it. I told him I was afraid to get involved because I felt I was not only deaf but also kind of dumb. He scoffed at this and said,

"I will be there for you and help you to get started."

To which I said, " You have no idea what you would be in for Fred, as not only do I feel dumb but it seems when I struggle so hard to understand what you're trying to tell me, I reach the point where I just have to shut down. When I reach that place I'm exhausted and I will snap out at you if you try to continue."

Fred said, "So what is the problem? We would stop and just shut down."

A young lad from White Oaks, whose hair I had cut for a number of years was now going to Western University. A few nights of the week he worked for Staples Business Depot. I chatted with him about a computer and he told me that since he was not on commission it didn't matter to him what I bought. But he would like to put a package together for me of what he thought would work best for me. He wanted me to stick with Hewlett Packard all the way. We settled on a 17 in. monitor, and the 6535-pavilion modem and the Desk Jet 612C printer plus a special connection cable, all of which along with the tax set me back $2,051.56

I was now the very proud owner of my very first and my very own computer, but unlike the new car I bought, I could not make it run.

The first thing I had to do now was buy a desk for the computer, I found this at Staples to, a "Jagger" work station by Bush furniture and it cost me with tax $345.00 It came in a large box. Fred and I put it together; it turned out to be a good desk.

Fred's son in-law, Bob Borisenko unpacked the computer and printer and put it all together and then connected me to a server.

From there Fred took over.

He arrived all bright and cheerful in the morning and started me out on the correct program where you get use to handling the mouse and opening and closing programs and how to send E Mail, open and shut down etc. This went on for days and I was not exactly happy at the progress. I don't know how he managed to survive and sometimes when he went out the door I was sure he would never come back. The next day he would be back, ever so cheerful again wanting yet more punishment. In the end it seems that you reach a point where you start to understand and are able to help yourself. The first thing you have to learn is that things have to be done the way the computer thinks, and you have to do all things in the correct order. Until you accept this you will continue to get into trouble. I will never be able to thank Fred enough for his time and patience and for proving to me that, …….. I was not as dumb as I thought I was. Every day or two I still learn something new about my computer, but I am happy that I can do the things I set out to do, and better then I ever hope to do it.

Yvonne Moves To London

Early in 2000 Yvonne sold her beautiful big house in Dorchester and moved to a smaller one in White Oaks not far from where she worked. Mike and I helped her move her boxes; and a mover handled the furniture, it was a very dirty day when she moved.

Everything seemed to be going well for everyone. I continued to cut hair and enjoyed it as a two-day paid outing which I spent with old friends, (my customers). Mike had renewed a friendship with an old friend Charlotte, who had lost her husband to cancer a year before Jigs passed away. She was also one of Jig's very best friends. I liked her right away and I was happy for Mike, as I knew he was not happy living alone. There was a problem though she was Mennonite and he a Catholic. Charlotte eventually became a Catholic and in time they got married.

In July 2000 Yvonne was not feeling well, and put in a very bad summer, not always being able to work. In November she had surgery and I had to work a few weeks in the shop alone. Her lease was up at the end of the year so rather then renew it she decided to take her business home to her house. She had a rear room with sliding glass doors out onto a covered deck. It all worked out perfectly. I painted the room a great antique shade of green. Mike and I helped her to move and hook up her plumbing and cupboards and place her chairs. It turned out to be a very nice looking shop and since then I am happy to say things have gone well for her. Yvonne had an extra chair, which she was going to sell along with some other equipment, but offered it to me if I wanted to cut a few head of hair at home. She felt her shop was not going to be big enough for two. So I took the chair home to my condo. Every Thursday I cut a few head of hair. I enjoy it as it keeps me in touch with a few of my older clientele some of whom I have cut for over forty years.

One of the reasons I had chosen this condo was because of the nice flowerbeds below my window. Two older brothers by the name of Smith had moved in here. The one was not well and appeared quite sick. He usually sat around in a wheel chair. The other one looked healthy enough and was trying to do the best he could for his brother. It was he who looked after the flowerbeds. I don't know how long they had lived here, but it seemed they had never been able to get totally unpacked. They had two small trucks both with a covered rear box. The one just sat there backed up to the sidewalk and was never moved. It was full of just about everything one can imagine. Every now and then Mr Smith would open the back and rummage through until he found what he was looking for. I remember visiting his condo once to ask about something and I saw boxes upon boxes, which had never got unpacked. Getting about in a wheel chair in that condo was not an easy chore.

The spring of 2000 arrived and people were out preparing their flowerbeds, and there I was on the second floor just itching to get involved. Mr. Smith had not yet touched his beds so one day I asked him if he needed any help with them. He told me he was not going to put them in that year as they were moving to a house in June, so if I wanted to take over the beds from him it was ok. So that was how I inherited my first flowerbed here. After it was dug up and the flowers in I could not help but notice how wild it looked on either side of our rear door. There were weeds and wild shrubs of all kinds growing in the hard clay soil amid rock and debris. Then to complicate the problem even more there was a down drain flooding the area. I decided to adopt this area too, as I park my car below my balcony and use this entranceway every day. It could stand to be beautified.

I took out all the weeds, wild shrubs and roots and added several bags of black garden soil. Bernie and Bonnie Holton gave me half a bag of peat moss they had left over. I went to Home Depot and bought some cement m-like flowerbed edging and put it on either side of the doorway and also under my balcony. I attached a long flexible drainpipe to the down drain, to shoot the water out and over the flowerbed.

Flowerboxes on Jack's Balcony

Soon the space below my balcony and around the rear doors was looking very much better; in fact it turned into one of the more beautiful areas of this building. It is not without cost and hard work. I kept wondering how so many people could just wander in and out of the building apparently blind to the effort of those who make life a bit more beautiful and enjoyable for them. However I have to remind myself that many people buy a condo just for that reason, to escape flowerbeds and yard work.

I have suffered an allergy for a number of years, dust, spore, mould, whatever and in the heat of summer it is worse so I find myself staying close to home on hot days.

One spring day while talking to Fred and Muriel next door I found that they were going to install a new kind of AC in their condo. I had never heard of it before. It was called a "Goodman Ductless Split AC" and is similar to central air as the compressor is located outdoors, in our case on the balcony. Copper insulated tubes run from the compressor to the unit located in your condo. A wireless remote control lets you control it to your comfort. George and Betty went for it to and when I found out just how well it worked I just had to put one in too. It is amazing and keeps the whole condo cool so easily and it also frees up your windows for letting in light. Perhaps best of all, it is very cost efficient to operate, much cheaper then window AC.

While it is quite expensive to put in, - about $2,400.00, with tax. I have no regrets. I was lucky in selling both my window AC for a fair price along with the Plexiglas to tenants in this complex. The year 2000 was an expensive year so no holidays.

When spring came in 2001 after a mild winter, I had the urge to take my Mustang out on the road for a long trip while it was still relatively new. It would have to be either in the early spring or the fall as my allergies did not let me function well in hot weather. There is not a lot of air conditioning in homes or motels in the west, so in all truths I could not find a place more comfortable than home. Besides my flowerbeds needed me.

My Sister Pearl raised Beautiful Cats

My Manx Cat Mandy Dies

Some time in August my cat Mandy stopped eating. There were no bowel movements for a number of days. For a few days I was not alarmed but when it stretched out to three, four and five days I knew I had to get her to a vet. My sister Pearl had been raising beautiful kittens while living in Russeldale and had great faith in the vets in the village of Kirkton. I put Mandy in her cage and drove to Kirkton. Mandy does not travel well, and when I took her out of the cage she was not about to have anyone but me handle her. With my help, the vet examined her closely. He said her hair was a thing of beauty and her skin or hide was nice and loose. Outwardly he could not detect a thing wrong with her So he suggested that if I really wanted to know if there was a problem he could do blood work. He added, "But that would be costly, at about $75.00."

I knew I would not forgive myself if she died and I might have done something to save her, so I told the vet we would proceed and do blood work. Mandy though would not hold still for him to draw blood, so he gave her a needle to make her settle down and get sleepy. After giving her a needle he left the room and I stayed with her. I remember yet seeing her gulp a few times but as I trusted the vet I thought it was ok. Actually she was struggling to breath. She suddenly was very still with her open eyes staring into space. I went to get the vet saying I was sure she was out, and maybe he should look at her.

When he saw her staring off into spare he quickly gathered her into his arms and rushed her to a back room, and called to another vet for assistance. After a few minutes he carried Mandy's lifeless body back into the room telling me he was sorry but she was dead. He said he had given her only the recommended amount in the injection and this had never happen to him before. This of course was of little comfort to me as I was in shock, and I didn't trust myself to talk just then so I just said,

"I will be back, I have to go for a walk."

I walked around the block, and I am not ashamed to say I shed a few tears for Mandy my cat, but I realized the vet was in a difficult position and very unhappy about what had happened. When I went back to the office they had put Mandy back into the cage for me. I asked about the billing and of course they said there was no bill.

While I was walking I had decided to drive on to Mitchell to Bill and Jeans, so often it seems it is Jean I turn to when life gets me down. I had arrived just in time for lunch; while we ate I pondered what to do about Mandy.

Jean's daughter Lori and Grant had just put there dog Spike to sleep. He was a brown Dachshund and very much a loving family dog. He loved nothing better than being under the table during family dinners and going from one to the other, secretly begging for handouts, which he usually got. Stiff, and sore from old age and arthritic they finally took pity on him and put him to sleep. He was buried in the lawn to the north of their garage.

Lori was at work in Stratford so I drove out to where Grant worked at a machinery dealership just east of Mitchell. Grant was very understanding of my sorrow as he still missed his dog Spike. I asked if he thought it would be ok if I buried Mandy somewhere out on the farm.

Grant said. "Burry her along side Spike. I know Lori would be happy about that as she keeps saying, poor Spike out there all alone, now he will have company."

So that was what I did. Bill made a nice wood box for Mandy and together we went out to the farm and dug a deep grave and buried Mandy next to Spike.

Lori and Grant's youngest daughter was only a little girl at the time and every day that fall she would go out and sit beside the graves and chat to Spike and Many. I wonder what she said?

With Mandy gone I had no reason not to be able to get out on the road in my Mustang for that nice long trip that had been smouldering away in the back of my mind.

My Very First "Mandy" a Manx cat

Chapter 9
A Great CANADIAN HOLIDAY TRIP
Friday September 14, 2001

Flower Boxes on Jack's Balcony

I was up early to be sure everything had been looked after. My Mustang was vacuumed, washed and waxed. My condo was clean and tidy and my flower boxes on the balcony were watered with care. The neighbours were given the keys to the condo and the mailbox, but I still had a last minute hair cut to do at eight o'clock. One of my long time customers called me the night before and said he could not wait until I got back, so he was coming over for his hair cut at eight AM. This proved to be a good thing though as he not only gave me $15.00 for his hair cut, but he and his wife helped me carry my things down from the condo and loaded it into my car, and then they saw me off.

My first stop was to be at my sister and brother in law's cottage at Maple Island north east of Parry Sound. For some reason I never seem to be able to drive up there by the same route. I feel that Ontario's road sign leave much to be desired. I don't actually get lost, but it is hard to follow the road numbers as the highways zig zag every which way hither and yonder. However I always get there. I arrived in time for supper and spent two quiet days with Arnold and Pearl; we caught up on the family, our health and social activities.

Their cottage sits high on the bank of the Magnetawan River in a park like setting, facing a great expansion of water like a huge bay, which starts off right there under the deck. The river here is more like a lake with a grand collection of poplar, cedar, spruce and pine all along the sides, then there's a sprinkle of oak and maple on the higher ridges. We took a boat ride on Saturday, down to the falls as they are called where the river drops several feet through a rocky gorge to flow on its way to Georgian Bay. On Sunday evening I took Pearl and Arnold out to McKellar for supper, and after that we took a long quiet drive through solid bush. As the sun went down and evening came on there is a great feeling of quietness and tranquillity out there, far from the warring world.

My Rio-Red 1999 Special Edition Ford Mustang

On Monday morning about 8:00 AM I said good-bye to Pearl and Arnold and started out on my long journey to Winnipeg. I think it was then that I wondered about the wisdom of starting out on this trip alone, at my age and with my deafness, all alone in a Silent World. It was overcast and cloudy all day, with a few drops of rain; there was just a hint of fall colour in the forest mostly with the poplar and birch. It was not a good day to use the camera. I guess I didn't really mind, as I wanted to make good time that very first day.

The speed limit is 90 km. so I had the cruise control on at 95. I seldom caught up with anyone but people were often passing me by. On this trip a traffic ticket I did not need.

By late afternoon I was driving through miles and miles of burned out bush on both sides on the highway. The fire was out but the smell of wood smoke hung in the air. Everything beneath the trees was gone and the whole forest stood bare, a blackened tragic and death for everything caught in its path. It was not a pretty sight.

As it started to get dark I noticed many NO VACANCY signs going up, so I thought it was time to find a place for the night. I was shocked to find out that because of the forest fire all the inns and motels were spoken for, for miles in every direction. They told me I would have to drive on to Nipigon about a two-hour drive to find a place. It was 11 pm when I got to bed, but one good thing about all this was that it was now just a nice day's drive to Winnipeg.

The next morning I was up early. As it had rained during the night the day started off cloudy and wet. I was now driving along the northern shore of Lake Superior but I could not see far out on the lake because of the clouds. I noted that the maple trees here were showing their first hint of red. So I hoped that I would be on time to see them in all their glory when I returned. Hopefully at that time the weather would be clear. I sometimes wonder if it is always raining around Thunder Bay or just when I pass by.

Twelve km. west of Thunder Bay is one of the more necessary stops I would have to make. It is the Terry Fox Memorial Park, with a bronze statue visible from the highway high on a cliff on the north side. The statue itself is one of the few really worthy works of art that has been erected in Canada for many years. It is also an inspiring site, and an all too young Canadian Hero truly worthy of it.

I saw tears in the eyes of many people who came there to pay their respects.

The sky was clearing by afternoon and so I got a glimpse of the Rainy Lake, then on to Fort Frances and past Lake of the Woods and on to Kenora. As I drew near the Manitoba border the hi-way seems to finally run straight. The border appeared rather suddenly and I was greeted with a great freeway. The land started to flatten out and for a while intermittent areas of bush of poplar and Manitoba maple dotted the countryside in fall colours of yellow and bronze. As you drive farther west bush gives way to true prairie and the land reaches out to the skyline.

I had not visited Winnipeg for many years so I was looking forward to it. With so much hype about Calgary and Edmonton, we are inclined to overlook the city of Winnipeg. It is a great city with a population of over seven hundred thousand. The downtown area has a large number of older more wonderful buildings still in excellent condition. These buildings were built when huge pillars and large building blocks were a norm. Perhaps it is because it has escaped much of the dust and smog from industrial pollution, that these old buildings look so remarkable today. It is the Chicago of the north. Unlike Calgary and Edmonton, which grew by leaps and bounds, Winnipeg gives off an air of a place where growth comes slowly but steadily. It seems more secure in its multi-type industries. It has two great rivers flowing into it, the Assiniboine River flowing in from the west, and the Red River flowing in from the south. In the heart of the downtown area, within a few blocks of Portage and Main the two rivers merge gracefully as the Assiniboine flows into the Red on a flowing angle; thus they merge without much flare. It's like a good marriage in which both benefit.

My long time friend Jerry Baltesson is a retired schoolteacher and lives in a penthouse in the heart of the downtown with a magnificent view from its 16th floor. Jerry's wife died of cancer a number of years ago. Our friendship goes back to the early nineteen forties when I first ventured west on what was called The Harvest Excursion, but that is a story I have already told you. Jerry and I had been in contact by e-mail and he was expecting me.

Assiniboine Park Bridge and Confederation Life Bldg

I told Jerry this story, just as I had told it to you a few chapters back. I told him of my train trip west and how I found my Uncle Fred the barber. It had much to do with what happened the next few days. The Confederation Life Building is visible from Jerry's balcony. It is within walking distance to the northeast. The next day we went for a walk to the historic corner of Portage and Main. Beautiful historic buildings, small green parks, flowerboxes and wide streets surrounded us. We then walked north to see the old Confederation Life Building. Somehow it seemed much smaller now than when I first came here in 1944. It appeared to be empty but still in good condition. The building that was next to it had been torn down exposing its sidewall of unfinished rough brick. I felt happy that I came to visit the site once more, as just maybe it will not be there too many more years. Jerry showed me the vacant lot where the old Leland Hotel once stood. It was good to walk the streets of Winnipeg once more, and remember.

Jerry wanted me to once again get the feeling of knowing Winnipeg. To know Winnipeg you must know its rivers. Sunday morning arrived sunny but brisk and the city was now very quiet. I found myself walking east with Jerry along the gravel path on the north shore of the Assiniboine. Looking back over my shoulder as far as one could see were huge rounded pillars carrying overpasses over the river, one after the other like dominos. That day we were heading east to the "Fork" so I could witness the exact spot where the two rivers merged. For some reason I expected to see a lot of action where the rivers meet, but the Assiniboine flows on an angle into the Red, which absorbs it with grateful need.

We walked a little farther around the bend and across the Red River stands the old French city of St. Boniface, which is now just a part of Winnipeg. The old but beautiful historic St. Boniface Cathedral still stands proudly on the east bank of the Red. Many years ago when Jerry lived in St. Boniface he took me to see this very old and beautiful Cathedral. Perhaps 20 years or so ago a great fire destroyed a large part of it. It was like many of those huge churches or cathedrals in Europe. It never could be heated in winter so they built a new cathedral along side, then preserved the old one for historic reasons. With Winnipeg's long and very cold winters it probably made sense, sad as it really is.

In the evening we drove out to The Assiniboine Park, I realized by now that Jerry wanted me to relive my first visit to Winnipeg knowing how close it was to my heart. As I walked through the flower gardens of multi colour in the Assiniboine Park I could almost feel my uncle Fred's presence and I wondered if he enjoyed that day in the park so long ago as much as I had. The sunset and darkness came on as we drove in quietness back to Jerry's Penthouse. Once there we sat down to chat in the glassed enclosed balcony with a pot of tea while watching the lights of the great city below, like a bed of jewels in the black of night flashing its colours. I was packed and ready to leave in the AM.

In the morning I left for Pincher Creek Alberta some 850 miles west as the crow flies. The speed limit on the Trans Canadian Highway in Manitoba is 100 km. and in Sask. and Alberta and BC it is 110km. So you can cover a lot of miles in a day on these straight highways. I seldom had to pass anyone but many including little old ladies passed me by. Again I didn't want to spoil my trip by getting a ticket. Winnipeg sprawls far to the west actually some sixteen miles. Once out in the open I watched the miles fly by.

The harvest appeared all but finished, but here and there I would find a combine working in the field, and by looking at the stubble I could tell much about the crop. While some parts of Manitoba had a fair crop most of it was poor, and as you drove farther west it got worse. By the time I got to Swift Current the ground was bare of stubble. All my life I had heard of the saying "The Bald Prairie." Now for the first time in my life I saw it. I remember seeing thin cows walking,

walking, looking for grass that did not exist, and seeing them standing knee deep in mud praying for water. This was not the west, as I knew it, and it was very sad.

The miles flew by and soon I realized I was going to be able to reach Pincher Creek that evening. I had passed through a time zone and that gave me an extra hour to drive by. I arrived in Pincher Creek about 8 PM. I had not stopped for supper so I went to a restaurant to eat. The waitress called Ron and Lenora to tell them I had arrived safely. When I arrived at my long time friends, Ron and Lenora Oddie the welcome was warm and the coffee hot. We sat and chatted till late as we had a lot to catching up to do. I always carry a pen and pad to help me understand what is said when I get stuck. It amazes me that neither Ron nor Lenora seem to ever tire of writing page after page of notes to be sure I understand what it is they want to tell me. Ron seems to get all his writing done while I am there, or so I have it figured, as I never hear from him on paper again until my next visit. However I do get many great letters from Lenora over the year keeping me informed on the weather, the crops, our mutual friends, and the bad eastern governments   So what is left for Ron to tell me?

Log Cabin up the Livingston Range North of Pincher Creek

Basically we like many of the same things, starting out with horses, and Hereford cattle but ending with Ontario and the federal government. Fortunately we both have a sense of humour and a great love for Canada. Westerners are a really weird lot of individuals. They have never met an easterner "personally" that they didn't liked, but collectively they feel we are the source of all their problems. Oh yes, there is a long list of things we are to blame for so I won't get started.

The next day was Sunday and I rested. At my age now I am in need of more Sundays per week. The days got a bit too hot and I missed my AC. The nights cooled the house down nicely and by morning it felt just right, but unfortunately

Lenore suffers from fibromyalga and needs the heat so the furnace comes on first thing in the morning and soon the house is uncomfortably hot again. Ron and Lenora live just a few miles southeast of Pincher Creek, with a view of the Livingston Mountain Range in the northwest. We decided to drive up to the Chain Lakes and have a picnic lunch. I volunteered to buy a bucket of Kentucky Fried Chicken, and Lenora built a great picnic lunch around that.

Pine Trees Grow in Rugged Outcrop North of Pincher Creek

It is a colourful drive north through real ranch country. Out there it's easy to visualize the west as it use to be. Here and there are old log houses and ranch buildings slowly decaying…weathered by westerly winds, bleached by the summer sun, and heaved by winter frost. They stubbornly refuse to accept their fate. Along the east side of a winding road is an outer crop of rock within the hillside. From these rocks stunted, weathered pine trees with flaying knotted branches struggle to survive against the hot dry summer sun and the ever-blowing year round winds from the Crows Nest Pass.

We came home via Cowley where there are many windmills working to create electrical power, stretching out miles in every direction. After many years of being ignored it seems they have finally won some recognition by the Alberta OIL Revenue rich government. There are no royalties to be collected from the wind.

Waterton Lake in Waterton Park

We took a drive down to Waterton Park, perhaps one of the less spoiled parks in Alberta. I have been there many times to dine and to take pictures. I am always amazed how the time of day reflects on the pictures one takes of Waterton Lake, with its many moods, sometimes looking angry and cold…other times mellowed by the setting sun and reflecting the beauty of lofty mountains along either side and always under the watchful eye of the great glacier from which it is fed. Ron treated us to a splendid lunch after which I spent the day with my camera. There are great pictures waiting to be taken and deer and goats willing to oblige even the worst of photographers. One of the sad sights here is the destruction being done by the Lodgepole Pine Beetle. It separates the bark off the trees and the tree dies. Luckily it only attacks the Lodgepole Pine, but there are thousands of acres of dead trees, a disastrous sight, and fodder for a great future forest fire to come. We drove home, knowing that this was my last evening visiting with my friends the Oddies. In the morning I would put my suitcases back in the Mustang and head off into the mountains.

Off Into Wonderland - The BC Interior

I took highway 3 west, going past the town of Frank and the Frank slide, where the old town lies buried under a rockslide. From there on through the Crows Nest Pass and down to Creston at the foot of the Kootenay Lakes. I love this town and its valley; here you will find something really different. It is the first valley where you will see large orchards of apple, pear, plum and peach trees. You will find everything from strawberry farms to dairy farms in the valley. I bought some fruit to take on my trip, and then I was back on the road to Castlegar where I spent the night. The next morning I drove on to Trail and to Okanagan Lake and valley to Penticton and on to Kelowna. I believe these two cities are the most beautiful cities in all Canada. Everything here is new and you will find everything from Canadian Tire to Staples, McDonalds, Burger King, or the Dairy Queen. There are tree planted boulevards rich in colour and lawns like London Life. They have it all, and Kelowna even has an International Airport. Also, many new apartments high-rises give it a neat skyline. From Kelowna, I drove up the east side of the Okanagan to Vernon and then west to the city of Kamloops.

Now I had always wondered what the country would be like in that huge area going northeast from Kamloops to Jasper. On the map it looks empty. The Highway is called, 'The Yellow Head Highway.' What I found was far beyond my expectations. Endless forests were highlighted in brilliant fall colours and reflected in its great rivers and lakes. It is an open country, which is very sparsely populated with people, where small villages and towns bear strange names I had never heard of before. The villages break the lonely highway and add comfort in the feeling that you are not alone. Everyone seems to own lots of horses and several large dogs.

A Russian Wolf Hound On Yellowhead Hwy.

Here and there are rustic ranches with herds of cattle and sheep, and green fields of alfalfa, already cut and baled into huge round bales for winter hay. The winter snow is so deep in this area that cattle cannot forage for food in winter or spring as they do in much of Alberta. So they have to be hand-fed. Fortunately they grow great alfalfa here for hay crops and pasture, but the season is too short to grow good grain crops. I drove for miles along the Thompson River, which rushes south from its high source, the tall mountain country of Jasper.

As you near Jasper Park the mountains get higher and higher with snow covered tops. Suddenly very high mountains seem to block your northern travels and the highway splits at a huge clover leaf, and goes in two directions east and west…It was very tempting to turn east to Jasper as I looked longingly at all those tall commanding snow capped mountains to the east, but I had planned on seeing the country between Jasper and Prince George. So I drove west. The highway seems to straighten out and the country is more open. Along here new land is being cleared from meadows and adjoining bush land. New ranch buildings and modest ranch houses make it look very appealing, and I wished I were fifty years younger. It was really a beautiful drive all the way to Prince George. I stayed there for the night because in the fall one does not drive at night in this country, as you just might meet a romantic moose on the highway and that is a love affair best avoided.

I was back in familiar country again as I drove north from Prince George to Dawson. It is wise to keep the gas tank full and eat when you can, as this is really an empty country. In the afternoon I arrived in Dawson and on to Grand Prairie by evening. One is struck by the suddenness that you are in open country and true prairie again. Up here they were still harvesting grain and it looked like a very good crop. I went to the same Inn in Grand Prairie that I had stayed at before. From there I had the clerk call Shelly my friend Mike's daughter in Dorchester to see if we could have dinner together. Shelly was born in Dorchester Ontario just outside of London and she has always called me Uncle Jack. She was home and said she would meet me at Kelsey's for dinner in twenty minutes. However it was an hour before she finally turned up and I was beginning to be afraid it was the wrong Kelsey's.

She said, "I am very sorry I am late but it is my dad's fault."

I said, "You can't blame your dad for anything now, as he is in Ontario and you are here." She said, " Would you believe it, right after I got your call my phone rang again, and it was dad wanting to know if I had seen or heard from you. I told him I was just going out the door to have dinner with you."

Supper was very enjoyable as Kelsey's do justice to beef steak. We lingered chatting long after we had finished eating. I know to Shelly I am someone from home - a close friend of her dad and mom, It seemed just a short time ago she was that little girl that played a joke on me. She had put a nice size rock in a basket of potatoes her mom gave to me.

I kept the rock and I call it a Shelly stone. She didn't want me to go before I had told her all about her dad back in Ontario. Her dad moved back to Dorchester from Creston after Shelly's mom died of cancer just a few years ago. I made a rather sad departure back to my room at the Inn. I have not mentioned here that I do not like motels or inns for when you travel alone and deaf, it is just a long lonely evening that you have to put in. Not one place where I stayed knew how to turn on the Caption on their room TV and as far as reading, I had read the paper in the many eating places and coffee shops during the day and after driving all day my eyes were not up to reading anyway. Then I don't sleep well anymore, and if I go to bed too early I will want to hit the road long before daylight.

Rising early the next morning I found out there was a healthy frost to clear from my windshield before starting out. At the outer edge of the city a work crew was working on a huge cloverleaf and in places the soil was cut away perhaps more than ten or twelve feet. It was a reminder of the stories I had heard about the number of feet of black soil all across the northern part of the Peace River country, foot upon foot of rich black soil.

It was another glorious sunny day, as I turned my Mustang towards Peace River. It just seemed as if fall was just continuously opening up to me everywhere I went. The open prairie looked good again after so many miles of mountains. Many farmers were in their fields combining the last few acres of what looked like a great crop of wheat. The stubble showed to my knowing eye that the harvest had gone well as it was rich in colour and thick enough to hold the straw aloft. I had lunch in Fairview, a beautiful small town made rather famous over the disappearance of a local doctor a few years ago. A second doctor was thought to be involved with his disappearance, as they had an ongoing feud. To this day the doctor has never been found.

Flat Top Hills at Peace River

As you near the Peace River great flat-topped hills appear in the northeast and you enter some really beautiful rugged country. The colour up close was amazing and the hills in the distance were in a soft haze against the pale sky. As yet you have not seen the river or town as it is in a deep valley. You arrive rather quickly; and you have a clear view of a large suspension Bridge at the foot of a long winding highway awaiting you.

The Peace River and its valley are impressive to the eye and seeping with history of yesteryears. Witnessing this great river and crossing it, gave me a feeling of being a part of something historic of Canadian value. The highway winds up the steep banks on the north side of the river and to your right you are looking down onto the flood plains below. Between the steep banks of the river you see the many vegetable gardens in the fertile soil of the river flats, all under irrigation from the river. As quickly as you come onto the river and the town you leave it all behind as it is situated in the deep valley. You rise from the valley to prairie once again and soon you are travelling through fields of wheat stubble and then areas of fenced grassland.

I stayed the night at a motel just east of Peace River.

The next morning I was off to High Prairie and while I have travelled to Peace River before, I had not been into the vast country west of there. To my surprise it is more like parts of Manitoba, lots of prairie but also areas of good bush lands. It is a good mixture of cattle and cropland. In many places new land is being broken and I feel there is room for several million new Canadians in parts of BC and this northern Alberta country. Along the highway I began to see signs, 'honey for sale', then a sign 'Garage Sale and Honey'. Well I have always been told the best honey in the world comes from the Peace River Country, so I thought I should stop and buy some. Here I found a nice house and all new buildings.

I was surprised by the size of the crowd they were drawing, as this place was far out on a very distant highway and houses here are far, far apart. When I parked the car a nice lady approached me and asked,

"Where in Ontario are you from?"

I said, "London."

She said, "Before you go be sure to go over there and speak to my husband as he came from Ontario." So I bought four 1kg pails of honey, and then I walked over and introduced myself to the husband. It turns out he used to live in Mount Forest a nice little town about 100 miles north of London. He had come out there about 20 years ago to keep bees and is very happy with the country and the way his business turned out. He has two great looking sons about 19 and 20 and a pretty little daughter he adores, very much younger. It always makes me feel good when I find that Canadians are much the same wherever you find them, friendly, happy healthy and prosperous, and very much interested in Canada as a whole.

He took me into his buildings, which were huge, insulated, and heated in winter. In there he had all kinds of professional equipment to process his honey, and everything was spotless. I asked him about his bees and the cold winters. He said when he first went there he expected to have to buy new bees every spring but he has not had to buy bees for a number of years, as they don't get the cold winters like they use to.

He added, "If you want to experience cold winters today you go to Winnipeg." This kind of story is repeated all over this North Country. For some reason the weather has changed and nowhere is it more obvious then in northern Alberta.

So I travelled on to High Prairie, which turned out to be a really modern and beautiful town more like a small city. It has all the things one would expect to find in a town a thousand miles south, beautiful new homes, landscaped and with nice green lawns. There are new shopping plazas and oh yes, there's McDonalds and Tim Hortons. These northern towns show the new growth and the prosperity of Alberta while many towns all over Ontario are dying. Soon I was driving along the southern shore of a long low lake. Its water was a dark cold blue. This is the Lesser Slave Lake. The east end of the Lake is the town of Slave Lake and again a very modern town that would put most of Ontario towns to shame. Then again Ontario works hard for its tax dollars, which is not oil, related? Ouch, my western friends are going to make me pay for that, but lets face it! Its true.

Travelling on I came to the town of Athabasca, a magical name that seems to have been stuck somewhere in the back of my mind ever since I first heard of it when I was a child in Public School, and now as if it was meant to be I am here… Here too of course is the Athabasca River, which actually starts out fed by glaciers hundreds of miles to the south in Jasper Park It winds its majestic way north through Whitecourt to Athabasca and on to Ft. McMurray then north to Lake Athabasca, where it feeds many lakes and rivers.

As my map shows vast empty spaces ahead I thought I had better top up the gas tank. Then as I drove out of town I saw a donut shop so just in case I thought I had better top up Jack too, with coffee and a donut. Remember I'm on vacation here, so nothing counts. As I parked my car a man stopped to look at it so I asked him,

"How is the highway ahead to Ft. McMurray?"

He said, "Oh great, in fact it just keeps getting better" I went in ahead of him as he continued to chat. Soon I had to tell him I was deaf. I got my coffee and donut and found a table and a newspaper. The man sat two tables away and again started to chat from that distance, but soon he beckoned me to join him. I told him he would find it difficult to chat with me, as I am stone deaf. He said,

"We will make out, no problem." So I found out he was from Newfoundland, and that there was a lot of people here and in Ft. McMurray from Newfoundland.

In the end it was a very enjoyable stop, and when I drove off the lot he shook my hand and wished me a safe trip. Again I had found a Canadian who just wanted to show his friendship, the kind of friendship that ties this country together.

I Drive North to Fort McMurray

Actually it was a bit late to start on the highway north to Ft. McMurray, yet too early to quit driving so I decided to drive on. The day had been perfect, a fresh very new and beautiful country to explore along with good weather and friendly natives, and so what could go wrong? As I drove north the land intermingled as it changed several times from great round bales of hay in fields of dark lush green alfalfa, which was already a foot high, to good bush in fall colour. I was surprised to see a lot of yellow tamarack and tall Lodgepole pine, mixed with poplar and aspen. The soft October sun hovered long and mellow low in the west making this drive one I would always remember.

The highway to Fort McMurray is good, built high for winter driving, but there are no villages and very few houses along the way, certainly not a place you would choose to run out of gas or have car trouble at any kind. Darkness came on and my gas tank was low, and frankly I was beginning to get a bit concerned, and the words of wisdom from my little sister pops into my head, She is the one that is always advising me to stop driving in the middle of the afternoon. But suddenly the lights of a great new city of about 50,000 lights up the night sky. All along the highway into the city are no vacancy signs, and I am hearing the voice of my little sister as she says,

"I told you so." I decided to pull into an inn and ask for advice. They were very friendly and helpful and offered to phone around and find a place for me. I had a wee bit of trouble following directions but finally found it. It was $123.00 for the night…and they asked me how long I would like to stay. I wish I had said…(about half a night).

It was late, perhaps after nine PM and I still had no supper, so as there was a restaurant connected to the inn, I thought I might as well eat right here. They already had my leg I might as well give them an arm too. In the morning I was up early, full of anticipation of seeing the sand tar works, as I have always been very much interested in it, - but first off to McDonalds.

While you will find most things very expensive in Ft McMurray breakfast at McDonalds, (or coffee and donuts at Tim Horton) will cost you exactly the same as you pay in London. So needless to say these places are thriving. But there is a problem in finding a good staff and keeping them as they have to pay their staff better here than in other places, as why work for less when you can make $70,000 working for Syncrude.

The sand tars works of Suncor and Syncrude are 50km north of the city; my inn had been in the south end thus I found myself driving through a long and beautiful city, far longer than it is wide. I could have been driving through any new city in North America except that there are no old or older, buildings visible. Its wealth is very obvious in its new cars and wide four-lane highway going north out of the city. It is said it takes 240 busses to take the sand tar workers from the city to the work site every morning. One could well imagine you were driving on one of Toronto's busy expressways.

In early times this was a trading post where the Indians brought their furs to trade with the French and thus saved them a long trip east to trade with the Hudson Bay Company.

In 1778 Peter Pond, a Scotch-American explorer built a house and trading post here, then with the Indians as guides he first marked the location of the tarry substance. The Indians referred to it as the Stinking Lakes. But nothing really happened here for hundreds of years until a half-hearted attempt to mine the tars started in 1964. But until world oil prices climbed and better methods for extraction was found things seem to sit still. The last 30 years has been good for Ft. McMurray, however no one here seems to have any ties to this city as everyone you talk to here comes from some place else. Sometime…somewhere…down the road, when they exhaust the sand tars, it will bust. Will this city with all its seemingly physical energy survive when its oil energy from the sand tars runs out??

One thing that I found very disheartening was that the Alberta Government, knowing where the big money is allowed them to build a huge Gambling Casino in the city. These guys work very hard for their money in a harsh climate and yes get paid well, but for many with no outside entertainment, they become addicted to gambling. I read that every available gal in the city is pregnant, so what else is a guy to do? They are not ready for BINGO yet!

The figures here are impressive, as this is perhaps one of the worlds greatest single oil resources, an estimated 2.5 trillion barrels, not all of which is recoverable with today's technology, but what is recoverable is more than the known reserves of Saudi Arabia.

It isn't a pretty sight, seeing these huge man made machines tearing up thousands of acres of riverbed and low lands, to launder it and then return it to the site where it came from. There are promises to reclaim and reforest the area as the project proceeds. Already the area that was first to be reclaimed and reforested has trees growing well above my head. It is a good start. Let me say, I am glad "I went there, and saw that" but I was happy to leave it all behind. Perhaps if I were fifty years younger I would want to be a part of it, to be involved, but as of now I am ready for a quieter more reformed life style in my condo back home in London. While I would say it is not for everyone, rest assured what is taking place in Ft McMurray now is very important to all of Canada and will some day be remembered as "Historical."

I returned to the city and stopped at Tim Horton's for an early lunch, soup and a biscuit, coffee and a donut. I had taken a few notes and I busied myself sorting them out for future reference and I am using them here. My penmanship at times leaves much to be desired, so it is best I don't wait too long to read my own notes so as to be sure things will be clear later.

Now it appeared for the first time that I was actually heading in a homeward direction, but first I was to visit Dave and Cathy Laing, in Edmonton. I was supposed to call them and let them know when I would arrive but I was having trouble getting them on the phone. What I didn't know was that Edmonton had changed their area code number from 403 to a 700 number the same as Grand Prairie and Dawson Creek. As I didn't take my TTY machine with me I had relied on some stranger to make the call. When they first got no answer, they would all kindly say, "Don't worry I will call again until I get them."

So I didn't know if they would be expecting me or not. It was another great day for driving and the miles were soon behind me and I arrived in Edmonton about six in the evening. To get to Laing's I had to drive from the north end of Edmonton to the south and I soon found myself on the Wayne Gretzky Freeway and traffic, traffic, traffic, but I was careful and kept to my lane and had no trouble, but it sure was not for the faint of heart. No one was at home at the Laing's. I found out after I got home that they never did get any message from me so were sorry that they had missed me.

Wayne Butler, my sister Jean and Bill's son lives in Red Deer and about an hour and a half drive south, so I decided to drive on to Wayne and Alana's. An hour later I stopped at a place for supper and I had some one call Wayne and let them know I was on the way. I arrived about eight o clock or so, and Wayne had just come home ahead of me. He did not look well and he could hardly talk. He said they were all just recovering from the flu. Well the last thing that I wanted was to catch the flu while en route on a holiday trip.

So I said, "Oh Wayne, I better not come in, I will go to a motel or inn."

But Wayne said, "No Uncle Jack, we would keep the kids away from you and you can sleep in the basement away from all of us."

This was not at all what I had hoped for, as I wanted to spend a few days with Wayne and family, and perhaps even dig up a few of his potatoes. You see I had visited Wayne a number of times over the years, and somehow it always coincides with digging Wayne's huge size Yukon potatoes. I am sure it was just by accident mind you, but it was a job I escaped from that year. I had the house and the computer all to myself the next morning as everyone was off to school or work. I was able to write a letter and E Mail it to everyone from Winnipeg, Mitchell, Stratford, London, and my cousin in Louisiana, U.S.A.

East To Oyen

It turned quite cold and windy overnight, the first really cold weather I had on this trip. I was now heading for Oyen, that little town away out east of here, near the Saskatchewan border where I had spent so much time so many years ago. I travelled south on the Calgary to Edmonton Freeway to Innisfail then straight east through what is called The Big Valley Country. This area was so very dry; there was just no pasture or water anywhere. It is here we cross the Red Deer River, which is always scenic to see. I stopped at Dry Island Buffalo Jump, along the Red Deer River where the Indians use to kill the buffalo for their winter meat; the view is terrific in a wild and forlorn way.

I feel I should perhaps refresh your memory as to why I am driving out to Oyen.

In 1919 my Grandfather's sister Rosena Butson was working in a restaurant in Chicago when a charming man en route home to his homestead in Alberta walked in for a meal. They chatted and found out they both came from the same part of Southern Ontario. He came from the Tavistock area and she came from the Mitchell area. He delayed his trip west to woo her and in the end she married him.

They travelled west together first going to the land title office in the town of Brooks east of Calgary where my aunt could register a quarter section homestead in he own name so as to enlarge their holdings. She picked the quarter section across the road from my Uncle Frank. Uncle Frank's ¼ was SW1/4 of 10-27-5-4. By chance, they had both chosen the most rock infested quarter sections in all Alberta. They spent the rest of their lives picking rock. Over the years they built a solid wall of rock five feet high across the front of their land to be used as a pasture fence. It still stands to this day as a testimony of their hard work.

It is worthy to note it took the Canadian Government over 50 years to complete the land survey to turn the Prairie Provinces into townships and the townships into homesteads. They started in Manitoba in 1869 and finished parts of Alberta well into the first quarter of 1900. Oyen itself was surveyed some time before 1905. The basic survey unit is a township. A township contains 36 sections, each being one-square mile or 640 acres. Row after row of townships were laid out starting at the American border and worked its way north.

The trouble was that although the townships were supposed to be constant in size, the earth is not flat. That is, the longitude lines converge as they head north. To compensate, and offset this a correction line was introduced between every few townships. Such a correction line was found a couple miles south of my uncle's.

Of Interest - One hundred years ago this year 2005 Saskatchewan and Alberta, were officially open for settlement. At that time the Canadian government offered one quarter section of land or 160 acres, free to anyone who wanted to homestead.

To continue - In the fall of 1944 World War 2 was still on and I was 15 coming 16, going deaf and driving my parents crazy. My dad and mother decided to let me go west. My mom had kept in touch with her Aunt Rosena. Aunt Rosena believed in Christian Science and Faith Cure and she wanted mom to let me go west to visit them, thinking the drier air and prayer might cure my hearing loss. She proved to be a dear old soul and I loved her dearly. Uncle Frank was a hard working big man with a booming voice. He had many big Clydesdale horses and if they didn't work hard or toe the line he called them many names with his booming voice. (Let's not go there) They were retired when I first visited them and rented the farm to a neighbour, an Englishman Harry Bull whom I met at that time. A few years later he had my Aunt write and see if I could come west and help him and his son Wm. harvest their crop in the fall. That is how I came to know the Bulls. I worked for them many years going west after the harvest was off on my dad's farm in Ontario.

All the years that I worked for the Bulls I never felt like a hired man. I guess I was my Aunt Rosena's nephew and soon everyone in the community knew me, as that. I sort of inherited other people's uncles and aunts and I respect them to this day. When you are young it is so easy to win the hearts of good people. All you have to do is open up and be honest and love them back.

So now you will know why I am on my way to Oyen.

It was cold windy, dry and dusty, when I arrived at Oyen and as it was 6 pm I went directly to a restaurant for supper. Then as the Mustang was very dirty by now I took it to a car wash to make sure it would look good when I arrived. This proved a real waste of time as I found the gravel road going out of town was freshly graded and my car was engulfed with dust, the kind of dust you only seem to find in the west. When I arrived out on the farm, one could hardly tell just what colour my car was. It was the colour of road dust. It gets into your car trunk, and in around the car doors. They just have to live with it. I well remember years ago when I worked there and often ate wonderful meals in the field, and I never had to use salt or pepper, as nature provided it. This is the stuff that makes those westerners so politically gritty. Amen!

Roy Jacques Windmill in the Sunset Oyen Alberta

No one was home when I arrived but the door was unlocked like so many other western homes this far out of the city. After knocking several times and then calling out I went in and made myself at home. Alma and Brian her son, arrived home shortly after.

They too, had supper in town but at a different place. We settled in for a long evening of chat, as I wanted to know about so many people and so many things. Their crop had been a total disaster as it had been a very poor year. Even what did grow got hailed out, and what was left the grasshoppers got. So you see you need to be a bit gritty here to even survive.

The next few days were windy and very cold. Every night there was a glorious sunset followed by a clear cold frosty night. I remember taking a picture of a windmill with the sunset beyond; I will share it with you here.

I visited with many old friends, the oldest being Lorne and Isabelle Sutherland 91 and 94 years old that fall of 2001. I called to ask if I could go over for a coffee with them. She said, "No you must come for dinner." They were a wonderful old couple with a great sense of humour and struggling to stay in their home as long as possible. I have a great respect for them, as they were the last of the older generation that were there when I first went west.

Since then Lorne has passed away and Isabelle is in the lodge in Oyen.

Brian Bull loves his tomatoes, so that year he planted a huge plot of them of perhaps fifty plants or more. He had watered them with precious water from the dugout until it had run dry. Up until then they had done well, but a hailstorm came and stripped all the leaves off the plants. Along with the hail came a lot of rain so the plants leafed right back out and then grew a vast crop of late green tomatoes on very stocky green looking plants. This left poor Brian in total frustration, as it was late in the fall and he needed a couple or three weeks of sunshine and warm weather, then he would have tomatoes galore. In mid October it was windy and cold and frost every night so we went out each evening at sundown and covered the plants with a tarp to save them for yet one more day. I understand they picked them green and took them to the house to ripen and for a while Brian and all his friends ate tomatoes at every meal.

One evening Alma's daughter Barbara came to have a visit. I noticed she and her mom in deep discussion in the kitchen. Then Alma beckoned me to come into the dining room where she led me to her buffet. Opening the glass door she pointed to a set of crystal, a tall water pitcher and glasses. She asked me if I recognized them,

I said, "I said yes they use to belong to my Aunt Rosena." When Aunt Rosena died Alma bought the crystal at the house sale. At that time she thought she would someday give them to Barbara. But now Barbara thought they should go back to my Aunt Rosena's family. Long ago my dad and mom had driven west in their mobile home and took my sister Jean's daughter Nancy with them. Nancy and Barbara got to know each other and so she asked me if I would give this Crystal to Nancy some day. I was overjoyed with this gift to bring home. Now you will understand when I say I feel like family. For now I have the Crystal in my cabinet, but some day it will go to Nancy to be handed down in her family. I will be sure to write down a bit of its history to go along with it. I know my Aunt Rosena would be very happy if she knew about this.

There is so much I could tell you about this place and these people, as they were so much a part of my life in my teens and twenties. I worked hard all day, and then I sat for hours in the evening listening to the stories the older folk would tell me. Other times we would gather around the piano singing songs in the evening. Later we all sat together at the kitchen table for coffee and goodies before heading for bed. We had the kind of bath every Saturday night that kept us clean for a week? On Sundays I visited my inherited Uncles and Aunts, who fed me as if I were royalty; such was life as I remember it so many years ago. It was hard to say goodbye to, such good friends - - - or "family."

When you're a long way from home, saying good-bye to good friends is never easy. I remember well when I use to work for Alma's father-in-law Harry Bull. He would speak to you well before the time of your departure and then go for a walk in the garden as he was just not good at saying bye to those he loved. When I questioned it, they told me,

"Dad does not like goodbyes." Being English, shedding a tear would not be proper.

I have a long time friend Grace Snell who lives in Acadia Valley perhaps twenty miles south of Bulls and I was to call for coffee before I left for home. Grace and Lenora Oddie of Pincher Creek grew up together (on horse back) here in the Oyen Country. Lenora had come up the night before to visit Grace, so I was to have my morning coffee with my two lady friends. This added a nice touch to my final farewell to Alberta.

Back on the road I travelled south on highway 41 on what they call the "Buffalo Trail." It is through very dry country north of Medicine Hat. First you pass over the Red River and later the Saskatchewan. This route bypasses the Canadian Force Base at Suffield, which use to be called "The British Block" and it was where they kept the prisoners of war during the Second World War. After the war some veterans eyed all the empty grass on which only antelope were pasturing. So they cut a gate in the fence and drove their cattle in. The army turned their head as long as they hired someone to herd the cattle and keep them away from the base. I fondly remember those wonderful days I spent riding a horse all day long herding cattle with a friend Deke Sutherland down in the British Block - part of the past, I will treasure.

The highway arrives at the Trans-Canada highway just east of Medicine Hat. I had hoped to make it to Winnipeg that night but as I drove on into Saskatchewan I began to feel tired. I had worried about this before I left home, but this was the first time while driving on the trip it had bothered me. So I pulled in on a vacant garage lot away out in the middle of nowhere and had a sleep. I was rested and back on the road, but I realized that I was not going to get anywhere near Winnipeg that day. As it grew dark I came to the town of Moosomin, which is in Saskatchewan but near the Manitoba border. Many years ago when I was on the way west with four others we stayed in this town overnight.

While it had grown a lot since then it is still just a small prairie town of a few hundred souls, very much like so many others I had just travelled through. One of the first few motels in town was all decorated up for Halloween, pumpkins and corn stalks witches and gravestones all under coloured lights. To me this said, that these people were a working part of this community, and they offered you perhaps just a bit more. Then the name of the motel was "Prairie Pride Motel" and I could not help but notice it. These people had pride and they showed it. When I registered, I was really surprised that they only charged $39.95 plus tax. This was by far one of the best values I had on my trip. Then came more! They served you breakfast in the morning. Most of my motel bills were in the $58.00 to $65.00 range, except for the northern cities like Grand Prairie and Ft. McMurray which were ninety to well over one hundred dollars.

I would ask for a single, but many tried to sell you a double first, as it is usually about ten dollars more. Then if you said "No" they would look again and say,

"Oh just a minute, there is one single left." It was always their last one? When you entered you would find two beds. Many of these motels did not measure up anywhere near "The Prairie Pride." Across the highway from the Prairie Pride was a brand new Dairy Queen restaurant so as it was handy I had supper there.

In the morning I packed my bags back into the car and decided to try the coffee. When I entered the office there was a man behind the desk.

He said, "My wife tells me you are from London Ontario so I wanted to meet you, and thought we could have breakfast together this morning. You see my mother came from Woodstock Ontario and right now she is down there visiting friends and family." It seems he was born out there and had never been east but his mom talked about London and Woodstock, and many places in the area. So he felt he would enjoy breakfast with me.

He offered coffee and orange juice, two slices of toast and your choice of four different kinds for home made jams. If that didn't please there was a basket of muffins. Now nowhere on my trip was there any place that came near to the value and the hospitality of "The Prairie Pride" but his mom came from Ontario, so what would you expect of the son, of an Easterner? When I left he gave me a pad and pen, compliments of "Prairie Pride."

During the night a snowstorm had passed through Manitoba and the fields had a light dusting of white stuff. I found out later that this same storm went all the way through Northern Ontario and on to London. It was the first snowfall of the season.

I arrived in Winnipeg about noon, and went to a Tim Horton's to eat. The manager there kindly called my friend Jerry to let him know where I was. Jerry said he would be in the downstairs entranceway waiting for me, so I could put my car in the Underground Parking again. It would not be wise to leave your car out at night in downtown Winnipeg.

It was good of Jerry to have me stay a second time. He knew I needed the break for the long drive home through Northern Ontario. So far I had been standing up to the driving really well, actually better than I had expected. I told Jerry all about my trip since I had left him. That afternoon we went shopping in the Bay and a mall all connected to Jerry's penthouse. You can walk inside to quite a number of stores and business places or cross the street in overhead walkways. Then there are many stores adjoined to one another from the inside. Thus in winter if the weather is bad you have no need to go outside, and that in Winnipeg-like winters is a real plus.

In the evening we found ourselves once again walking along the Assiniboine River, only this time walking upriver, west on a gravel-packed path, past great pillars and under bridges, the river itself looking quiet and gentle in the evening. Many people walking looked like tourists, and others with dogs would be local.

We walked by the Fork Theatre and we could see the Fort Gary Hotel with its revolving restaurant on top. From here we had a great view of the downtown. We could also see the old Union Station with its green copper dome. It seeps in memory for me of other times, when I was so very young and arrived in Winnipeg on the train fresh from the farm, with a guardian angel looking over me.

Soon we came to a wide set of many steps leading up the hillside to the parliament buildings. Atop the steps is a giant statue of Riel, probably the most revered hero to this day in Manitoba and the west. Sometimes I look at history feeling great shame, sadness and deep regret, as we cannot, just wipe out our yesterday's mistakes, yet many keep the pain alive and pass it on to their children. Thankfully in time we all learned the truth, and that was, it was our governments blunder that created a historic tragedy, one we cannot live down. Riel's statue stands rightfully on the parliamentary lawn in Manitoba capital, a haunting reminder to us all of past mistakes.

I was back on the road again and soon into the lakes and forest of Northern Ont. Snow was under the spruce and pine trees where it was sheltered from the sun. Now I'm going home. There were feelings of a deep satisfaction, of happiness, and at times melancholy.

Now the north was in full fall colours, but it was mostly in shades for yellow, bronze, brown and gold for that first day. I made great time and my Mustang thundered by Thunder Bay and far beyond Nipigon to Schreiber where I stayed overnight at "The Villa Bianca Inn."

Back on the highway the next morning I had some breathtaking views of the shores of Lake Superior, many deep bays of shallow inlets edged with fall colour and those awesome waves coming in off the lake. Here again was our maple, which was sadly missing in yesterday's drive. I drove east past Marathon where the highway turns inland and there are fewer maples, but near Wawa the maples are back with great gusto and a great show of endless parades of colours so wondrous, so splendid. At times I rein in my Mustang and take time to take some pictures to look again and to really appreciate it.

As you near Sault Ste. Marie, the great show continues and there are even more Maples enveloping the highway on either side. On this trip my timing could not have been better. Out on the prairie or in the mountains, or back here in northern Ontario, my Guardian Angel has certainly worked overtime.

I really had planned on staying overnight somewhere and driving on to London the next day, But when I arrived in Parry Sound about seven PM it seemed I had a choice of my own bed or one more night in a motel. I had driven to my sister's cottage from London to here many times after work so I decided I would head for home. I made good time and soon took the turn off from the 400 highways to Horseshoe Valley and on to Stayner.

I had taken this old Ontario Atlas car book along, but it was ten years old. It seems our good government has gone ahead and changed the numbers on many highways then forgot to put up new signs to guide us. This of course is to confuse us. Confused travellers take more time en route to get from here to there thus spending more money, and this means more tax dollars. Anyway I was soon driving south (I think it was south) getting more confused as the miles passed by. I entered village after village with no visible sign to tell me where I was. As almost everything was closed I didn't want to knock on someone's door, besides you know how we men hate to ask for directions. It's not a manly thing to do?? If I can find my way all across Canada I should not get lost at home.

I came to a corner in some unknown village and there was a donut and coffee shop open, so I had a perfect excuse to stop, using the coffee and donut as a cover up. I asked a man sitting there if he knew this country, and he did, so I showed him my map book and after looking at it,

He said, "No wonder you're lost. All the numbers on the highways are wrong." So he set about drawing a map on the back of his paper place mat. The waitress came along and added a few more lines to it. So I thanked them and was soon back driving in another direction, which seemed all wrong to me but then was it the map, the coffee or I.?

Soon I came to a biggy corner and the sign said in big letters, "to Waterloo," but an even bigger more impressive sign said, to the 401. Well naturally I thought it meant the 401 was closer or just around the corner. So I turned that way. I drove for miles and miles always expecting the 401was just ahead. Little did I know I was driving in more or less an eastwardly direction towards Toronto to get to the 401. I did get there but it was a long trip from there back to London hemmed by giant transport trucks all driving like maniacs. Ah! London and Home but first I stopped at the all night A&P to pick up milk and bread and then home to my own bed. Ah! It never felt so good; I hope you have enjoyed travelling along with me. It was a great trip, but it was good to be home again

Time For Another Kitty

Late in the fall with the prospects of a long cold winter ahead of me, my thought turned to getting another cat. I decided to visit the humane society on Clarke Side Road. There were many sad and pitiful eyes hopefully looking out of their cages at me, saying,

"Take me, take me home, I'm a good kitty." I chose a black short hair cat about 2 years old, de-clawed and neutered to be picked up at five PM the next day.

The next day was Thursday and I was cutting hair. One of my customers, Jack Thompson came in for a haircut and while I was cutting hair he asked me if I was thinking of getting another cat anytime soon. I told him it was funny that he asked, as I was to pick one up at five o'clock that night at the humane society. He had a few snap shots with him of a cat that had come to his place a few weeks ago and stayed for lunch. It apparently liked it, so stuck around on the front porch. They let it in to eat and then turned it outside again hoping it would find its way home. But by now the nights were getting cold and they were letting it in for the night and putting it out in the morning. They liked it a lot but his wife Jean was a bit allergic to a cat so they were looking for a home for it. The pictures he showed me were of a nice looking cat but long and lean. He was both de-clawed and neutered. I told him I would come over and take a look at it.

I took the cage along with me just in case I liked the cat, but I really did feel I would prefer the black cat at the humane society. When I arrived the cat was sitting on Jean's lap at the far end of the chesterfield. I sat down on the other end where I could get a good look at it. The cat got up and without hesitation walked down the chesterfield and settled down on my lap and looked up at me and said,

"I'm ready whenever you are, so let's go home."

I Still Have My Second Mandy 2005
He's a Puuurfect Cat

So how could I resist. Jack told me if by chance I didn't want it after a few days to just bring it back. I brought the cat home and he didn't make strange at all. He spent perhaps twenty minutes going from room to room to check things out and then hopped up on my lap and I could feel a thankful vibration, a big, big song from his thankful heart. He knew he had found a home. He is a grey and black Ocelot cat but I call him a "Lap-cat" as whenever I go to sit down he comes on the run. Many times he flies onto my lap even before I hit the seat. At first it seemed a bit much, but now I would miss him if he were not there.

He watches a lot of TV so I try not to watch too much violence. He does get upset when animals fight. Sometimes when there are cats, dogs or birds on the screen he jumps off my lap and sits up close to the screen on his hind legs looking in as if ready to jump. He proved to be a very loving cat, to me and to all my friends who come to visit. He loves company. While trying to think of a proper name for him I would forget and call him Mandy. Since he started to respond to Mandy I decided to keep the name although he is a male cat. .

Don The Computer Guy

Over the winter of 2002 /2003 I was having more than my share of computer problems. While trying to explain a problem to my friend Nevol Huddleston, he said he would ask Don Peever, a friend of his at work if he knew how to solve it.

Don works at the hospital and he loves to play with computers. Rather than try to answer the problem to Nevol he said he would come over and take a look at it. He arrived and in a few minutes my problem was solved. However as everyone knows when you are learning how to handle your computer you are going to mess up time and time again. So I found myself forever calling on Don to see if he could come over and help me with yet another problem.

I was embarrassed at the number of times I asked him for his help. I wanted to pay him for his service, but he would not take any money. So I invited Don and Nevol to go out to lunch and I picked up the bill. When I drove Don home he gave me a lecture saying that he paid his own way and I was not to do that again. He claimed that he enjoyed solving computer problems and all he wanted from me was my friendship. I realized then I had found a good friend.

At Christmas time I thought I would surprise him with a crisp one hundred dollar bill in a Canada Trust envelope along with a note thanking him for all the help he had given me the past year. Certainly he had earned it several times over, but he simply refuse the bill on moral grounds, saying he just could not take it.

He told me he would like to look after my computer for me, but if he was to do this, he didn't want anyone else to touch it, so things would stay as he set them.

Don truly has a great gift and he is exactly what every senior citizen needs when they go to buy their first computer, a computer guy along with every computer.

We work well together. I mess up and he fixes.

Life Moves On - New Friends – Old Friends

The years have rolled by and I find myself looking more often at the obituaries than the funnies. It is sad and perhaps eerie to see the names of people you once knew as capable, strong and vibrant leaders of the community listed among the dead. Perhaps the one good thing about getting older is that it is now easier to make friends. People trust older people, letting down their guard and enjoy a chat. It seems the people who live in condos tend to move more frequently then those who live in houses, thus it is always sad to make a new friend, only to find that they are moving to a house, out of town or even out of the province.

My friend Bonnie Holten had told me about her husband Bernie's failing health. You see Bernie was born with Spinda-Bifida. As a baby he was not expected to live. However with determination to succeed he had a very successful life and for a number of years was purchasing manager for Benson Hedge Tobacco Company before they shut down. Later he worked in Timken Bearing Company in St Thomas where he met and married Bonnie.

His health began to fail in the nineties. About the same times Bonnie also had health problem, so they were forced into early retirement and at that time bought a condo here.

Bernie had his mother, Ruth Holten moved in down from me. She is a great neighbour and every now and then arrives at my door bearing gifts of homemade goodies. It's her motherly instincts; she can't help herself.

In the few years I lived here I came to know Bernie well as I went down to their condo and shampooed and cut his hair and trimmed his beard for a number of years. Bernie's health continued to worsen and in 2002 he was confined to a wheel chair. In January 2/ 2003 he passed away. Bonnie's health continues to worsen and in the fall of 2003 Bonnie sold her condo and moved to an apartment in St. Thomas to be closer to her sister Jackie.

Ken and Bonnie Burke had moved in down the hall from me and we became good friends. Ken was working at a plant in St Thomas and drove back and forth every day. Bonnie it seems kept busy looking after her family and Ken, gossiping with the neighbours and buying yet another pair of shoes. Ken had a new motorcycle his pride and joy and he and Bonnie would often go on long rides out into the country. Their son also had a bike and often went along with them.

In 2002 they sold their condo here and moved to a house in St Thomas. The following year they moved to New Brunswick to where they originally came from. They have asked me to come down and visit them; some time soon I must do that.

In January 2004 my good friends Mike and Charlotte sold their home in Dorchester and bought a place in Fenwick. I am not at all happy about that, as I liked to have them close to me in Dorchester. However Mike has bought and sold places all his life. It seems he always hopes the next place is going to be home, but for some reason it eluded him.

At the time of writing May 21, 2005 Mike called me to tell me he had just sold the place in Fenwick after spending almost a year and a half remodelling it. He now plans to return to BC in search of his dream. Most likely to Osoyoos or the Okanagan valley area. I am glad I know where I want to be....here in London.

I feel that the years have been kind to me, as this fall Oct. 17th, 2005 I will be 77 years old. I don't feel at all old.. I am contented with where I am in life and what I am doing. After all these years of travel it is important to arrive at your destination. I feel it has been, but a journey from 1928 until now 2004. A long wonderful journey. Now don't write me off just yet; I plan to be around for at least another twenty years, err I feel I'm almost at my best now.

Friends
Jack and Daisy

For a number of years until she passed away
<u>Daisy,</u> The Burmese Mountain Dog,
at Susan's Pet Grooming Shop, next door
came to visit me at the shop every morning.
"I think it was love"

Chapter 10

A TIME TO REFLECT

There are times when I sit in my lazy-boy in a silent world and contemplate. My thoughts wander back over the years to a time, a place or to someone I once knew, perhaps we shared a few moments or a few years. We each left our footprints on the sands of time. We can reflect on the past, but time itself marches forever on. I have found that life is but a journey that takes us from here to there. Life is also much like an echo. What you send out comes back to you, of that I am very sure. I am also aware that while I lost a whole dimension of life when I lost my hearing I was given something else in its place - eyes that both see and understand perhaps better than the average person and a memory that as yet, has not failed me.

People who hear seldom give thought to the wondrous gift they have; in fact they spend much of their time trying to turn it off. Thus they seldom really listen to what they hear, so turning themselves off, becomes a way of life for them

If they were to lose their sight they would listen to understand better what they hear. Thus when you lose your hearing, I believe you see more clearly and understand better what you see.

I know many of you will wonder how I feel about my deafness. I can truly tell you that at this time in my life I don't waste much time thinking about it. I have accepted a Silent World, to me it is now what we call spilt milk. I have found my own ways of dealing with it, while it is not always easy, I have learned to cope.

However every time I see a deaf child my heart goes out to him or her, as I know the Silent World they are going to have to learn to live in. It is a world, which they will have to adjust to, as the world will not adjust to them. They will always have to try just a bit harder in life to prove themselves, as few people will accept them as equals. People seem to add the stigma of not being too bright to deafness. The deaf will always have to go that extra mile, as nothing much will come to them if they don't do everything in life just a bit better then average.

Your friends and family will find it difficult and time consuming to visit or to communicate with you. People who claim to be your friends may wish you well but will not take the time to learn how to make a Bell Relay System (BRS) call. They don't seem to understand what a blessing the Bell Relay phone system is to the deaf. To us it opens a door from a Silent World to the real world, but to many it is just a complication like a computer and they don't feel they need it. So they leave you on your own in your Silent World.

In reality it seems, if you want to stay in touch with someone it will be up to you to make the phone calls and do the visiting. This sometimes can hurt your pride, so perhaps you have to develop a wee bit thicker skin. Whenever someone actually reaches out to you and wants to be your friend and keep in touch you will know he or she is a very special person. In them you have a friend indeed..

For the most I feel I have accepted my deafness as fate as I have had to so that I could get on with my life. Thus when I am alone in my everyday living I find I can all but forget that other people have hearing. Then something happens that brings me back to reality and I feel, well… lonely, lost, something is amiss. It was Helen Keller, who said,

"Blindness separated people from things, deafness separates people from people."

From my personal experience I know it is true I have friends and family members I wish I could be closer to but they are busy and you only slow them down; thus your deafness separates you from them. It is wise to protect yourself. Never let your expectations or dependency on others rise too high, then you won't get hurt or disappointed when you are left alone, overlooked or not included.

Everyday I count my blessings as I see many neighbours, my friends and family with real problems both physically and mentally. It is then I know I am blessed as I have health and security, and some true friendships old and new. This is something neither better hearing nor money can buy.

Life is but a journey that takes you from here to there. During that lifetime, every thing you have ever done, every one you have ever met, every experience you have ever had, rubs off on you and makes you, who you are. We in turn rub off on others, making life much like an Eternal River with no end.

Look at your grandchildren or the children of all those you have loved and rubbed shoulders with. It's not only the way the children look but also the way they think, the way they talk or walk that reflects who they are. During their lifetime they will be moulded by all the people they come to know, by all the things they have ever done and all the experiences they have ever known from their past, into their future. Life on earth as we know it will end but the Eternal River flows on.

On the east side of Mitchell there is a beautiful large green cemetery. It has many trees and manicured lawns. There within a stone throw of my dad and mom's old house on Arthur Street is a gravestone with my name on it.

When I started to write a few lines on my family history for my memoirs I had no idea that it would end in a book.

A Special Thank You

Special thanks, to my neighbours Fred and Muriel Halle for their encouraging words, which kept me pounding away on my computer keyboard.

To Don Peever, for the excellent and tireless work he did on my pictures. I know he was aware I would never ask him to do anything he could not do. Thus I often pushed him into doing the impossible. You did a great job Don, thank you.

Then a special thank you to Ralph and Eleanor Smith of Goderich for doing the proofreading of my book. For their guidance their suggestions and their encouraging words. You never failed me. Without you I would not have got the job done.

Jack's Balcony Wall

Epilogue
The Long Winter of 2005

Writing this book has been a great challenge to me. While in many ways I am happy to have it finished, I have to admit it has been a labour of love. Perhaps the timing was also good as this winter I found out I have to start to watch my health.

I may be deaf, but throughout my life I have always enjoyed great health. As my oldest niece Linda Canniff told me just recently, she always thought of her Uncle Jack as being invincible. Nothing could happen to him or keep him down for long. After weathering my growing up years, and my deafness I believed it was true, somehow I would always manage to bounce back on my feet and come out on top. For some time now I was aware I had diabetes, but my sugar count reading was always what I thought acceptable. In early 2005 something happened to humble me, to remind me just how vulnerable we are to life's problems In other words welcome to the real world, we may be lucky for a time but few, if any of us can escape it forever.

It was January of 2005 and for the third time in the last six months I had a sty on my right eyelid. I had read in a book that the only way to rid yourself of a re-occurring sty was to have surgery. I asked my family doctor about it and he flatly rejected the idea of surgery. He wanted me to continue with pills and eye drops.

Later, on a Friday night in early February, I could not sleep and I was walking the hall in pain. The next day two neighbour ladies came knocking on my door to find out just how bad it was. They wanted me to let them call the Ivy Eye Clinic.

I think perhaps my neighbour Muriel poured it on telling them I was already deaf and she didn't want to see me lose an eye. So they said to rush me in right away. Ann Barns, another neighbour offered to drive me in. Within an hour I was flat on my back on a table, with two doctors peering into my face.

I remember one was an older doctor who coached the younger doctor about the procedure and what had to be done. Then he left the room. The younger doctor seemed very confident and I rather liked his style. When he went to put a needle in my eye he kindly told me it was going to hurt, but is spite of that I was not to move. I reasoned, that this made a lot of sense.

After he gave me the needle he left the room. Ann who had stayed with me and was seated close by held a note over my head saying, the doctor said he would be gone for ten minutes and when he returns he will give you a second needle.

The doctor returned and began slapping towels all about my head with wild abandon as I lay there thinking about that second needle, but it never came.

As I looked up through my bad eye I could make out that the doctor had an instrument in his hands much like an open paper punch. It had an open eye on one end and a hammer on the other. He slid the eye in under the eyelash and they turned on a long screw which pulled the hammer down onto my eyelid and pushed it through the open eye of his instrument. Then all at a sudden he flipped the thing up on my forehead turning my eyelid inside out ooouch!. It hurt a lot and I was very uncomfortable.

I still wondered about that second needle. Would I not feel it?. Was it possible he had forgotten it.?

"No no, after all this was, 'The Ivy Eye Clinic' and world renown."

I still had blurry vision and much feeling, but I knew very well what was going on. The doctor took his knife and much like my mom use to cut the extra piecrust off the pie pan, the doctor cut the flesh off around the sty. I felt each and every cut, cut, cut, and I guess half way through I let out a low moan and Ann heard the doctor say ,

"Oh I believe he is in pain, I better give him that second needle."

There are times when you should never say,

"Better late then never" and this was certainly one of them.

When it was over he slapped a huge amount of bandages and gauze and tape on my face making me look as if I had one of those extreme makeovers.

Ann needed something to steady her nerves after trying hard not to watch all this .Thus we ventured into the hospital's Tim Horton's. Somehow I fitted right in there with other patients all about me. Much more so than I would at just any Tim Horton's out there in the city.

I slept very well that night. Perhaps it was just the feeling that it was now over and all I had to do was heal. The next day I had one of the world's greatest looking black eyes. But at this time of my life I no longer take any pride in a black eye. It seemed the pain got worse over the day and the eye looked swollen, red and angry. The next night after the late news I decided I just had to get out of my condo for a wee while as I knew I was in for another sleepless night. So as Tim Horton's is just across the street I thought I would do something really sinful to get my thoughts off my pain. I would walk over to Tim Horton's for a coffee and a donut.

However when I went out the rear door I found out it was pouring rain. As I had been driving up until now and it was just before midnight with little traffic, I was sure I could drive over without a problem. I was very careful backing out of my parking space as I noted I could not see well to the rear or to the side. I was driving south off the lot when a small car backed out suddenly right in front of me. I braked fast but I was sure it was going to be too late. I sat still not wanting to take my foot of the brake as I might move ahead and come in contact with the car. While I had the right of way there is not much comfort in being right in such a situation. The car moved forward and I drove on. I will never know who it was.

Now a strange thing happened! Half way to the street, everything turned grey as if someone had turned off the light switch. I stopped the car not knowing what had happened. It cleared so I thought I would continue, but in that instant it went grey again. I knew something had happened but I didn't understand it. I thought I better turn around and park the car. It was then I realized I could not see to the side well enough to turn around. It seemed I could only see straight ahead. So I reasoned I would drive to the street and make a u-turn and drive back to my parking spot.

I tried to do this but I was afraid to make that u-turn as I could not seem to see behind me. In the end I drove straight ahead through the green light to Tim Horton's and had my coffee and donut and then back home and parked the car. That was the last time I drove my Mustang for weeks. It sat on the parking lot all winter.

That night the pain was so bad I could not sleep. My neighbour Muriel checked on me the next morning and called the Ivy Eye Clinic again and they said once more to bring me right in. Again it was Ann who drove me to the hospital. Two doctors looked at me and told me I had a stroke. They made an appointment for me to see a doctor, a specialist in ophthalmology at the University Hospital the very next morning.

He turned out to be a very grumpy little old man who seemed very unhappy with his job and his earthly burdens. His hall was full of sore and sad-eyed patients all … …..waiting…..waiting..

When he found out I was deaf he would not even look me in the face. Here was a man who had earned a wall full of plaques in his lifetime, but had never learned how to be comfortable with a deaf person. How sad. Whenever I spoke to him he answered by speaking directly to Ann. It was easy to see he was uncomfortable and had no patience for deaf people. He said that it was as stroke and he would arrange for me to have an MRI as fast as possible by putting me on an emergency list. I was to come back to see him on the Friday, three days hence.

You can imagine my surprise when I got an early morning phone call from the University Hospital the next morning asking me to be in at 11:30 am for my MRI.

Of course I said yes I would be there, but I had no idea how I would get in unless I took a taxi. Again it was good neighbours that came to my rescue. George and Betty Vezeau offered to drive me in. George had an MRI a couple or more years ago so could lead the way. They would stay with me and help me through it.

Two days later Ann drove me back to keep my appointment with the specialist. This time he was just a bit better. He told us that because of the stroke I had what is called 3rd. nerve palsy. Which means the 3rd muscle behind the eye is paralysed.

This time the doctor did put his hand kindly on my shoulder and said,

"I now you're worried about this more then other people might be because of your hearing loss, but I assure you it will heal, although it will take at least six weeks, and then you will have to upgrade your glasses."

The six weeks were of hard cold winter weather, which seemed forever in passing. I was house bound and bored to death. Driving the car was simply out. I could not see to use my wheels to go anywhere,. and the weather was too frigid cold to go out walking. I could not watch much TV,. and I had to use the computer sparingly. Although it was not exactly safe for me to walk about to the local stores I managed to keep things afloat. It was dangerous for me to go shopping in stores as it seemed I would cut corners a bit too short and bump into things. I'm sure the next day scratch and dent sales had something to do with me being in their store.

I have been back for my six week check up and it seems they think everything will turn out ok in the end. This week I was in for my eye check to upgrade my glasses to the tune of $350.00 just for the lens, o-h-h-h the pain. It seems the muscle behind the eye has been pulled and I need these special lens to help pull the eye back into focus. My new glasses would be ready for me in one week.

The week went by and the time came for me to pick up my glasses. Again it was Ann who drove me to the clinic. For so long now I had been seeing double, I was beginning the think I was rich as it seems I had two of everything. I had two Rio red Mustang cars and two very large plump tomcats and two rather lean wallets all of which made me, oh so comfortable, amid all of my new-found blessings.

I was not sure what to expect of my new glasses, but I had hoped for a miracle.. When I put them on my prayers were answered, I had my sight restored instantly.

I was handed one of those laminated pages to read. My eyes roamed from the top of the page to the bottom and the printed words leaped out at me all the way down to the small print in the very last line. I read that line off flawlessly. It seemed every one was surprised. Didn't they think I could read?

Tuesday April 12th, 2005 I received word that Mrs. Carl Eisler had passed away. That was the mother of Bruce who went west with me in the fall of 1955. It was his sister Carolyn (Mrs Earl Paulen) who played the piano for me when I sang. There was a second brother Hugh whom I never really got to know very well. Visitation would be at the Lockhart Funeral Home on Wednesday the 13th. This would be the first time I had driven the car since the night of my stroke.

It went very well, and I was both pleased and surprised. The next day I even took the car to the car wash and got the winter grime washed off. There are times now that I almost forget I had a stroke or trouble with my eye. Life is good again.

Every day I greet the morning with contentment as I know I am one day better.

Spring is in the air and it is a time when all life is renewed. I feel in tune with nature as I watch yet another spring unfold. This one has a special meaning to me.

The End

But boys cannot appreciate their priceless joy until too late

And those who own the charms I had will soon be changed to men;

And then, they too will sit, as I and backward turn to look and sigh

And share my longing, vain, to be a carefree boy again.

By Edgar Guest

www.ingramcontent.com/pod-product-compliance
Lightning Source LLC
Chambersburg PA
CBHW082106230426
43671CB00015B/2620